HEWLETT-PACKARD
DATA SYSTEMS

D1377315

Semiconductor Memory
Design and Application

TEXAS INSTRUMENTS ELECTRONICS SERIES

Carr and Mize ▪ MOS/LSI DESIGN AND APPLICATION

Crawford ▪ MOSFET IN CIRCUIT DESIGN

Delhom ▪ DESIGN AND APPLICATION OF TRANSISTOR SWITCHING CIRCUITS

The Engineering Staff of Texas Instruments Incorporated ▪ CIRCUIT DESIGN FOR AUDIO, AM/FM, AND TV

The Engineering Staff of Texas Instruments Incorporated ▪ SOLID-STATE COMMUNICATIONS

The Engineering Staff of Texas Instruments Incorporated ▪ TRANSISTOR CIRCUIT DESIGN

The IC Applications Staff of Texas Instruments Incorporated ▪ DESIGNING WITH TTL INTEGRATED CIRCUITS

Hibberd ▪ INTEGRATED CIRCUITS

Hibberd ▪ SOLID-STATE ELECTRONICS

Kane and Larrabee ▪ CHARACTERIZATION OF SEMICONDUCTOR MATERIALS

Luecke, Mize, and Carr ▪ SEMICONDUCTOR MEMORY DESIGN AND APPLICATION

Runyan ▪ SILICON SEMICONDUCTOR TECHNOLOGY

Sevin ▪ FIELD-EFFECT TRANSISTORS

Semiconductor Memory Design and Application

GERALD LUECKE, M.S.E.E.
Manager of Advanced Technology, Texas Instruments Learning Center

JACK P. MIZE, Ph.D.
Staff Consultant, Texas Instruments Learning Center

WILLIAM N. CARR, Ph.D.
Professor of Electrical Engineering, Southern Methodist University

Edited by
Robert E. Sawyer

McGRAW-HILL BOOK COMPANY

New York   St. Louis   San Francisco   Düsseldorf   Johannesburg
Kuala Lumpur   London   Mexico   Montreal   New Delhi
Panama   Rio de Janeiro   Singapore   Sydney   Toronto

Library of Congress Cataloging in Publication Data

Luecke, Gerald, date.
  Semiconductor memory design and application.

  (Texas Instruments electronics series)
  Includes bibliographical references.
  1. Computer storage devices.   2. Semiconductors.
I. Mize, Jack P., date, joint author.
II. Carr, William N., date, joint author.
III. Title.
TK7895.M4L83   621.3819′58′33   73-8908
ISBN 0-07-038975-6

1234567890 HDBP 76543

*The editors for this book were Tyler G. Hicks, Beatrice Carson,
and Linda B. Hander, and its production was supervised
by Teresa F. Leaden.   It was set in Fototronic Times Roman by
York Graphic Services, Inc.*

*It was printed by Halliday Lithograph Corporation and bound by
The Book Press.*

Contents

Preface

Rapid change is the byword for the present era of the evolution of the use of semiconductor devices for the storage function in memory systems. Decoders, buffers, and drivers are common in peripheral circuitry, but the main storage component is just now finding its way into systems for field use.

There has been much literature on storage functions, but little attempt has been made to present a comprehensive view of them and of the design and applications of the semiconductor components that fulfill these functions. This book was written for that purpose. If the authors' objectives have been met, it will serve as a good overview text. This book is aimed primarily at the hardware circuit designer who is going to use the semiconductor storage elements and build larger memory systems.

With the rapid changes that are occurring it was difficult to select the emphasis for the material. The authors have attempted to picture the present state of the art, indicate what has happened in the past, and project the direction for the future. They have made a conscientious effort to present an objective evaluation of the position of semiconductors in relation to other storage media.

The authors had a strong motivation to provide material that would be read and used; it is their hope that basic ideas and techniques are presented in sufficient detail to be understood and used to give the designer a start. After that, he should be able to carry his specific design to a successful conclusion.

This is not a book that teaches the intricate details of the design of monolithic semiconductor integrated circuits; however, it does cover enough semiconductor processing and monolithic design to enable the user to become familiar with the design goals, the progress to those goals, and the details that help to make his application decision easier. It also describes specific applications and the design details of specific storage elements sufficiently to interest the experienced designer. A general background is assumed in semiconductor integrated-circuit processing terminology and in circuit design theory. Senior engineering students should be able to easily understand the information if they have been exposed to a course on semiconductor devices.

Chapter 1 provides an overview. The storage functions are categorized and characterized, and the media that provide the functions, including semiconductors, are identified. A discussion on price projections is intended to instill confidence that these projections will be accomplished. Chapters 3, 4, 5, and 6 concentrate respectively on the design objectives and characteristics of sequentially accessed storage, bipolar and MOS random access storage, and fixed program storage. From these chapters the reader should obtain important terminology and guidelines for evaluating semiconductor storage elements.

Since process and fabrication are intimately related to design and performance, a chapter, Chapter 2, is devoted to the arsenal of available and future semiconductor technologies.

How to use storage elements in a memory system is the subject of Chapters 8, 9, 10, and 11. Sequentially accessed memory and read only memory applications (Chapter 8) include MOS shift registers and both MOS and bipolar ROMs. Some enlightening cost-effective techniques are suggested for multipliers and random logic.

Bipolar random access memories with capacities to minicomputer mainframe size are the center of discussion of Chapter 9, but the material on the general topics of loading, timing, and output fan-out is applied throughout Chapters 10 and 11.

In Chapter 10 the applications of MOS storage elements to random access memories are discussed again with capacities to minicomputer mainframe size. However, the newer n-channel developments and their applications, especially the interface, suggest the use of these devices for larger mainframe memories. General topics peculiar to MOS are included and can be applied independently. Several important monolithic peripheral circuits are included. The important difference between driving p-channel and n-channel MOS devices is included in the discussion of the continuing p- and n-channel developments.

The application discussions end with large mainframe memory (Chapter 11). The two-level memory and the fast buffer memories (ECL) required are presented, including a cost-performance evaluation that indicates the cost effectiveness of an all-semiconductor two-level memory. Certain designers need a high-speed large-capacity mainframe memory. Chapter 11 concludes with a discussion of such a system.

No discussion of the use of semiconductor memories is complete without the subject of reliability. The material presented in Chapter 7 represents, in the opinion of the authors, the position of the reliability data. It is minimal as concerns storage elements directly, and it is full of projection but, even so, worthy of publication.

The authors are indebted to many people without whom this task could not have been accomplished. Billy Martin and Clinton Kuo and their colleagues, especially Johannes Gruenert and Norishisa Kitagawa, were invaluable in providing design and process details on bipolar and MOS devices, respectively. Projections on the future of semiconductor storage elements were obtained from the following: Charles Phipps, Jerry Moffitt, Daniel Baudouin on economics, Jim Schroeder and Ed Ward on MOS device characteristics and processes, and Earl Wilson, Steve Baird, and Wilton Workman on bipolar device characteristics and processes. Mike Cockran, Gene Cavanaugh, Kurt Boehnke, Gaylon Kornfuehrer, Daren Appelt, and Bill Wray contributed significantly to the applications material and Pat Hawkins to the circuit analysis. Ann Mize provided the manuscript typing.

The authors are grateful for the extensive editing provided by Robert Sawyer; his fine work is apparent throughout the book. Finally, a book such as this could not be completed without management involvement, assistance, and encouragement, and this Don Scharringhausen provided.

Gerald Luecke
Jack P. Mize
William N. Carr

Semiconductor Memory
Design and Application

1

Memory Functions and Economics

1.1 INTRODUCTION

The advent of discrete semiconductors and the technological follow-on, e.g., the monolithic integrated circuits, have had significant impact on the performance, cost, reliability, maintainability, physical size, and architecture of the central processing units of digital computers[1,2,3] and of all varieties of digital systems.

The use of semiconductors has now started to spread to peripheral equipment and is having the same strong impact there as it did in other digital systems.

Memory, of course, is one of these peripherals. This discussion examines elements or media that perform the storage function. These elements, or media, are called storage elements. When they are organized and combined in a particular arrangement, they are referred to as a memory or memory system.

Such memory systems fall into functional categories, and these functional categories relate to the type of application of the memory.

Increasing emphasis has been placed on the application of semiconductor memory to these categories.[4,5,6] It is the purpose of this book to identify these storage system functional categories; discuss the media that serves them; show how semiconductors serve them; provide some design principles that are applied in designing the storage elements; tell where the memory systems are applied and how; and analyze the advantages and disadvantages, including reliability and costs, of the semiconductor storage elements.

This chapter identifies the storage functional categories and discusses the characteristics of the categories and the major application areas. It also identifies how semiconductors provide the storage elements for each category and concludes with a discussion of the economic goals for semiconductor storage elements. Since the price projection for semiconductor storage elements will have a significant impact on digital systems by providing more bits per second per dollar, it is important that the engineer designing semiconductor storage elements into a system know the basis for these price projections. If he understands, he will gain confidence that these projections will occur as he sees the data develop.

1.2   THE THREE CATEGORIES OF STORAGE FUNCTIONS

The three categories chosen for storage functions are: sequentially accessed storage, random access storage, and fixed program storage.

Before examining sequentially accessed storage in detail, let us look briefly at random access storage and then return with greater detail later. As shown in Fig. 1.1, random access storage involves choosing an address randomly. The address locates a bit of information which is received at the output. Each bit of information can be located with approximately the same time delay. For example, the arrival of the information for address $X_0 Y_0$ at the output is the time indicated at A from $t = 0$, which is when the address is applied. The time shown at B is for the information at $X_1 Y_1$. $X_n Y_n$ information arrives at time C. All times are approximately the same. The time variation over all bits from randomly chosen addresses fits into a narrow band. Thus, the term *random access* is used for this type of storage.

1.2.1   Sequentially Accessed Storage

Description.   Sequentially accessed storage provides data with varying time delays from a reference point, depending on the position of the data in a time sequence. Figure 1.2 shows the use of paper tape as the storage media. The state of the bits in the digits is identified by the presence or absence of holes in the tape. The digits are separated physically in series on the tape.

The bits in the digit are sensed as they move by $t = 0$ as shown in Fig. 1.2a. The timing diagram of Fig. 1.2b shows the timing sequence of the data sensed at the output. Digit 1 arrives at t_1, digit 3 at $3t_1$, digit 5 at $5t_1$. Data at the output have a varying time delay from t_0 depending on the position in the time sequence. Thus, the term *sequentially accessed* is used for this type of storage.

Other media may have different characteristics than paper tape; they may require more or fewer bits, and they may store these differently than paper tape—for example, magnetic bits on magnetic tape—but the basic sequentially accessed concept still is valid.

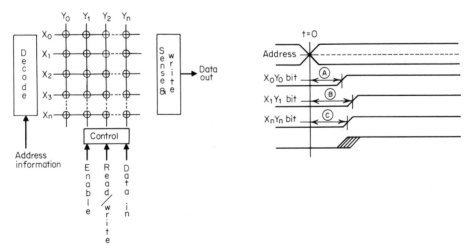

Fig. 1.1.   Random access storage.

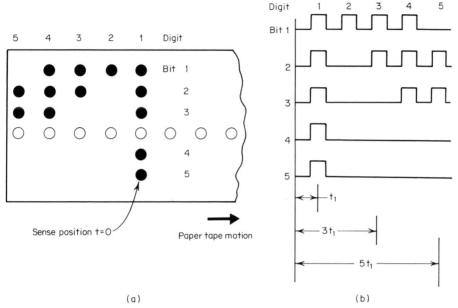

(a)   (b)

Fig. 1.2. Sequentially accessed storage.

When the sequentially accessed data are received, they are normally presented for use in two formats. One of these formats, shown in Fig. 1.3, is bit-serial digit-serial. In this format, data are presented at the output one bit at a time, separated by a time interval. The second of these formats, shown in Fig. 1.4, is bit-parallel digit-serial. In this format, the number of bits in the code for the digit are all presented at the same time: in parallel in the same time interval.

In bit-serial digit-serial format, four clock times are required to identify all the bits in a digit because only one bit is at the output at a given time. In bit-parallel digit-serial format, all the bits to identify a digit come out in parallel. Digit 1 is at the output at t_1, and digit 2 at t_2.

In mass memory, seven- and nine-channel magnetic tape storage and magnetic disk with fixed heads are examples of bit-parallel digit-serial. Magnetic disk storage with one movable head per surface is an example of bit-serial digit-serial.

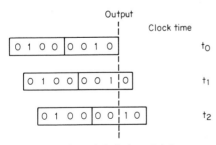

Fig. 1.3. Bit-serial digit-serial format.

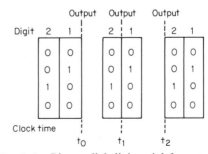

Fig. 1.4. Bit-parallel digit-serial format.

Major Application Areas for Sequentially Accessed Storage.   The major applications for sequentially accessed storage divide into two areas as shown in Fig. 1.5: mass memory for computers, and temporary storage for peripherals, terminals, and office equipment.   Peripherals and terminals have refresh memories and buffer I/O memories.   Office equipment uses temporary storage for calculators and buffer I/Os.   Sequentially accessed storage is used in these applications because it provides an economical solution for both large-capacity mass memory and small-capacity temporary storage.

Most designers are aware that the mass memory market is served by paper tape, punched cards, magnetic tape, and magnetic disk.   Semiconductors, at the present time, do not serve this market; however, semiconductors do provide the solution for temporary storage.   To understand the advantages of SCs in this application, the characteristics of the media used for mass memory will be examined.

Access times of paper tape, magnetic tape, and magnetic disk are very slow: from milliseconds to minutes.   These media provide permanent storage and nondestructive readout but have the major disadvantage, in addition to slow access times, of poor reliability of the mechanism that moves the media.   It is all mechanical and thus suffers from the problems of adjustment, critical tolerances, and short-term periodic maintenance.

An examination of the characteristics of low-capacity storage applications shows that such applications are not permanent, but temporary.   Therefore, semiconductors can be used because volatility is no problem and they can also provide some distinct advantages to the designer.   They have submicrosecond to microsecond access times.   They are all-electronic, thus eliminating mechanical failure and providing improved reliability.   They also enable retention of the desired, nondestructive readout.

Semiconductor Shift Registers Are the Main Ingredient for Temporary Storage.   The semiconductor storage element that serves the temporary storage requirement is the shift register.   Following the data formats presented, as shown in Fig. 1.6*a,* the shift register has a basic element that is bit-serial digit-serial.   Bits are inserted at the input and are presented at the output in clock time sequence, after an initial time delay of N divided by the clock frequency.   Now, as shown in Fig. 1.6*b,* it is quite easy to convert to bit-parallel digit-serial operation by paralleling the basic elements.   Similarly, other simple modifications and additions can be made to shift registers to provide new applications.

For example, as shown in Fig. 1.7, just the addition of input gating to a shift register (this can be done on the same chip) allows the shift register to recirculate the data and perform the function of a refresh memory for a CRT terminal.

Office equipment	Temporary storage
Peripherals and terminals	Refresh memory buffer for I/O
Computers	Mass memory

Fig. 1.5.   Applications of sequentially accessed storage.

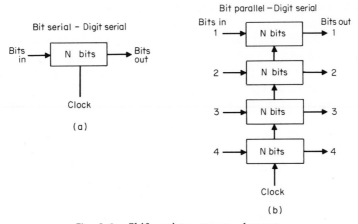

Fig. 1.6. Shift register storage elements.

This is a significant advantage of the semiconductor solution. Wide varieties of combinations of the two data formats integrated with other logic can be provided in an individual dual-in-line package with as many as 5,000 bits being used presently and emphasis continuing for even high density.

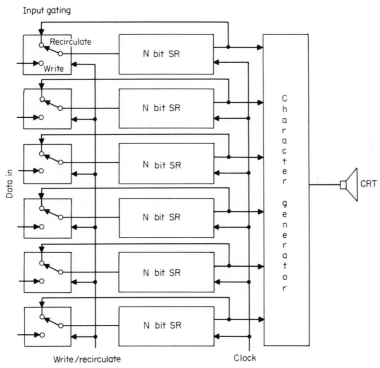

Fig. 1.7. Refresh memory for CRT.

Outlook for Semiconductors in the Mass Memory Market. The statement was made that the mass memory market is not presently served by semiconductors. Will it ever be? If so, when? Although no precise answers can be provided at this time, the objectives and design goals that face the semiconductor manufacturers can be outlined, and the progress being made toward those goals can be indicated. To do this, the characteristics of the mass memory market must be examined.

First, the capacity of the mass memory media varies. As illustrated in Fig. 1.8, using representative increments of the media, it can be seen that the capacity increases from 120,000 bits for 200 ft of paper tape to 4 billion bits per machine for a magnetic disk.

Second, the bit rate for mass memory increases dramatically. Including both the punch and read rates for paper tape and speeds up to 200 in. per sec for magnetic tape, the bit rate increases from 900 bits per sec for paper tape to 4.5 megabits per sec for magnetic disk, as illustrated in Fig. 1.9.

Third, access time decreases for the various mass memory media as illustrated in Fig. 1.10. Because, as was mentioned for sequentially accessed storage, the data are stored in a time sequence, access time does include varying latency times. The latency time is traversed at the rates indicated for paper tape, punched cards, and magnetic tape. The access time is given directly for magnetic disk and, as illustrated, it is 8.5 milliseconds (ms) for magnetic disk.

The last characteristic concerns cost. What is the cost? E. Holland[7] has presented data which are summarized in Fig. 1.11. The total system cost per bit is plotted against capacity in bytes. The cost starts at 1.25 cents per bit and extends below 1.25 millicents per bit.

Judging from the information shown in Fig. 1.11, it is clear that in capacities of mass memory greater than 10 million bytes any of the media from fixed head disk to moving head disks and tapes provide per bit system costs from approximately 10 to 130 millicents per bit.

Thus, the goals that semiconductors must meet to serve the mass memory market are clear: high density, low cost, and access time shorter than magnetic disk. The specific numbers are defined in Table 1.1.

Semiconductors are already being tried as solutions to storage elements for the mass memory application. One such solution is a long chain of shift registers using present technology. Another solution, which has been in the research and development laboratories and should emerge as a product in the near future, is arrays of

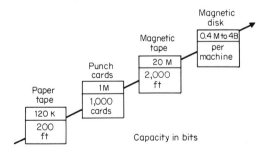

Fig. 1.8. Mass memory capacity.

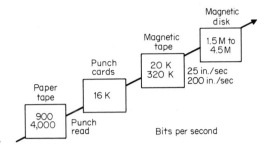

Fig. 1.9. Mass memory bit rate.

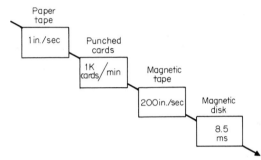

Fig. 1.10. Mass memory access time.

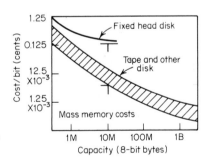

Fig. 1.11. Mass memory system cost per bit versus capacity in bytes.

Table 1.1   Objectives for SCs that Serve the Mass Memory Market

High density	10^5 to 10^6 bits per sq in.
Cost	Tens of millicents per bit
Access times	Less than 8.5 ms

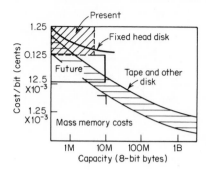

Fig. 1.12. Estimate of SC solutions.

charge coupled devices[8] and/or bucket brigade devices. An estimate of how these devices fit onto the cost-capacity plot of Fig. 1.11 is shown in Fig. 1.12.

To summarize, there are semiconductor solutions for temporary storage, and the industry is working on solutions for mass memory that have an acknowledged disadvantage of volatility. It will be interesting to see if the all-electronic solution can overcome this disadvantage.

1.2.2 Random Access Storage

Random access storage has been described, but further discussion is necessary. Refer to Fig. 1.13, which repeats Fig. 1.1. The address information, usually in binary code, selects a bit of information at random by decoder action. The storage must be enabled and in the read mode for reading. Control signals are present to accomplish this. The bit information passes to the sense amplifier and is received at the output. For receipt of the information at the output from any of the randomly selected bits there is only a small variation in the access time from any bit location. Obviously, there is addition control and interface circuitry to write information into the memory before it is read.

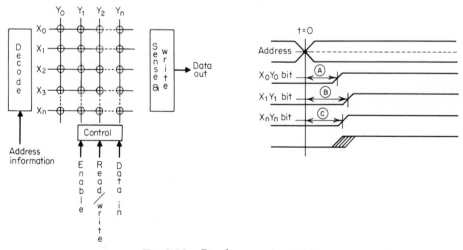

Fig. 1.13. Random access storage.

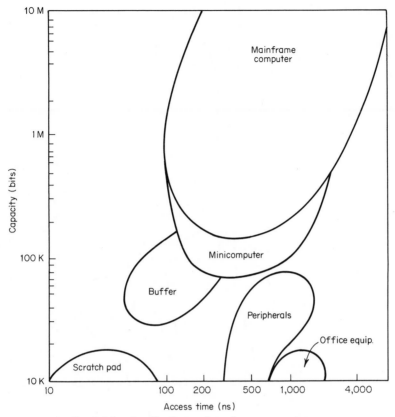

Fig. 1.14. Applications of random access storage.

Applications. Figure 1.14 shows where random access storage is being used. This illustration is generalized, so consider it in that light. The plot is for capacity of the storage system in bits versus access time in nanoseconds. The boundaries are typical values.

The major application of random access storage has been as a mainframe memory in computers, from the small minicomputer to the largest scientific computer. Capacities range from 64,000 bits to tens of millions of bits, the latter an extended memory application. Access times are from 100 ns to microseconds.

Buffer stores center in the 64,000-bit capacity, with access times at 100 ns. Scratch-pad memories that range in size from 256 bits to tens of thousands of bits have access times from 10 to 80 ns. Small local store and slower buffer memories are the storage requirements for peripherals extending up to tens of thousands of bits with access times to microseconds. Office equipment uses very small and slow memories which have capacities below 20,000 bits and microseconds access times.

During the past 15 years the dominant product for these applications has been one using magnetics as the storage media. This is illustrated in Fig. 1.15. Cores have had the broadest market coverage. Prior to semiconductors, core systems

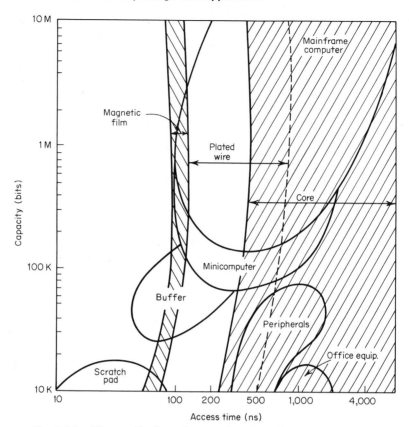

Fig. 1.15. The application of magnetics to random access storage.

provided the most economical solution at the performance required. Their typical speed range extends from 250 ns upward to 10 μsec.[9,10]

Plated wire systems, pursued only selectively, have demonstrated speeds down to 75 ns and up to 600 ns.[11] Magnetic film systems, now used only for isolated applications, have typical speeds below 100 ns.

Core Advantages. Why has core had such wide usage compared to the other magnetic media? The major reason is because core has provided a low-cost, high-capacity storage medium. Coupled with this, core storage systems have been designed for a wide performance range of access and cycle times, 250 ns to 10 μsec, nonvolatile storage, a nondissipative storage element, and an excellent reliability history. The reliability, to a large degree, has been a function of the support circuitry and not the core itself; the core itself seldom fails after it is in place.

Core System Disadvantages. Core systems have their disadvantages, the major one being limited speed performance. In fact, for storage requirements with cycle times below 200 ns, the cost per bit is not generally economical using cores. In addition, cost increases as speed increases. For example, increasing the speed performance of a core system from 1-μsec cycle time to 250-ns cycle time increases the cost by a factor of from 4 to 8 times.[12] This is because of higher manufacturing costs due to small cores and more expensive support circuitry.

There is another disadvantage associated with cost: Cost increases as the size of the memory decreases. This is directly related to the disadvantage that there is a pronounced interface between the storage media and the support circuits that are used with it. Different technologies and different packaging are used.

To emphasize these two points further, a major portion of the core system costs have been support electronics. Requirements are 250-to-500-mA drive circuits and sophisticated sense circuitry. These are expensive by themselves but result in low cost per bit if the number of bits serviced is large. However, as the number of bits is decreased, the cost of the support circuitry becomes a larger percentage of the memory system cost. Therefore, cost per bit increases. For example, a reduction in size of a memory system from 1 million bits to 64 thousand bits increases the cost per bit two to five times.[12,13]

Destructive readout is another disadvantage. Each time data are read from the memory they must be rewritten back into the memory, extending the cycle time of the system.

Core System Progress. Despite the disadvantages described, core has maintained its position in the face of competition because it has kept pace by improving its performance and reducing costs.

DeVoy and Moore in the *Honeywell Computer Journal* of 1971 have traced the cost reduction of core systems. They showed designs using 3D-4wire, 3D-3wire, and $2\frac{1}{2}$ D.[13] Their findings reveal that a memory of 16K words using a 3D-3wire design has been reduced in cost by a factor of 4 from 1966 to 1970. Cost of 4K-word and 8K-word memories was also reduced, but in a smaller proportion. In addition, they showed that in 1966 the $2\frac{1}{2}$ D design was the most economical of the three types for larger systems; in 1970 it was 3D-3wire. In other words, design improvements as well as cost reductions were made with performance also increasing. From 1963 to 1972 the core system speeds have increased by a factor of 6 to 8.[14]

Many factors, such as printed circuit frames, automated assembly, organizations that require less support circuitry and provide for fewer interconnections and lower-cost core stringing, and low overseas labor costs, have contributed to the lowering of cost. However, a major cost reduction has been the change from discrete to integrated-circuit support circuitry. Not only did this reduce packaging costs, but the subsequent reduction in integrated-circuit costs by semiconductor manufacturers resulted in additional system cost reductions.

An example of cost reduction is shown in Table 1.2. The cost reduction of each portion of a memory system is listed when the costs were compared for the years 1968 and 1970. The hardware costs used in the system remained the same, so no

Table 1.2. Core System Cost Reduction, 1968 to 1970

Stack	50 percent
I/Cs	50 percent
HDW	Same

cost reduction occurred there. However, both the stack costs and the peripheral overhead circuit costs dropped by 50 percent, and consequently half of the cost reduction was due to reduced IC costs.

Some additional cost reduction is apparently available for core systems through the use of tape cores, still more automated assembly, still further reduction in integrated support circuits, and a revival of the 2D design, especially for large systems. However, many feel that the fat has been trimmed and only small reductions remain. Only time will tell.

Semiconductor Solution for Random Access Storage. Semiconductor storage elements also satisfy the requirements of random access storage. Let's examine semiconductor storage elements in detail and see what characteristics they have, what applications they will satisfy, what they will cost, and whether they will replace core.

Applications. To the previous figure for random access storage applications (Fig. 1.14) a line has been added to illustrate in Fig. 1.16 the applications that the semiconductor storage elements can satisfy. SC memory systems meet the full range of random access storage requirements with bipolar systems meeting the high speed requirements for access times of 10 to 200 ns and MOS systems meeting the remainder.[15,16] N-channel MOS units with high speed performance (see Chap. 10) cause an overlap down to 100 ns.

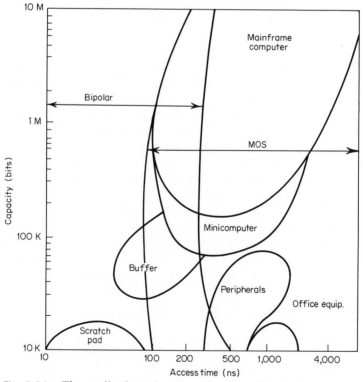

Fig. 1.16. The application of semiconductor random access storage.

Cycle time, ns	SC
10–200	Bipolar, ECL, TTL
100–400	N-MOS, P-MOS, C-MOS
400–800	P-MOS, N-MOS, C-MOS
800 up	P-MOS

Fig. 1.17. SC technologies for memory system speed.

Figure 1.17 shows how the MOS and bipolar technologies presently may be further segmented according to system speed, and it also demonstrates the wide range of performance of semiconductor elements for memory systems. The order of appearance of the technology under the SC column indicates its priority in satisfying the fastest speed most economically. SC memories using ECL circuitry have access times of less than 10 ns and are used for small scratch-pad memories with 10- to 30-ns cycle times. TTL memories have access times from 35 to 120 ns, depending on the speed/power tradeoffs, and are used in buffer memories, control memories, and high-speed mainframe memories with cycle times under 200 ns. N-channel MOS memories lead the way in MOS for highest performance, giving system speeds as fast as 100 ns. Since the n-channel MOS technology is not as mature as p-channel MOS, it will cost more initially but will still be below the high cost of its magnetic competitor. The established p-channel MOS will provide the most economical solution for the system speed ranges above 400 ns until challenged for that position by n-channel.

Characteristics. The second area deals with semiconductor memory system characteristics. A wide speed-performance range is only one characteristic. To help you recall what was said about core, a comparison will be made to core system characteristics. Semiconductor memory systems have an obvious speed advantage, satisfying the highest speed requirements, whereas core does not. This has been covered previously, so it is not included in the following table.

Table 1.3 shows a comparative analysis of the remaining vital performance characteristics of core and semiconductor memories.

Examining the table, it can be seen that core systems have had low costs for a wide range of performances. However, costs have increased for small sizes and for higher speeds. An advantage for SCs, besides the fact that systems have low costs and a wide performance range, is that the cost per bit tends to remain constant regardless of size. This is because the support circuitry does not change; there is just more of it. Architectural planners of computer systems feel this will have a significant impact on distributing smaller segments of storage throughout the machine, with systems performance thus increasing without paying a premium of higher costs. Both semiconductor and core memory systems can handle capacities of millions of bits.

SC memory has a nondestructive readout, an advantage over the destructive readout for core because it eliminates the time needed to rewrite data into the memory.

Table 1.3.   Comparison of the Performance Characteristics of Core and Semiconductor Memories

Performance characteristic	Core	SC
Cost/bit	Low	Low
	Up at small size	Constant with size
	Up at higher speed	
Capacity	Millions of bits	Millions of bits
Readout	Destructive	Nondestructive
Interface	Pronounced	Common
Packaging	Different	Common
		Small size
P_D	No P_D for element	P_D element
Storage volatility	Nonvolatile	Volatile
Reliability	Established	Being established
Use	Has customer acceptance	Needs customer acceptance

Core systems have pronounced interface between the storage element and the surrounding circuits. The packaging between storage element and other hardware is, therefore, quite different. SC memory systems have a common interface between surrounding circuitry and the storage circuitry. Even the interface between MOS and bipolar, which previously called for voltage translation circuits, is now being solved by designing the MOS for compatible logic levels. For the translations that remain, special monolithic circuits are being designed.

The common interface gives common packaging. With such common interfaces, systems are easily designed and implemented from smaller component packages into larger systems, and systems of a variety of organizations and capacities are configured easily from a common parts list. Such systems are reduced by at least a factor of 4 in physical size compared to their core system counterparts.

Core memory elements do have a power dissipation advantage because the storage element does not dissipate any power while the SC storage cell does. MOS storage dissipates microwatts per bit; bipolar dissipates milliwatts per bit. This advantage for cores disappears when the total system power is included—even when bipolar is used.

SC storage is volatile; core storage is not. This means that data will be destroyed if power is lost or, in the case of dynamic MOS storage elements, the data would disappear if they were not refreshed. This is a disadvantage for the SC memory system. However, only for in-line process control systems and special military systems is this a serious problem; because of the low power dissipation of SC storage elements, especially MOS, back-up systems using batteries have been very successfully applied.

When a storage element needs refreshing, as in noncritical data processing systems, the user has been willing to take the system time to refresh the volatile storage. It amounts to only 1 to 2 percent system time lost—time when the memory system is not available to the computer because it is being refreshed.

Core does have a good established reliability and certainly has customer acceptance. SC storage is at a disadvantage because the data to establish the reliability

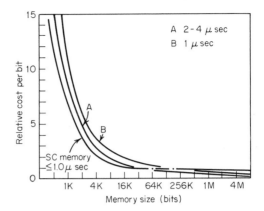

Fig. 1.18. 1972 systems costs: SC versus core.

are not yet available. It is this lack of an established reliability base that has hindered the commitment of SC memory designs to systems. Logic monolithic ICs have an excellent record of reliability. The same manufacturers are producing SC memory products and are building the reliability data base. As semiconductor memory systems demonstrate comparable reliability trends—field data are now beginning to appear—this barrier will disappear.

System Costs. The third area of comparison is memory system costs. Discussions of semiconductor storage element and SC memory system advantages and disadvantages are somewhat academic if these units are not used. They will not be used in high volume if the system cost does not compete with the core memory system costs.

The status of semiconductor memory systems cost compared to core systems cost is summarized in the chart in Fig. 1.18. Relative cost per bit is plotted against capacity. These costs are through 1972.[12,17,18] We see that the relative cost of a semiconductor memory system made up of dynamic MOS and with a cycle time less than 1 μsec is lower than the cost of a slow core memory (cycle time of 2 to 4 μsec) out to a capacity of 64K bits. After this, the core memory costs are lower. When equal cycle time systems are compared, that is, 1-μsec cycle times, the capacity approaches 256K bits for equal costs. The core memory system is lower in cost than the SC memory in large capacities.

As the production volume of catalog SC storage elements rises, the cost will decline. Consequently, the system's cost will reduce such that the differential shown between core memory systems and SC memory systems will reduce to zero, and SC memory will be lower cost than core, even in large capacities. For mainframe memory systems the advantage for SC compared to core is projected as 2 to 1 for 1975.

1.2.3 Fixed Program Storage

Introduction. The third category of storage is fixed program storage. As shown in Fig. 1.19, a typical fixed program storage element has an address input and a normal matrix, but instead of the bit information varying at each bit position, it is fixed. This is accomplished by providing coupling at the crosspoints in the matrix which are required to be a 1 (using the data notation of 0 and 1) and omitting the

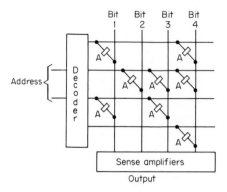

Fig. 1.19. A typical fixed program storage.

coupling at the crosspoints in the matrix which are required to be a 0. The letter A represents the coupling elements. The coupling element in present-day electronic fixed program storage is either inductive, capacitive, conductive, or optical.[19,20] There is normal address decoding and the normal sense circuitry, but with the majority of fixed program storage the write circuitry is omitted, and in this example data are written into the storage system when the unit is fabricated.

There are fixed program storage units where all 1s are written into the matrix during fabrication and 0 positions are programmed in electrically. The fuseable SC read only memories are examples. Also, units exist that contain write circuitry to alter the coupling at each bit position, such as the "floating gate" or charged dielectric MOS structures; in such units, the data are changed very seldom.

Characteristics. The basic characteristics of fixed program storage are: (1) it is considered a special application of random access storage in which the storage is fixed after programming, and (2) operation is in the read mode only, after the storage is programmed. Data are written only once for units that are programmed during fabrication or, for units that can be altered either electrically or from a radiation source, the data are changed very seldom. An alterable fixed program store that has the data changed periodically—with long periods of time between writing in new data, but fast access times on reading data—is called a read mostly memory system.

Obviously, random access storage can perform the same function that a fixed program storage can perform, but random access storage would have to rewrite after a read. If the application uses a fixed program storage system, then comparisons to determine if a fixed program storage element or a random access storage element is to be used for such read mostly applications show that the cost per bit favors the fixed program storage element. Reasons for this will become apparent after further discussion.

Applications. Fixed program storage finds use in many applications such as: instruction lists, look-up tables, code converters, keyboard encoders, character generators, microprogramming, and math function tables. In these applications the fixed program storage can be represented by a common diagram, as shown in Fig. 1.20a. The fixed program storage converts the input given to output data that exists as fixed data in the storage element. We need only change the name on the fixed

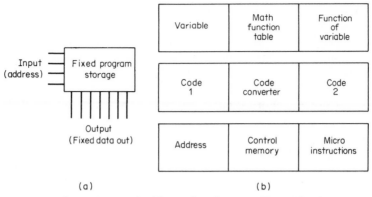

Fig. 1.20. Several examples illustrating the versatility of fixed program storage.

program storage box and it describes the application. Figure 1.20*b* lists several examples. A table for simple mathematical functions has an input of the variable with the output being the mathematical function of that variable. For code conversion, the input is code 1, the output code 2. A control memory for microprogramming has an address as an input and microinstructions as the output.

Other applications in computers are worthy of mention.[19] The first application is that in which fixed program storage is used for emulation. In such an application a computer is made to look like an entirely different computer, and it operates from programs prepared for an entirely different kind of computer. The second application is one in which fixed program storage is used for the special start-up programs for computers. In this application special functions are stored in the fixed program storage to initiate the system which is necessary because there is no information stored in the main memory. The third application uses a fixed program store for the location of faults in the computer. Such an application is very useful because the fault may prevent the normal diagnostic program from being entered or from operating in the computer.

Semiconductor Solutions. The semiconductor solution for fixed program storage is a component normally called read only memory or read only store. Either such semiconductor units are programmed during fabrication at the factory by using special masks in the slice process, or some form of electrically alterable programming is provided for programming by the user. Fabricated specially for each program required, the mask used for factory fabrication of the program is a unique mask for that store, and semiconductor units prepared in this manner are known as factory programmed units.

Advantages. The advantages of fixed program storage are: low cost, high density, speed, common interface, packaging, cost independent of size, nonvolatility, and electrical programmability. Many of the advantages shown are similar to those for random access storage.

When compared to other techniques, SC fixed program storage offers significant improvement in the cost of fixed program storage. As discussed previously, random access memory provides a very low cost potential. But fixed program storage has an even lower cost potential for the *same unit volume,* primarily because the matrix cell requires only one device to provide the coupling element shown in Fig. 1.19, and therefore, the chip size is smaller by as much as a factor of 2 compared to random access storage.[21]

Also, SC storage has the advantage of high density compared to other types of fixed program storage. For example, a read only SC memory with 2,000 bits per dual-in-line package, attached one package per sq in., has a density of 310 bits per sq cm. This is 40 to 60 times better than a capacitive fixed program storage system with a bit density of approximately 5 bits per sq cm.[19] A corresponding reduction in physical size for a total store fabricated from these packages results from this high-density SC storage.

Speed is another advantage semiconductors provide when they are used for fixed program storage. When a read only memory is used for control memory micro-programming, several microinstructions must occur per cycle of main memory; in fact, the ROM cycle may have to be four to five times faster than the random access memory—therefore, the emphasis is on speed.

As with random access storage, semiconductor read only memories have had no problem meeting the speed requirements. In fact, they provide speeds comparable to logic gates, and thus, are used as logic gates. This improved speed is particularly apparent when random logic is replaced with read only memory bits. Additional information concerning this application is discussed in Chap. 8.

The advantages of common interface, packaging, and approximately constant cost per bit independent of memory size are the same advantages that have already been discussed for random accessed storage, and thus, they need not be discussed again.

SC fixed program storage is nonvolatile, which is a significant advantage for the SC fixed program storage, because, unlike the SC random access storage, which is volatile, the information remains fixed even though power is removed from the unit. Of course, non-SC types of fixed program storage exist that are also nonvolatile, but they are slower and do not have the density that SC storage provides.

The last advantage of SC fixed program storage is its electrical programmability. As mentioned earlier, semiconductor storage units can be designed to be electrically programmable, providing the equipment designer with the opportunity to change the program in the unit as he designs his system. External currents or voltages are applied to program the unit. Units of this type are provided both in MOS and bipolar, with bipolar being of two types: one type has a fuseable link where a conductive path is opened; a second type uses an avalanche technique to form a conductive path.

MOS units, as yet, do not have the capability to be programmed by fusing. They are programmed by storing charge on a floating gate or in a dielectric structure, and in the process, these charges must be neutralized by some form of radiation, or by injecting a like amount of opposite charge carriers.

Electrically programmable units are particularly useful in the early stages of equipment design. As these first designs evolve and change, the programs in the fixed store change. If an electrically programmable unit has been designed in, it can be altered quite easily in the system designer's facilities. After the design is complete, and if the system volume is large, a unique mask can be fabricated for the device and factory programmed units, either MOS or bipolar, used in the final system design.

Items of Concern. Three factors presently pose problems with fixed program storage. The first factor is reliability, which has been discussed previously when describing random access storage. The same statements that apply to random access storage also apply to fixed program storage. However, a reliability base is being established presently and after trend lines are apparent, this reliability barrier will disappear.

The second problem factor is programming costs. Because the manufacturer incurs programming costs for programming units to a system designer's specification, these costs are included as one-time program costs to the user. For factory programmed units, these costs are principally the cost of the mask; for electrically programmable units these costs are the logistic costs plus the yield loss. A yield loss must be a factor because certain parameters cannot be tested until the units are programmed, and the user will experience this yield loss as he programs the units in his plant because the same parameter limits cannot be verified until the unit is programmed.

Depending on the volume, these programming costs can be significant. With the one-time factory programming costs in the hundreds of dollars—if only 10 factory programmed units are ordered—the cost per bit could increase significantly because of the programming costs. In high volume there is little noticeable impact on cost per bit; for small quantities, the electrically programmable units help maintain programming costs at a minimum. However, more silicon area is required for the electrically programmable type. Therefore, you should expect the cost per bit to be higher than that of the factory programmed type.

The third problem factor is a delivery time delay required to prepare the program for the factory programmed units. In the past, such time delays have been as long as 8 to 10 weeks. However, significant progress is being made by industry by using computer software to reduce this time to 2 to 4 weeks.

Performance Capabilities of Semiconductor Fixed Program Storage Elements. Figure 1.21 details the performance capabilities of the semiconductor fixed program storage, listing the capacities, power dissipation per bit, and access time of bipolar and MOS devices. Bipolar storage is available with access times from 35 to 100 ns, in capacities from 256 to 8,000 bits, and with power dissipation per bit from 0.1 to 1 mW. MOS

Bipolar capabilities	MOS capabilities
Capacities Per pkg.—256 to 8K P_D/bit—0.1 to 1 mW Access time—35 to 100 ns	Capacities Per pkg.—1K to 16K P_D/bit—0.05 to 0.2 mW Access time—300 ns to 1.5μsec

Fig. 1.21. Performance capabilities of semiconductor fixed program storage.

has capacities to 16,000 bits, with access times from 300 ns to 1.5 μsec, and with power dissipation in the microwatts per bit range.

For fixed program storage, the emphasis certainly will continue to be on finding ways to improve density and, because of the control memory, to increase speed.

1.3 PRICE PROJECTIONS FOR SEMICONDUCTOR MEMORIES

As mentioned at the beginning of this chapter, circuit designers and system designers must have confidence in the projected cost of storage element bits before they will commit these units to memory systems. This section provides projected prices for semiconductor storage bits and establishes the basis used for making these projections. The target year is 1975.

1.3.1 Market Growth

A market projection will establish the data base such as shown in Fig. 1.22. There are two curves in this plot: The bottom curve represents the total accumulated number of digital logic gates used in end equipment plotted versus time; the top curve represents the total number of storage bits used in end equipment plotted versus time.

A number of techniques are available for estimating the market growth. The technique used in Fig. 1.22 examines the various electronic end equipment market segments and projects the end use of SC functions based on these markets with these functions expressed as the lowest level functions relatable across the semiconductor technologies.[23] The lowest level of a logic function is a gate; the lowest level of a storage function is a bit.

History through 1972 is used as a base, and the expected growth for logic gates and storage bits is projected on these curves through 1980. Logic gates grow by a factor of 10 based on established growth rates prior to 1972.

Based on expected trends in end equipment and memory design related to factors that have been discussed, storage bits are projected to grow at a rate three to five times that of logic gates. That is, more storage will be used per logic gate, resulting

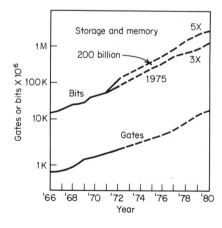

Fig. 1.22. Market growth of logic gates and storage bits.

in the total storage market increasing by a factor of 30 to 50 during the 10-year period.

Our interest is in the number of total storage bits in 1975. Projections from different sources vary, but they seem to fall between 170 billion to 210 billion bits. The point chosen for this discussion for 1975 is 200 billion bits, which includes all domestic types of storage, MOS and bipolar ROMs, RAMs, and shift registers, plus magnetic core. It does not include mass memory. The question naturally arises: What is it going to cost the manufacturer per bit for the SC bits of storage in his equipment? The next section examines that part of the problem.

1.3.2 Prices

The prices of semiconductor components have decreased continuously over the past 10 years, caused primarily by technological advances, but also forced by the competitive nature of the market. Price declines follow a learning curve. The basic concept of a learning curve is that after a product is in mass production, each time the cumulative production doubles, the unit price reduces by a constant percentage. Such a curve is plotted in Fig. 1.23, which is a curve for IC gates. Electronic Industries Association published data form the data base for the solid curve, and the trend is projected to continue. The price line falls at a 70 percent rate; that is, if the price of a gate is 10 cents at a given number of accumulated units shipped, if that volume doubles, the price of the gate will be 7 cents. The prices of other types of semiconductor integrated circuits, if studied individually, may vary somewhat in their learning curve from this slope, but, on the average, they follow the 70 percent learning curve. If the technologies used for SC memories are compared to those used for logic gates, at this time it is estimated that SC memories will follow a 70 percent learning curve. Such a curve is plotted in Fig. 1.24 with price per bit shown on the vertical axis.

Examining the limited data provided by 1970 and 1971 history, a cost point is established for the average price per bit of 1 cent in 1971; a 70 percent learning curve is shown from this point. The total number of bits delivered as they accumulate with time is plotted on the lower axis. For example, the accumulative storage bits at the midpoint of 1970 is 1 billion bits; for 1972 it is 10 billion bits. To determine the average price for the year, the midpoint of the volume is taken for that year.

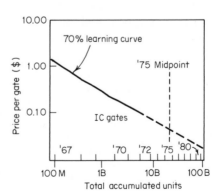

Fig. 1.23. Learning curve for IC gates.

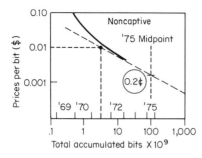

Fig. 1.24. Price projections for noncaptive semiconductor storage bits.

The learning curve shown in Fig. 1.24 is for the noncaptive SC storage bits. To obtain the accumulated bits versus time, the appropriate assumptions were made of percent penetration for semiconductors and percent captive versus noncaptive. These were varied for the different years and various combinations were tested to arrive at the time distribution shown in Fig. 1.24. Several of the cases tested are shown in Table 1.4.

For 1975, the learning curve projection of Fig. 1.24 indicates that the average price per bit of semiconductor storage will be 0.2 cent per bit. The learning curve is plotted through the midpoint in 1971, as if the manufacturing process were completely established in full mass production. Obviously, the semiconductor memory market is not yet at that point and thus the deviation from this curve in the early history of the product.

1975 will be considered in more detail to see if a price projection for MOS and bipolar storage bits can be determined.

The major portion of the market is random access storage with the remainder consisting of shift registers and read only memory. Presently, the major portion of the random access storage is core. Because the semiconductor product to compete with core is dynamic MOS, a major portion of the market will be MOS, with read only memories for fixed program storage also destined to be primarily MOS.

Even though the semiconductor read only memory component has lower cost potential at the same volume than random access memory, semiconductor read only memory will be used much less than semiconductor random access memory. Shift registers will continue to be supplied by MOS with only a small percentage bipolar.

Based on these assumptions, a present estimate of the semiconductor market by memory categories and the technology is shown in Fig. 1.25. As can be noted, MOS technology will be used for 80 percent of the storage bit requirements and bipolar for 20 percent.

Table 1.4. SC Penetration and Noncaptive Percentage (1975)

Case	1	2	3	4
SC bits (billions)	200	200	170	220
Percent SC	60	40	60	60
Percent mag	40	60	40	40
Percent noncaptive	60	60	60	60

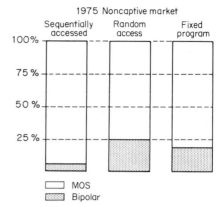

Fig. 1.25. Estimate of 1975 SC market by categories and technology.

The question remains: What is the projected average price per storage element bit for MOS and bipolar storage elements?

These can be projected by assuming volume variations, SC penetrations, and non-captive percentages, as in Fig. 1.25 and Table 1.4. The data shown in Fig. 1.25 on technology percentages are coupled to the above assumptions to obtain the spread of bit costs. The result of the analysis at the present time indicates that the average price for MOS storage element bits in 1975 is between 0.1 and 0.2 cent per bit and for bipolar storage element bits between 0.3 to 0.5 cent per bit.

REFERENCES

1. W. F. Jordan, Main Memory: Past, Present and Future, *Honeywell Computer J.*, **5**(2): 52–57(1972).
2. C. J. Walter, Impact of Fourth Generation Software on Hardware Design, *IEEE Comput. Group News*, **2**(4): 1–10(July 1968).
3. E. C. Joseph, Memory Hierarchy: Computer System Considerations, *Comput. Des.*, pp. 165–168, November 1969.
4. D. A. Hodges, Large-capacity Semiconductor Memory, *Proc. IEEE*, **56**(7): 1148–1161(July 1968).
5. R. J. Petschauer, Trends in Memory Element and Subsystem Design in the 1970s, *IEEE Comput.*, **3**(6): 12–17(November/December 1970).
6. L. C. Hobbs, Present and Future State-of-the-Art in Computer Memories, *IEEE Trans. Electron. Comput.*, **EC-15**(4): 485–501(August 1966).
7. E. Holland, Minicomputer I/O and Peripherals, *IEEE Comput. Group News*, **3**(4): 10–14(July/August 1970).
8. W. S. Boyle and G. E. Smith, Charge-coupled Devices—A New Approach to MIS Device Structures, *IEEE Spectrum*, **8**(7): 18–27(July 1971).
9. T. J. Gilligan, 2½ D High Speed Memory System: Past, Present, Future, *IEEE Trans. Electron. Comput.*, **EC-15**(4): 475–485(August 1966).
10. J. R. Brown, Jr., First- and Second-order Finite Memory Core Characteristics and Their Relationship to System Performance, *IEEE Trans. Electron. Comput.*, **EC-15**(4): 475–485(August 1966).
11. S. Waaben, High-speed Plated-wire Memory System, *IEEE Trans. Electron. Comput.*, **EC-16**(3): 335–343(June 1967).

12. T. W. Hart, Jr., and D. D. Winstead, Semiconductor Memory Systems—What Will They Cost? *Electron. Eng.,* pp. 50–54, September 1970.
13. D. D. DeVoy and D. W. Moore, A Case for Increasing the Modularization of Large High Performance Digital Memories, *Honeywell Computer J.,* **5**(2): 58–65(1971).
14. R. A. Henzel and D. L. House, Semiconductor Memories and Minicomputers, *IEEE Comput.,* **4**(2): 23–29(March/April 1971).
15. R. F. Graham, Semiconductor Memories: Evolution or Revolution, *Datamation,* June 1969.
16. R. A. Farley, Modular MOS Memory Challenges Core in Data Buffering, *Comput. Des.,* pp. 38–41, September 1969.
17. E. DeAtley, The Big Memory Battle: Semis Take on Cores, *Electron. Des.,* pp. 70–77, July 19, 1970.
18. G. E. Moore, Semiconductor RAMs—A Status Report, *IEEE Comput.,* **4**(2): 6–10 (March/April 1971).
19. R. Dussine, Evolution of ROM in Computers, *Honeywell Computer J.,* **5**(2): 79–87(1971).
20. F. Filippazzi, A New Approach to Permanent Memory, *IEEE Trans. Electron. Comput.,* **EC-16**(3): 370–731(June 1967).
21. B. T. Murphy, Cost-Size Optima of Monolithic Integrated Circuits, *Proc. IEEE,* **52**(12): 1537–1545(December 1964).
22. W. Taren, Semiconductor Memory Systems: How Much Do They Really Cost? *Electronics,* **143**: 94–97(October 12, 1920).
23. R. Graham and M. E. Hoff, Why Semiconductor Memories, *Electron. Prod.,* **11**: 28–34(January 1970).

2

The Semiconductor Technology Arsenal
for Storage Elements

2.1 CHARACTERISTICS OF THE DESIRED SEMICONDUCTOR STORAGE ELEMENT

Seven basic design goals must be considered when evaluating the array of semiconductor technologies available for performing the storage function. These goals directly affect the characteristics of semiconductor storage elements. The first and foremost goal is *economy* consistent with the level of performance required including speed, reliability, and other factors. Economy is measured in terms of cost per bit. The primary competition of semiconductor memory is, of course, magnetic devices such as core, plated wire, drum, and tape. To be competitive, semiconductor random access memories and fixed program memories must be in the tenths of cents per bit range. Sequentially accessed semiconductor mass memory must attain a cost goal of tens of millicents per bit. Projections indicate these economic goals will be attained by the mid-seventies. Whatever technologies are selected must be compatible with these economic estimates or must lead to further cost reductions.

A second design goal is that of *low power dissipation per bit*. This is important since it is desirable to constrain our overall electronic system to a physical size which is as small as possible. Resulting heat dissipation becomes a major factor working within this constraint.

A third characteristic to be attained and one which is interrelated with low power dissipation is *speed performance*. Achieving high-speed performance, defined in terms of bit rate, access time, or cycle time, is important because it enables data processing time within the electronic system to be kept minimal. The result is more effective use of the system. Fundamental limitations arise when attempting to achieve fast switching speed and low power dissipation simultaneously. In practical terminology, power dissipation and operating speed are related through the so-called speed/power product. The resulting numerical product is determined by the characteristics of the chosen device technology. Expressed in units of *energy*, the speed/power product is, therefore, directly related to the efficiency with which a logic or memory function can be performed. The speed/power product concept, as it relates to the various technologies, will be considered in detail later in this chapter.

25

A fourth desirable goal to be achieved is *small area per bit*. The area per bit will, of course, directly affect the overall *system* size. Encouraging possibilities offered by semiconductor storage elements are demonstrated by a comparison of 4K bits of MOS semiconductor random access memory with 4K bits of magnetic core, Fig. 2.1. In addition, the cost per bit is directly related to the silicon area per bit required for a given semiconductor storage function. So for maximum economy, considerable design effort is expended reducing the silicon area per bit.

Nondestructive readout and nonvolatility of the memory cell can be considered simultaneously as the fifth and sixth design goals. Nondestructive readout is desirable because, with its realization, data processing time is not wasted recirculating data back into the memory cell after the read operation. Nonvolatility is desirable because it permits the cell to maintain its memory content despite possible power-supply disruption; reprogramming after reenergizing of power supplies is, therefore, unnecessary. Magnetic memory elements suffer from destructive readout, but do offer nonvolatility; *semiconductor* memory cells suffer from volatility, but offer nondestructive readout.

The required *reliability* of the semiconductor memory element is the seventh design goal. The mean time between failures (MTBF)[1] of a memory system determines the repair and maintenance cost, as well as the system availability. Assessment of the *system's* mean time between failures requires a knowledge of the failure rates of the *components* which comprise the system. The approximate failure rate that could be allowed for a 1,024-bit RAM used in a 10 million bit memory system, where the repair frequency is once every month, is 0.007 percent per 1,000 hours per 1,000 bits. Although these low failure rates are presently available with existing circuits, the technology must be utilized in such a manner as to increase the reliability and the mean time between failures in order to implement even larger machines with improved reliability. Thus, particular attention must be given to semiconductor technologies such as diffusion, oxide growth, ion implantation, metalization, bonding, and packaging. This attention is essential because new semiconductor storage

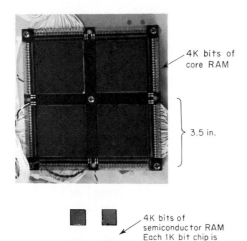

4K bits of core RAM

3.5 in.

4K bits of semiconductor RAM
Each 1K bit chip is 115 mils by 145 mils

Fig. 2.1. Area comparison of 4,096 bits of MOS RAM with 4,096 bits of magnetic core.

elements are continually being developed which require fabrication techniques whose resulting product reliability has not been established previously.

2.2 REVIEW OF PRESENT-DAY SEMICONDUCTOR MEMORY CIRCUITS

Since much present-day technology is directed toward using bipolar devices in semiconductor memory circuits, let us begin our analysis with these devices. The bistable flip-flop, Fig. 2.2, consisting of two cross-coupled inverters, has been the basic storage cell adopted for bipolar random access memories (RAMs) and also serves as the basis for presently available bipolar *sequentially accessed* memory elements (shift registers). With two stable states, the flip-flop memory cell stores information in the form of 1s and 0s. The storage states are stable (static operation is possible) until an externally applied signal changes the situation. Enjoying high yield, the cell has good operating speed capabilities and provides a cost-effective design.

The simplicity of bipolar *fixed program or read only memory* (ROM) is illustrated by the representation of the memory matrix shown in Fig. 2.3. Because of its simplicity, ROM circuitry requires only small area per bit. Therefore, many more bits of *ROM* can be fabricated on a given size chip than is the case for *RAM* and *sequentially accessed memory* circuits.

In an effort to reduce area per bit in bipolar RAMs, emphasis has been given to circuitry which departs from a static mode of operation with classical flip-flops to that of a dynamic mode of operation featuring greatly simplified circuitry. The operational basis of this circuitry is charge storage on the capacitance of reverse-biased p-n junctions.[2] Because of leakage current, memory cells which operate on the principle of charge stored on p-n junction capacitance eventually lose their information content and must be refreshed at intervals less than a few tenths of a

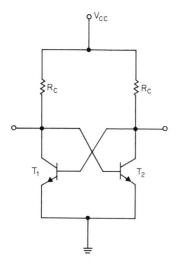

Fig. 2.2. The basic bistable flip-flop (bipolar technology).

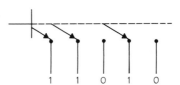

Fig. 2.3. Representation of the basic bipolar ROM circuit.

second. Such circuits are operated, therefore, in a dynamic mode and are referred to as dynamic memory circuits. These contrast with the *static* operation of flip-flop memory elements. Developmental efforts will undoubtedly continue to reduce the device count and silicon area consumed per bipolar memory cell. Further discussion of dynamic bipolar circuit operation is presented in Chap. 4.

Shifting our attention to MOS circuitry we find that the basic flip-flop is also employed for statically operated RAMs and shift registers. Examples are shown in Fig. 2.4a and b, respectively. The trend, however, as evidenced by numerous commercial products, is to *dynamic* operation with device count and silicon area per bit effectively reduced. An example of one type of *dynamic* shift register is shown in Fig. 2.5 (*cf.* Chap. 3). A number of dynamic RAM circuits are now commercially available, and the basic circuitry for these 4-, 3-, and 1-MOS transistor dynamic RAM cells is shown in Fig. 2.6a, b, and c, respectively. The design and application of these cells will be presented in Chaps. 5 and 10, respectively. Discussion in this chapter focuses on fabricational aspects of these circuit elements.

The MOS ROM is similar to its bipolar counterpart because of its extreme simplicity (Fig. 2.7). Resulting MOS ROM cells are small (1 transistor per cell) and, as with *bipolar,* many more bits of MOS ROM can be fabricated on a given size silicon chip than for MOS RAM and sequentially accessed memory circuits.

2.3 THE CONCEPT OF SILICON REAL ESTATE

2.3.1 Introduction to Silicon Processing

(a) MOS. By way of introduction to the concept of silicon real estate and the importance of reducing the silicon area per bit consumed by memory circuitry, let us first consider the fundamental steps of MOS and bipolar integrated-circuit fabrication.

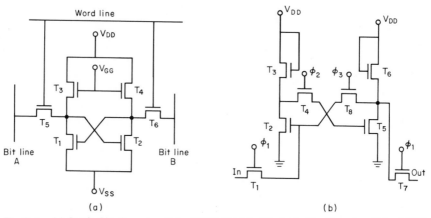

Fig. 2.4. (*a*) Static flip-flop circuit for MOS RAM; (*b*) static flip-flop circuit for MOS shift register.

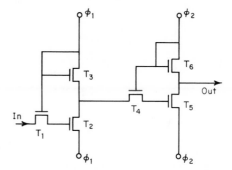

Fig. 2.5. One bit of dynamic shift register circuitry.

Figure 2.8 summarizes the basic process sequence for the formation of standard p-channel MOS circuits. The process is initiated at A with n-type silicon wafers approximately 14 mils thick and of $\approx$1 to 4 Ohm-cm resistivity. A layer of silicon dioxide (i.e., glass) of $\approx$5000 Å thickness is thermally grown on the surface of the silicon wafer at elevated temperature (typically 1000°C) at B. The top of the oxide layer is then coated with a photosensitive emulsion which is referred to as photoresist at C. After curing the photoresist, a photomask (usually a glass transparency), shown

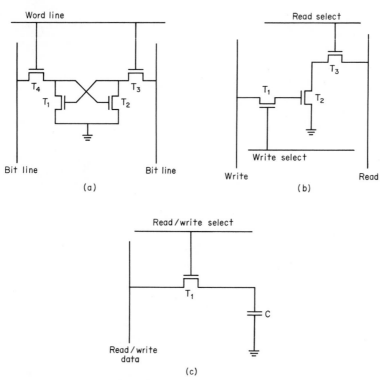

Fig. 2.6. Dynamic MOS RAM cells: (*a*) 4-transistor; (*b*) 3-transistor; (*c*) 1-transistor.

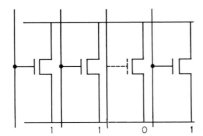

Fig. 2.7. Representation of a basic MOS ROM circuit.

in Fig. 2.9, possessing many repetitive patterns of the desired configuration is placed in contact with the surface of the photoresist and exposed to light. The photomask can also be used for a projection-type exposure of the photoresist. Development of the exposed photoresist pattern takes place in a manner analogous to that used in classical photography. With desired areas of the photoresist thereby selectively removed, as shown in D of Fig. 2.8, the silicon wafer is then immersed in a hydrofluoric acid solution, and silicon dioxide areas are selectively removed by etching

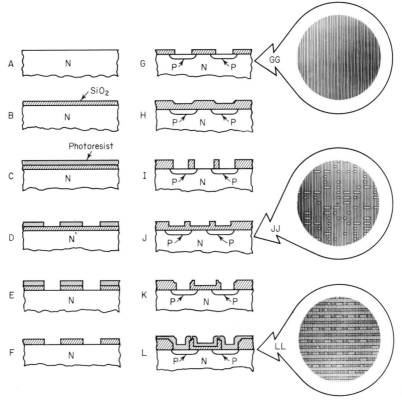

Fig. 2.8. Basic process sequence for the formation of standard p-channel MOS integrated circuits. Inserts GG, JJ, and LL are photomicrographs of the IC chip at various process steps.

Fig. 2.9. Photomask for a 3-in. diameter silicon wafer.

at E. The photographic emulsion is etch resistant to hydrofluoric acid, hence the term "photoresist."

When the oxide etch process step is completed, the photoresist pattern is stripped from the slice with the appropriate chemicals at F. The slice, accompanied by many others that have been similarly processed, is then inserted into a furnace and p-type regions are formed, as shown in G, by the process of boron diffusion at approximately 1000°C. Note that the regions of silicon dioxide present serve as masking barriers against the boron so that only the desired regions such as source, drain, and interconnection areas are made p-type.

The foregoing procedure is called a batch process since numerous devices can be formed simultaneously on each slice and many slices can be etched and diffused in a given process step. The various regions that have been etched in the oxide and which will be diffused with boron atoms are shown at a magnification of 100X in Fig. 2.8 insert GG. This is an example of an MOS ROM geometry. Here the source and drain regions for the decoder section of the ROM take the form of long stripe areas. On completion of boron diffusion to a depth of a few microns, the silicon slices are removed from the diffusion furnace and returned to the oxidation furnace until ≈13,500 Å of oxide is formed, as shown in H.

A second photolithographic step is performed next. In this step, careful alignment of the photomask is maintained with respect to the pattern that resulted from the p-diffusion process. This is made possible by the step which was formed in the oxide. Mask alignment must be accurate to within a few microns. On completion of alignment and exposure, oxide etching again takes place and source, drain, and gate regions are cleared (I). When this procedure is completed, a very clean, ≈1200 Å oxide is grown (J). The gate-oxide regions of the decoder section of the ROM are shown in insert JJ of Fig. 2.8.

Formation of the gate oxide is followed by a third photolithographic step, which establishes contact holes by selectively etching the oxide (K).

Aluminum metalization of the slice then takes place, followed by a fourth photomasking step to selectively remove aluminum with an appropriate etch solution. Source, drain, gate, and interconnecting metal regions are formed with this processing step (L).   A protective layer of glass is then deposited over the entire circuit, basically completing the process.   The resulting slice is shown in insert LL of Fig. 2.8.

(b) Bipolar.   Fabricating standard *bipolar* integrated memory circuits is somewhat more complicated than fabricating MOS circuits.   For bipolar circuits, circuit fabrication is initiated with a silicon wafer on which *previous* processing has been performed.   Epitaxial silicon is thus used in the first process step.   In the epitaxial materials preparation, n-type single-crystalline silicon has been grown on a p-type silicon substrate by the hydrogen reduction of silicon tetrachloride at a temperature of 1200°C.   N-type impurity dopant has been added to the gas flow.   A sheet of n-type silicon of 0.2-mil thickness has thus been formed on top of the p-type substrate (A in Fig. 2.10).   Prior to the epitaxial deposition, selective n+ regions (i.e., regions of heavy n-type dopant) have been diffused into the substrate.   The purpose of these regions is to obtain low collector series resistance in the completed circuit, thereby ensuring high switching speed.   It should be noted that these epitaxial slices are about a factor of 3 to 5 times more expensive than the silicon starting material used in MOS.   Insert photo AA shows the starting material after the subdiffusion step and prior to the epitaxial deposition.   The first process step consists in thermally oxidizing these pre-prepared epitaxial slices of several mils thickness (B).   Then employing the previously discussed photolithographic techniques, holes are etched in the oxide in preparation for isolation diffusion.   Note that preparation is being made to form thousands of different p-diffused regions on a single wafer, and that boron diffusion will be simultaneously formed in many wafers when they are positioned in the diffusion furnace (C).   Insert CC of Fig. 2.10 shows a portion of a

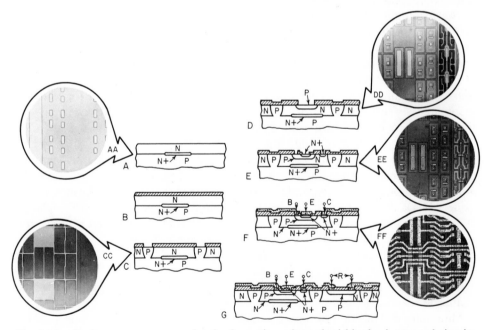

Fig. 2.10.   Basic process sequence for the formation of standard bipolar integrated circuits. Inserts AA, CC, DD, EE, and FF are photomicrographs of the IC chip at various process steps.

bipolar RAM slice after diffusion isolation where p-diffused moats form isolated n regions on which transistors and resistors will be structured. In the next step, the photolithographic process is used to form holes in the oxide where p-base regions or p-resistor regions are desired (D). So again, the slices are returned to the boron-diffusion furnace with results shown in insert DD of Fig. 2.10.

After the latter diffusion is completed and followed by suitable oxidation, a photolithographic process is used to cut holes in the oxide, this time for n^+ emitter structures and n^+ collector contact regions (E). Diffusion of the n^+ emitter structures is performed in a furnace containing phosphorus. Insert EE of Fig. 2.10 shows a portion of the wafer after emitter diffusion. Finally contact holes are etched in the oxide and aluminum is deposited on the slice. The metal is then selectively removed (F) in a photomasking step to define the desired interconnection pattern (Fig. 2.10 insert FF). A protective glass layer is then usually deposited on the completed wafer. Contact holes must be cut in the deposited glass layer in order to bond connecting wires between chip and package terminals. The finalized transistor structure with base, emitter, and collector contacts denoted as B, E, and C, respectively, as well as a resistor structure with contacts denoted as R is shown in G of Fig. 2.10.

2.3.2   MOS Bipolar Comparison

Processing conventional *bipolar* ICs involves more photolithographic and diffusion steps than those required for MOS. These process operations have costly labor content in them. The additional process steps of bipolar offer increased opportunities for yield loss in manufacturing. Furthermore, the starting material for bipolar circuits is more expensive than for MOS circuits. These factors, plus the fact that the circuit density of MOS can be compacted on silicon by a factor of ≈ 5 greater than that of bipolar, result in the greater cost per bit of bipolar semiconductor memory storage compared to MOS memory storage. The additional cost of bipolar is offset, however, by its superior *speed* performance, which is a factor of 10 to 100 times greater than standard p-channel MOS.

The speed advantage of bipolar arises from the basic parameter of transconductance (g_m). Recall that

$$g_m \equiv \frac{\Delta I_{\text{out}}}{\Delta V_{\text{in}}} \qquad (2\text{-}1)$$

and if it is required to charge or discharge a load capacitance C, i.e., swing between 0 and 1 state, the time taken when using a constant current source is

$$t \propto C \frac{\Delta V}{\Delta I} \qquad (2\text{-}2)$$

If charging or discharging takes place through the active device over the same voltage swing, then from Eqs. (2-1) and (2-2)

$$t \propto \frac{C}{g_m} \tag{2-3}$$

Hence the greater the g_m, the smaller the switching speed. (Switching speed is expressed in units of seconds.)

The transconductance g_m of the bipolar transistor is given by

$$g_m = \frac{I_E}{KT/q} \tag{2-4}$$

where I_E = emitter current, KT/q = 0.026 V at 300°K, and for the MOS transistor operation in the saturation region,

$$g_m = \frac{\mu\epsilon_{Ox}\epsilon_0 W}{t_{Ox}L} \mid V_G - V_T \mid \tag{2-5}$$

where μ = surface carrier mobility

ϵ_{Ox} = dielectric constant of SiO_2, 4.0

ϵ_0 = 8.85 · 10^{-14} F/cm

W = channel width

L = channel length

t_{Ox} = gate-oxide thickness

V_G = gate voltage

V_T = threshold voltage

It can be shown from Eqs. (2-4) and (2-5) and the current-voltage expression for the MOSFET operating in the saturation region

$$I = \left[\frac{\mu\epsilon_{Ox}\epsilon_0 W}{t_{Ox}L}\right]\left[\frac{(V_G - V_T)^2}{2}\right] \tag{2-6}$$

that for equal operating current values typical of memory circuitry, the g_m for the bipolar transistor is greater than that of the MOSFET by a factor of ≈ 100. Also, since

$$\frac{g_m(\text{bipolar})}{g_m(\text{MOSFET})} \propto \frac{I_E}{\sqrt{I_D}} \tag{2-7}$$

the g_m values of the bipolar transistor become even more favorable in comparison to the MOSFET as conduction current increases.

Furthermore, g_m of the bipolar transistor is essentially fixed by nature through values of K, T, and q [cf. Eq. (2-4)], while the g_m of the MOSFET is dependent on technology through the dielectric constant ϵ, μ, W, L, t_{Ox}, and V_G[cf. Eq. (2-5)]. Nevertheless, it appears unlikely that straightforward modifications of MOSFET technology can bring the g_m values of the MOSFET into a competitive position with those of the bipolar transistor—at least in the foreseeable future.

Thus, from these very basic considerations, it becomes apparent that bipolar plays its major role in *performance* (i.e., circuit speed), whereas MOS plays its major role in *economy*. These two basic principles should be used as guidelines in the employment of technology for developing semiconductor memories.

2.3.3 The Role of Silicon Real Estate

(a) Yield. With the foregoing considerations in mind, the discussion will turn to terms such as *silicon real estate, area per bit,* and *cell area,* and the minimization of the latter two quantities. Recall that minimization of cell area is required for system size reduction as well as for achieving maximum economy.

For a semiconductor storage element such as the 1,024-bit bipolar RAM shown in Fig. 2.11, considerable engineering effort has been expended designing and fabricating the circuitry onto as small a silicon area as possible. The area utilized by the circuit is referred to as silicon real estate. The design goal is to achieve the greatest circuit density possible on a given silicon area, in accordance with good engineering practices and overall product reliability. Since memory cell size thus becomes important, a figure of merit for a given technology and circuit form is expressed in terms of square mils per bit.

Now, if memory circuits (*chips*) such as shown in Fig. 2.11 are fabricated on 3-in. diameter silicon wafers (Fig. 2.12) with batch processing methods, it will be found at final test that not all the circuits will function properly; hence, not all the chips from a 3-in. silicon wafer will be usable. This implies that a manufacturing *yield* must be considered. The yield is less than 100 percent mainly because of:

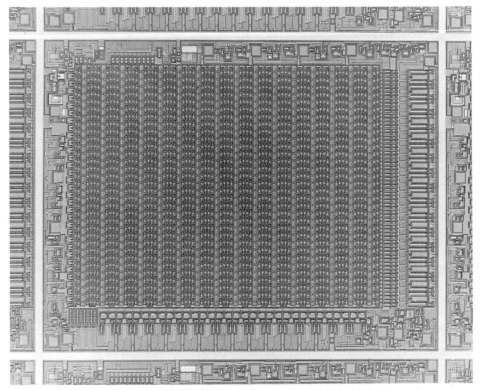

Fig. 2.11. Photomicrograph of the SN74S204 1,024-bit bipolar RAM.

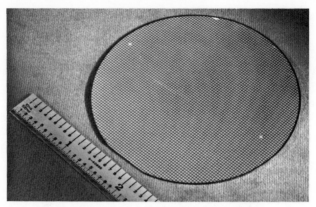

Fig. 2.12. A 3-in. diameter silicon wafer.

1. Materials defects
2. Defects in the photomasks
3. Pinholes in the oxide regions
4. Improper mask alignment
5. Defects in the photoresist
6. Processing errors such as over-etching, slice breakage, etc.

Yield is thus the percentage of acceptable memory circuits (chips) produced by a particular process. The number of potential flaws a circuit can encounter is a function of the *area* which the circuits occupy on the silicon wafer. The larger the required area, the more defects likely to be encountered and the lower will be the expected yield for a given defect density per unit area. Since it is desirable to obtain the maximum complexity in a memory chip, it is, therefore, necessary to minimize the area per bit or area per memory cell to obtain the highest yield possible. The memory cell is compacted both through improved *circuit design* (for example, reducing the device count) and through improved technology. An example of the latter is the refinement of photolithographic techniques which result in smaller device geometries.

(b) Circuit Costs. Since manufacturing yield will ultimately determine circuit costs, it is necessary to make quantitative statements concerning this important factor. A survey[3] of the present situation indicates (Fig. 2.13) that a 20 to 30 percent yield improvement per year can be expected for a given chip area as the semiconductor manufacturer gains experience with the technology. Consequently, the chip *area* for a given yield will increase with time. Thus, at any given design time, there is an optimum chip size[4] for a given technology which will minimize the projected system cost per memory bit. This situation is summarized generally in Fig. 2.14. The chip area is therefore made large to accommodate as many memory bits as possible on a given chip and within a single package. Yet it is not designed so large that yield loss significantly increases the cost per chip.

Recently, for new designs, the chip size for minimum cost per bit memory elements has been ≈175 × 175 mils for bipolar and ≈225 × 225 mils for MOS. MOS

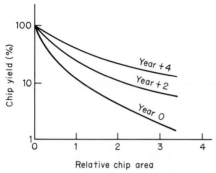

Fig. 2.13. A steady yield improvement can be expected for a given chip area as the semiconductor manufacturer gains experience with the technology.

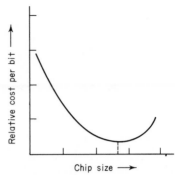

Fig. 2.14. Relative chip size versus relative cost per bit.

enjoys the larger chip size since process simplicity provides inherently higher yields than does the bipolar process.

2.4 ANALYSIS AND COMPARISON OF SEMICONDUCTOR MEMORY TECHNOLOGIES

2.4.1 Bipolar

(a) Standard TTL. The basic technology used for fabricating TTL logic circuitry has become the major form of technology adopted for implementation of various types of bipolar memory circuits. This technology employs epitaxial material, as previously described, plus buried collector regions in the epi material. Electrical isolation between devices is achieved with p-diffused regions as previously explained (Fig. 2.10). Interestingly enough, one example of a bipolar 64-bit RAM uses a memory cell which has a multiple-emitter structure reminiscent of TTL logic circuitry, Fig. 2.15.

One cell of a 256-bit bipolar RAM circuit which also employs standard TTL technology is shown in Fig. 2.16. This is often referred to as a diode coupled cell[5]

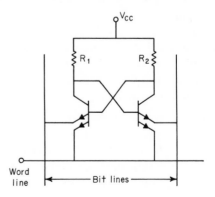

Fig. 2.15. Bipolar RAM memory cell using multiple-emitter structures.

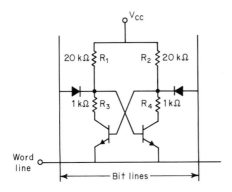

Fig. 2.16. Bipolar RAM memory cell using diode coupling.

wherein conventional p-n junction diodes or Schottky diodes are utilized. As a result of the diode coupling, R_1 and R_2 do not significantly affect access speed and they can be made large ($\approx$20K Ohms) to obtain low-power dissipation per memory cell. The formation of these relatively large resistances is the first notable departure from standard TTL technology because the resistors have been compacted in order to conserve silicon real estate. These resistors have sheet resistivities greater than 1,000 Ohms per square (as opposed to 120 Ohms per square for standard TTL technology), and they are formed in a p-diffusion process step that is separate from that of p-base diffusion. The resulting size of the cell shown in Fig. 2.16 is 38 sq mils.

To obtain the required circuit density and resulting chip size for a 1,024-bit bipolar RAM requires that cell size be reduced further. Without this reduction the overall chip size would be excessive and the resulting yield-economic characteristics would be unfavorable. Cell size has thus been reduced to 11.5 sq mils in the SN74S204 bipolar 1,024-bit RAM shown in Fig. 2.11. In this bipolar RAM, high-density bipolar memory devices are fabricated with a *composed masking* approach. In the standard approach a separate mask, which is used for each oxide removal and diffusion step, must be very carefully aligned, thus requiring additional spacing between images to compensate for misalignment and mask registration offset between the different layers. In the composed masking approach, all of the images are "composed" on a single mask, resulting in near-perfect alignment over the entire slice. This is achieved by using multiple dielectric layers, SiO_2 and Si_3N_4, which respond differently to various etchants, thereby permitting the master pattern to be composed in a single exposure. As a result, no additional spacing between images is required to compensate for misalignment or mask registration offset. The method thus achieves smaller components with higher density. The composed masking approach is compared to standard masking in Fig. 2.17 and is characterized by the following features:

1. It provides the density necessary for present-day bipolar memory requirements. An 11.5-sq mil cell is realized for the SN74S204, a 1,024-bit RAM.
2. It eliminates or minimizes the need for new and potentially difficult processing steps identified with alternate approaches. Standard, high-production-volume epitaxial films of $\approx$5-micron thickness can be used. Also, the

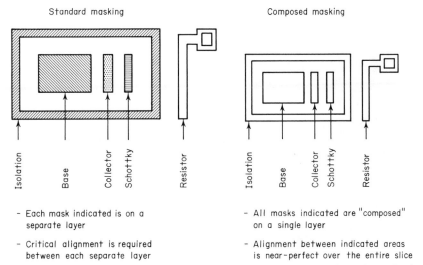

Standard masking   Composed masking

– Each mask indicated is on a separate layer	– All masks indicated are "composed" on a single layer
– Critical alignment is required between each separate layer	– Alignment between indicated areas is near-perfect over the entire slice

Fig. 2.17. Comparison of the composed masking method to that of standard TTL masking.

composed masking processing steps are near standard, eliminating the need for new techniques of oxide or moat-etch isolation.

3. It minimizes exposure to new reliability problems associated with new techniques since the processes used are basically those of standard TTL technology with Schottky-diode coupling.

A comparison of the 38-sq mil cell employed in the 256-bit RAM to that of the 11.5-sq mil cell of the 1,024-bit RAM realized with composed masking is shown in Fig. 2.18. It should be noted further that high sheet-resistivity diffusions for compacting resistors, in addition to two-level metalization for dense interconnections to silicon, also contribute to the small cell size of the 1,024-bit bipolar RAM cell. Also, it is obvious that the 1,024-cell technology can be retrofitted back to the 256-bit RAM to reduce its cell size accordingly.

(b) ECL. Process technology very similar to that of TTL has been used to fabricate emitter-coupled logic (ECL) random access storage cells. The ECL form of storage cell (Fig. 2.19) provides the shortest access time of all semiconductor methods. Since it is a time-consuming process to bring a transistor out of saturation, this speed performance is achieved by preventing the transistors in the cells from entering into the saturation region. ECL is thus a form of circuitry in which transistors are switched between two well-defined levels in such manner that *they never saturate*; instead the transistors remain in the active or current mode of operation. One of the major design factors to prevent transistor saturation in the *on* state is achieved by using very low value load resistors, R_L. This type storage cell thus draws constant current, except during switching transients. For this reason, relatively high power consumption typical of unsaturated circuit operation is experienced.

The basic technology employed for ECL storage circuitry is similar to that of TTL: epitaxial material and p-diffusion isolation. However, the emphasis for ECL is

(a)   (b)

Fig. 2.18. Comparison of the SN74200 256-bit RAM cell and the SN74S204 1,024-bit RAM cell.

speed, dictating low stray capacitance, close component spacing, and careful control of base-emitter input characteristics. Also, f_t of the transistors in ECL circuits must be higher than for TTL, necessitating extremely shallow and narrow base regions in ECL circuit transistors. All these considerations cause added process complexity for ECL. Double-level metalization is required, but metal migration is a more severe problem in ECL circuits than TTL circuits because of the higher current values experienced with ECL.

It is really, however, the *circuitry* of the two approaches that differs. For example, the so-called ECL memory cell requires a constant current supply which is shared among a number of cells. Also, the peripheral ECL circuitry requires a voltage

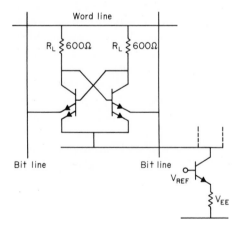

Fig. 2.19. ECL form of memory cell.

reference generator. Furthermore, the OR-NOR decode ECL circuitry, with its multiple base-emitter structures, consumes more silicon area than the TTL multiple-emitter structures within a *single* base region of a TTL NAND decoder. All these factors contribute to the projected costs of ECL RAMs being a factor of two to three times the costs of TTL RAMs.

Although ECL is, therefore, the most costly, it enjoys the fastest switching speed of all semiconductor RAMs. As a consequence, these memory elements find their widest usage in fast scratch-pads and buffers. Improvement in price structure will be achieved by closely related development of technology and circuit innovation. In general, the technology methods being developed for the more advanced TTL RAM cells will be applicable to ECL RAMs. To date, only the beginning of the ECL RAM technology has been witnessed.

(c) CDI and Isoplanar Technology. Let us now turn to a discussion of bipolar processing methods which represent somewhat major departures from standard TTL fabrication techniques. One of these is called *collector diffusion isolation* (CDI),[6] and the other is referred to as *isoplanar*.[7] CDI is designed to simplify and minimize the number of bipolar IC processing steps in an effort to compete with the process simplicity and resulting economics of MOS. The goal of isoplanar is to increase circuit density by compacting component areas. These two structures are compared with standard TTL in Fig. 2.20. Note that the CDI structure differs from standard TTL in that:

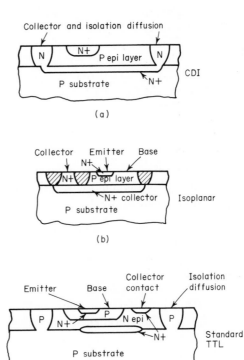

Fig. 2.20. Comparison of standard TTL with CDI and isoplanar structures.

1. It uses an epitaxial layer for the base structure, thereby eliminating the base-diffusion step.
2. It combines the deep collector contact and isolation step.

Although the resulting CDI circuitry is no denser than standard TTL, several process steps associated with standard TTL such as base diffusion and isolation diffusion have been eliminated. The simplicity of the CDI process is achieved, however, at the cost of lower collector-base breakdown voltage, higher reverse current gain, higher collector-junction capacitance per unit area, and less control over base width in comparison to standard TTL. The method is, therefore, incapable of the high-speed performance attainable with Schottky TTL or ECL.

By way of introduction to the isoplanar process, note in Fig. 2.20 that standard bipolar TTL integrated-circuit fabrication requires burying the collector of the transistor beneath an epitaxial layer through which contact is made. Also, p-diffusion regions isolate the collector region of one transistor from the collector region of an adjacent device. The space between the isolation and base is required mainly for accommodation of a depletion layer which results from reverse bias applied to the isolation junction and to the collector-base junction. In the isoplanar process shown in Fig. 2.20, the isolation regions consist of selectively grown oxide formed to the depth of the buried collector. The depletion layers which accompany diffusion isolation are thereby eliminated, and silicon real estate is conserved. The contact to the buried collector is surrounded by an additional oxide region located between the base region and the collector sink area. The space between isolation and base in the standard TTL fabrication can, therefore, be eliminated with isoplanar processing. This results in a savings of up to 40 percent in chip area for a given memory function. Also note that an epitaxial base can be used for isoplanar. As a further bonus, the process requires only five photomasking steps. Improved yields in circuit fabrication should accompany this process simplification. Finally, it should be noted that when silicon area utilization of the composed masking and isoplanar processes are compared, both processes are approximately equally effective (*cf.* Table 4.2).

2.4.2 MOS

(a) P-channel. The other mainstay of semiconductor memory technology is MOS. Several of the important properties of the MOSFET that make it attractive as a memory element are:

1. *Self-isolation.* Isolation diffusions are not required, and this conserves silicon real estate.
2. *High input resistance.* This readily permits storage of information on the gate of the device. Thus, dynamic circuit operation with low device count per cell is possible.
3. *Bilateral symmetry.* Gate and source are interchangeable with respect to current flow through the device. This feature gives rise to circuit design innovations.
4. *Active or passive operation.* The device can exhibit effectively high sheet resistance and serve as a load resistor permitting memory cell size reduction.
5. *Process simplicity.* This results in high fabrication yields which, in turn, provide high functional complexity and favorable economics.

The process details of p-channel MOS circuitry were summarized earlier in this chapter. The semiconductor industry initially chose p-channel devices for circuit fabrication mainly because of the magnitude and sign of the fixed charge value (Q_{SS}) at the silicon–silicon dioxide interface. This charge was such as to form p-channel devices of the *enhancement* variety (normally *off*), which is the desired state for a logic or memory device. Conversely, n-channel devices are usually *depletion* mode (normally *on*). The p-channel structure was, therefore, utilized and has advanced to an elegant state of refinement during the past 10 years. We will not attempt to trace these developments but will only elaborate on one particular process development which will undoubtedly play a significant role in MOS memory circuitry. That process development is the *self-aligned gate process*.

(b) The Self-aligned Gate Process (P-channel). In the standard p-channel process for MOS (Fig. 2.8), the gate metalization was aligned to the source and drain regions *after* their formation. To ensure alignment, gate metalization provides a source-drain overlap of a few tenths of a mil. This overlap not only generates parasitic capacitance, degrading circuit speed through the Miller effect; it is also wasteful of silicon area. This could be remedied by reversing the process order: that is, first *defining* a *gate region* and then using *that* region for alignment of source and drain edges. This would be, in essence then, a self-aligned gate process—a process reducing source-drain overlap to approximately 50 μin.

The concept of the self-aligned gate process is shown in its most fundamental aspect in Fig. 2.21. Note that the process sequence for the self-aligned gate method is to define the gate areas and then perform the source and drain diffusions. This procedure contrasts with the standard process in which source and drain are defined, followed by a photomasking step of metal-gate alignment. Now, of course, a refractory gate material must be used for the high temperature diffusion masking of source and drain regions in the self-aligned gate process. The conventional gate

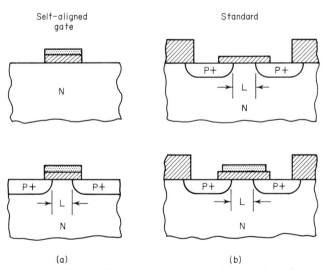

Fig. 2.21. Comparison of gate formation by self-aligned gate process and standard process.

material, aluminum, would volatilize at the temperatures associated with source-drain diffusion. Several refractory materials and methods are available for forming the required refractory gate region. At present, the most popular method uses deposited polycrystalline silicon. Thus, this particular technique is referred to as the *self-aligned silicon gate* process.[8] The silicon gate shown in Fig. 2.21 is doped p-type simultaneously with source-drain diffusion, thereby ensuring sufficient electrical conductivity for the silicon gate as it serves as a level of interconnection. Not shown in Fig. 2.21 is an oxide deposition over the silicon gate with standard aluminum interconnection patterns in turn formed over the insulating oxide layer.

Still another self-aligned gate process is the self-aligned thick-oxide (SATO) process shown in Fig. 2.22. In this process, silicon nitride defines the gate region and also serves as a protective "cap" over the gate region to shield that region from oxide growth during later steps in the process. Not shown in Fig. 2.22 is an oxide layer of a few hundred Angstroms thickness located over the gate region between silicon and silicon nitride. This thin oxide layer passivates the silicon surface in a manner that stable and reproducible threshold voltage values result, values which have not been achievable to date with the silicon–silicon nitride interface.

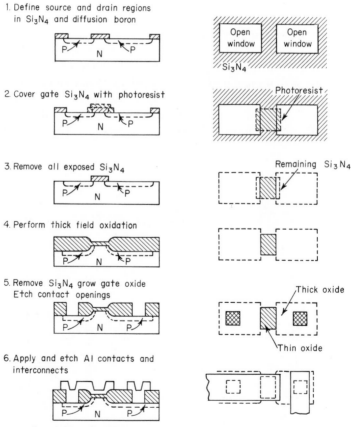

Fig. 2.22. SATO process fabrication steps (abbreviated).

(c) N-channel Silicon Gate.   Although the self-aligned silicon gate process was first applied to p-channel memory storage elements, the present trend is toward utilizing n-channel silicon gate processing.   Advances made in working with and understanding p-channel processes have basically made this trend toward n-channel processes possible.   The technology has taken this direction because:

1. Electron carriers in n-channel devices have mobility values which are a factor of 2 to 3 times higher than those of hole carriers in p-channel devices.   Hence, g_m for n-channel devices is correspondingly higher which, in turn, results in increased switching speed.
2. Operation with $+5$-V power supplies is possible with n-channel silicon gate MOS circuitry.   This low-voltage operation results from the low threshold voltages of these devices.   Accompanying depletion layers are, therefore, relatively narrow, and channel length can be reduced resulting in further compacting of memory circuitry.
3. Low-voltage operation makes these circuits TTL compatible.

Therefore, when these features are coupled with the accompanying advantages of silicon self-aligned gate structures such as reduced Miller capacitance and increased operating speed, small device area, and three levels of interconnection (diffused tunnel regions, silicon gate extensions, and aluminum interconnections), then approximately a fivefold density increase compared to standard aluminum-gate p-channel technology can be realized.   A factor of ≈ 2 increase in speed also results. The conservation of silicon real estate, of course, provides n-channel silicon gate circuitry with the potential for further improvement in the economic position of MOS.

A five-photomask, n-channel silicon self-aligned gate process sequence is shown in Fig. 2.23.   The process is initiated with a p-type substrate which has been thermally oxidized (A).   A moat-etch oxide removal is then performed (B).   In step C, an ≈ 1200-Å thick gate oxide is thermally grown.   Then a photomask and etching step cuts holes in the oxide which will later be used for silicon gate contacts to n^+ diffused regions (D).   This is followed by deposition of polycrystalline silicon which will form the gate regions and interconnections to the gate (E).   The "polysilicon" is then patterned with a photomasking step, and the resulting pattern is used as a mask for oxide etching (F and G).   This is followed by n^+ diffusion of source, drain, silicon gate, and contact regions (H).   A layer of silicon dioxide is then deposited (I), followed by a photomask and etching step for aluminum contact holes (J).   Aluminum metalization and selective removal of aluminum to form the top level of interconnection then completes the major steps of the process (K).

The resulting configuration for an n-channel silicon gate, 3-transistor MOS dynamic RAM cell[9] just prior to aluminum metalization is shown in Fig. 2.24.   In that figure, the memory cell circuit is compared to its form in monolithic silicon structure.   In evidence is the source region of T_1, polysilicon gate 1 with contact hole.   (Note that aluminum has not as yet been applied.)   The drain of T_1 and source of T_2 are common.   Then note polysilicon gate 2 to diffused drain 3 (gate 3 with contact hole and source 3).   This cell occupies an area of approximately 3 sq mils, but layouts have been implemented which are between 1 and 2 sq mils.

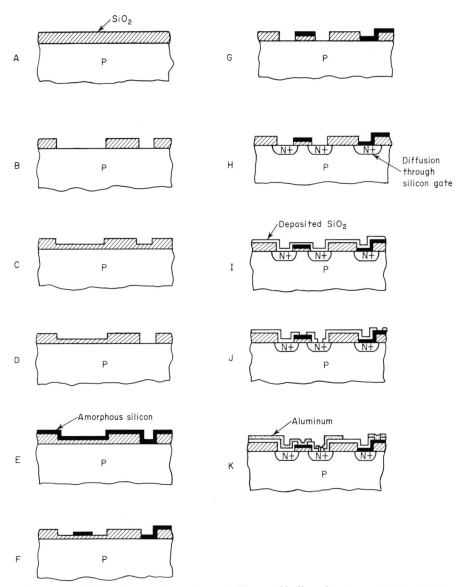

Fig. 2.23. A five-photomask, n-channel silicon self-aligned gate process sequence.

(d) CMOS. Another technology which has received considerable attention is that of complementary MOS (CMOS).[10] This technology combines both p-channel and n-channel transistors on the same substrate, as shown in Fig. 2.25. The n-channel transistor is normally the driver device and the p-channel transistor is the load. Only one transistor of the pair is normally on except during the switching mode. This arrangement leads to extremely low standby power and high-speed operation. Operating frequencies of 20 MHz are readily obtained with CMOS. The circuitry

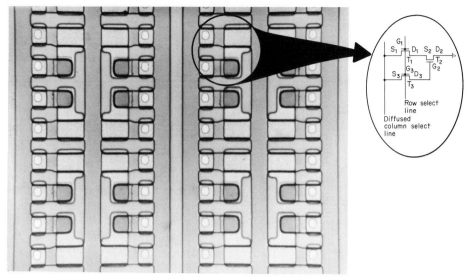

Fig. 2.24. Photomicrograph and circuit diagram of 3-transistor n-channel silicon-gate MOS dynamic RAM cell.

thus exhibits operating speed comparable to many bipolar devices and offers the ultimate in speed/power product for MOS. Other features are high noise immunity, TTL compatibility, single power-supply operation, and relative insensitivity to temperature variation. The low power dissipation makes battery operation readily feasible, and this brings semiconductor memory performance a step closer to non-volatile operation.

Unfortunately, economic problems arise when CMOS technology is applied to circuitry for the industrial memory markets. These problems result from the complexity of the required fabrication technology. For example, CMOS requires two additional diffusions and photomasking steps compared to standard single-channel

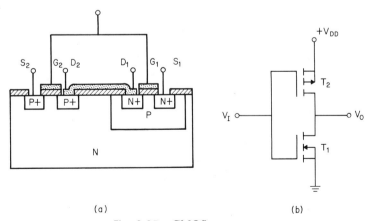

(a)   (b)

Fig. 2.25. CMOS structure.

MOS. Also, CMOS demands electrical isolation to preserve n- and p-channel devices as separate entities, as shown in Fig. 2.25. Therefore, source and drain regions are not shared and must be separately interconnected with metalization. Numerous contact holes result as shown in Fig. 2.26. All this results in an intolerable consumption of silicon real estate, at least as far as industrial markets and resulting costs are concerned.

As a result, CMOS is not best suited for large memory arrays possessing stringent economic constraints. Most applications for CMOS will probably be those requiring low power or battery operation, or where power supplies are noisy and poorly regulated. Such applications include automotive equipment, gas and water monitoring systems, aerospace circuitry, and wrist watches.

(e) Silicon on Sapphire. Silicon-on-sapphire (SOS) technology can be applied to improve the performance of conventional CMOS.

The starting material is obtained by epitaxially growing a 1-micron thick, single-crystalline, n-type silicon layer on a single-crystalline wafer of sapphire (Al_2O_3). The resulting configuration is shown at A in Fig. 2.27. A silicon dioxide film is then grown on the surface of the silicon, and the photolithographic process is used to form an appropriate silicon dioxide mask. The silicon dioxide is used as a mask during the selective etching of the silicon film. N-type silicon regions, isolated by sapphire, result as shown at B. Diffusion of the required p, n^+, and p^+ regions is made with standard oxidation and photolithographic techniques as shown at C and D. A thick layer of silicon dioxide is then deposited and appropriate channels are etched

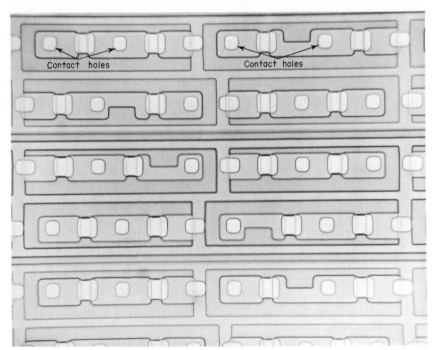

Fig. 2.26. Photomicrograph of CMOS shift register prior to metalization.

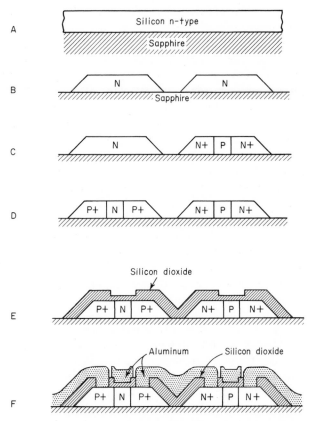

Fig. 2.27. Basic process sequence for the formation of SOS CMOS integrated circuits.

in the oxide over the gate regions. This step is followed by $\approx 1000\,\text{Å}$ oxide growth over the gate regions (E). Finally, contact holes are etched through the oxide and aluminum contact gates and interconnections are formed at F by methods previously discussed.

The major benefits arising from the SOS complementary symmetry configuration are (1) the aluminum interconnections are essentially free from parasitic capacitance since they are isolated from ground by the thick slab of sapphire dielectric, and (2) source and drain junction capacitances have been reduced by the presence of silicon-sapphire interface regions which exhibit essentially zero capacitance. The high speed and low power dissipation resulting from the reduced capacitance values have made possible a new family of semiconductor memory circuit products. These include a 256-bit shift register having 10 times the speed of standard p-channel MOS static shift registers as well as 256-bit RAMs with 50-ns access times which also provide a factor of 10 power reduction in comparison to equivalent bipolar RAMs.[11] Disadvantages of the method are the costs incurred with the single-crystalline sapphire substrate as well as accompanying process complexity.

(f) Ion Implantation. The process of ion implantation is often used to adjust threshold voltage values by implanting dopant ions in the gate region after formation of source and drain areas. The implanted ions can be of either the p- or n-type

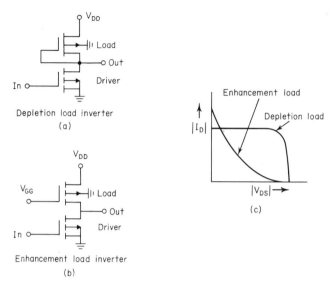

Fig. 2.28. Comparison of enhancement-load and depletion-load inverter configurations.

doping variety. The implanted doping level is controlled by the ion accelerator beam current and implant time. The method can be applied to p- or n-channel devices, to self-aligned devices, to CMOS, and in many other ways. One of the most significant applications of the method has been the forming of p-channel depletion-mode loads for p-channel enhancement-mode drivers all on the same silicon chip.[12] The combination results in a very efficient inverter configuration. This is demonstrated in Fig. 2.28c, where depletion-load and enhancement-load inverter configurations shown in Fig. 2.28a and b are compared. The plot shows the near-constant current load line of the depletion-load device compared to the nonconstant current load line of the enhancement-load configuration. The result is that the depletion-load inverter exhibits superior switching speed. Another point of comparison is that the depletion-load device presents a very high dynamic impedance to the driver device. Depletion loads can, therefore, be fabricated with minimum geometry since it is the *mode* of device operation and not the *size* of the device (W/L value) that determines, to first order, its effective resistance as a load element. Circuit density can thereby be increased. Other advantages are: the depletion-load arrangement is similar, in a sense, to CMOS because the resulting circuitry is insensitive to power-supply variations; internal voltage swings are essentially equal to the supply voltage; and operation takes place from a single voltage supply. Also because the gate-to-source voltage of the depletion-mode load remains constant during the switching transient (i.e., constant current is supplied to the active device), the speed/power product is improved compared to that of the enhancement-mode load circuit.

Disadvantages of the method are primarily economic, in that an expensive ion accelerator is required and the technique is difficult to adapt to multiwafer batch processing.

(g) Charge Coupled Devices (CCDs). From previous comments it should be understood that the motivating factor of circuit economy provides the major drive for additions to the arsenal of semiconductor storage devices. Probably the outstanding example of this is the development of charge coupled devices (CCDs).[13] These devices have no pre-prepared p-n junctions, and the circuitry does not require load devices or flip-flop configurations. Instead, CCDs store minority-carrier charges in potential wells created at the silicon surface and transport these charge packets along the surface by moving the potential wells. Zeros and ones are represented by absence or presence of charge in the wells. The potential wells are produced by applying a voltage to conducting electrodes formed on the surface of an insulator which covers the semiconductor. The applied potential thereby drives the semiconductor surface into the depletion mode. In its most elementary form, the structure that accomplishes this function consists of an array of aluminum electrodes spaced about 0.1 mil apart that overlay the insulator SiO_2 which has been grown on a silicon substrate. Figure 2.29 illustrates the concept of a CCD fabricated on an n-type silicon substrate. A sufficiently large negative potential has been applied to all electrodes to produce surface inversion. No inversion layer is present, however; only a depletion layer because a negligible number of minority carriers are present in the transient state. The surface will remain depleted for times on the order of seconds before thermally generated minority carriers accumulate. This happens because of the low density of surface- and bulk-generation centers in silicon. If minority carriers (holes in this example) are introduced by methods which will be described, they will collect at the surface where the minimum of the potential well is located. With the accumulation of minority carriers in a depletion well, electric-field lines terminate on these carriers, causing a decrease in both the depletion-layer width and the surface potential.

Charge can be generated for the input of a CCD array by several means. Again, considering the most basic implementation, Fig. 2.30 illustrates a method of injection that uses a gate electrode to produce an inversion layer adjacent to a diffused p-n junction diode formed in the bulk silicon. The diffused p region serves as a source of minority-carrier holes which support the inversion layer and are transported to the first element of the CCD array. An alternate method involves minority-carrier generation under the CCD electrodes by incident light. In this latter mode of operation, the entire CCD array can be operated as an imaging device and has the built-in features of image storage and scanning.

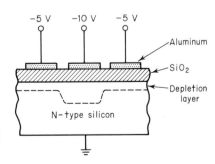

Fig. 2.29. Representation of an elementary CCD configuration.

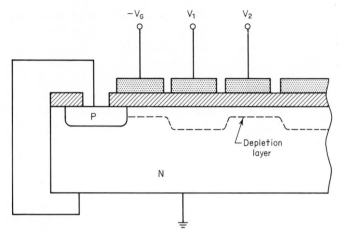

Fig. 2.30.   Charge injection from p-diffused region and gate electrode for CCD array.

As a method for detecting charge at the output of a CCD array, consider Fig. 2.31 where a diode at the end of the array is reverse-biased to voltage V_o. V_o is more negative than any of the surface potentials used for transfer.   When charge, in the form of holes, is transferred to the p region, an output current I_s is produced and an output voltage is developed across R.

CCDs can thus perform memory, shift register, delay line, and imaging functions. An example of their efficient use of silicon real estate is evidenced in the layout for a CCD 64-bit multiplexed shift register (Fig. 2.32).   Circuit density greatly exceeds present forms of MOS/LSI and will be greater than 500,000 elements per sq in. for future CCDs.

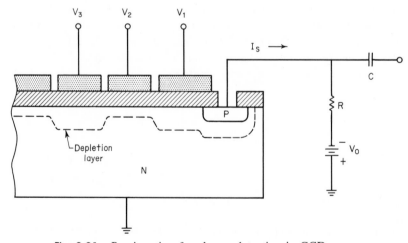

Fig. 2.31. P-n junction for charge detection in CCD array.

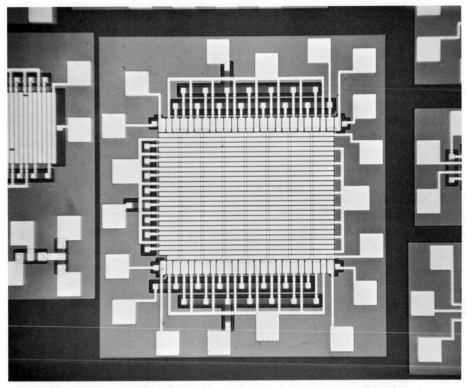

Fig. 2.32. Photomicrograph of a CCD 64-bit multiplexed shift register.

2.5 COMPARISON OF SPEED/POWER PRODUCTS

The various technologies can be related to a figure of merit called the *speed/power product*. When transistors are used for amplifiers, figures of merit are reasonably straightforward, e.g., noise figure, power gain, bandwidth, and so forth. In switching applications this is not true because the switching speed and power dissipation depend greatly upon the type of circuitry employed. There are, however, fundamental limitations relating switching speed and power dissipation for the various technologies. The resulting speed/power products are summarized in Table 2.1.

First note that propagation time through a logic gate is indicated as t_p and power dissipation per gate as P_D. These are minimal numbers; hence, we strive for as small a value as possible for the speed/power product. The speed/power products must be used with caution since minimal values exist for the two components that comprise the product. This figure of merit is, however, indicative of the energy required to perform a logic function. In general, it is desirable, as with most other physical systems, to conserve energy. As such, the speed/power product becomes one of the characteristics in addition to economy, speed performance, size, power dissipation, and reliability which must be considered in system design.

Table 2.1. Comparison of Speed/Power Products for the Various Technologies

Type of technology	t_p, ns	P_D, mW	Speed/power product, picojoules
TTL	10	10	100
TTL$_S$	3	20	60
ECL	2	25	50
MOS	200	0.1	20
CMOS	30	0.05	1.5
SOS	5	0.02	0.1

2.6 SUMMARY OF PACKAGE TECHNOLOGY

The *packaging* of semiconductor memory elements is similar to the packaging of digital ICs. Memory elements are, therefore, available in ceramic and plastic packages with 16-, 18- and 22-pin configurations as shown in Fig. 2.33. Also shown is an example of some new interface drivers that are being packaged in an 8-pin plastic package.

Twisted pair wiring and two-sided circuit boards have been adequate for handling the speeds of standard TTL. But to use some of the Schottky TTL and ECL circuitry, it has been necessary to employ multilayer, controlled-impedance circuit boards. Manufacturers such as Texas Instruments, Inc., employ computer programs to design and supply such multilayer boards for the system designer.

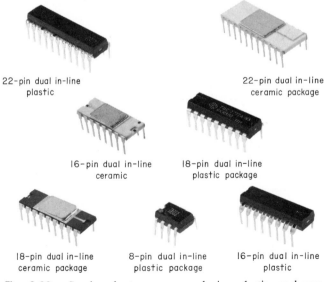

22-pin dual in-line plastic

22-pin dual in-line ceramic package

16-pin dual in-line ceramic

18-pin dual in-line plastic package

18-pin dual in-line ceramic package

8-pin dual in-line plastic package

16-pin dual in-line plastic

Fig. 2.33. Semiconductor memory device plastic packages. Configurations are 16, 18, and 22 pins. Also shown is an 8-pin package for interface devices.

Table 2.2.   Summary of the Techniques That Are Being Applied to Reduce the Silicon Area Per Memory Bit

Design element	Bipolar	MOS
Layout rules	Reduced line width and spacings	
Device structures		
Active	Composed masking	Self-aligned gate
Passive	High sheet resistivity	Depletion load
Metal interconnections	Two-level metal	Silicon gate
Circuitry	Schottky diode coupled cell	Dynamic cell (3-transistor)

2.7   CONCLUSIONS

Let us summarize the techniques that have recently been applied to reduce the silicon area per memory bit and which are shown in Table 2.2.   For bipolar circuits, line widths and component spacings have been significantly reduced by more stringent layout rules.   In addition, the composed masking method has improved masking techniques and, consequently, bipolar device structures.   For MOS structures, self-aligned gate processes have been developed.   For bipolar structures, resistors with high sheet resistivities are employed, and for MOS, depletion loads have been developed.   Metal interconnection efficiency has increased by using two-level for bipolar and silicon gate for MOS.   Bipolar circuitry has been improved by using Schottky diode coupled RAM cells.   MOS circuitry (particularly the 3-transistor RAM cell) has been effectively advanced through dynamic operation of memory circuitry.

The impact of these developments is evident when the resulting area reductions in going from the older 256-bit RAM design are compared to the newer 1,024-bit RAM design.   These comparisons are shown in Table 2.3.   It will be noted that tightening up of the layout rules for bipolar reduced the cell area by 20 percent. Improvements in device structures resulted in 40 and 15 percent reductions in active and passive bipolar component areas, respectively, and 10 percent for MOS.

Table 2.3.   Cell Size Reduction in Bipolar and MOS RAMs (percentage)

	Reduction in area 256-bit versus 1,024-bit	
Design element	Bipolar	MOS
Layout rules	20	
Device structures		
Active	40	10
Passive	15	
Metal interconnections	25	20
Circuitry		70

Table 2.4.   New Developments Which Will Benefit MOS and Bipolar Designs

Design element	New development	Bipolar	MOS
Layout rules	New masking and photo-resist techniques	X	X
	Electron beam		
Device structures			
Active	New isolation techniques	X	
	Thin epilayers	X	
	Ion implantation	X	X
	N-channel		X
	Charge coupled devices		X
Passive	High resistivity with diffusion or ion implantation	X	X
Metal interconnections	Two-level metal improvements	X	X
Circuitry	New cell (greater functional capability per device)	X	X

Advances in metal interconnection techniques account for 25 percent in bipolar and 20 percent in MOS. The dynamic circuit techniques of MOS have been most effective in reducing cell area by 70 percent!

In the future, new masking and photoresist techniques will benefit both MOS and bipolar. Table 2.4 lists some of the techniques. New isolation techniques and thin epitaxial layers will aid bipolar technology. Ion implantation will be used for both bipolar and MOS. N-channel and CCDs will result in significant advances for MOS. High sheet resistivities will aid bipolar and MOS, and depletion loads will continue to advance MOS. Further refinements in multilayer metalization will occur for both bipolar and MOS. New forms of memory cells which depart from the classical flip-flop are foreseen in the form of CCDs. All this will result in a greater functional capability per device.

REFERENCES

1. G. W. A. Dummer and N. B. Griffin, "Electronics Reliability-Calculation and Design," p. 40, Pergamon Press, London, 1966.
2. J. Mar, A Two-terminal Transistor Memory Cell Using Breakdown, *IEEE J. Solid-state Circuits,* **SC-6**: 280–283(October 1971).
3. G. E. Moore, What Level of LSI Is Best for You? *Electronics,* **43**: 126–130(February 16, 1970).
4. B. T. Murphy, Cost-Size Optima of Monolithic Integrated Circuits, *Proc. IEEE,* **52**: 1537–1545(December 1964).
5. D. L. Lynes and D. A. Hodges, Memory Using Diode-coupled Bipolar Transistor Cell, *IEEE J. Solid-state Circuits,* **SC-5**: 186–191(October 1970).
6. B. T. Murphy, S. M. Neille, and R. Pedersen, Simplified Bipolar Technology and Its Application to Systems, *IEEE J. Solid-state Circuits,* **SC-5**: 7–14(February 1970).

7. D. Peltzer and B. Herndon, Isolation Method Shrinks Bipolar Cells for Fast, Dense Memories, *Electronics,* **44:** 53–55(March 1, 1971).

8. L. L. Vadasz, A. S. Grove, T. A. Rowe, and G. E. Moore, Silicon-gate Technology, *IEEE Spectrum,* **6:** 28–35(October 1969).

9. J. A. Karp, W. M. Regitz, and J. Chou, A 4,096-bit Dynamic MOS RAM, *ISSCC72 Dig. Tech. Pap.,* pp. 10–11.

10. R. W. Ahrons and P. T. Gardner, Interaction of Technology and Performance in Complementary Symmetry MOS Integrated Circuits, *IEEE J. Solid-state Circuits,* **SC-5:** 24–29(February 1970).

11. A. K. Rapp and E. C. Ross, Silicon on Sapphire Substrates Overcome MOS Limitations, *Electronics,* **45:** 113–116(September 25, 1972).

12. R. Crawford, Implanted Depletion Loads Boost MOS Array Performance, *Electronics,* **45:** 85–90(April 24, 1972).

13. W. S. Boyle and G. E. Smith, Charged-coupled Semiconductor Devices, *Bell Syst. Tech. J.,* **49:** 487–493(1970).

3

Sequentially Accessed Design

3.1 INTRODUCTION

Storing and transferring digital information is one function which is common to essentially all data processing equipment and which can be performed in either a sequential or random fashion. The sequential form of accessed storage with semiconductor technology will be discussed in this chapter. Data bits are arranged in this form of storage so that each has a unique time delay from a reference point. The data are then moved toward the output where the binary state of each data bit is made available consecutively for processing within the digital computer, communication, control, or display system.

The sequentially accessed form of memory storage is probably most clearly illustrated by its implementation using magnetic tape.[1] In this example, data bits are recorded and stored in a serial mode on the tape. Controlled movement of the tape results in a corresponding movement of the data bits toward the output where the data can be accessed consecutively one bit at a time. If desired, several magnetic tape heads can be employed to access the data in a parallel mode as the tape is moved under the heads.

Quartz delay lines[2] and magnetostrictive delay lines[3] are also categorized as sequentially accessed memory elements. Pulses (bits of information in the form of 0s or 1s) serially enter these ultrasonic delay lines and are available at the output after a delay time determined by the length of the line and the pulse propagation velocity down the line. The delay time is made long compared to the pulse time and, therefore, a sequence of 1s and 0s can be stored serially within the delay line and presented at the output in a serial sequence. If it is desired to hold the data in the delay-line memory register for an extended period of time, an amplifier can be added in a closed loop arrangement as shown in Fig. 3.1. Data can thereby be fed back into the delay line and circulated until the desired time of processing. Delay lines have thus found application as sequentially accessed memory storage elements in data processing machines—particularly in those types which transfer and operate on data one bit at a time.

A variety of electronic devices referred to as shift registers (SRs),[4] the central topic of this chapter, also effectively perform the sequentially accessed storage function.

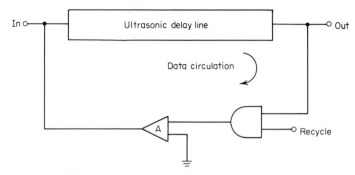

Fig. 3.1. Recirculation of data through an ultrasonic delay line.

An electronic shift register (SR) is a circuit in which digital information can be stored temporarily while, during the processing operation, a clock pulse controls the transfer of data from one shift register stage to the next. A serial SR consists of n cascaded stages of delay elements called cells or bits. A flip-flop circuit, activated by a clock pulse, constitutes one form of shift register cell implementation.

An example of a 4-bit SR implemented with clocked R-S flip-flops is shown in Fig. 3.2. At a time interval determined by the successive application of a clock signal, each digit stored in the cells of the SR is shifted one unit to the right. The input digit occupies the left-most cell, A, and the digit in the right-most cell D is shifted out for data processing. For example, a logic 1 could be clocked through the register as:

$$1 \longrightarrow 0000$$
$$1000$$
$$0100$$
$$0010$$
$$0001$$
$$0000 \longrightarrow 1$$

Thus, in the electronic serial SR the data march along from left to right on command of, and in synchronization with, a clock pulse.

The treatment of data by the electronic SR thus differs markedly from that of the ultrasonic delay line. In the delay line, data bits travel down the line in an analog fashion governed by the characteristic ultrasonic wave velocity and amplitude decay. Input-to-output delay time is, therefore, constant but the number of bits n in transit down the line can vary. Conversely, in the electronic SR, input-to-output delay time is a controlled variable, whereas the number of bits and bit positions along the line is fixed. The signal is of constant amplitude as it moves through the SR because of the regenerative action of the flip-flop circuitry which constitutes the n cells of the register. The characteristics of the electronic SR are contrasted to the ultrasonic delay line in Fig. 3.3 where an 8-bit SR and a delay line containing 8 bits of information are shown.

The SR can be modulated timewise without losing stored data, since the orderly transfer of information from one stage to the next takes place on command of a

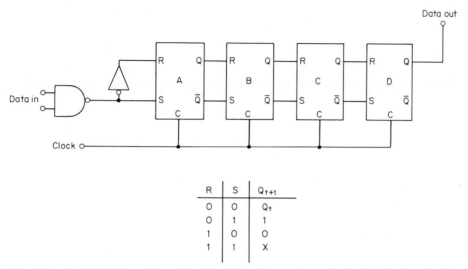

R	S	Q_{t+1}
0	0	Q_t
0	1	1
1	0	0
1	1	X

Fig. 3.2. A 4-bit shift register with 4 R-S flip-flops used as electronic binaries for the register.

clock signal. For the case of the *static* SR, data flow can actually be stopped and held in a fixed position indefinitely without losing the data. This, of course, assumes that power is continuously supplied to the elements comprising the register. If supply power is interrupted, data will be lost. Therefore, because of the potential loss of these data, the electronic SR is referred to as a volatile memory element.

Electronic SR configurations can be constructed to reverse the conventional direction of data flow through the register, thus making the data shift left on

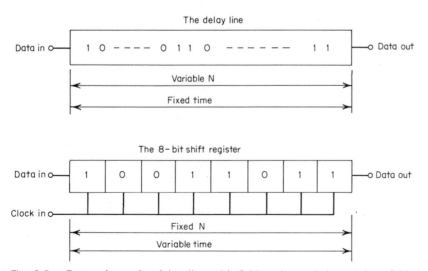

Fig. 3.3. Comparison of a delay line with 8 bits of stored data and an 8-bit shift register with 8 bits of stored data.

command of a clock pulse. SRs which have the capability of moving the data in *either* direction are referred to as shift-right shift-left registers. These features, coupled with the capabilities of time modulation and logic control of the clocks of an SR, and hence, the data therein, are of great convenience in configuring electronic memory systems. The operational flexibility of the electronic SR in conjunction with favorable access times and low cost brings these semiconductor circuits to an ever-increasing role of importance as memory storage elements.

The conventional mode of SR operation for data storage features bit-serial input and bit-serial output. Bit-parallel output can be obtained by addition of metalized patterns for individual connection to the output of each cell of the register. In addition, if it is desired to retain the data stored in the SR, a circulating mode of operation can be achieved as shown in Fig. 3.4. In this feedback mode of operation, the output states are recirculated to the input of the register and the data path is closed in a manner analogous to the recirculating delay line configuration of Fig. 3.1. Thus, this technique provides a means for storing data until the propitious moment when it must be transferred on for processing. The feedback mode of SR operation is, for example, ideal for use in CRT refresh operation within a data terminal.

It is not our purpose, however, to explore the applications of electronic SRs in this chapter. Shift register applications will be discussed in Chap. 8. Instead, the intent at this point is to detail the various semiconductor approaches to the sequentially accessed storage function which presently hold promise. These include the SR methods of MOS and bipolar as well as bucket brigade and charge coupled devices. A comparison of these various techniques will be given, and the trends with extrapolation to possible future memory storage capabilities of these approaches will be summarized.

3.2 MOS SHIFT REGISTERS

3.2.1 Introduction

MOS technology provides the systems designer with integrated circuits of high complexity.[5] To achieve the maximum benefits of this available complexity, the design principle of maximizing the circuit complexity to package pin ratio arises. This principle is derived from the fact that as the number of package pins increase,

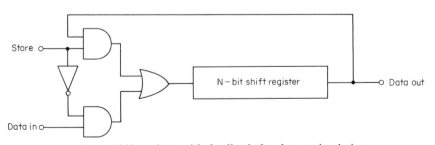

Fig. 3.4. Shift register with feedback for data recirculation.

the chip cost, package cost, and assembly costs increase also. The serial SR requires only a single input and output regardless of the number of interstage cells. It is, therefore, probably one of the best examples of an MOS memory product that achieves a high circuit complexity (bit density, in this case) per package pin. Various circuit approaches to the MOS SR function are available,[6] however, so let us direct our attention to the relative advantages and disadvantages of several MOS SRs and analyze the design trade-offs.

In the design of all SRs, two data storage elements per SR bit must be included. These elements are referred to as master and slave. If the particular SR employs two alternate clocks, the data are transferred from master unit to slave unit during one clock phase and from slave unit to the following master during the second clock phase. The requirement of one master and one slave unit per bit arises from the fact that it is impossible to receive a new digit from the preceding section and simultaneously transport a stored digit to the next SR section on a single memory element without mutual interference. This concept will become evident from a consideration of the design examples given in this chapter.

3.2.2 The Three-phase Static SR

An example of a three-phase SR employing a clocked, bistable flip-flop element is shown in Fig. 3.5a.[7] W/L values representative of channel width to channel length ratio are indicated adjacent to each device. The master section of the cell comprises T_2, T_3, and C_1; whereas, T_5, T_6, and C_2 form the slave section. Clocking and controlling the cell is performed with T_1, T_4, and T_7. The capacitors C_1 and C_2, essential to cell operation, are formed by clever use of gate capacitors and parasitic elements indigenous to circuit fabrication, thereby reducing circuit complexity.

Data can be held in fixed position within each cell with one cell isolated from the other by maintaining T_4 and T_7 on and T_1 off. This type cell, therefore, operates down to dc clock frequency and is referred to as a static cell.

To have the static cell assume a form analogous to other MOS SR cells which will be studied and compared, it has been redrawn in Fig. 3.5b. Note that the static cell consists of two inverters T_2-T_3 and T_5-T_6 coupled by T_4. T_7 closes a feedback loop, locking the data into the cell at frequencies down to dc. T_1 is used to clock data into the cell. This entire arrangement has been represented in block form in Fig. 3.5c.

Existing output data from the cell are maintained during the clock cycle by storage on C_2 of Fig. 3.5a. Thus with ϕ_1 on and ϕ_2, ϕ_3 off, data are transferred out of the cell and new data are transferred into the cell through T_1 where they are stored on C_1. From the timing sequence of Fig. 3.5d, ϕ_1 turn-off is followed by turn-on of ϕ_2 and ϕ_3. The turn-on of ϕ_2 is made faster than that of ϕ_3 in order that the SR bistable flip-flop will be set so that information will move from left to right along the SR chain. Thus, for example, a logical 1 can be clocked into the shift register by ϕ_1 and appear at node B inverted as a logical 0. The logical 0 is then clocked through T_4 to the gate of T_5 and storage node C. The logical 0 appears inverted at the output of T_5 and the resulting logical 1 is clocked by T_7 back to the gate of T_2. A logical 1 has thus been entered and stored in the register cell. The logical

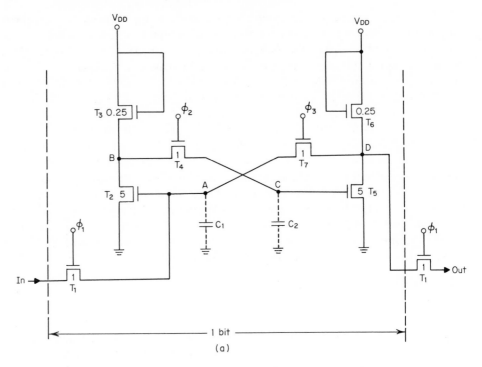

(a)

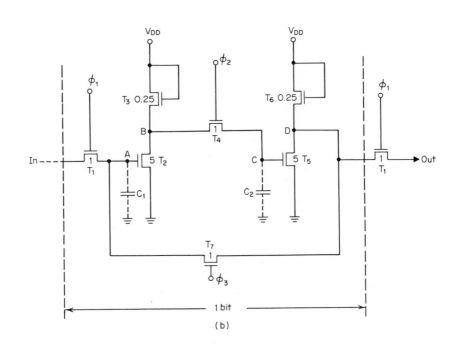

(b)

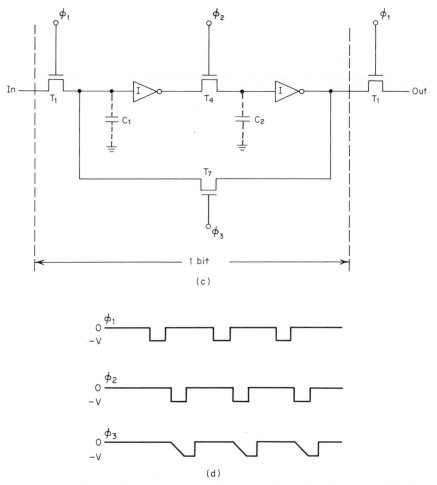

Fig. 3.5. (a) The clocked flip-flop performs the static shift-register function. (b) Conventional circuit diagram of the static shift-register bit. (c) Block diagram of the static shift-register bit. (d) Timing diagram of the clock phases for the static shift register.

1 is clocked out of the cell and into the next cell by activation of clock phase ϕ_1 after ϕ_2 and ϕ_3 have become inactive. A logical 0 is shifted through the cell in a similar manner.

The W/L values for the MOSFETs used in the SR cell are given in Fig. 3.5a and b. The beta ratio for the inverters is approximately 20. Recall that the beta ratio β_R is defined as W/L of the driver device divided by W/L of the load device. A beta ratio of approximately 20 is required for proper definition of 0s and 1s resulting from inverter output voltage swings. The transfer devices T_1 and T_4 and the feedback device T_7 can be minimum geometry devices with $W/L \approx 1$. T_2 and T_5 have W/L values greater than 1 to provide a g_m large enough to obtain the required switching speed. Although T_3 and T_6 have W/L values smaller than 1 to provide the proper logic swing, their W/L values are large enough to ensure the required 0 to 1 transition time.

The area per bit of the static SR is inherently large since three clock lines and a feedback transistor T_7 are required. Therefore, to prevent the chip size of static SRs of length greater than 500 bits from becoming excessively large, it is necessary to utilize a process featuring self-aligned silicon gates with three levels of interconnect. Present performance of p-channel static SRs is:

1. Length to 1,024 bits per package
2. Dc to 4 Mhz operation
3. 1 mW per bit power dissipation
4. Silicon area per bit
   (*a*) 34 sq mils (conventional)
   (*b*) 17 sq mils (silicon self-aligned gate)

3.2.3 The Two-phase Dynamic SR (Ratio Type)

Many electronic systems do not require SR operation down to zero frequency. Instead, a recirculating mode of operation (Fig. 3.4) can often be employed. Also, conventional clocked delay-line programming with direct passage of data through the register at some minimum frequency can be utilized. If the dc mode of operation can be discarded, then certain design changes in the static SR of Fig. 3.5*b* can be made, resulting in performance and economic benefits. The major design change is to eliminate transistor T_7 and accompanying clock line ϕ_3 of Fig. 3.5*a*, which together provide the necessary latch for dc storage. Operation of the resulting cell can then be extended down to some minimum (but not zero) frequency, and the mode of operation is referred to as *dynamic*. The dynamic SR cell thus enjoys smaller area per bit in comparison to the static cell.

Two features of the MOSFET make dynamic SR operation feasible. They are: (1) its bilateral nature permits current to flow equally well in either direction, and (2) extremely high input resistance allows temporary data storage on the gate of the device by means of charge stored on gate and parasitic capacitance.

The first dynamic SR to be considered is shown in Fig. 3.6*a*. The circuit utilizes a ratio-type design. The beta ratios of T_2-T_3 and T_5-T_6 are greater than unity. Thus, high gain inverters are employed as in the static SR. The dynamic, ratio-type SR cell is represented in block diagram form in Fig. 3.6*b*. Operation of the cell can be understood by considering a logical 0 at the input. This data bit is transferred to the gate of T_2 by activation of T_1 with clock phase ϕ_1. The clock timing diagram is given in Fig. 3.6*c*. The logical 0 charges parasitic capacitance C_1, and data are temporarily stored at node A. After ϕ_1 turns off, a nonoverlapping clock pulse ϕ_2 comes on and activates T_4, transferring the inverted input pulse at node B to the gate of T_5 and node C. Thus, logical 1 is presented to T_5, resulting in zero charge on C_2. Any charge remaining on C_2 from a previous logic bit is removed by conduction through T_2. The logical 1 on the gate of T_5 appears as a logical 0 at node D. Then on return of ϕ_2 to its inactive state and with turn-on of nonoverlapping clock pulse ϕ_1, the logical 0 is transferred out of the SR cell onto the next stage and new data are shifted into the cell. A logical 1 is transferred through the cell in a similar manner.

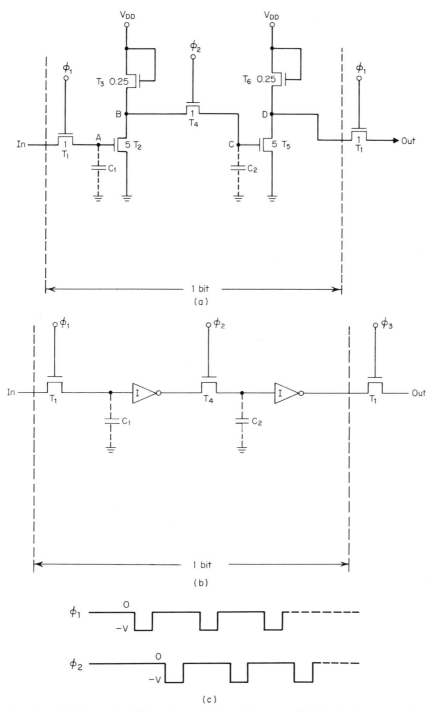

Fig. 3.6. (*a*) Dynamic shift register of the ratio type. (*b*) Block diagram of the ratio-type dynamic shift register. (*c*) Timing diagram of the clock phases for the ratio-type dynamic shift register.

The master and slave storage elements of the SR (Fig. 3.6a) are simply parasitic capacitors C_1 and C_2. The data transfer elements of the cell are MOS transistors T_1 and T_4. Since T_1 and T_4 are bilateral, they can either charge or discharge nodes A and C, respectively. Cell operation, however, depends on continuous clocking of the alternate clock phases. If the clocks are stopped for too long an interval, the SR cell can lose its information. For example, assume data have been transferred by ϕ_1 to node A and then ϕ_1 has gone off and remained off. If a logical 0 is stored at node A, leakage current from the drain-substrate junction of T_1 will eventually discharge node A to the 1 state. Clock phase ϕ_2 must be activated for data transfer before node A is discharged. Therefore, dynamic SRs have a minimum operating frequency which is temperature dependent through the temperature dependence of the leakage current. The minimum operating frequency is governed by the time required to discharge C_1 or C_2 by the leakage current of the drain-substrate junction of T_1 or T_4, respectively. The discharge time at room temperature is calculated assuming that junction leakage current is not voltage dependent as:

$$t = \frac{CV}{I} \approx \frac{0.1 \text{ pF } (10 \text{ V})}{10^{-10} \text{ Amp}} \approx 10 \text{ ms} \tag{3-1}$$

where I = junction leakage current
  C = junction capacitance
  V = logic swing (volts)

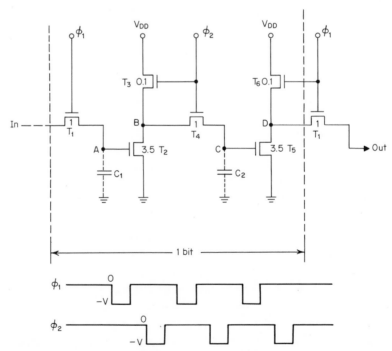

Fig. 3.7. Dynamic shift register of the ratio type with clocked load devices (right-handed version).

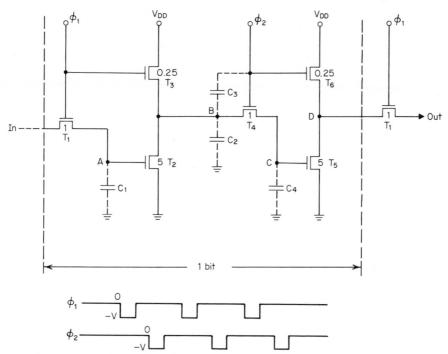

Fig. 3.8. Dynamic shift register of the ratio type with clocked load devices (left-handed version).

Power dissipation in the dynamic, ratio-type SR can be reduced by clocking the load devices of the inverter stages as shown in Fig. 3.7. With clocked load devices, the inverter stage draws less power, since even though the driver devices may be held in an *on* state by charge stored on the gate node, current cannot flow until the load device is activated by the appropriate clock phase. Power is thereby conserved. A penalty paid for this design advantage is that clock-line capacity per cell has been increased by the addition of the clocked load gates. This implies that the clock generators must have greater drive capability for this type of cell in comparison with the dynamic SR of Fig. 3.6*a*.

Figure 3.8 pictures a left-oriented version of the dynamic cell of Fig. 3.7. Although both cells have similar performance characteristics, their operation is somewhat different. This becomes apparent when we consider the process of clocking a logical 0 through the cell of Fig. 3.8. Thus, if a logical 0 appears at the gate of T_2 (Fig. 3.8), it is inverted to a 1 at node B when ϕ_1 is active. Charge is stored on C_1. With ϕ_1 off and nonoverlapping clock phase ϕ_2 active, T_2, which is held in a conducting state by the charge on C_1, removes the charge from the gate of T_5 if a logical 0 had previously existed at that point and stores a logical 1 on the gate of T_5. A logical 1 on the gate at T_5 appears inverted as a logical 0 at the drain of T_5. Then on application of ϕ_1, the logical 0 will be clocked out of the cell and new information clocked into the cell. Note that if a logical 1 is clocked into the cell with ϕ_1, then a logical 0 appears at node B charging capacitor C_2. On activation of ϕ_2, charge on C_2 is transferred to C_4 and a logical 0 is presented to the gate of

T_5. It is necessary that parasitic capacitor C_2 be made several times larger than C_4 since charge sharing between these capacitors reduces the size of the logical 0 signal. To obtain a more comfortable noise margin, parasitic capacitor C_3 acts as a booster to impart additional logical 0 value to node B on activation of ϕ_2. The boosting must be done with care, however, since excess coupling through C_3 will destroy a logical 1 stored on node B.

Present performance capabilities of p-channel, two-phase, dynamic ratio-type SRs with clocked loads are:

1. Length to 1,200 bits per package
2. Operation: min. 500 Hz; max. 5 MHz
3. 0.5 mW per bit
4. Silicon area per bit = 12 sq mils (p-channel technology with silicon self-aligned gate)

An example of a 4 × 256-bit, two-phase dynamic, ratio-type SR is shown in Fig. 3.9. Chip size is 127 × 130 mils.

3.2.4 The Two-phase Dynamic SR (Ratioless Type)

In a ratio-type SR cell, the *on* resistance of the load devices is much greater than that of the driver devices. The large beta ratio is required in these types of cells in order to maintain the logical 1 state at a level below the threshold voltage of the following stage. To maintain this required *off* level and to ensure comfortable noise margins, the load transistor must have 10 to 20 times the resistance of the driver transistor; it, therefore, occupies a correspondingly large area in comparison to the driver transistor. Switching times of the inverters within the SR cell are of course limited by the longest RC time constant present. For the ratio design, this turns out to be the time constant of the load transistor and associated capacitance. The maximum frequency of operation can be increased if the load resistor can somehow be reduced and made equal to the driver transistor (beta ratio then equals unity). Also, equal resistance values for load and driver devices imply that their geometrical sizes will be small and equal, resulting in conservation of silicon real estate. Both these features are realized in the two-phase, ratioless-type, dynamic SR cell shown in Fig. 3.10. The circuit uses minimum geometry devices throughout. The ratioless design permits no dc paths through the inverter stages. Power dissipation is therefore proportional to clock frequency F:

$$P = CV^2F \tag{3-2}$$

It is also interesting to note that the circuit of Fig. 3.10 is similar to that of Fig. 3.8 except that ratioless inverter design is employed with modified clocking.

Operation of the cell (Fig. 3.10) can be explained as follows. When ϕ_1 is active (logical 0), parasitic capacitance C_2 charges to a 0 through T_3. When ϕ_1 becomes inactive (logical 1), transistor T_2 turns on if the input level was a 0 and discharges C_2. For a 1 input, T_2 stays off and C_2 remains charged. When nonoverlapping clock ϕ_2 turns on, T_4 is activated. This results in C_2 sharing its charge with C_4. Capacitor C_2 must be made large enough so that after charge sharing with C_4, a sufficient 0 or 1 level voltage will be exhibited by C_4. The charge stored on C_2

Fig. 3.9. A 4 × 256-bit, two-phase dynamic, ratio-type shift register (chip size is 127 × 130 mils).

is boosted also by introducing a small extra charge from clock pulse ϕ_2 coupled through C_3. Care must be taken that parasitic capacitance C_3 is not so large that ϕ_2 will destroy the noise margin of a logical 1 stored on C_2. Finally, when ϕ_2 becomes inactive (logical 1), the data on C_4 are transferred to the output through interaction with the following stage in a manner analogous to transfer of data from C_1 to C_2.

Additional booster capacitors C_A and C_B (Fig. 3.11) can be added to the two-phase dynamic, ratioless SR to increase speed performance by 30 percent. This improvement arises, for example, from the coupling of clock pulse ϕ_2 to node C through C_B. The resulting signal further enhances the transfer of a logical 0 from node B to node C. Parasitic capacitors C_A and C_B values range from ≈ 0.03 to 0.1 pF. Like other booster capacitors, the values must not be excessive, for if this were to occur, a logical 1 at node B might be transferred as a "mini 0" to node C, resulting in loss of data.

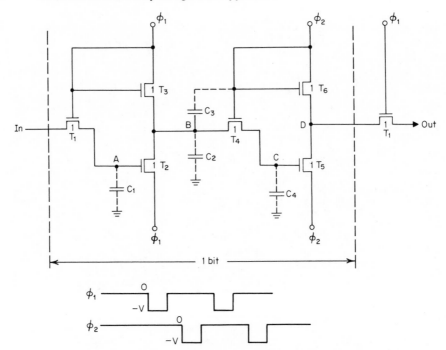

Fig. 3.10. Dynamic shift register of the ratioless type.

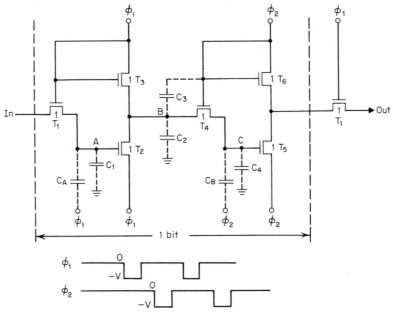

Fig. 3.11. Dynamic shift register of the ratioless type with booster clocking.

The ratioless dynamic SRs of Figs. 3.10 and 3.11 introduce large capacitive loading on the clock-drive circuitry. The clock-line capacitance can be reduced by adding another transistor to the inverter stages. This ratioless, dynamic cell has 8 transistors and is shown in Fig. 3.12. Clock drivers for ϕ_1 and ϕ_2 are then loaded only with the gate capacitance of the individual transistors. Source and drain junctions clocked in Figs. 3.10 and 3.11 are now connected to ground or to the V_{DD} supply. Area of the cell has been increased slightly by the addition of the two minimum geometry load transistors.

Operation of the circuit of Fig. 3.12 can be explained as follows. When ϕ_1 is activated (logical 0), the input voltage charges node A. Transistor T_4 is concurrently in a conducting state and node B is precharged to a logical 0. When nonoverlapping clock pulse ϕ_2 is activated, T_3 is turned on and the dynamic state of T_2 determines whether node B should be discharged. For example, if node A has stored a logical 0, then node B will be discharged through T_3 when ϕ_2 is active. If node A had stored a logical 1, then T_2 would not be in a conducting mode and the logical 0 at node B would not be discharged when ϕ_2 is active. An effective inversion of the input voltage thus appears and is stored at node B. Clock pulse ϕ_2 brings about charge-sharing between C_2 and C_3 and also precharges node D to a logical 0. (Note as in previous examples $C_2 \gg C_3$.) When ϕ_1 is reactivated, "sampling" again takes place to determine if the voltage at node D is to be discharged to ground. This type action then proceeds down the SR chain.

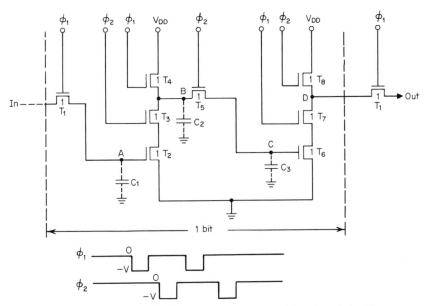

Fig. 3.12. Dynamic shift register of the ratioless type with reduced clocking power requirements.

3.2.5   The Four-phase Ratioless Dynamic Shift Register

The maximum operating frequency of the two-phase dynamic SR cell of Fig. 3.10 is limited by the value of C_2. Recall that transfer of a logical 0 from node B to node C requires that C_2 must be made several times larger than C_4. Minimum device geometry does not naturally provide the large capacitance C_2 desired at node B. Therefore, considerable area is expended bringing C_2 to its required value. The silicon area savings obtained by designing with minimum geometry transistors has thus been compromised. For the above reasons, effort is made to design and utilize a ratioless-type circuit that does not depend on gated charge-sharing. The desired performance is achieved with a four-phase SR cell.[8]

The first four-phase SR cell to be considered is shown in Fig. 3.13. The circuit is ratioless and minimum geometry devices are employed throughout. Four non-

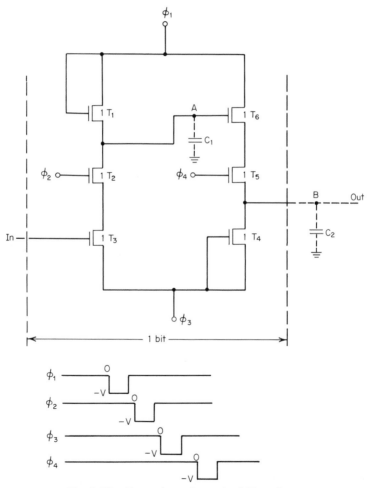

Fig. 3.13.   Four-phase dynamic shift register.

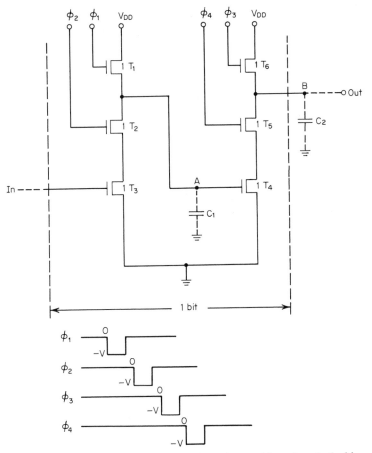

Fig. 3.14. Four-phase dynamic shift register with reduced clocking power requirements.

overlapping clock pulses are used in order to avoid interference of adjacent information bits and to prevent formation of dc paths during shifting. Clock pulse ϕ_1 unconditionally charges node A through T_1, independently of the logic condition on the input line since ϕ_2 is off. When ϕ_2 turns on, node A is conditionally discharged through T_2 and T_3 if a logic 0 is applied to the gate of T_3. The input information has been shifted in inverted form to node A. A corresponding shift and inversion of the information at node A is then made to node B by a successive application of nonoverlapping clock pulses ϕ_3 and ϕ_4. This results in the elimination of charge-sharing between two capacitors connected by a transfer gate and attendant problems.

The clock-drive requirements of the cell under consideration can be relieved somewhat by minor circuit modifications as shown in Fig. 3.14. In the latter circuit, the clock drivers need only charge the gate capacitances of the minimum geometry devices while V_{DD} precharges p-n junction capacitances as well as node A and node

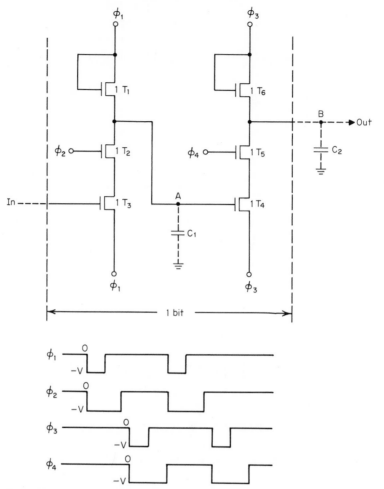

Fig. 3.15. Four-phase dynamic shift register featuring overlapping clock pulse operation.

B.   The penalty for achieving reduced clock-drive requirements is the addition of the V_{DD} line which contributes to enlargement of the cell size.

As has been seen in this chapter, many of the SR design variables concern clocking considerations.   Another example of this can be seen by noting that generation of four separate nonoverlapping clock pulses is the major limitation to obtaining high-speed operation for the SR cells shown in Figs. 3.13 and 3.14.   A somewhat simpler clocking scheme in which the clock phases can overlap without permitting a dc path through the master and slave sections of the four-phase SR is shown in Fig. 3.15.   Explanation of circuit operation is essentially identical to that of Fig. 3.13.   Design considerations are also similar.   The circuit layout of Fig. 3.15, however, is $\approx$30 percent larger than the nonoverlapping clocked four-phase SR; this is caused by the additional routing of clock lines ϕ_1 and ϕ_3.

Thus, four-phase ratioless SRs enjoy small cell size, low power dissipation, and high operating speed. Relatively complex clock-drive circuitry is required, however. Performance of four-phase cells can be summarized as:

1. Length to 1,200 bits per package
2. Operation: min. 500 Hz; max. 10 MHz
3. ≈ 0.090 mW per bit at 1 MHz
4. Silicon area per bit ≈ 17 sq mils (standard p-channel technology)

3.2.6 Complementary MOS Shift Registers

Complementary MOS (CMOS) SRs are constructed from two basic building blocks defined as *inverters*[9] and *transmission gates*.[10] An inverter (Fig. 3.16a) consists of one p-channel and one n-channel enhancement-mode MOSFET connected in series. When the voltage at the input of the inverter is $+V_{DD}$ (logic 1), the gate-to-source voltage (V_{GS}) of the n-channel device is equal to V_{DD} and the device is on, while the p-channel MOSFET is off. A very low impedance path is thus formed between ground and output; a very high impedance path exists between V_{DD} and ground. The output, therefore, approaches ground (logical 0). Conversely, when the input voltage approaches ground, the output approaches V_{DD} (logical 1) with the p-channel device on and the n-channel device off. The output of the CMOS inverter thus can swing essentially over the full range of supply voltage. Also, since in either logic state one MOSFET is on while its complement is off, dc current is never permitted to flow in the inverter and ratioless design can be employed.

The CMOS transmission gate, Fig. 3.16b, is formed by the parallel connection of p- and n-channel enhancement-mode devices. An analysis of the configuration reveals that the gate-to-source voltage of both n- and p-channel devices never simultaneously equals the threshold voltage of the devices. One of the parallel

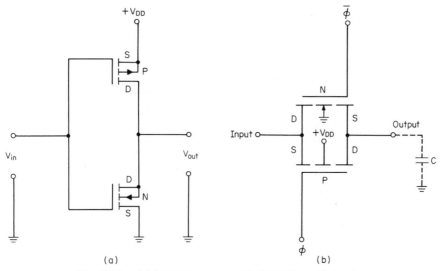

Fig. 3.16. (a) MOS inverter. (b) CMOS transfer gate.

devices is always in the triode region of operation, and therefore a threshold voltage drop is not "lost" in switching with the transmission gate. Another way of looking at this is to visualize that one of the two devices is always being operated as a drain-loaded configuration regardless of the value of input and output voltages. Recall that the single-channel transmission gates (transfer gates) of the enhancement-mode variety employed in the SRs considered previously in this chapter operate as source-follower circuits in which a threshold voltage is lost in the switching process. As a result of the full supply voltage being available to drive the storage capacitance of each stage, the CMOS transmission gate is considerably faster (RC time constant is smaller) than that of the single-channel MOS transmission gate.

CMOS transmission gates and inverter stages are combined to form SRs of dynamic and static designs in Fig. 3.17a and b, respectively. The transfer of data

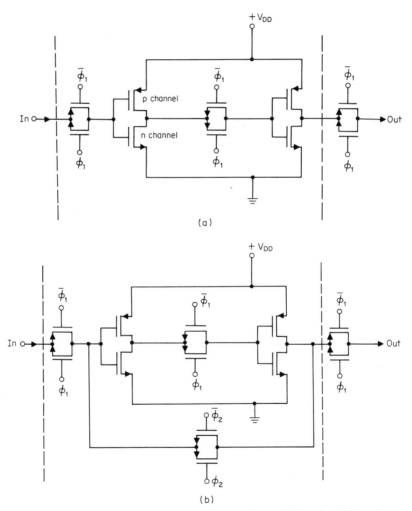

Fig. 3.17. (a) CMOS dynamic shift register. (b) CMOS static shift register.

through the CMOS SR is performed with a single transient for each shift of data rather than by an unconditional charge followed by a conditional discharge as in the case of four-phase and some of the two-phase dynamic SRs. This feature leads to power conservation in the CMOS SR. As a further result, clocking of the CMOS SR therefore is relatively straightforward with two clock pulses 180° out of phase being required.

From the discussion of the CMOS inverter, it is evident that CMOS SRs consume no dc power other than that defined by the product of the supply voltage and the leakage current. Ac power dissipation is directly proportional to the frequency of operation through the term $P_{AC} = CV^2F$.

As pointed out above, CMOS SRs utilize ratioless design; this feature tends to offset the requirement for large-area silicon consumption characteristic of CMOS. Recall from Chap. 2 that CMOS circuitry generally consumes more silicon real estate than does the single-channel MOS variety because isolation diffusions, guard bands, and numerous contact holes are required. In general, however, the CMOS SR cell size remains large—comparable to that of the p-channel static SR. This feature, coupled with increased process complexity, has, to date, relegated the CMOS SR to use in special high-performance applications rather than in the high-volume memory market.

Another favorable characteristic of CMOS circuitry contributing to its high-performance characteristics is liberal noise margins. Noise margins are approximately 45 percent of the power-supply voltage. This high value of noise immunity is a result of: (1) change of state of the inverter at $\approx$50 percent of the supply voltage, (2) the "steep" transfer characteristics of the inverter, and (3) the output swing which approaches the supply voltage within several millivolts. The liberal noise margins thus relax the power-supply regulation requirements. This characteristic, coupled with low power consumption, readily permits standby battery operation bringing us a step closer to achieving a nonvolatile semiconductor memory element. Also important is the fact that the supply voltage requirements of CMOS SRs make the circuits directly TTL compatible.

Performance characteristics of present-day CMOS SRs can be summarized as:

1. Length to 128 bits per package
2. 20 MHz operation
3. $\approx$0.010 mW per bit at 1 MHz
4. Silicon area per bit with standard technology
    (a) 40 sq mils (static)
    (b) 30 sq mils (dynamic)

3.3 PROBLEMS ASSOCIATED WITH MOS SHIFT REGISTERS

3.3.1 Generation of Clock Phases

Let us now examine some of the problems associated with the use of MOS SRs in system design. The first observation is that the internal MOS SR bit requires more than one clock phase as well as controlled timing between the phases. For reasonably slow operation ($\approx$4 MHz or less), all the phases can be generated on the

MOS chip from a single, low-level, low-capacitance clock driver. For high-speed operation (greater than ≈ 4 MHz), the multiple clock phases must be generated by external bipolar circuits because the integrated MOS clock-driver switching speed cannot match the MOS SR speed. But even in high-speed operation, the slow phase III of the static register or two phases of some of the four-phase dynamic SRs can be generated on the chip while the critical high-speed clock phases are generated externally.

3.3.2 Shift Register to System Interface

A second question pertains to the interface between the MOS SR and the system. If the MOS SR interfaces with MOS logic, there is no problem. But if the MOS SR must interface directly to a bipolar TTL logic system, then either the MOS SR must interface directly to the TTL or a level translator must be used. With low-threshold MOS technology now well established, the trend is toward making a direct interface between MOS and TTL. In fact, MOS SRs are now available that generate all internal clocks from a single TTL level external clock, as well as accept TTL levels at the data input and also drive a TTL load directly at the output. Therefore, unless the ultimate in speed is required, these registers offer a significant decrease in external circuit complexity as well as the elimination of all clock drivers and interface components.

3.4 CHARACTERISTICS OF BIPOLAR SHIFT REGISTERS

Bipolar medium-scale integration (MSI) provides 4- to 8-bit SRs of high operating speed (25 MHz). Circuit implementation is accomplished with integrated R-S flip-flops and required gates as shown in Fig. 3.18. Bit length is limited because of the silicon cell area required to form the basic bit which can be as large as a few hundred square mils. Cell area is large because the bipolar transistor occupies more area in IC form than does the MOSFET.[11] In addition, bipolar transistor input impedance is relatively low. This means the base of the transistor cannot be used for information storage and storage processing as easily as the gate of the MOSFET. Therefore, the device count per bit of SR is higher for bipolar than for MOS since latching circuitry must carefully be provided on all information storage nodes in the bipolar SR. Cost per bit of bipolar MSI SRs is presently in the 10 to 50 cent range. The data rate is fast, however, and parallel accessing is provided. The devices, thus, find application in sequential decoding, multiplexing, and frequency division. Generally, they are not used to perform the delay-line memory function.

Although this discussion has pertained to commercially available bipolar SRs, it should be noted that development efforts throughout the industry are resulting in advances toward lower power dissipation and higher circuit density coupled with simplified processing for bipolar LSI. For example, increased circuit density is being achieved in these efforts by combining functions on a single island of diffusion, reducing the requirements for area-consuming isolation regions and the number of interconnections.[12] Although these efforts are primarily directed toward bipolar RAM circuitry, these advances are being applied to SRs. Therefore an improved situation for bipolar SRs in the next year or two should be witnessed.

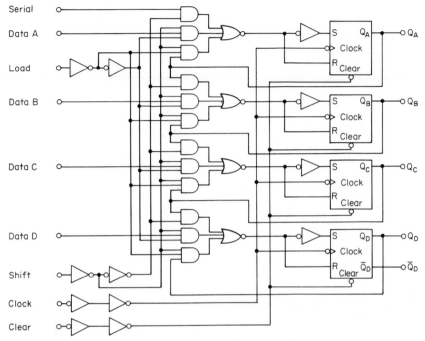

Fig. 3.18. Bipolar MSI shift register.

3.5 MOS SHIFT REGISTER PRODUCT PERFORMANCE WITH TIME

Now let us return to the world of MOS and view the progress which has been realized with MOS SR products during the past several years. Figure 3.19a shows the trend in silicon real estate utilization per SR bit as a function of time. Reduction in area per bit has been made possible mainly through process developments such as the self-aligned silicon gate and improvements in photolithographic techniques. Figure 3.19b indicates the increase in the number of bits per package as a function of time caused by a combination of the results of Fig. 3.19a with those of both yield improvement programs and circuit innovation. Of primary importance, however, are the results shown in Fig. 3.19c which depict the price trend per MOS SR bit with time. These results have been made possible, of course, by the previously indicated advances.

3.6 INTEGRATED SHIFT REGISTER ARRAYS

Arrays of SRs can be combined to form useful data processing functions.[13] An example of this is the silo array of SRs shown in block diagram form in Fig. 3.20. A silo memory reads out stored data in a first-in/first-out mode. It is used for interfacing a fast telephone line with a slow data transmission unit or a magnetic tape (or other medium operating at electronic speeds) with a keyboard operating at human speeds. In a sense, a silo register is an information buffer that stores data which can move rapidly and sporadically to the silo buffer while at the same

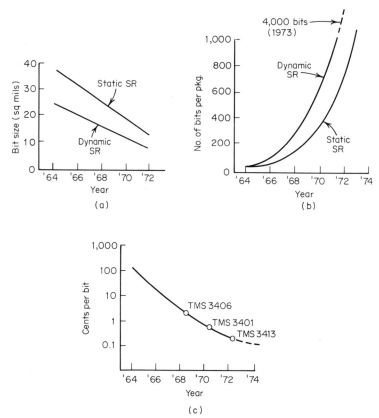

Fig. 3.19. Developmental progress of MOS shift registers: (*a*) bit size versus time; (*b*) bits per package versus time; (*c*) cents per bit versus time.

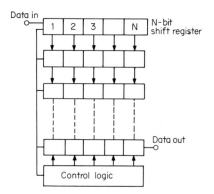

Fig. 3.20. Silo shift register array block diagram.

time the silo buffer releases the information at a relatively slow and semiuniform rate. In the block diagram example of Fig. 3.20, the data are entered serially into the top row which consists of an n-bit serial SR. When this row is filled with data, the n-bit SR empties its data in a parallel mode to the next row and the data continue to drop down through the silo array. The data are extracted serially at the data output at a semiuniform rate that is determined by the data content state of the silo. A fully integrated MOS silo SR is shown in Fig. 3.21. It consists of 6-bit registers which are stacked 12 rows deep. The general features of this geometrical arrangement are shown in the integrated-circuit layout of Fig. 3.21.

Silo storage operation is almost completely independent of the total electronic system because the silo requires only data-in and data-out lines plus a few signals from an associated control logic unit. The basic function of the control logic is to

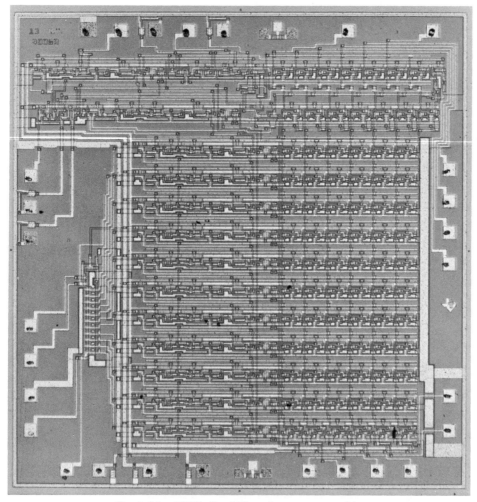

Fig. 3.21. MOS silo shift register memory chip.

provide signals that permit proper loading and unloading of the silo memory. Thus, control logic performs bookkeeping on the content state of the silo register to ensure that the data are entered and extracted at a rate such as to prevent silo overflow.

3.7 FUTURE DIRECTIONS

3.7.1 Introduction

It will be recalled that presently a suitable semiconductor form of circuitry is not available for the mass memory market. Let us, therefore, discuss several semiconductor approaches that may find application in mass memory products for this market.

3.7.2 Charge Coupled Devices (CCDs)

CCDs store minority-carrier charge in potential wells created at the surface of a semiconductor and transport the charge in packet form along the surface by moving the potential wells.[14] The potential wells are produced by applying a voltage to conducting electrodes formed on the surface of an insulator covering the semiconductor. The potential wells are moved along the surface by appropriate application of potential to the various electrodes. Presence or absence of charge in the wells is representative of 1s or 0s, respectively. The sequentially accessed memory function can thus be performed with CCDs. The fundamental operating principles of CCDs have been presented in Chap. 2.

As a practical configuration for a CCD array intended to perform the dynamic shift register function, consider the two-phase structure shown in Fig. 3.22. The two-phase device uses overlapping gate electrodes that effectively eliminate any coupling problems which might arise from the 0.1-mil field-plate gaps in the more elementary structure described in Chap. 2. The problems associated with high photolithographic resolution required for 0.1-mil metal spacings are also alleviated by the overlapping two-level gates. The asymmetrical potential wells of the two-level gate structure ensure directionality of charge flow by extending each phase electrode over two thicknesses of channel oxide. The structure can be fabricated by using polycrystalline silicon gates overlapped by aluminum gates and isolated from each other by an SiO_2 layer. Charge is moved through the CCD array by alternating the clock pulse potentials as shown in Fig. 3.22. In this way coded information (0s and 1s) can be shifted along the array. A variety of geometries other than this two-phase structure utilize these same basic concepts in CCD array design.

Perhaps the most important problem associated with CCD technology is that of incomplete charge transfer from one plate to the next as well as the fall-off of transfer efficiency with increasing clock frequency. Description of the problem involves the dynamics of free carrier motion, including the mechanisms of diffusion and drift. Trapping at interface states must also be considered. Experimental results indicate that for material systems and geometries used to date, these effects are present but are not sufficiently large to preclude useful applications of CCDs. In fact, a major improvement in charge transfer efficiency can be obtained by simply operating the CCD shift register with a constant small amount of charge input—a trickle charge

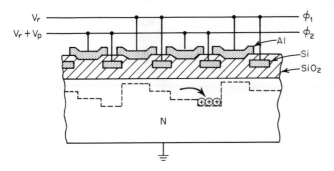

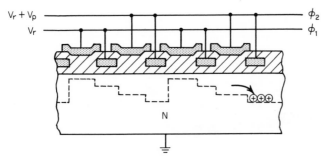

Fig. 3.22. Clocking of charge through a multilevel, two-phase CCD.

referred to as a "fat zero."[15] The fat zeros serve to keep fast interface state traps filled, thereby resulting in negligible charge-transfer loss.

CCDs thus perform the SR function with a power dissipation per bit of 5 μW at a clock frequency of 1 MHz. Power dissipation varies approximately linearly with clock frequency. Operation with p-channel technology to 10 MHz and with n-channel to 50 MHz is thought to be feasible. Area per bit is $\approx$1 sq mil. Circuit density therefore exceeds present forms of MOS/LSI and is greater than 500,000 elements per sq in.

The structure of the CCD[16] is compared to the MOS configurations in Fig. 3.23. The trend is obvious: simplified processing, potentially high yields, and increased circuit density, all resulting in improved system economics. These characteristics, coupled with the inherent circuit simplicity of the CCD (note memory circuitry no longer need be implemented with load-active devices arranged in flip-flop configurations), promise a bright future for this new technology. A 4,096-bit CCD SR representative of the current state of the art (Fig. 3.24) has been reported by Collins et al.[17]

3.7.3 Bucket Brigade Devices (BBDs)

The basic concepts for an electronic delay line of variable delay, now referred to as a bucket brigade or analog shift register, were initially defined by Janssen[18]

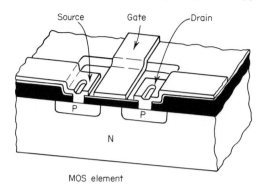

MOS element

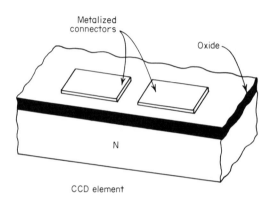

CCD element

Fig. 3.23. Comparison of bipolar versus MOSFET and the CCD in cross-sectional view.[16]

(Fig. 3.25). The amplifiers are buffer amplifiers with unity gain and infinite input impedance. Transfer of analog information along the electronic delay line is caused by alternately actuating all even-numbered and all odd-numbered switches. For example, all even-numbered switches can be activated at times $T/2$, $3T/2$, $5T/2$. The time delay per section can be varied continuously by varying the period of the switching pulse.

An MOS/LSI version of Janssen's electronic delay line has been fabricated by Sangster.[19] The basis for its operation is a chain of storage capacitors and charge transfer circuits functioning as an analog or digital shift register. Sangster refers to the circuit as having bucket brigade capacitor storage, a name which derives from the operational resemblance of the circuit to the historical fire brigade. The shift register uses two complementary clocks with a frequency equal to the sampling frequency applied to the input signal. Signal delay can thus be accurately controlled, or if required, can be changed electronically. Due to the absence of dc gate currents, signal attenuation is negligible. The circuit structure is shown in Fig. 3.26. The storage capacitors are formed by the enlarged gate areas and accompanying p regions. No interconnection pattern between adjacent stages is necessary because the drain of one stage also forms the source of the following stage. Sangster has fabricated a p-channel enhancement-mode analog shift register comprising 72 stages with 8-pF storage capacitors on a 60×95-mil chip.[19] The circuit uses two clock

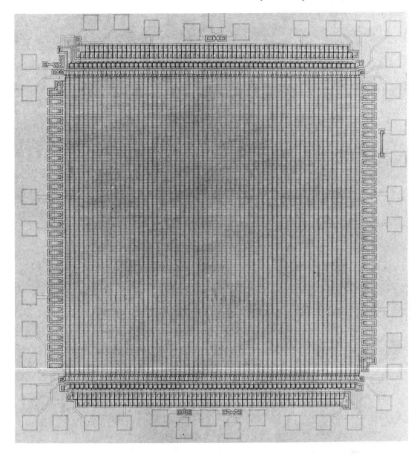

Fig. 3.24. A 4,096-bit n-channel CCD shift register.[17]

signals of 5-V amplitude and has been operated at clock frequencies between 100 Hz and 3 MHz. The circuit has been used experimentally for speech processing and audio delay. This is an early experimental model. More recently, 512-bit MOS bucket brigade structures have been fabricated[20] for use as an audio delay line. As the technology develops, small bucket brigade cells ≈ 1 sq mil will become

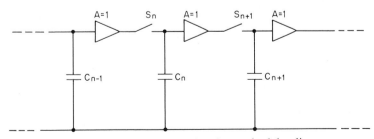

Fig. 3.25. Schematic of the electronic delay line.

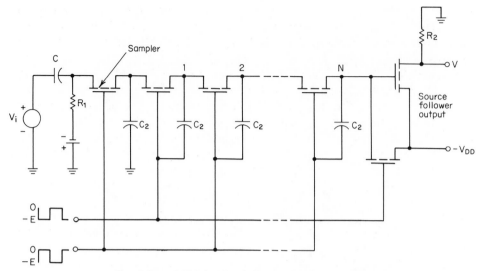

Fig. 3.26. MOS bucket brigade circuit structure.

available for digital storage, thus providing greater than 500,000 bits per sq in. Power dissipation will be $\approx$5 μW per bit.

Berglund and Strain have made a comparison of fabrication and performance characteristics of CCDs and BBDs.[21] They find the two methods are quite similar with respect to silicon area limitations, voltage, current, and power requirements. High- and low-frequency operating limitations originate in both methods from the same mechanisms and are numerically equivalent to within less than a factor of 2. CCDs require no diffused areas in their active regions and may offer less critical mask alignment for the two-level electrode structure, compared to BBDs. Also, at intermediate frequencies, both methods are capable of transfer efficiencies greater than 99.9 percent. The residual inefficiency of the BBD is caused by nonzero dynamic drain conductance of the MOSFET; the CCD intermediate frequency performance is limited only by interface-state trapping of mobile charge carriers and thus the CCD holds promise for higher efficiency charge transfer than the BBD.

3.7.4   The Magnetic Bubble Device (MBD)

Magnetic bubble devices[22] comprise a new technology which is akin to semiconductor technology because the material can be processed with existing photolithographic methods. Magnetic bubble devices store data bits in the form of magnetic bubbles moving in thin films of magnetic materials. The bubbles are cylindrical magnetic domains whose polarization is opposite to that of the thin magnetic film in which they are formed. The bubbles are stable over a considerable range of conditions and can be moved from point to point in the film with high velocity. The sequentially accessed memory function can thus be performed with magnetic bubble technology. The devices have the potential to be as inexpensive as magnetic disks if the technology can be developed. For the magnetic bubble memory, information is stored in states of magnetization on (or in) a thin magnetic film. The data can travel in two dimensions in the film, and bubble memory data manipulation can be performed without readout followed by write-in (i.e., the bubble memory is nonvolatile).

Magnetic domains form the basis for the bubble technology. They have their origin in powerful localized fields within ferromagnetic material which are capable of aligning molecular magnets parallel to one another. The size and shape of the domains are determined by a balancing of several forces that minimize the sum of the magnetic energy, the exchange energy, and the magneto-crystalline energy. Only in single crystalline material with few defects can one obtain domains of the required simple geometric form.

Let us consider a thin wafer of specially prepared single-crystalline, magnetically anisotropic material and place the wafer in an external magnetic field perpendicular to the wafer (Fig. 3.27a and b). As the field strength is raised, all the domains will suddenly contract (as viewed with polarized light) into small circles called bubbles (actually these are cylinders seen on end). Raising the external field still further causes the bubbles to shrink until they finally disappear. Each bubble acts like a very small magnet which floats in a sea of magnetic field opposite in polarity to the bubble. The bubbles can be easily pushed in any direction with a magnetized iron wire. The bubbles, of course, repel one another and maintain uniform spacing because they are all similarly polarized.

A search has thus been made for a material that gives rise to small bubbles that can be moved at high velocities: i.e., require $\approx 10^6$ bubbles per sq in. with mobilities which allow data processing rates of $\approx 10^6$ bits per sec. The required material has been found in synthetic garnets with the general formula of $Y_3Fe_5O_{12}$. The garnets readily lend themselves to materials engineering—with bubble diameters of 3 microns yielding bubble density of $\approx 10^6$ per sq in. that can be moved stepwise at the rate of 10^6 per sec. The energy required to move a garnet bubble through a distance of four bubble diameters is only 4×10^{-14} joules!

So, in summary, effort is being made with this technology to create compact domains inside sheets of magnetic material and move these domains about in two

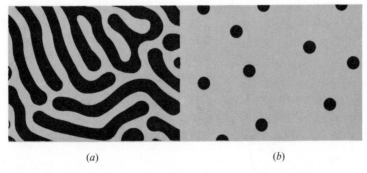

(a)   (b)

Fig. 3.27. Magnetic domains:[23] (a) strip domains present in a thin sheet of terbium orthoferrite with no bias applied; (b) bubble domains with magnetic bias applied perpendicular to the material.

dimensions by exerting unbalanced magnetic forces on the domain walls. The magnetic domains (bubbles) serve as data storage.

One magnetic field access approach to moving the domain bubbles involves applying a rotating magnetic field to the wafer in conjunction with a pattern of thin-film permalloy T's and vertical bars which have been previously formed on the wafer with a photolithographic process (Fig. 3.28a).[23] In the full rotation of the field, the bubble will travel, as a result of magnetic forces arising from the induced magnetic poles in the permalloy pattern, from the center of one T to the center of the next, thereby moving a bubble from left to right (Fig. 3.28b).[23] With the field rotating 100,000 times per sec, a bit rate of 10^5 bits per sec is obtained and the SR function realized.

A bubble generator can be made by utilizing a hairpin conductor that is separately energized. If a bubble is present, it is pinched at its waist and fissions into two bubbles. Conversely, the bubbles can be annihilated by passing them through a region of high magnetic bias that shrinks the bubble to less than its minimum stable diameter.

The presence of a bubble signifies a 1 and the absence of a bubble signifies a 0. A bubble can be detected by employing the Hall effect. Indium antimonide is presently considered to be the best material for this type sensor. The magneto-resistance effect can also be used for the detection of magnetic bubbles. Here, materials such as Permalloy can be employed.

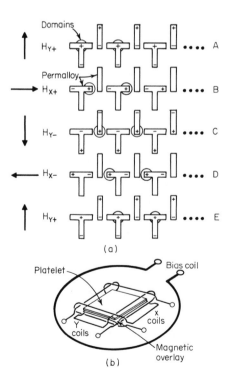

(a)

(b)

Fig. 3.28. T-bar propagation:[23] (a) Cylindrical domains are attracted to positive magnetic poles that appear when the rotating field is directed along a long dimension of a T or bar. As the field rotates clockwise, the positive poles appear immediately to the right of the domains, causing them to propagate toward the right. (b) Bias and propagation fields are provided by a coil arrangement, as shown.

At present, research efforts in bubble devices are focused on materials technology and methods of bubble propagation. A 1,000-bit magnetic bubble shift register has been described in the literature.[24] Although processing of material requires only a few steps for device realization, a great amount of research and development remains to be done before these devices will be practical in industrial memory applications. Mastery of the bubble technology must be accompanied by achievement of cost goals in the 10 millicents per bit region.

3.8 CONCLUSIONS

This chapter can be summarized with the following conclusions:

1. During the next several years, MOS/LSI will fill the major requirements for sequentially accessed temporary storage. One possible exception is that of high bit-rate requirements at and above 25 MHz for short SR chains—then bipolar will be used.

2. Static MOS SRs will be employed if dc storage is required; but then storage will be limited to $\approx$1,000-bit chains per silicon chip. Dynamic MOS SRs will be used where up to 4,000-bit chains are required in the absence of required operation at frequencies down to dc. CCD dynamically operated arrays will effectively perform the shift register function for chain length greater than 4,000 bits in the near future.

3. There appear to be feasible semiconductor solutions on the horizon for mass memory where the objectives for mass memory are (a) tens of millicents per bit, (b) 10^5 to 10^6 bits per sq in., and (c) access time less than 8.5 ms. Possible solutions to these requirements are charge coupled devices (CCDs), bucket brigade devices (BBDs), or magnetic bubble devices (MBDs).

4. The minimum energy required to write a logic bit with the various technologies and methods is:
   (a) 10^{-12} joules for bipolar
   (b) 5×10^{-13} joules for MOS
   (c) 10^{-13} joules for CCDs and BBDs
   (d) 4×10^{-14} joules for MBDs

An energy theorem has been given by Landauer[25] which states that only a few KT or $\approx 10^{-20}$ joules should be required to write a logic bit. The theorem has its origin in fundamental considerations of thermodynamics. The amount of energy required to perform the memory function is of importance since this defines the electrical efficiency with which a computer system will function.[26] Whether the approximately six order of magnitude gap in performance between devices presently fabricated and the theoretical limit can be closed is not clear. It does appear, however, that substantial progress has been made toward that direction during the past several years, and that semiconductor devices and circuits will play an increasing role in sequentially accessed storage design.

REFERENCES

1. R. Petterson (contributing editor), Digital Magnetic Tape Equipment, *Comput. Des.*, **5**(5): 34–37(May 1966) and **(6)**: 36–46(June 1966).
2. E. K. Sittig and F. M. Smits, Recirculating Ultrasonic Stores: An Economical Approach to Sequential Storage with Bit Rates Beyond 100 MHz, *Bell Syst. Tech. J.*, **48**(3): 659–674(March 1969).
3. Z. Kitamura, H. Tevada, and S. Hidaka, The Magnetostrictive Film Transducer for Ultrasonic Delay Lines, *IEEE Trans. Magn.*, **Mag-2**(3): 206–207(September 1966).
4. N. R. Scott, "Electronic Computer Technology," p. 316, McGraw-Hill Book Company, New York, 1970.
5. W. N. Carr and J. P. Mize, "MOS/LSI Design and Application," McGraw-Hill Book Company, New York, 1972.
6. L. M. Terman, MOSFET Memory Circuits, *Proc. IEEE,* **59**: 1044–1058(July 1971).
7. General Instrument Corp., *Tech Spec. MEM 501,* May 1965.
8. L. Cohen, R. Rubenstin, and F. Wanlass, MTOS Four Phase Clock Systems, *NEREM Rec.,* pp. 170–171, 1967.
9. J. R. Burns, Switching Response of Complementary-symmetry MOS Transistor Logic Circuits, *RCA Rev.,* pp. 627–661, December 1964.
10. J. R. Burns and J. J. Gibson, "Complementary Field Effect Transistor Transmission Gate," U.S. Patent 3,457,435, July 22, 1969.
11. R. M. Warner, Comparing MOS and Bipolar Integrated Circuits, *IEEE Spectrum,* **4**: 50–58(June 1967).
12. S. K. Wiedmann and H. H. Berger, Small-size Low-power Bipolar Memory Cell, *IEEE J. Solid-state Circuits,* **SC-6**: 283–288(October 1971).
13. R. Percival, Dynamic MOS Shift Registers Can Also Simulate Stack and Silo Memories, *Electronics,* **44**: 85–89(November 8, 1971).
14. W. S. Boyle and C. E. Smith, Charge Coupled Semiconductor Devices, *Bell Syst. Tech. J.,* **47**(4): 587–593(April 1970).
15. W. S. Kosonocky and J. E. Carnes, Two-phase Charge-coupled Shift Registers, *ISSCC72 Dig. Tech. Pap.,* p. 132.
16. L. Altman, New MOS Technique Points Way to Junctionless Devices, *Electronics,* **43**: 112(May 11, 1970).
17. D. R. Collins, J. B. Barton, D. C. Buss, A. R. Kmetz, and J. E. Schroeder, CCD Memory Options, *ISSCC73 Dig. Tech. Pap.,* pp. 136–137.
18. J. M. L. Janssen, *Nature,* **4291**: 149(January 26, 1952).
19. F. L. J. Sangster, *ISSCC70 Dig. Tech. Pap.,* pp. 74–75.
20. L. Boonstra and F. L. J. Sangster, Progress on Bucket-brigade Charge Transfer Devices, *ISSCC72 Dig. Tech. Pap.,* p. 140.
21. C. N. Berglund and R. J. Strain, Fabrication and Performance Considerations of Charge-transfer Dynamic Shift Registers, *Bell Syst. Tech. J.,* **51**(3): 655–703(March 1972).
22. A. H. Bobeck and H. E. D. Scovil, Magnetic Bubbles, *Sci. Am.,* **224**: 78–90(June 1971).
23. G. Lapidus, The Domain of Magnetic Bubbles, *IEEE Spectrum,* **9**: 58–62(September 1972).
24. I. Danylchuk, Operational Characteristics of a 1,000 Bit Garnet Y-Bar Shift Register, *J. Appl. Phys.,* **42**: 1358–1359(March 1971).
25. R. W. Landauer, Irreversibility and Heat Generation in the Computing Process, *IBM J. Res. Develop.,* **5**: 183–191(1961).
26. O. G. Folberth, The Ultimate Speed-Power Product of Logic Transistor Circuits, *Proc. IEEE,* **54**: 1125(August 1966).

4

Bipolar Random Access Memory Design

4.1 INTRODUCTION

4.1.1 Definition of the Random Access Memory Function

Random access memories[1] can be defined as structures in which a computer stores information and from which information can be obtained without first searching through a large amount of irrelevant data. This form of memory can be accessed in a random fashion thereby saving time. In this application, the most efficient organization of the data is one in which the computer can write into or read out of any data storage location in a random fashion; hence, the term random access memory (or RAM). Any location within the RAM can be reached without regard to any other location. At the selected location, data can be written (stored) in the memory and retrieved from it. A RAM is sometimes called a direct access memory because any location can be addressed in approximately the same time interval as any other location. Thus for receipt of the information at the output, there is only a small variation in access time from any of the storage locations.

RAMs are utilized in the computer as scratch-pads, buffers, mainframe memories or as mass storage. The greatest portion of RAMs in today's computers take the form of magnetic cores. Because of its importance the magnetic core has probably played as large a role in advancing the computer industry as has the transistor.

4.1.2 Why Bipolar RAMs?

Magnetic cores[2] have been widely used for the RAM function because they provide a low-cost, high-capacity storage medium. Their range of access times is 250 ns to 10 μsec. Magnetic core systems, however, have their disadvantages, and speed performance is the major one. Each time data are read from core memory, they must be written back into the memory, and it is this destructive readout characteristic of core that degrades the speed of the magnetic core RAM. Since, in many cases, the RAM stores information that is currently being used by the computer, a most important property of the RAM is its speed. How fast the information can be entered and retrieved from the memory significantly affects how fast the computer will operate. Bipolar transistor systems meet the high-speed RAM requirements for access times of 10 to 200 ns in addition to providing the feature of nondestructive readout. Bipolar RAMs thus operate in a region not possible with magnetic systems.

As a further consideration, the support circuitry for cores (sense amplifiers, line drivers, and receivers) becomes a large percentage of the memory system cost as the bit capacity decreases. Semiconductor memory systems, however, have a common interface and technology between surrounding circuitry and storage circuitry. With commonality of interfaces, systems can be configured and reduced in size more readily. These factors, coupled with rapidly improving economic characteristics of bipolar MSI and LSI, make semiconductor technology a strong contender for selected RAM functions. This chapter is directed toward defining the trends in bipolar RAM performance and economics from which engineering decisions can be reached pertaining to the proper use of bipolar RAMs.

4.1.3 Bipolar RAM Design Considerations

The bistable flip-flop (Fig. 4.1) consisting of two cross-coupled inverters has been the basic storage cell adopted for the bipolar RAM. Simple to design, the cell has good speed-performance capabilities and provides high-yield, low-cost components. The inverter of Fig. 4.1 consists of a transistor and collector load resistor R_C. In this flip-flop cell, one transistor is on, keeping the other transistor off. When the *off* transistor is forced into the *on* state by an external signal, the initially *on* transistor turns *off*. The flip-flop can, therefore, have two stable states, and it will remain in either of these states until an external signal changes the situation. The two stable states are used to store information in the form of logic 1s and 0s.

Power dissipation and physical size of the cell are second only to operating speed as parameters of interest in this chapter. Power dissipation is important because it can limit packing density. Since computers are becoming faster and smaller, the trend is to fit more circuitry into smaller volume. Cell size is related to silicon real estate consumed which in turn plays a major role in determining circuit and system economics. Finally, it should be noted that the flip-flop memory element is, of course, volatile—its information content is lost if power is removed from the cell.

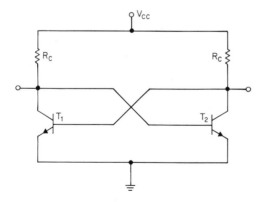

Fig. 4.1. Bistable flip-flop circuit.

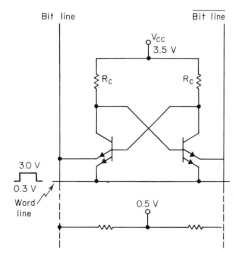

Fig. 4.2. Multiple-emitter RAM memory cell (TTL).[3]

4.2 BIPOLAR RAM CELL CIRCUITRY

4.2.1 The Multiple-emitter Cell

The widely used multiple-emitter RAM memory cell is shown in Fig. 4.2.[3] The cell is designed with high load resistance for low standby power, yet with sufficient readout current so that it will operate over a 0 to 70°C range for commercial applications and a −55 to +125°C range for military applications. The multiple-emitter cell is read by raising the word line from 0.3 to 3.0 V. This action transfers the standby current from the word line to the bit line connected to the *on* transistor. A relatively low impedance current-sensing amplifier detects the memory state by the presence of bit line current in the *on* side. During the read mode, the differential voltage on the bit lines must be kept relatively low, $<(V_{BE} - V_{SAT})$, to avoid disturbing the cell. Data are written into the cell by lowering the voltage on one bit line to produce a differential bit line voltage of $>(V_{BE} - V_{SAT})$. The transistor with the lowest emitter voltage will be turned on. The stored data are maintained when the word line is lowered to 0.3 V. When the cell is not selected, the word line is kept low and cell current continues to flow through the word line. Under this condition there is no signal current at the bit lines and the content of the cell is not sensed. Similarly, raising or lowering the voltage on the bit line will not affect the state of the flip-flop. The circuit is gold-doped for high-speed operation. The speed of accessing the memory cell depends largely on the amount of current available from the cell for sensing. To maintain consistent and fast switching speed, the collector load resistance R_C of the cell must be relatively small and not have large variations. The multiple-emitter cell has been used successfully in 64-bit and 256-bit RAM components.

4.2.2 The Diode Coupled Cell

The SN74200, a 256-bit RAM, uses, however, a diode coupled cell.[4] The circuit shown in Fig. 4.3 operates in a different mode from that of the multiple-emitter

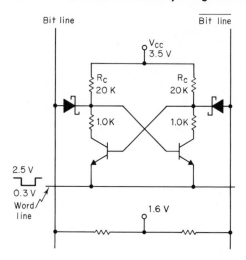

Fig. 4.3. Diode coupled cell.[4]

coupled cell. The circuit is particularly suited for the Schottky TTL process because the two added gating diodes can be of the Schottky variety and fabricated within the collector regions of the flip-flop transistors, keeping the cell size small. The 1K-Ohm resistors are integral parts of the transistors as they are fabricated in integrated-circuit form.

Operation of the diode coupled cell shown in Fig. 4.3 is as follows: V'_{CC} is at 3.5 V and the word line is at 2.5 V. This voltage, in conjunction with the 20K-Ohm load resistors, gives a standby power of less than 75 μW with one transistor quiescently on. Since R_C does not significantly affect access speed, R_C can be made large to reduce power dissipation. The word line voltage also determines the back-bias voltage on the Schottky-barrier diodes connected to the digit lines. The quiescent bit line voltages are approximately 1.6 V. The cell is addressed for reading by pulling the word line down to 0.3 V. This forward-biases the Schottky coupling diodes on the addressed cell, resulting in a read current of approximately 0.3 mA from the 1.6-V supply and presenting a differential voltage on the bit lines. The stored data are read by sensing this differential voltage. During the write operation, the bit line connected to the side of the cell to be written is raised to 2.8 V by a low-impedance driver. The word line is held near ground potential. This causes a current of $\approx$1 mA to flow through the cell if the cell transistor connected to this bit line is on. The voltage that is developed across the 1K-Ohm resistor at the *on* transistor is sufficient to turn on the *off* transistor. The write operation is complete when the *off* transistor has been forced *on* and regeneration completed. If the cell is in the desired state prior to the write cycle, however, no change in state results.

An important advantage of the diode coupled cell is that read current is substantially greater than standby current. This helps obtain *short* read access time. With the multiple-emitter cell, read current is limited to a value determined by the supply voltage and the load resistor. Both diode coupled cells and multiple-emitter cells require regeneration to complete the write cycle. The advantages of the diode coupled bipolar transistor memory cell compared to the multiple-emitter memory cell are lower power consumption and a more favorable speed/power product.

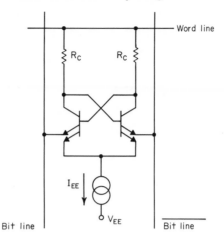

Fig. 4.4. Multiple-emitter RAM memory cell (ECL).

4.2.3 The ECL Memory Cell

A third class of memory cells is shown in Fig. 4.4. This circuit is reminiscent of emitter-coupled logic (ECL) circuits. A given bit is selected by raising the word line voltage. Writing or reading of the memory cell is very similar to that of the multiple-emitter cell of Fig. 4.2 except that the voltage across the selected cell is higher than that across the unselected cell. Therefore, a large sense current is available from the flip-flop when it is selected. When the flip-flop is not selected, the voltage across its supply terminal is quite low, and low standby power is maintained. The collector resistors (R_C) are selected so that for the constant current source value, the transistors are never operated in the saturation mode which would degrade speed performance. The ECL RAM is another example of a nondestructive accessed memory.

4.3 PERIPHERAL CIRCUITRY FOR RAMS

4.3.1 A 2-word, 3-bit-per-word RAM Design Example

Some form of addressing and sensing must be provided for RAM cells in order to realize a useful storage function. To obtain a basic understanding of these peripheral circuits, let us consider a hypothetical and very elementary 2-word, 3-bit-per-word memory array, shown in Fig. 4.5. The multiple-emitter memory cell is used in the example. Note that a word select line is provided for each of the two words (rows) and that a single line for writing or reading is provided for the memory bits in each column. One side of all bit cells is tied to a fixed reference potential. The peripheral circuitry, which will be discussed initially, consists of sense amplifiers, write amplifiers, and write enable gates.

(a) Writing a 0. To write a logic 0 into a single cell (i.e., write a single bit):

1. Address the desired word (row); i.e., raise the word line high (1).
2. Place write enable at low (0).
3. Data in low (0).

4. This results in write/read line high causing T_1 to turn off and T_2 to turn on. The cell has a logic 0 written into it.
5. The word line will return to low (0) when the address is changed.

(b) Writing a 1.   To write logic 1 into a single cell (i.e., write a single bit):

1. Address the desired word (row); i.e., raise the word line high (1).
2. Place write enable at low (0).
3. Data in high (1).
4. This results in write/read line low causing T_1 to turn on and T_2 to turn off. The cell has a logic 1 written into it.
5. The word line will return to low (0) when the address is changed.

(c) Reading.   To read: Assume the case where a logic 1 is stored in a cell with T_1 on and T_2 off.

1. Address the desired word (row); i.e., raise the word line high (1).
2. Hold write enable in its read position, i.e., high (1).
3. This results in read current flow into the appropriate sense amp.

Operation of the circuitry for the write amplifiers and sense amplifiers (Fig. 4.6) is relatively straightforward and can be readily integrated on the silicon chip with the memory cells.   A clever arrangement of diodes within the sense amplifiers

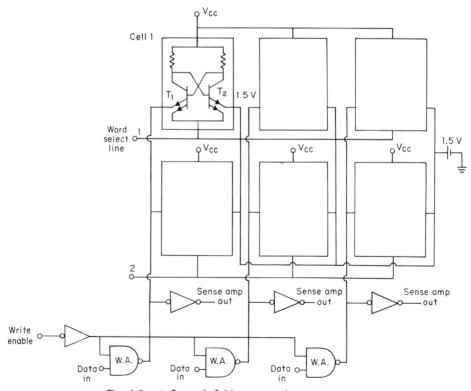

Fig. 4.5.   A 2-word, 3-bit-per-word memory array.

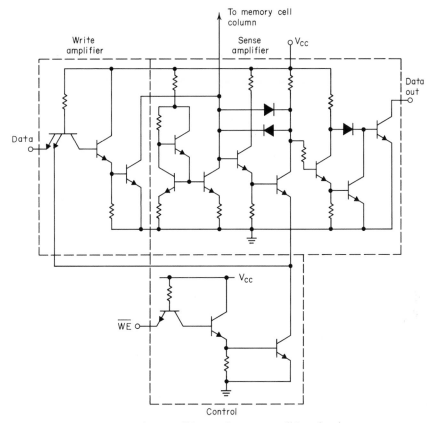

Fig. 4.6. Write amplifier and sense amplifier circuitry.

permits writing and sensing to take place on the same line, yet when sensing, no change of potential is presented to the bit cells within the memory matrix. The outputs of the sense amplifiers must also be made compatible for bus-line interconnection.

4.3.2   The 64-bit SN7489 RAM Design Example

Now, of course, a 2-word–3-bit per word semiconductor memory would be quite limited in usefulness. It thus becomes desirable to place as many cells as possible plus associated addressing and sensing circuitry on a silicon chip. It is apparent from the previous example how the rows and columns of the memory array can be extended to greater values. In practice, row extension can become quite large. Consider, for example, the case where 16 rows (words) exist accompanied by 16 package pins for word address. A desired numerical reduction in the 16-pin requirement can be realized by using a 1-out-of-16 decoding circuit (Fig. 4.7). This decoder consists of a simple arrangement of logic gates, which results in the capability of being able to select a given word (row) with application of the proper logic signals to only 4 pin-outs instead of the previously required 16. So therefore, an address decoder is added to the peripheral circuitry to minimize package pin count required

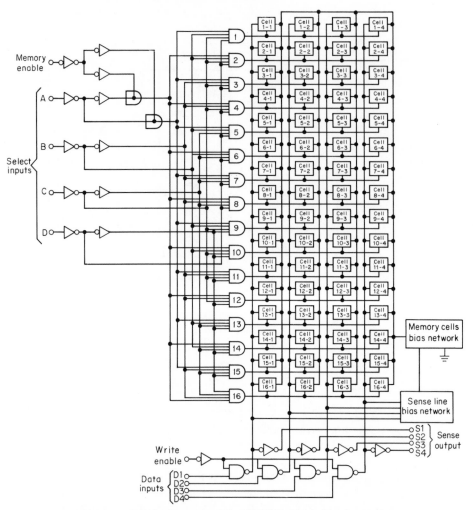

Fig. 4.7. Block diagram of the SN7489 64-bit bipolar RAM.

for word address. Note that memory enable in this design is implemented in the input buffering rather than in the output circuitry.

These circuit concepts and organization methods have been brought together and constitute a 64-bit SN7489 bipolar RAM circuit. This silicon chip (Fig. 4.8) is used for scratch-pad memory with nondestructive readout. It is a fully decoded memory organized as 16 words of 4 bits each. Typical access time is 33 ns. It features inputs that are diode-clamped for noise suppression and are buffered to reduce the input loading. All four column bits are brought out with column decode. Open collector outputs provide *wired-AND* capability.

A summary of the 64-bit RAM characteristics shows that:

Cell size = 62 sq mils
Total area per bit = 163 sq mils

t_{pA} (access time from address application) = 60 ns (max)

t_{pAE} (access time from enable application) = 50 ns (max)

p_D per bit = 5.8 mW (typically)

p_D total = 375 mW (typically)

I_{LF} = (input load factor) = 1.6 mA (Input load factor is a measure of the signal amplitude that an input gate requires for activation.)

4.4 THE 256-BIT SN74200 BIPOLAR RAM

The 256-bit bipolar RAM (SN74200) is organized as 256 × 1 (i.e., 256 words of 1 bit each). The chip is fully decoded. All inputs are buffered and clamped. Architecture of the 256-bit RAM is given in Fig. 4.9. Note there are eight address, one data in, one write enable (or read enable), and three active memory enable decode inputs. The three active memory enable decode inputs are an aid in expanding the 256-bit RAM into larger memory systems. The one data output features *three-state output*[5] instead of the conventional open-collector operation.

Let us digress for a moment and define *three-state switching*. The push-pull output of TTL circuits (Fig. 4.10) consists of 2 transistors in series between voltage supply and ground with the circuit output between these transistors thus making the wired-OR function impractical for these TTL outputs, i.e., outputs of a number of these gates cannot arbitrarily be connected to one another because the logic 0 and

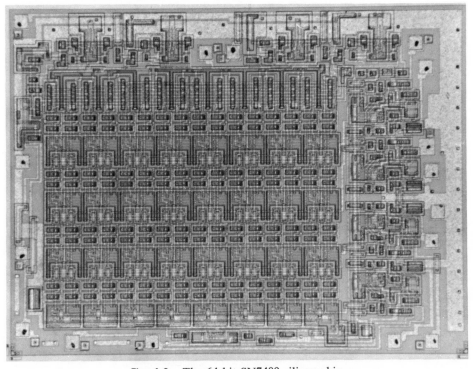

Fig. 4.8. The 64-bit SN7489 silicon chip.

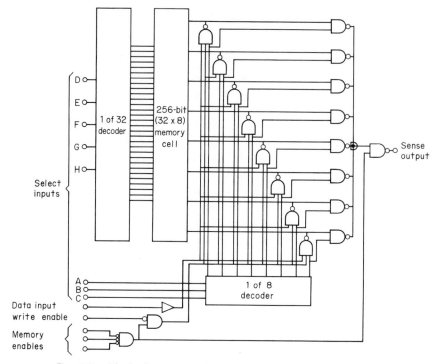

Fig. 4.9. Block diagram of the 256-bit SN74200 bipolar RAM.

1 outputs would be incompatible with each other. To overcome this limitation, the push-pull output of a TTL circuit can be clamped off with an added transistor as shown in Fig. 4.10. This effectively disconnects the output stage of the TTL gate, thereby permitting a wired-OR connection to the output. With the *three-state*

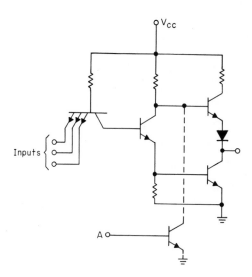

Fig. 4.10. TTL gate with three-state switching.[5]

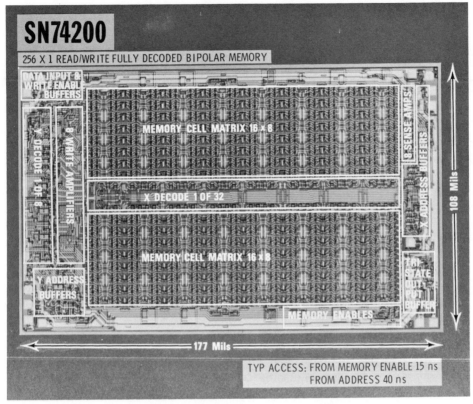

Fig. 4.11. The SN74200 256-bit RAM chip.

feature, the system must choose one particular gate among those connected to a wired OR, switch it on, and keep all others switched off. For this reason, the output of the three-state gate is more correctly referred to as a "bused" configuration, rather than a true logic OR. A typical application wherein memory expansion is required, such as interconnection of numerous 256-bit RAMs, is facilitated with the presence of the three-state output. The output of the 256-bit RAM can supply at least 10.3 mA when the voltage is 2.4 V, thereby providing the necessary current for 256 loads.

The storage cell for the 256-bit RAM uses diode coupling to the bit lines. The chip is pictured in Fig. 4.11. Note the organization of circuitry on the silicon chip—two 16×8 memory matrices, X and Y decode, write amplifiers, and sense amplifiers. Features of the SN74200 256-bit RAM are:

Cell size $= 38$ sq mils
Total area per bit $= 74$ sq mils
$t_{pA} \approx 70$ ns (max)
$t_{pAE} \approx 40$ ns (max)
$P_D = 1.9$ mW per bit (typical)
$I_{LF} = 1.0$ mA (max)

4.5 ECL RAMS

To this point in the discussion, consideration has been given to what is referred to in the industry as transistor-transistor logic (TTL) RAMs. It should again be noted that emitter-coupled logic (ECL) RAMs also exist. The basic cell was shown in Fig. 4.4. The ECL RAM is employed when the ultimate in speed is required. For example, presently available 16-, 64-, and 128-bit fully decoded ECL RAMs have typical access times of 5 to 15 ns. In general, however, cell sizes for these circuits are larger than those of TTL RAMs since circuit complexity is greater. Also, increased power dissipation which accompanies high-speed operation tends to constrain the basic cell size of ECL RAMs. As pointed out in Chap. 2, this increased cell size, coupled with increased fabricational complexity for the ECL RAM, results in projected costs of these devices being a factor of 3 to 5 times those of TTL RAMs during the next two to three years.

4.6 THE 1,024-BIT BIPOLAR RAM

The 1,024-bit bipolar RAM (SN74S204) is organized as 1,024 $\times$ 1 to be compatible with a standard 16-pin package. This results in the following pin-outs:

$$
\begin{array}{lr}
\text{Address} \dots \dots \dots \dots \dots & 10 \\
\text{Input} \dots \dots \dots \dots \dots & 1 \\
\text{Output} \dots \dots \dots \dots \dots & 1 \\
\text{Write enable} \dots \dots \dots \dots & 1 \\
\text{Chip enable} \dots \dots \dots \dots & 1 \\
\text{Power } (V_{CC} \text{ \& ground}) \dots \dots & \underline{2} \\
\text{Total} \dots \dots \dots \dots \dots & 16
\end{array}
$$

The physical cell arrangement on the chip is in the form of a 32 $\times$ 32 matrix with 5 to 32 line X and Y decoders as shown in Fig. 4.12. The resulting chip is shown in Fig. 4.13. Memory cells are Schottky-diode coupled.

Now, to obtain the required circuit density, cell size had to be reduced and electrical interconnections to the diffused components had to be made very dense. The size of the memory cell is as dependent on the interconnecting metalization that must be made to a cell as it is on the size of the components that make up the cell. But, the economics of manufacturing the storage element must be within bounds; therefore, the objective was to make use of as much standard technology as possible. The resulting process, thus, uses self-aligning composed masking for dense active components, high-sheet resistivity diffusions for compacting passive components, and a two-level metalization for dense interconnections to the silicon. As shown in Chap. 2, much closer component spacing is achieved with self-align composed masking because mask alignment tolerances between certain steps in the process are reduced significantly.

As more bits are incorporated on the chip, more levels of decode are necessary. To keep the delays to a minimum in all the areas of decode—matrix, sense, and write—the memory uses Schottky technology throughout. Speed performance for the 1,024-bit storage element compared to the 256-bit is approximately the same

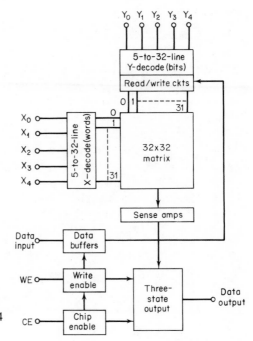

Fig. 4.12. Block diagram of the SN74S204 1,024-bit RAM.

(60 ns), but the power dissipation per bit is reduced by a factor of 5 (i.e., from 1.9 mW per bit to 0.42 mW per bit). The following specifications for the 1,024-bit RAM result:

Organization: $1,024 \times 1$
Cell size = 12 sq mils
Total area per bit = 22 sq mils
$t_{pA} \approx 45$ ns (typical)
$t_{pAE} \approx 15$ ns (typical)
P_D per bit = 0.42 mW per bit (typical)
P_D total = 425 mW (typical)
$I_{LF} = 0.4$ mA (typical)

A summary comparison of the 64-, 256-, and 1,024-bit bipolar RAMs is given in Table 4.1. Note that as the complexity of the storage element has been increased in number of bits from 64 to 1,024, the cell size has been reduced by a factor of 5 down to 12 sq mils per bit. In addition, the power per bit has been reduced by more than a factor of 10, providing a significant advantage when applying these storage elements to larger systems.

A normalized figure of merit has been used to compare storage elements. Like logic gates, a speed/power product has been used. This product multiplied by the total area per bit indicates how well the silicon area is being utilized. The smaller this latter figure of merit value, the better the storage element. The 1,024-bit figure of merit is improved by almost a factor of 100 to 1 over that of the 64-bit.

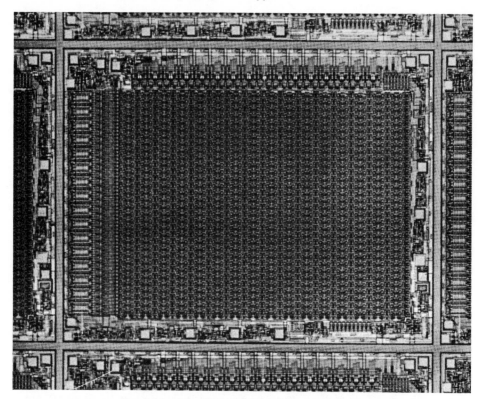

Fig. 4.13.   The SN74S204 1,024-bit RAM chip.

The design of a fully decoded 4,096-bit RAM chip is guided mainly by the consideration of achieving minimum memory cell size which results in appropriate manufacturing yields. Figure 4.14 is a plot of cell area versus bit complexity for resulting bars of 18K and 24K sq mils. Note the permitted cell sizes for the 256-bit and 1,024-bit RAMs. The data points indicate the actual design values. From Fig. 4.14 it can be deduced that the cell size for the 4,096-bit RAM must be less than 4 sq mils to obtain a chip size no larger than 24K sq mils and therefore compatible with appreciable manufacturing yield. This is about a factor of 3 down in cell area from the 1,024-bit RAM cell which we have just discussed. Clearly, some very

Table 4.1.   **Performance Summary of 64-, 256-, and 1,024-bit Bipolar RAMs**

RAM	$t_{pA},$* ns	Cell size, sq mils	A Area/bit, sq mils	P P_D/bit, mW	Figure of merit $t_{pA} \times P \times A$
64-bit	60	62	163	5.8	57
256-bit	70	38	74	1.9	10
1,024-bit	70	12	22	0.42	0.65

*Worst case.

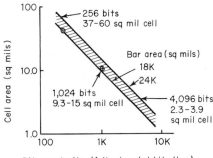

Fig. 4.14. Cell area versus bit complexity for bars of 18K and 24K sq mils.

innovative design and technology utilization must be employed to reach this goal. Let us examine some of the techniques which may prove effective in fabrication of the 4,096-bit bipolar RAM.

4.7 NEW SEMICONDUCTOR TECHNOLOGY HORIZONS FOR BIPOLAR RAMS

4.7.1 The Two-diode Array

An electronically variable memory cell consisting simply of two diodes has been proposed by Waaben and Waggener.[6] This basic memory cell, illustrated in Fig. 4.15, consists of two series-connected diodes having different minority-carrier storage times and therefore, different recovery times from forward conduction. In the example, one diode (D_2) is a conventional structure with minority-carrier storage time of 20 ns; the other element (D_1) is a Schottky diode with essentially zero minority-carrier storage time. To write a 1, a forward current I_f is conducted through both diodes, causing each diode to accumulate a charge. Subsequently, when the polarity of drive voltage is reversed, a reverse-diode minority-carrier current flows. If the minority-carrier current flow is taken as zero in the Schottky diode, then the available minority carriers from the conventional diode charge the Schottky diode to a voltage which is determined by the corresponding charge displaced from the capacitance of the Schottky diode. This charge represents a stored 1.

To read the 1, a voltage with a constant rate of rise is applied to the memory cell in the forward direction. After a finite time delay, C_1 associated with D_1 becomes charged sufficiently for D_1 to go into forward conduction. The previously written and stored charge determines the timing of turn-on of D_1. The stored charge

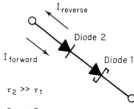

Fig. 4.15. A two-diode memory cell array.[6]

in a cell is detected by sensing this flow of charge through the leads which connect the voltage drive to the cell. The 0s are distinguished from 1s by the two distinctly different time responses of current flow through the addressed cell.

In operation, the cells of the array must be refreshed every 1/20 sec with the refresh cycle lasting about 50 ns. Read/write time is $\approx$100 ns. The six orders difference of magnitude refresh to revisit time can be effectively used either by scanning through all cells sequentially or by operating with a sequential refresh and random read/write mode. Memory standby power and refresh power are each $\approx$1 nW per cell at room temperature. Area per bit is $\approx$10 sq mils. Processing is relatively simple. Yields should be high, and favorable economics should result.

4.7.2 The Two-terminal Transistor Memory Cell Using Avalanche Breakdown

A transient charge storage memory cell consisting of a simple two-terminal transistor structure using junction breakdown has been proposed by Mar.[7] The cell (Fig. 4.16) consists of a bipolar transistor with its base floating, except for the presence of junction and parasitic capacitances. The two charge states of the cell correspond to the case where both junctions are strongly reverse-biased (state of maximum stored charge, the 0 state), and the case where both junctions are weakly reverse-biased (state of minimum charge is the 1 state).

Applying a positive pulse, which is insufficient to avalanche the collector-base junction, across the cell causes a 0 to be written. After removal of this pulse, both junctions are strongly reverse-biased because of charge storage in the base.

To write a 1, a large positive voltage sufficient to avalanche the collector-base junction is applied across the cell. Collector-base breakdown creates an excess of majority carriers which cancel the charge depletion at the junction, leaving both junctions weakly reverse-biased.

To read a cell, a moderate-sized positive pulse is applied, and the resulting charge flow observed. If the voltage is applied to a 0-state cell, then only a small transient charge will flow. On the other hand, when sensing a 1 state, the transistor will enter active conduction allowing considerable charge to flow from emitter to collector. Provision must be made for refresh of these memory cells since charge stored on the reverse-biased back-to-back p-n junctions is limited by leakage current to storage times of $\approx$0.1 sec.

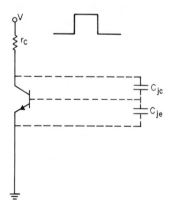

Fig. 4.16. Two-transistor memory cell using avalanche breakdown.[7]

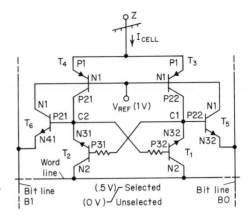

Fig. 4.17. The Wiedmann-Berger memory cell.[8]

The fabrication of this memory cell is simplified by the absence of base contacts. Cell size can probably be made as small as ≈ 1 sq mil. Read and write time is ≈ 10 ns. For a 4,096-bit 100-ns cycle time, the average power dissipated is estimated at 10 μW per bit.

4.7.3 The Wiedmann-Berger Memory Cell

An interesting advanced RAM cell design that exhibits dc stability (i.e., requires no memory refresh) has been proposed by Wiedmann and Berger.[8] This cell is a novel bipolar structure featuring extremely low standby power and small size. Designed to achieve maximum compatibility with bipolar integrated-circuit processing, the cell is fabricated using complementary lateral multicollector PNP transistors as switchable current-source load devices in conjunction with inversely operated NPN transistor flip-flop elements. The circuit diagram is shown in Fig. 4.17. Using constant-current load devices results in extremely low dc power dissipation and small cell size. The inversely operated transistors T_1 and T_2 permit a common n-type bed for all transistors of a common word, enabling the entire cell to use unidirectional isolation pockets. Thus, single-level metalization is possible because the isolation pockets can be utilized for connection lines. Reading and writing into the cell is similar to the method for the multiemitter bipolar cell described earlier in this chapter. With conservative dimensions (e.g., 0.4-mil metal line width) cell size is 14 sq mils. For access time of 10 ns and write time of 80 ns, power dissipation of a 512-bit array is ≈ 0.5 mW per cell. Standby power dissipation is less than 0.1 μW per cell.

Further extension of these developments using current injection logic, I^2L, has been reported by Wiedmann[9] wherein a cell size of 3.1 mil^2 has been employed. This results in a 4K bit storage element of projected size 150 mils $\times$ 160 mils with 50-ns access time and a 0.1-μW per bit standby power.

4.7.4 Fabrication Methods

(a) Isoplanar. A savings in silicon real estate is the promise of the *isoplanar process*[10,11] being developed for fabricating bipolar circuits. It will be recalled from discussion in Chap. 2 that, for conventionally fabricated integrated circuits, the collector of the NPN transistor is buried beneath an epitaxial layer through which contact is made. Also, a p-type region isolates the collector region of one transistor from the collector region of an adjacent device. The space between the isolation and base is required to accommodate a depletion layer resulting from the reverse bias applied to the isolation junction. In the isoplanar process, the p-diffused isolation regions are replaced by selectively grown oxide isolation regions formed to the depth of the buried collector: isolation depletion layers are thereby eliminated. An additional oxide region, located between the base region and the collector sink area, surrounds the contact to the buried collector. The region between the p^+ isolation and the base in the conventional IC can therefore be eliminated, resulting in a savings of up to 40 percent in chip area. To realize the full promise of isoplanar, however, the process must not be metal limited, i.e., metal interconnection line widths must be reduced to 0.2-mil width and 0.1-mil spacing. Since the isoplanar process reduces cell size, more RAM bits per square mil can be placed on a chip. This, coupled with the simplified photomasking steps that the process allows, results in improved yields in circuit fabrication.

It should be noted, of course, that the standard bipolar integrated-circuit process has several years of successful manufacturing experience behind it. Composed masking techniques introduce only minor modifications to these standard processes. In comparison, isoplanar is a relatively new process and must be developed over a period of time into a well-established process, compatible with mass-production methods. In addition, when special layout rules resulting from composed masking are applied to the standard process, then 1,024-bit RAM cells fabricated with isoplanar and standard process provide the results as shown in Table 4.2. Furthermore, it should be pointed out that the isoplanar process presently used is an epitaxial-base process, and the control of the epilayer can be difficult. For example, the layer must be thin or resulting oxide isolation humps become too large, causing abrupt steps in the interconnecting metalization. If the epilayer is too thin, then punch-through will occur in the transistor structures. Conversely, if the epilayer is too thick, then beta of the transistors may be too low or switching times excessive. Considerable development effort will, therefore, be necessary to enable isoplanar to become a truly efficient method.

(b) CDI.[12] A process method, designed to simplify and minimize the number of processing steps in an effort to compete with MOS, is *collector diffusion isolation* (*CDI*). The CDI process discussed in Chap. 2 differs from conventional bipolar fabrication with composed masking in two ways: (1) it uses the epitaxial layer as the base region, eliminating the base diffusion step, and (2) it combines the deep

Table 4.2. Comparison of 1,024-bit RAM Produced with Composed Masking and Isoplanar Processes

Production process	Cell size, sq mils	Area/bit, sq mils
Composed masking	12	22
Isoplanar	10	19

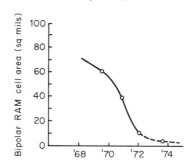

Fig. 4.18. TTL RAM cell size versus time.

collector diffusion contact and isolation step. These techniques eliminate several processing steps of the conventional method. The simplicity of CDI fabrication is achieved at the cost of lower collector-base breakdown voltage, higher inverse current gain, and higher collector junction capacitance per unit area. Switching speed remains, however, equal to that of conventional TTL circuits (4 ns per gate), and power dissipation is low: 6 mW per gate. Process controls problems do result, however, because of the exceedingly thin, 0.08-mil epilayer required for this method.

4.8 BIPOLAR RAM PROGRESS WITH TIME

4.8.1 Cell Size

Figure 4.18 shows TTL RAM cell size versus time. Cell size reduction has been made possible through technology and design innovations, such as narrow epilayers, small geometries, high sheet resistivities, composed masking, Schottky diodes, and other factors. Yield improvement programs have also contributed to this advance.

4.8.2 Economics

The continually improving economic position of bipolar RAMs reflects the conservation of silicon real estate achieved to date in RAM cell fabrication. This is graphically demonstrated in Fig. 4.19, where price per bit is plotted as a function of time. Extrapolation of the data to 1975 indicates that bipolar memory will then be selling at 0.4 ± 0.1 cent per bit!

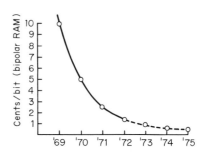

Fig. 4.19. Economic trend of bipolar RAMs.

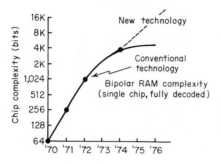

Fig. 4.20. Bipolar RAM chip complexity versus time.

4.8.3 Chip Complexity (Bits per Package)

The *complexity* of bipolar RAM chips (fully decoded) is plotted versus time in Fig. 4.20 with forecasts given for future chip complexity. Considered in the forecasts are two cases: (1) conventional technology employment and (2) new technology (which we have previously discussed in this chapter).

4.8.4 The Speed/Power Product Figure of Merit

Access time for bipolar LSI RAMs has remained fairly constant with time. Typical values are 30 to 40 ns. The all-important speed/power product per RAM bit is improving with time, however, as shown in Fig. 4.21. Recall that low speed/power products represent the desired condition. The primary cause for the dramatic improvement in speed power per bit shown is that of increasing the complexity of fully decoded RAMs. Higher complexity results in a much-improved utilization of the decoding power and accounts for most of the improvement. In addition, lower standby power cell approaches are being used. Techniques to power-down large portions of the overhead circuitry of a fully decoded memory are currently under development throughout the industry and promise a further reduction in power dissipation. With power-down methods, it is possible for the system power per bit to approach that of the holding power of the cell itself.

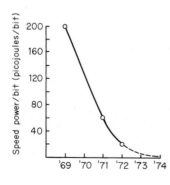

Fig. 4.21. Bipolar RAM speed/power product per bit versus time.

4.9 CONCLUSIONS

1. The main criteria in appraising monolithic memories are bit density, power dissipation, performance, and economics. Several bipolar RAM schemes have been proposed which are compatible with low power dissipation and high bit density.

2. The next bipolar RAM design hurdle is the 4,096-bit chip. Technology and circuit innovation which are developed for achieving the 4,096-bit RAM may be attractive for retrofitting into the 64-, 256-, and 1,024-bit bipolar RAMs for improved performance and/or economics. An example of retrofitting advanced technology such as composed masking, two-level metalization, Schottky diodes, etc., into the 256-bit SN74200 bipolar RAM thereby resulting in the SN74S200 device is shown in Table 4.3.

3. Advances in technology and cell design should result in availability of fast bipolar RAM cells at 0.3 to 0.5 cent per bit by 1975.

Table 4.3. Summary of Results Achieved by Retrofitting Advanced Technology into the 256-bit Bipolar RAM

Design element	SN74200	SN74S200
Cell area, sq mils	38	13.5
Total area per bit, sq mils	74	39
t_{pA}—typ/max, ns	45/70	33/50
t_{pAE}—typ/max, ns	20/40	21/35
P_D per bit—typ, mW/bit	1.9	1.7
ILF—typ/max, mA	0.6/1.0	0.025/0.25 PNP input
(t_{pA}) $(P_D$ per bit), pJ/bit	85	51
Temperature, °C	0 to 70	0 to 70

REFERENCES

1. J. K. Hawkins, "Circuit Design of Digital Computers," p. 379, John Wiley & Sons, Inc., New York, 1968.

2. A. P. Malvino and D. P. Leach, "Digital Principles and Applications," chap. 12, McGraw-Hill Book Company, New York, 1969.

3. R. Rice, W. S. Sander, and F. S. Greene, Jr., Design Considerations Leading to the ILLIAC IV LSI Process Element Memories, *IEEE J. Solid-state Circuits,* **SC-5:** 174–181(October 1970).

4. D. J. Lynes and D. A. Hodges, Memory Using Diode-coupled Bipolar Transistor Cell, *IEEE J. Solid-state Circuits,* **SC-5:** 186–191(October 1970).

5. J. Sheets, Three-state Switching Brings Wired OR to TTL, *Electronics,* **43:** 78–84(September 14, 1970).

6. S. Waaben and H. A. Waggener, 100-ns Electronically Variable Semiconductor Memory Using Two Diodes Per Memory Cell, *IEEE J. Solid-state Circuits,* **SC-5:** 192–196(October 1970).

7. J. Mar, A Two-terminal Transistor Memory Cell Using Breakdown, *IEEE J. Solid-state Circuits,* **SC-6:** 280–283(October 1971).

8. S. K. Wiedmann and H. H. Berger, Small-size Low-power Bipolar Memory Cell, *IEEE J. Solid-state Circuits,* **SC-6**: 283–288(October 1971).

9. S. K. Wiedmann, High Density Static Bipolar Memory, *ISSCC73 Dig. Tech. Pap.,* pp. 56–57.

10. D. Pelkzer and B. Herndon, Isolation Method Shrinks Bipolar Cells for Fast, Dense Memories, *Electronics,* **44**: 50–55(March 1, 1971).

11. V. A. Dhaka, J. E. Muschinske, and W. K. Owens, Subnanosecond ECL Gate Circuit Using Isoplanar II, *ISSCC73 Dig. Tech. Pap.,* pp. 172–173.

12. B. T. Murphy, V. J. Glinski, P. A. Gary, and R. A. Pedersen, Collector Diffusion Isolated Integrated Circuits, *Proc. IEEE,* **57**: 1523–1527(September 1969).

5

MOS Random Access Memory Design

5.1 INTRODUCTION

5.1.1 Definition of the Random Access Memory Function

Random access memories can be defined as structures in which a computer stores information and from which information can be extracted without first searching through a large amount of irrelevant data.[1] In this application, the most efficient organization of the data is one in which the computer can write into, or read out of, any data storage location in a random fashion without regard to its physical position relative to other locations in the storage unit; thus the term *random access memory* or *RAM*.

5.1.2 Why RAMs?

Rams are utilized in the computer as scratch-pad, buffer, and mainframe memories. At the onset of the 1970 decade these functions were almost exclusively performed by magnetic devices.[2,3] In the next generation of computers, MOS/LSI will be speedily adopted for buffer and mainframe memories. Following is a summary of the advantages of MOS/LSI for performing the RAM function.

1. *Nondestructive Readout*. Readout of a MOS RAM does not affect the content stored. Readout of magnetic core is destructive and hence affects the content stored. Therefore, with MOS RAM it is unnecessary to perform a write after every read operation as must be done with core memory. The possible exception to be noted in this comparison is the 1-transistor MOS RAM cell for which readout is destructive.
2. *Fast Operating Speed*. Access times as low as 150 ns, with on-chip decoding, are possible for p-channel MOS circuitry. Shorter access times can be obtained by off-chip decoding or by using n-channel technology. Minimization of access time is of importance since its compression gives the systems designer more time to perform other necessary operations, such as parity check.
3. *Low Power Dissipation*. Power dissipation is typically less than 1.0 mW per bit for static design, and less than 0.5 mW per bit for dynamic.

4. *Compatibility.* Semiconductor memory systems are entirely self-compatible because they enjoy common interface and technology between sensing and decoding circuitry (i.e., overhead circuitry) and the storage element itself. With commonality of interfaces, systems can be configured to desired size more readily.

5. *Economy.* MOS memories are presently more economical than magnetic core for small and medium-size systems. This has happened while circuit innovation of MOS RAM systems is still in its early stages of development.

6. *Versatility.* New and very promising memory cell configurations are made possible by certain operational and physical characteristics of the MOSFET device (for example, the infinite input resistance and bilateral nature of the device).

This chapter traces the advances of MOS memory cell development, considers design fundamentals, discusses technology interplay, and summarizes the performance and economic characteristics of these memory elements. It also summarizes some of the recent developments and points out the directions in which they can lead us.

5.2   STATIC RAM CELLS

5.2.1   Introduction

The bistable flip-flop, shown in Fig. 5.1, is the basic form of memory cell first used in MOS RAM circuitry. The active devices, T_1 and T_2, are connected to their respective load resistors, T_3 and T_4, to form two cross-coupled inverters. Note that load resistors have been implemented with MOS transistors. MOS load resistors exhibit high resistance per unit area permitting fabrication of the flip-flop memory cells with high circuit density and high yield resulting in low cost.

In the flip-flop, one transistor is normally on; this in turn keeps the other transistor off. The flip-flop has two stable states, either of which can be chosen by application of the proper external signal. The two stable states can thus be used to store logical 0s or 1s in memory form. Since stable states exist unless purposely disturbed, the cell is referred to as a static memory cell. The static cell stores each bit of data on a latch and requires no refresh cycle and no clocks.

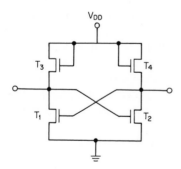

Fig. 5.1. The MOS bistable flip-flop.

Information is, of course, lost if power is removed from the cell for time intervals which exceed a few milliseconds. This gives rise to a common characteristic of semiconductor memories, namely that of *volatility*.

5.2.2 The 8-transistor Static RAM Cell

An 8-transistor static RAM cell is shown in Fig. 5.2. The circuitry represents a static memory cell featuring two-dimensional decode.[4] There are 256-bit arrays of these memory cells available commercially. The two-dimensional decode for these circuits employs 16X address lines and 16Y address lines. Any one of the 256 bits in the memory can be selected by turning on an X address line in coincidence with a Y address line. Power dissipation for this circuit is ≈ 1 mW per bit. The 8-transistor cell requires ≈ 35 sq mils of silicon real estate per bit. Although it is not particularly efficient in terms of space and power required, it does allow use of simple peripheral circuitry.

It should be noted at this point that a design goal is to reduce the device count and thereby simplify the RAM cell circuitry. This has been accomplished, and it is possible to simplify the cell until only 1 transistor and 1 capacitor perform the entire function. But that's getting ahead of our story, so let us return to the static cell and see how it can be simplified.

5.2.3 The 6-transistor Static RAM Cell

The silicon real estate required by the 8-transistor cell can be reduced by combining the address circuitry with the bit lines. Figure 5.3 shows a 6-transistor RAM cell in which this has been accomplished. Note that in this circuit column select gating transistors are used. Double-rail transfer of data is also employed. This cell finds use in fully decoded memory arrays in which decode from address bits located on the chip determines the particular cell of the memory matrix in which the read or write operation will be performed. The 2 cross-coupled transistors, T_1 and T_2, serve as memory storage elements. T_5 and T_6 are transistors that connect or isolate a given storage cell from the sense-bit lines. The word select line controls the *on* or *off* condition of T_5 and T_6.

In the storage mode, the cell maintains one of its two stable states. The word select line is held high (close to V_{SS}) and T_5 and T_6 are, therefore, off. The cell

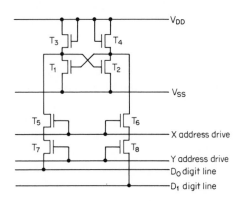

Fig. 5.2. An 8-transistor static RAM cell.

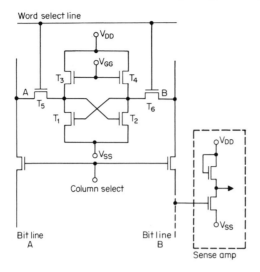

Word select line

Fig. 5.3. A 6-transistor static RAM cell.

is then isolated from its sense-bit lines. To change the information stored in the cell (i.e., to write data in), the sense-bit lines are connected to the p-channel MOS cell by applying a low-level state (V_{DD}) to the gates of T_5 and T_6 (therefore, T_5 and T_6 are thereby turned on). Then, for example, if bit line A is brought low to V_{DD} and bit line B is held high (close to V_{SS}), T_1 will turn off and T_2 will turn on. This memory state is locked into the memory cell at the completion of the write operation when the word select line is returned to V_{SS}.

To read the contents of a cell, at least one of the sense-bit lines must contain sensing circuitry capable of determining the state of the storage cell. The sensing circuitry can be simply an MOS inverter, as shown, which senses the contents of the cell when the word select line is activated.

If it is desired to organize 64 of these memory cells into 16 words of 4 bits each with on-chip decoding, a 1-out-of-16 word (or row) decoder will be required. The basic circuitry for the word decoder with 4 binary inputs (A_0 through A_3) is shown in Fig. 5.4. As an example, consider the case where the zeroth word is to be activated. This will occur when A_0, A_1, A_2, and A_3 are all high (ground), i.e., (1111) in positive logic, and the word line will then go low (to V_{DD}). If, for example, the first word is to be activated, then A_0, A_1, A_2 must all be high and A_3 must be low, i.e., (1110). The situation is continued to the fifteenth word where A_0, A_1, A_2, and A_3 must all be low, i.e., (0000) in order to activate that, and only that, particular word line. It should be pointed out that in order to reduce gate delays, decoders are usually buffered by amplifiers capable of driving the capacitance associated with the numerous input lines of the decoder.

For the array in this example, only four columns of memory cells exist. These columns can readily be decoded and addressed with MOSFETs placed in series with the bit lines, which can then be properly activated. Thus, for a 64-bit RAM organized as 16 words of 4 bits each, the following terminals would be required:

4	address lines for word (row) select
3	lines for V_{GG}, V_{DD}, and V_{SS}
4	data-in lines
4	data-out lines
1	chip enable
1	write line
1	read line
18	total

The 6-transistor MOS cell provides several advantages. First, because of its static nature, reading and writing are straightforward and the cell need not be refreshed. Second, readout is nondestructive. Third, power dissipation is ≈ 0.9 mW per bit. Power dissipation could be reduced by clocking the power supply from a high voltage to a low voltage, placing the circuit in a dynamic mode of operation. The consequences of dynamic operation will be analyzed in detail later in this chapter.

A major disadvantage of the 6-transistor static cell is the large cell size required by the 6 transistors (≈ 25 sq mils). Cell size has been reduced by using n-channel technology; see Chap. 10. It appears difficult, however, to reduce the device count since a flip-flop configuration plus addressing transistors are required. Only by deviating from a classical flip-flop configuration can the device count be reduced in the memory cell. Fortunately this can be accomplished in MOS technology by utilizing what is referred to as a *dynamic* cell.

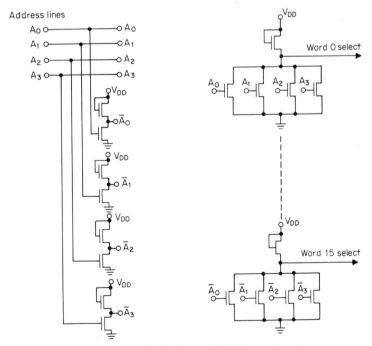

Fig. 5.4. Word decoder with 4 binary inputs.

5.3 DYNAMIC RAM CELLS

5.3.1 Introduction

The nearly infinite input resistance of the MOSFET provides a temporary data storage node which can be used to simplify RAM cell circuitry. Using this capability, information can be stored for a finite length of time on the gate of the MOS device. The p-n junctions which are inevitably connected to the gate regions and the accompanying junction leakage currents are small enough so that charge can be stored on the gate capacitance and gate parasitic capacitances for times of milliseconds to tenths of seconds. Of course, some electrical method must be provided for refreshing the gate prior to loss of data. It will be recalled that it was this type storage that permitted successful operation of MOS dynamic shift registers; this type storage will also provide the means for operation of the dynamic RAM.

5.3.2 The 4-transistor Dynamic RAM Cell

As a first example of dynamic RAM cell circuitry, let us consider how a static cell such as the 6-transistor configuration previously discussed can be operated dynamically in a 4-transistor configuration, thereby realizing a reduced device count. To achieve the configuration, the load transistors of the flip-flop are operated in a clocked mode and the load transistors are simultaneously used as elements by which the cell can be accessed as shown in Fig. 5.5. The cell will thus hold information which has been set into it, when T_3 and T_4 are activated by clock pulse ϕ. When the clock voltage turns off, T_3 and T_4 are off and the charge on C_1, resulting from the previously set condition of T_1 *on* and T_2 *off*, will gradually leak off through the drain junction of T_2 and source junction of T_4.

The cell will eventually lose its information content and therefore must be refreshed. This can be done quite simply by turning T_3 and T_4 back on with a clock pulse, ϕ. At 70°C, the clock pulse must come on every 2 ms and stay on for a few hundred nanoseconds to restore the charge on capacitor C_1. The flip-flop, of course, remembers the state it should be in, since prior to refresh all the charge (and hence voltage) was not permitted to be lost from C_1. The refresh method for this cell is, therefore, quite direct and is probably the simplest in operation of all dynamic cells which we will consider.

To utilize this 4-transistor cell in a memory array, the overhead circuitry shown in Fig. 5.6 must be employed. The cell is refreshed by the row (word) select line,

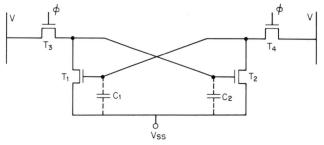

Fig. 5.5. A 4-transistor dynamic RAM cell.

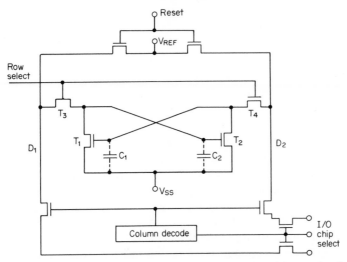

Fig. 5.6. The 4-transistor dynamic RAM cell with overhead circuitry.

which must be activated every 2 ms. The column decode and chip select complete the path to the output, and the differential current that exists on the lines is sensed for reading the state of the cell. Writing is accomplished by forcing line D_1 or D_2 to ground with external signal application when the cell is selected by the row select line.

Advantages of this cell are its high speed, short cycle time, and straightforward refreshing method. Disadvantages are that the writing operation is complex and the cell size is fairly large, ≈ 15 sq mils. This form of RAM cell is popular, however, and its application in a 1,024-bit RAM configuration will be presented later in this chapter. Meanwhile, let us determine what can be done to further reduce the device count and cell size in MOS dynamic RAM cells.

5.3.3 3-transistor Dynamic RAM Cells

When discussing the dynamic operation of MOS circuits, it has been noted that charge (i.e., information) can be temporarily stored on the gates of MOS transistors. Thus a logic 1 can be represented by sufficient charge storage to turn the device on. A logic 0 can be represented by a low charge state resulting in an *off* state condition for the device. This basically implies that it should be possible to make a major departure from the classical flip-flop arrangement in the design of a dynamic RAM cell. Such is the case for the 3-transistor cell shown in Fig. 5.7.[5] Operation of this circuit is as follows. Transistor T_2 is the information storage element where charge stored on capacitor C determines the state of T_2. Transistor T_3 connects T_2 to data out when T_3 is activated by a read select signal. T_1, when activated by a write select signal, transfers input data to the storage element T_2. T_1 also provides refresh of the information storage element T_2 by means of a clocked refresh amplifier which is connected between the read and write lines, thereby closing the

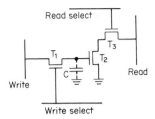

Fig. 5.7. The 3-transistor dynamic RAM cell (3-2-2 configuration).

loop on the memory cell (Fig. 5.8). A single refresh amplifier can, therefore, service an entire column of cells in a memory array.

A memory cell shown in Fig. 5.7 is often referred to as a 3-2-2 cell since it has 3 transistors, 2 address lines, and 2 digit lines. These descriptive numbers are important because they relate to cell size, which must be minimized. This cell is used in the type 1103 RAM.[6] Cell area achieved is $\approx$6 sq mils. The separate read and write lines to the cell make it inherently fast.

Now there are other configurations of 3-transistor dynamic RAM cells. For example, the 3-1-2 configured cell shown in Fig. 5.9 has the advantage that one address line serves both read and write select functions resulting in reduced cell size. Unfortunately, a race condition develops unless read and write address pulse shapes and voltage levels are very accurately tailored. This disadvantage has hindered the adoption of this particular cell.

Another configuration, the 3-2-1 cell, is shown in Fig. 5.10. Read and write signals are presented on a common line, resulting in cell size reduction to $\approx$5 sq mils with p-channel technology. This cell is relatively easy to refresh. Since the cell forms a loop on itself (the read/write line is a common bus), the cell refreshes itself in a complementary manner and refresh amplifiers are eliminated. This cell is often referred to as an *inverting cell*.[7] A data control register must be provided to keep track of the refresh status, but that turns out to be a relatively simple requirement for a matrix array of cells. The 3-2-1 cell configuration thus holds promise for MOS RAM applications.

The available 3-transistor dynamic RAM cells are characterized by access times less than 300 ns, 0.1 to 0.5 mW per bit power dissipation in the active mode, and less than 10 μW per bit dissipation in the standby mode. Silicon area required for these cells of p-channel variety is $\approx$5 to 8 sq mils.

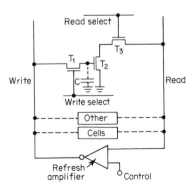

Fig. 5.8. The 3-transistor dynamic RAM cell with overhead circuitry.

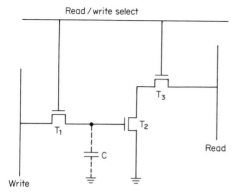

Fig. 5.9. The 3-transistor dynamic RAM cell (3-1-2 configuration).

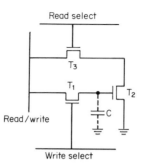

Fig. 5.10. The 3-transistor dynamic RAM cell (3-2-1 configuration).[7]

5.3.4   The 1-transistor Dynamic RAM Cell

What further reduction in component count can be made for the MOS dynamic RAM cell? Let us consider the ultimate—a 1-1-1 configuration. Such a cell features 1 transistor, 1 address line, and 1 digit line. Cells of this type have been successfully fabricated,[8,9,10,11] and they take the circuit form of 1 transistor in series with a storage capacitor, as shown in Fig. 5.11. The transistor serves as a switch, permitting charge flow either into or out of the capacitor storage element when read or write select is activated. This cell's major problem is that of obtaining a large enough voltage swing to read information out of the cell easily. This problem arises because of the large ratio of bit-sense-line capacitance C_2 to cell-storage capacitance C_1. Thus, in the readout of the original voltage stored on capacitance C_1, a reduction of the initial voltage across C_1 will occur as indicated in Fig. 5.11. This results in a voltage sensing problem and poor noise immunity. In design, the ratio of bit-sense-line capacitance C_2 to cell capacitance C_1 is therefore held to a value of less than 10 to 1. To further alleviate the problem, the following design steps can be taken: The storage capacitance of the *cell* can be *increased,* the storage capacitance of the sense lines can be *decreased,* or the sensitivity of the sense amplifiers can be *increased.*

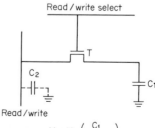

Fig. 5.11. The 1-transistor dynamic RAM cell (1-1-1 configuration).[8]

$$V_R = V_i \left(\frac{C_1}{C_1 + C_2} \right)$$

The capacitance of the sense lines consists of the gate overlap capacitance of the cells plus the junction capacitance of the p-diffused read/write data bus. Without departing from standard fabrication techniques, this implies that ≈ 1 sq mil per cell is occupied by the thin-oxide MOS storage capacitor C_1. The resulting large area of thin oxide required for a 4,096-bit RAM matrix contributes to yield loss. Therefore, design development is required to minimize this capacitance. Special design is also required for increase of sensitivity of the sense amplifiers.[9,10,11] In addition, readout of this particular cell is *destructive;* therefore, overhead circuitry is required to internally rewrite the data into the cell after it is read. This circuitry can also be used to refresh the cell at periodic intervals. A disadvantage of the 1-transistor cell is the large ratio of overhead circuitry required in addition to the sense amplifiers.

These factors are balanced, however, by the advantages of the cell such as high speed (≈ 300 ns access time), small cell size (≈ 2 sq mils), and simple cell structure. Note that the component spacing is not as critical in the 1-transistor cell as it is in the 3-transistor cell. Adoption of the 1-transistor cell thus depends upon the answer to this question which relates to manufacturing: Is the dominant factor the simple structure, or the large area of thin oxide required for the storage capacitors? Until this question is resolved, further development efforts will continue for *both* the 1-transistor and the 3-transistor MOS RAM cells.

5.4 PRODUCT EXAMPLES

5.4.1 The TMS1103

To obtain an appreciation of the overhead circuitry required for the basic memory cells which we have discussed, let us consider the circuit details of some of the popular MOS RAM products. The first example will be that of the TMS1103.

The TMS1103 is organized as 1,024 words of 1 bit each. For simplicity, Fig. 5.12 pictures only 2 of the rows with 2 cells per row, and 2 columns with 2 cells per column. When considering the overhead circuitry for the array, the refresh amplifier will be discussed first. It will be noted that a single refresh amplifier will service all the cells of a column. The refresh amplifier is an inverting amplifier. This is demonstrated by following a logical 1 signal at the source of T_1, which results in a 1 on the gate of T_2, a 0 on the source of T_3, a 0 on the gate of T_4, a 1 on the source of T_5, and a 1 returned to the source of T_1. The path to the gate of T_2 is closed through T_1 being on because of the row decode signal being applied to the gate of T_1 through the control circuit of $\bar{R}$. The extra circuitry shown is for precharging and disconnecting the refresh amplifier during writing.

Now let us examine how a row would be selected. A row decoder is also shown in Fig. 5.12. A row decoder is required for each row. For the first row decode: $A_0 = 1, A_1 = 1, A_2 = 1, A_3 = 1$, and the line is at V_{DD}. Now sending the V_{DD} signal on through a chip enable source follower results in activation (turn-on) of T_3. With read select at V_{DD}, T_3 is on, and cells of that particular row have been prepared for the read cycle.

To select the desired column, the same form of decode circuitry as employed for row decode is used to activate the read/write bus line attached to a particular

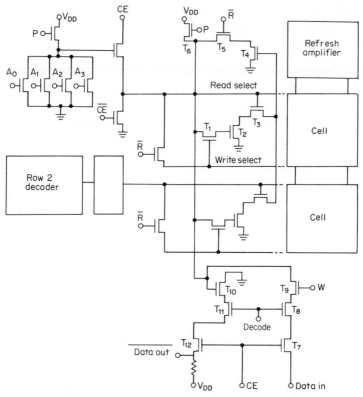

Fig. 5.12. Cell and overhead circuitry for a 2-row, 2-column matrix of the TMS1103.

column. Figure 5.12 shows the overhead circuit detail of how data are written into a given cell. Consider a logical 1 input on the source of T_7. With chip enable active, T_7 will be on and a 1 will appear on the drain of T_7. With T_8 and T_9 on, the 1 will be fed to all rows of a single column. But the 1 will be stored only on that particular cell in that column which has received a proper row address. In the read mode, T_9 will be off; therefore, the data output activates T_{10} either on or off depending on the bit line data. Current will flow through T_{10}, T_{11}, and T_{12} if the data state is such that T_{10} is activated. The current will be zero after an initial discharge of the digit line, if T_{10} is off. The data output thus comes down through T_{11} and appears on the drain of T_{12} as a complemented data output signal. Now it becomes evident how the column decoder functions. Column decoder operation, therefore, is similar to row decoder operation except that the row decoder activates the actual memory cells; while the column decoder activates the data-in and data-out bus lines by turning on transistors T_8 and T_{11}.

Operation of the TMS1103 always proceeds through a timing cycle. Clock, precharge, chip enable, and write must always be provided in a timed sequence. Although the details of the timing diagram of the TMS1103 will not be presented in this chapter, its complexity can be visualized (*cf.* Chap. 10). In fact, operation of the TMS1103 is essentially based on a critical race condition set up by the various input signals. Also there must be an overlap between precharge and chip enable. These timing pulses must therefore be accurate to within several nanoseconds.

In general, the accurately timed input signals are generated by TTL or ECL high-speed logic gates. Level shifters are required to connect these logic levels to MOS levels. Since the signal lines to a TMS1103 memory board array have characteristic capacitance values of a few hundred picofarads, a few hundred milliamperes are required to charge these lines in tens of nanoseconds. This means that the line driving circuitry must be capable of generating these current values. The capacitive loading can also produce ringing if the leads from the line drivers have significant inductance. Therefore, series damping resistors of 10 to 100 Ohms are usually required in the level-shifter output leads. Power dissipation for the TMS1103 is 400 mW operating and 50 mW standby.

5.4.2 The TMS4062

The TMS4062, another 1,024-bit MOS dynamic RAM, affords an interesting comparison to the TMS1103—particularly with respect to overhead circuitry. The TMS4062 is organized as 1,024 words of 1 bit each. Again for ease of understanding, let us consider a 2-row by 2-column portion of this RAM shown in Fig. 5.13.

The TMS4062 utilizes a 4-transistor storage cell which was discussed earlier in the chapter (*cf.* Fig. 5.6). The first feature to be noted is that a feedback loop around each cell for cell refresh is not required as it was for the 3-transistor cell of the TMS1103, since refresh can essentially take place "automatically" for the TMS4062. (The cell is refreshed every time it is addressed.) Since the memory cell of the TMS4062 is essentially a flip-flop, refresh is accomplished by merely applying V_{REF} voltage intermittently in order to restore the flip-flop cell to its maximum charged state. So activation of the word line serves to refresh the cell. This inherently simple refresh cycle results in a relaxation of the critical timing sequences which existed for the TMS1103.

Row decode circuitry (Fig. 5.13) is similar to that previously shown in this chapter. A circuit of this type is required for each row of the array.

Column decode is accomplished in the read/write circuitry. To understand how this takes place, consider the circuitry of Fig. 5.13. For the write condition with a logical 1 appearing at T_1 and a logical 0 at T_2, this information appears differentially at the output of T_3 and T_4 if the chip select is active and if the column decode is selected, so that T_3 and T_4 are in the conducting mode. The data bit is then entered into the cell in that particular row which has been activated.

To read a column, again consider the schematic of Fig. 5.13. With the column decode properly activated, T_3 and T_4 are in the conducting mode; and with chip select active, the data appear differentially at the output terminals. Again the simple overhead circuitry utilized throughout the device is to be noted. A differential current of 100 μA must be sensed to read the storage element data. This function is performed with an external bipolar sense amplifier. The differential output when connected to a differential amplifier provides good common-mode noise rejection.

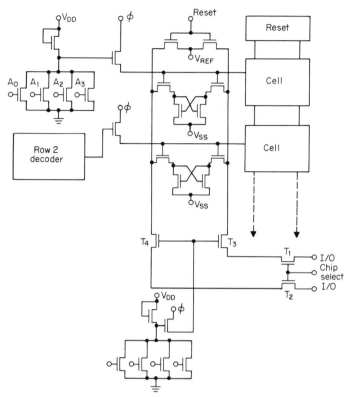

Fig. 5.13. Cell and overhead circuitry for a 2-row, 2-column matrix of the TMS4062.

Even though the TMS4062 is processed with the conventional and well-established silicon-oxide-aluminum gate, p-channel process, it has an access time of 150 ns and a cycle time of 290 ns. Its noncritical timing cycle simplifies the design of the overall memory system. Refreshing occurs every 2 ms, and the chip need not be selected during refresh, since word address provides the required refresh signals. Power dissipation of the TMS4062 is typically 180 to 250 mW total operating, and only 2 mW total standby.

The consequence of simplified overhead circuitry is summarized in Table 5.1, where the TMS4062 characteristics are compared to the TMS1103. Note that the overhead-area to cell-area ratio is approximately 50 percent larger for the TMS1103 than for the TMS4062.

Table 5.1.   Comparison of the TMS1103 with the TMS4062

RAM	Cell size, sq mils	Bar size, mils	Ratio of overhead area to cell area
1103	6.0	115 × 145	1.7
4062	10.8	146 × 163	1.1

5.5 MOS TECHNOLOGY AND RAM CELL DESIGN

When examining the interplay of technology with MOS RAM cell design and fabrication, we should be guided by three goals for memory system design. They are:

1. Economy
2. Versatility (or ease of use)
3. Performance

5.5.1 P-channel and P-channel Silicon Gate Technology

Today's most *economical* process for MOS/LSI is probably that of p-channel enhancement-mode device fabrication on (111)-oriented n-type silicon, with silicon dioxide gate insulation and aluminum metal gate field plates that also serve as interconnecting leads. This process accounts for $\approx$50 percent of present MOS/LSI production. As previously mentioned, the TMS4062 is fabricated by this particular process. Resulting threshold voltage is ≈ -3.5 V. Therefore, noncompatible TTL power supplies are needed for the resulting circuitry. In addition, TTL interfacing requires buffering by means of additional circuit components. It is therefore desirable to perturb the process in an effort to obtain lower threshold voltages. This is accomplished by merely changing the silicon material from (111) orientation to (100) orientation. Since the interface charge is lower on the (100) than on the (111), threshold voltage then becomes ≈ -2.0 V, and direct interfacing to TTL can be accomplished. Unfortunately, carrier mobility and hence, circuit speed, is lower for a given device geometry on (100)-oriented silicon than on (111) silicon. The factor is $\approx$25 percent.[12]

The situation can be remedied, however, if the aluminum gate field-plate material is changed to p-type silicon,[13] since the gate-to-silicon work function is thereby altered. This results in the threshold voltage at the (111)-oriented slices being lowered to ≈ -2.0 V. The high mobility of the (111) orientation is thereby enjoyed, in conjunction with low threshold voltage which permits direct interfacing to TTL for the signal lines on some designs. Clock amplitudes, however, are still high voltage. In addition, the presence of the silicon gate results in a savings of silicon real estate as well as further enhancement of circuit speed. The basic reason for this is that silicon is a refractory material and when positioned in place as the gate field-plate structure of the MOSFET, it can then delineate the source and drain diffusion edges in the high-temperature diffusion process. This results in the gate being self-aligned, as shown in Fig. 5.14 and as discussed in Chap. 2. The fact that the source and drain regions are self-aligned permits tightening the layout rules and thereby shrinking the cell size and overhead circuit area in the memory array.

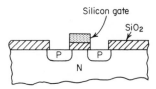

Fig. 5.14. The silicon self-aligned gate structure.

Also, since the gate region is self-aligned, gate overlap capacitance to the source and drain regions can be reduced in a controllable fashion in comparison to the standard process. This results in improving operating speed by a factor of ≈ 2.

The process for producing p-channel silicon-gate circuitry (summarized in Chap. 2) employs 5 photomasks, and is not especially complex. Note also that the upper surface of the silicon gate can be oxidized, and conventional aluminum leads can be positioned over the silicon gate. Thus, with the presence of p-diffused tunnel regions, essentially three levels of interconnections exist and can be employed to further reduce the silicon area required for the RAM function. It should be pointed out that the TMS1103 RAM is fabricated by a p-channel silicon gate process.

5.5.2   N-channel Technology

Let us next consider the impact of n-channel technology on MOS RAM design. The n-channel device offers a factor of 2 to 3 carrier mobility advantage (depending on crystal orientation and substrate doping level) over p-channel devices. In general, the value of Q_{ss} (interface surface charge) is such that in order to make these devices in the normally *off* state with sufficient threshold voltage (i.e., enhancement mode), a reverse-bias substrate power supply is required. Flexibility in choice of threshold voltage and substrate doping level is thereby obtained at the expense of the additional power supply. If an n-channel design were made with the same voltages and device geometries as the p-channel design, the current levels would be increased by the mobility ratio while the circuit delays would be decreased correspondingly (that is, if the circuit capacitances were the same in both cases).

Another advantage of the n-channel process is the low threshold voltage obtainable. This permits direct interface between these MOS circuits and bipolar TTL circuitry. So, in summary, n-channel devices offer an improvement chiefly in circuit performance when compared to p-channel devices.

5.5.3   N-channel Silicon Gate Technology

At present, however, the trend is not toward n-channel with aluminum gate, but instead is directed toward n-channel with silicon gate.[14] Here again, as discussed in Chap. 2, the self-aligned structural features of a silicon gate process permit a reduction in required circuit area, attained through tighter layout rules, as well as speed increase through reduction of parasitic capacitance arising from the gate-source and gate-drain overlap region. So the n-channel, silicon gate process offers an improvement in performance through increased speed, and in economy through more efficient use of silicon real estate. Some improvement in versatility (ease of use) also results because V_T is low and a direct interface to TTL circuitry is thus made possible. Of course, certain processing problems arise in the fabrication of n-channel with silicon gate. But as has happened to so many other semiconductor device processing problems—as the process is utilized in more designs—the problems are overcome through simplification and experience.

5.5.4   Ion-implantation Technology

Selective ion implantation of boron in silicon has been used to fabricate depletion-load p-channel devices on the same chip with p-channel enhancement-mode devices.[15]   This combination results in the realization of very efficient inverter configurations for MOS integrated circuits—that is, efficient in the sense of silicon real estate consumption and improved speed performance.

The enhancement- and depletion-load inverter configurations and their resulting load lines have been compared in Chap. 2.   The near-ideal load line of the depletion-load device provides essentially a constant-current source, thereby improving switching speed in contrast to the enhancement-load case.   Also, the essentially horizontal load line of the depletion-load device presents a very high dynamic impedance to the driver device; therefore, minimal geometry dimensions can be used in load device design since it is the mode of device operation that determines the effective resistance generated by the device.   This results, then, in a reduction in required size of the load devices.   In addition, a separate ion-implantation process step can be expended on the enhancement-mode driver devices to lower their threshold voltage values.   This ensures low supply-voltage operation of the circuitry.

To date, ion implantation to achieve these configurations has been used in RAMs only in the overhead circuitry, and not in the actual memory cells.   The major advantages of ion implantation accrue to the overhead circuitry rather than the RAM cell itself.   When overhead circuit content is appreciable, then the advantages of ion implantation significantly reduce the area required for this circuitry and provide, for example, TTL compatibility, single power-supply operation, and conservation of silicon real estate.

5.5.5   CMOS Technology

CMOS technology offers the advantages of:

1. Very low power
2. Very low voltage
3. High noise immunity
4. High-speed operation (equivalent to low-power TTL)

These advantages are all counterbalanced in RAM design by the unfavorable economics associated with the process—or more accurately stated—resulting from the process.   Recall from Chap. 2 that not only is the CMOS process complex, but it requires device isolation coupled with numerous contact holes for necessary interconnections resulting in an intolerable consumption of silicon real estate.   At the present time, it appears that the role of CMOS is in circuitry for aerospace and in circuits for automatic meter reading, wrist watches, and automotive applications.   Its role is not in RAMs.   N-channel with silicon gate is less costly and will probably be as fast.

5.6   RECENT DEVELOPMENTS

5.6.1   The N-channel 4,096-bit RAM

From the foregoing statements it appears that n-channel with silicon gate will be the technology on which innovations in MOS RAM cells will be based.   Let us see to what extent this statement holds true in the light of recent developments.

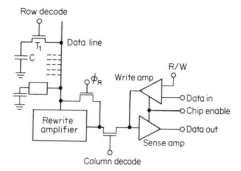

Fig. 5.15. The 1-1-1 dynamic memory cell with overhead circuitry.

Two approaches are available for fabricating a 4,096-bit MOS dynamic RAM. The first uses the previously described 1-1-1 memory cell as shown in Fig. 5.15. Recall, the data are stored on capacitor C and when T_1 is energized by the row decode the data appear on the data line. As shown in Fig. 5.15, the data are amplified in a rewrite amplifier for each column and pass through the column decode to the output sense amplifier. After the data appear, the ϕ_R signal closes the feedback path to rewrite the data onto the capacitor C of the selected cell. Refreshing is then accomplished by energizing ϕ_R and selecting rows of devices with the row decode. The memory cell is a simple structure and occupies an area of approximately 2 sq mils.

The memory cell employed in the second approach has a 3-1-1 configuration as is shown in Fig. 5.16. Such a cell has 3 transistors, 1 address line, and 1 digit line for reading and writing.[16] In a matrix array of these cells, the address line serves as row select and the bit line serves as column select. The memory cell for the device uses three minimum-geometry transistors and occupies an area of 1.8 sq mils. To present the proper signal phase to T_1 in the refresh mode, it is necessary that the row select voltage be three-state. Reading of the cell is accomplished during the intermediate level of the three-state signal, and writing of refresh is accomplished during the high level of the signal. To conserve power, the high level is turned off as soon as information is properly gated into the cell. The bilateral nature of MOS transistor T_1 also contributes to making this refresh mode of operation possible.

A single column line allows transfer of information into or out of the 3-1-1 cell. This line connects to a column amplifier which is used to sense the information

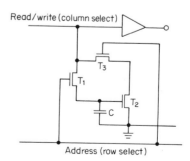

Fig. 5.16. The 3-1-1 dynamic memory cell.[13]

present in the cell, or to write new information into the cell. A ground line is shared between two adjacent columns of cells, contributing one-half of a connection per cell. The layout of this cell is presented in Chap. 2.

Organization of this RAM, featuring the (3-1-1) configuration, is 4,096 words by 1 bit. A 12-bit address buffer routes input signals so that address is decoded into 1 of 64 rows and 1 of 64 columns. The design objectives are to have only one clock, TTL compatible inputs, 0.1 mW per bit operating power dissipation, and 1 μW per bit standby, and medium speed operation with access times of approximately 300 ns.

5.6.2   The Charge Pump RAM Cell

The charge pump RAM cell reported by Burke and Michon[17] combines the simplicity and performance of a static RAM cell with the packing density and silicon area conservation characteristics of the dynamic cell. The circuit diagram for this new cell is shown in Fig. 5.17. It bears a remarkable resemblance to the 6-transistor cell discussed earlier in the chapter. The important difference is in the load devices T_3 and T_4. The design goal is to reduce their physical size in comparison to that utilized in the 6-transistor static cell. Recall that for desired low power dissipation, their effective resistance must be large; for static operation, this requires that the devices themselves be large.

In the charge pump case, a fixed amount of charge is transferred from source to substrate whenever the channel is formed, and is extinguished by a charge pump supply to the gates of T_3 and T_4. The sequence is shown in Fig. 5.18: (*a*) depicts the quiescent condition, (*b*) shows the channel from source charges diffusing into the inversion layer, and (*c*) shows the mobile charge returning to source as the immobile charge recombines. Thus a current proportional to pump frequency flows into the substrate. As shown in Fig. 5.19*a*, this results in the formation of a constant-current supply, which makes the ideal load device (ideal because the load line is horizontal). The load resistor can therefore be reduced to minimum geometry and still maintain the high load resistance. This implies also that the desired low power dissipation will be achieved. A conventional load characteristic is displayed for comparison in Fig. 5.19*b*.

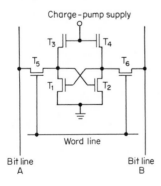

Fig. 5.17.   The charge pump RAM cell.[17]

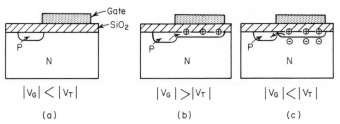

$$|V_G| < |V_T|$$

(a)

$$|V_G| > |V_T|$$

(b)

$$|V_G| < |V_T|$$

(c)

Fig. 5.18. Operation of the charge pump RAM cell:[17] (a) quiescent condition; (b) channel formation; (c) mobile charge returning to source as immobile charge recombines.

It should further be noted that the charge pump configuration is also inherently faster than the conventional load-active pair because of the constant-current charging and discharging capability of the pump device. The 6 transistors of this new configuration, however, contribute to making cell size fairly large, ≈ 15 sq mils. But this is balanced, of course, by the modest on-chip overhead circuit requirements for a 6-transistor RAM cell. Resulting characteristics of the charge pump RAM cell are compared to a typical 3-transistor commercially available RAM cell in Table 5.2. The major disadvantage of the charge pump RAM cell is the uneconomical use of silicon real estate. Its cell size is a factor of 7 larger than the n-channel dynamic cell.

The charge pump cell, however, offers advantages in speed, power, and operating simplicity. Although the device characteristics as they result from p-channel proc-

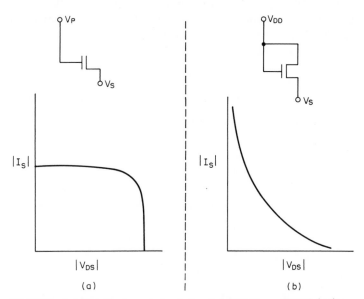

Fig. 5.19. (a) Constant current supply of charge pump RAM device. (b) Load characteristic for conventional device.

Table 5.2.   Comparison of Characteristics of a Charge Pump RAM Cell and a 3-transistor RAM Cell

RAM cell	Standby power, μW	Active power, μW	Cell size, sq mils	Cycle time, ns
Charge pump (in development)	0.1	100	15	100
3 XTR dynamic (TMS1103)	5	500	6	500–600

essing have been described, n-channel with silicon gate would of course lead to higher packing density and improved utilization of silicon real estate.

5.6.3   The Internal Refresh Dynamic RAM Cell.

A 3-transistor MOS dynamic RAM cell reported by Walther and McCoy[18] incorporates a method for refresh within the cell such that the system designer need not concern himself with the details of cell refresh. The schematic for this self-refreshing cell is shown in Fig. 5.20. When data are written into the cell, the addressing transistors T_3 and T_4 are on at the same time as the write transistor T_2. The bit of data is then stored on node A, across capacitor C_M. Before a read cycle, node F is discharged to ground by chip enable. A read is performed by energizing X_0 and the read line to the cell. If the bit of data stored in the cell is a 0, the output will remain a 0, because T_1 is off. Coupling between nodes A and B is low because the gate voltage of C_M is below V_T.

C_M is a gated capacitor of the form shown in Fig. 5.21. When the voltage on the gate (node A) is below the threshold value for C_M, then the capacitance coupling between B and A is quite small. When the voltage at node A is above the threshold value, then an inversion layer forms and the capacitance between nodes B and A

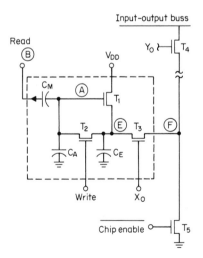

Fig. 5.20.   The self-refreshing dynamic RAM cell.[18]

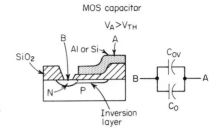

Fig. 5.21. MOS gated capacitor for the internal refresh memory cell.

increases significantly. Thus when the bit of data stored in the cell is a 1, a large capacitive coupling exists between the read line and node A. As the read line is energized, the gated capacitor C_M causes a large portion of the read voltage to be added to the voltage previously stored at node A of Fig. 5.20. The gate of T_1 is then raised to a voltage much higher than V_{DD}, and the output is pulled toward V_{DD} through transistors T_1, T_3, and T_4. The capacitor C_E is also charged toward V_{DD}. C_E plays an important role in the self-refresh operation of the cell, since it serves as the source of refresh current. In the read mode, all the cells in the memory array that contain a logic 1 have capacitor C_E charged to approximately V_{DD}. When the read line returns to ground and the write line goes to logic 1, T_2 is turned on and charge is transferred from node E to node A—and the cell has refreshed itself.

An n-channel silicon gate 1,024-bit MOS dynamic RAM that utilizes this cell exhibits access times of, typically, 75 ns.[18] Overhead circuitry has been minimized as a result of the self-refreshing feature. Chip size is 116 × 128 mils, indicating excellent use of silicon real estate.

5.7 MOS RAM PROGRESS WITH TIME

5.7.1 Cell Size

MOS RAM cell size versus year is depicted in Fig. 5.22. Cell size reduction has been made possible by the trend from the static cell to the dynamic, by self-aligning gate processes, and by n-channel devices. The two extreme data points represent

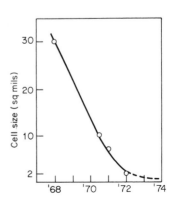

Fig. 5.22. MOS RAM cell size versus year.

the 30-sq mil area required for the 8-transistor static RAM cell of 1968, and the 2-sq mil area of the 1- and 3-transistor dynamic RAM cells of 1972. Since overhead circuitry contributes to the final chip size and manufacturing yield, the cell size in itself does not tell the whole story. The chip area consumed by overhead circuitry required for decoding, cell refresh, and TTL compatibility must therefore always be considered.

Reducing the area of the RAM cell further will require a major modification in fabrication technology. It is difficult to see how the device count can be decreased much further! For example, electron beam techniques might be introduced in the photolithographic process. This would permit a factor of ≈ 10 reduction in circuit layout dimensions. This approach must, however, also offer the favorable economics of present technology; at this time it is not clear how this will be accomplished.

5.7.2 Chip Complexity

Figure 5.23 shows the trend in chip complexity: the number of memory bits per chip versus year. The two extreme data points represent the 1968, 256-bit static RAM, and the recent 4,096-bit dynamic RAMs. This trend has been made possible chiefly by utilizing dynamic cells with low device counts. Careful design attention has been given to overhead circuit requirements. Technology advances such as n-channel with self-aligned silicon gate innovation, as well as general yield improvement programs, have also contributed to this advance.

5.7.3 Power Dissipation

The trend in MOS RAM cell power dissipation in microwatts per bit versus time is shown in Fig. 5.24. Reduction of this important parameter is necessary for achieving higher packing densities and smaller-sized electronic equipment. Reduction of power dissipation has been made possible through circuit innovation and employment of technology which permits operation from lower-voltage power supplies. The trend is toward 5-V operation, which also results in ease of use in system application.

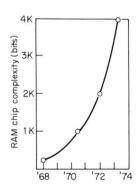

Fig. 5.23. MOS RAM chip complexity versus year.

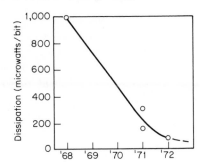

Fig. 5.24. MOS RAM cell power dissipation versus year.

5.7.4   Economics

The combination of silicon real estate conservation through increased circuit density, coupled with the learning curve effect (i.e., higher manufacturing yields), has resulted in the dramatically improved economic position of MOS RAMs. Price per bit is plotted as a function of time in Fig. 5.25. A selling price of ≈ 0.1 cent per bit is forecast for 1975! This represents a factor of 100 price decline when compared to the 1968 status.

5.8   SUMMARY

In summary of this chapter, four major conclusions can be drawn. They are:

1. The guiding principle of MOS RAM design is that of economy. Performance of MOS RAMs will probably never attain that of their bipolar counterparts. MOS should be able to maintain a factor of 3 to 5 economic advantage over bipolar in RAM applications during the next several years if continued attention is given to further economic improvements resulting from design and process innovations.

2. Ease of use in systems is the next most important design consideration and benefit offered by MOS RAMs. Here reference is made to TTL compatibility, 5-V power-supply operation, ease of interface to the "outside world," simple timing sequences, and the like.

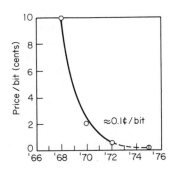

Fig. 5.25.   MOS RAM price per bit versus year.

3. Performance improvement such as increased operating speeds and lowered power dissipation can be realized through clever design. These efforts, however, must be kept in harmony with achieving the important objectives of economy and ease of use within the system.
4. Significant technical progress to increase MOS storage element packing density has been made during the last five years, and significant progress is in view for the next five years. This should result in the use of the technology in an efficient manner and on a wide scale.

REFERENCES

1. Burroughs Corporation, "Digital Computer Principles," p. 341, McGraw-Hill Book Company, New York, 1969.
2. J. W. Forrester, Digital Information Storage in Three Dimensions Using Magnetic Cores, *J. Appl. Phys.*, **22**: 44–48(January 1951).
3. N. R. Scott, "Electronic Computer Technology," chap. 10, McGraw-Hill Book Company, New York, 1970.
4. J. Schmidt, Integrated MOS Transistor Random Access Memory, *Solid-state Des.*, **6**: 21(January 1965).
5. W. M. Regitz and J. Karp, Three Transistor-cell 1,024-bit 500 ns MOS/RAM, *IEEE J. Solid-state Circuits,* **SC-5**: 181–186(October 1970).
6. L. L. Vadasz, H. T. Chua, and A. S. Grove, Semiconductor Random-access Memories, *IEEE Spectrum,* **8**: 40–48(May 1971).
7. W. Martino and B. F. Croxon, The Inverting Cell Concept for MOS Dynamic RAMs, *ISSCC72 Dig. Tech. Pap.*, pp. 12–13.
8. L. Cohen, R. Green, K. Smith, and J. L. Seely, Single-transistor Makes Room for More Memory on an MOS Chip, *Electronics,* **44**: 69–73(August 2, 1971).
9. C. W. Lambrechtse, R. H. W. Salters, and L. Boonstra, A 4096 Bit One-Transistor per Bit RAM with Internal Timing and Low Dissipation, *ISSCC73 Dig. Tech. Pap.,* pp. 26–27.
10. R. Proebsting and R. Green, A TTL Compatible 4096 Bit N-Channel RAM, *ISSCC73 Dig. Tech. Pap.,* pp. 28–29.
11. K. U. Stein and H. Friedrich, A 1-mil² Single Transistor Memory Cell in N-Silicon Gate Technology, *ISSCC73, Dig. Tech. Pap.,* pp. 30–31.
12. D. Colman, R. T. Bate, and J. P. Mize, Mobility Anisotropy and Piezoresistance in Silicon P-type Inversion Layers, *J. Appl. Phys.,* **39**: 1923–1931(1968).
13. L. L. Vadasz, A. J. Grove, T. A. Rowe, and G. E. Moore, Silicon-gate Technology, *IEEE Spectrum,* **6**: 28–35(October 1969).
14. R. Abbot, H. Gopen, T. Rowe, and D. Bryson, N-channel Goes to Work with TTL, *Electronics,* **45**: 107–110(May 8, 1972).
15. J. Macdougall and K. Manchester, Ion Implantation Offers a Bagful of Benefits for MOS, *Electronics,* **43**: 86–90(June 22, 1970).
16. J. A. Karp, W. M. Regitz, and J. Chow, A 4,096-bit Dynamic MOS RAM, *ISSCC72 Dig. Tech. Pap.,* pp. 10–11.
17. H. K. Burke and G. J. Michon, The Charge Pump Random-access Memory, *ISSCC72 Dig. Tech. Pap.,* pp. 16–17.
18. T. R. Walther and M. R. McCoy, A Three Transistor MOS Memory Cell with Internal Refresh, *ISSCC72 Dig. Tech. Pap.,* pp. 14–15.

6

Fixed Program Semiconductor
Memory Design

6.1 INTRODUCTION

Fixed program memory refers to those types of memories into which data normally can be written only one time. Generally these memories are called ROMs, an acronym for read only memory. In addition to being called ROM, a fixed program memory is also known as read only store (ROS), fixed memory, permanent memory, and dead memory. The data content of most fixed program memories is determined during manufacture. An exception is programmable ROM in which data content can be determined by the end user.

The fixed program memory, or ROM, has been around a long time. The primitive lock and key used by the ancients was perhaps the first example of a ROM application. The key for the lock was programmed with a single word. The data transfer from the key to the lock mechanism was a parallel operation. The output code from the ROM controlled the mechanical locking and unlocking function.

More recently, techniques for sequentially addressing the fixed program memory have evolved to provide a series of coded words for control applications. Perhaps the first sequentially addressed ROM was designed into the mechanical control structure of early cloth weaving machinery in eighteenth-century textile mills. These ROMs used wooden fingers (address lines) which probed a flat, two-dimensional matrix into which programmed holes were drilled. The wooden or metal card matrix memory found extensive use in the control section of Jacquard looms.[1] Thousands of Jacquard looms, without electronics, have been built during the past 150 years. Many are still in operation all over the world.

This chapter concentrates on the design of semiconductor ROMs. Several examples of application are given to illustrate the ease of programming. The chapter will first present coding techniques useful in ROM application. Later we will review specific ROM on-the-chip circuitry for MOS and bipolar technologies.

Read only memory has a name which is self-explanatory. If one removes the write capability from a RAM, a ROM results. The ROM, with this reduced capability, generally is available at lower per bit prices than is RAM. Still, it is a random access memory, because the access time is independent of data location. Read only memories are chosen for designs where a fixed program is desired and speed or economy requirements permit their choice over the more common RAM memories.

The ROM exists in many forms. We can classify the ROM into three categories according to the difficulty in changing the program data in memory. The *standard ROM* refers to memories in which the data stored are never changed following packaging. The most common standard semiconductor ROM is this type where the data are programmed in during manufacture by means of a custom masking process step.

A second category of ROMs are termed *programmable ROMs*. The programmable ROMs require times of microseconds to seconds for writing in the desired program. The programmable ROM uses such things as fusible links, metal migration, scribing open one leg of a circuit, or rerouting a wire for writing.

The third category of ROMs are those that can be reprogrammed time and time again. These reprogrammable ROMs have relatively slow write times compared with RAMs and therefore are given a different name. The reprogrammable ROM is also called a read mostly memory (RMM).

The standard ROM is generally arranged in a rectangular matrix. The matrix with associated circuitry indicated is shown in Fig. 6.1. Semiconductor fixed store memory cells are generally arranged into a two-dimensional matrix as shown in Fig. 6.1. This two-dimensional matrix is convenient for parallel binary address (W lines) and parallel binary output (B lines). The W and B lines are commonly referred to as word and bit lines, respectively. The mode of addressing for the ROM of Fig. 6.1 is random access. The coupling mechanism between the word address lines and the specific bits sensed is indicated in Fig. 6.1 by the symbol ⵗ. In electronic ROM memories, the coupling may consist of resistive, capacitive, optical, inductive, diode, or active device elements. The coupling mechanism employed in the semi-conductor ROM is an active device, or in some cases, a diode.

The resistive or conductive coupling element provides several benefits. It reduces circuit complexity of ROMs with discrete elements. The resistive element reduces parasitic signals that may develop more readily with capacitive or inductive coupling. The amplitude of the readout signal from the resistive coupling element is

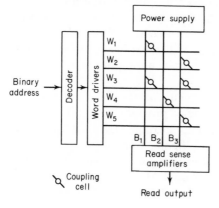

Coupling cell

Read output

Fig. 6.1. Diagram of a fixed store memory with the memory cells arranged in a rectangular matrix.

a steady-state (static) voltage and does not require differential sensing of a transient voltage or current pulse. The resistive coupling allows one to obtain a readout signal with little dispersion in amplitude even at higher speeds. Using coupling elements, such as discrete resistors, does not presently compete in either cost or packaging density with integrated-circuit technologies.

The inductively coupled ROM has found application only in very small memories. The capacitively coupled ROM can be fabricated at low cost, but requires bulky rack space. The most common optical ROM is the punch card reader, with the more advanced forms using a high-power laser to burn holes in the recording media. The read function determines the presence or absence of these holes and can use a spontaneous photosource such as a light-emitting diode (LED).

Each type of ROM has, for previous designs, been chosen by computer manufacturers[2] as solutions to diversified applications—a situation very different from that of RAM memories where ferrite core technology has been the dominant factor. The IBM 360-50 uses a capacitor ROM with a 500-ns read time and is expandable to 255K bits. The IBM 360-40 uses an inductively coupled ROM with a 625-ns read time with expansion available to 260K bits. The CDC G-140 computer uses a resistor-matrix ROM with a 350-ns read cycle and 66K capacity.

MOS or bipolar integrated-circuit technology provides the most cost-effective ROM solution for most electronic systems design situations. Monolithic semiconductor technology provides an increase in bit density of one to two orders of magnitude over most competing approaches. It is possible to integrate the ROM matrix together with word address and bit output decoding circuitry on a single substrate. In monolithic semiconductor ROM, the coupling elements used are generally active devices. MOS ROM uses an MOS transistor at each programmed bit location in the matrix and is coded by varying the thickness of the gate dielectric. The bipolar ROM is correspondingly programmed through a connection to a transistor emitter in each memory matrix cell.

6.2 IMPLEMENTATION OF LOGIC AND COUNTING FUNCTIONS USING ROM

The application of integrated-circuit techniques to ROM has opened a range of new applications, in addition to permitting replacement in existing designs. The applications for ROM presently include code conversion, table look-up, arithmetic logic, control logic, and character generation. An introduction to ROM implementation is given in this chapter, while additional application detail is presented in Chap. 8.

ROM most basically is a combinatorial logic network with an arbitrary logic function defined for each word address. A ROM can be substituted for logic. The versatility of random combinatorial logic provides a very powerful design vehicle for many applications.

6.2.1 Code Conversion: Gray to Decimal

Perhaps the most instructive task to perform now should be to investigate the logical operation of a specific ROM. A code converter for implementing a single-decade decimal equivalent of the Gray code listed in Table 6.1 is suitable for this

Table 6.1.   Four-bit Gray Code
with Decimal Equivalent Values

Gray code				Decimal
A	B	C	D	Q
1	1	1	1	0
0	1	1	1	1
0	0	1	1	2
1	0	1	1	3
1	0	0	1	4
0	0	0	1	5
0	1	0	1	6
1	1	0	1	7
1	1	0	0	8
0	1	0	0	9

purpose. The word address for the Gray code requires one line for each Gray code bit and another for the complement. The output consists of 10 bit lines to specify one decimal decade.

The actual logic (NOR, NAND, and so forth) implemented by the ROM depends upon the specific coupling element used. When a diode or resistor is used, the ROM, without any inverters added, performs positive AND logic. Similarly, if an NPN bipolar transistor with multiple emitters (one emitter for each Gray code input line) is used in the ROM matrix, the logic implemented by each column is positive AND. When the inverter is cascaded into each ROM bit line, the overall logic function performed by the ROM is positive NAND. When p-channel enhancement-type MOS devices are used in the ROM, positive NAND logic is directly implemented without using the cascaded inverter. When n-channel enhancement-type MOS devices are used in the ROM, a negative NAND function is directly implemented. For our designs we will refer to ROM circuits that provide NAND logic. The reader should remember that the inverter may or may not be required in the actual ROM structure, depending upon the technology used.

The ROM matrix of Fig. 6.2 has been coded for the Gray code to decimal conversion of Table 6.1. The inverters are included in this example and thus refer to a non-MOS technology. The decimal output line goes to a logic 0 corresponding to the Gray input.

The ROM is programmed as a collection of NAND gates with high fan-in. Each column of the memory in Fig. 6.2 represents a positive-NAND gate with a fan-in at each coupling node point. The decimal output 0 line (Q_0) is obtained from the input function $Q_0 = ABCD$. Thus, each coupling element in the matrix provides a coded binary 1, and the absence of a coupling element provides a logic 0. Coding for the decimal 0 is programmed into the matrix through the input bits $A = B = C = D = 1$. The decimal line Q_1 is obtained by programming $\bar{A} = B = C = D = 1$. The complete code conversion for a single decimal decade requires 8 input or word address lines and 10 bit lines output. Thus the ROM matrix size in this example is 80 bits.

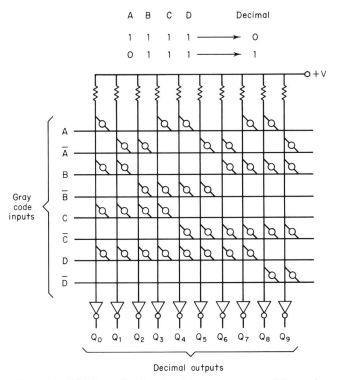

Fig. 6.2. ROM matrix that has been programmed for code conversion.

The logical equivalent of the ROM in Fig. 6.2 including inverters is shown in Fig. 6.3 for the decimal lines Q_0 and Q_1. The other decimal lines are omitted from Fig. 6.3 for schematic simplicity. The single ROM matrix can be used to implement single-level logic. We will limit the discussion in this chapter to NAND logic.

The logical complexity can be increased by adding a second ROM in cascade with the first as shown in Fig. 6.4. Suppose we wish to simultaneously convert the Gray code of Table 6.1 further into a standard BCD code. The code conversion for this is given in Table 6.2. Also, let's assume for this design that we are using

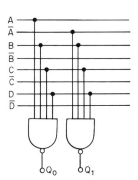

Fig. 6.3. Logical equivalent of the ROM lines that select the decimal 0 and the decimal 1. (Inverters at the output are omitted.)

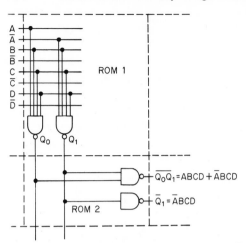

Fig. 6.4. Logic complexity of ROM logic can be extended by using more than one ROM matrix.

MOS ROMs with p-channel enhancement-type devices. This MOS ROM will not require the inverters that were used previously in Fig. 6.2. The Gray-to-decimal conversion is taken directly from the schematic of Fig. 6.2 and forms the upper ROM of the new design in Fig. 6.5a. A second ROM performs the decimal-to-BCD conversion. The W-, X-, Y-, and Z-bits can be programmed into the lower ROM by inspection of Table 6.2. The W (most significant) BCD bit requires selection of two decimal lines, namely 8 and 9. These two lines are selected by programming in a 1 at these two locations in the lower ROM of Fig. 6.5a. The line $\overline{W}$ forms the complement of W and is obtained by selecting the remaining 8 decimal lines. Referring back to Table 6.2 one notes that the X line requires selection of decimal lines 4, 5, 6, and 7. These same decimal lines are programmed for selection into the lower ROM at the four corresponding cell locations. Similarly, the lower ROM of Fig. 6.5a is completed by reference to Table 6.2.

Table 6.2.   Tabulation of Conversion Combinations with BCD and Decimal Equivalents to the Gray Code

Gray code	Decimal	1-2-3-4 BCD		
A B C D	Q	W X Y Z		
1 1 1 1	0	0 0 0 0		
0 1 1 1	1	0 0 0 1		
0 0 1 1	2	0 0 1 0		
1 0 1 1	3	0 0 1 1		
1 0 0 1	4	0 1 0 0		
0 0 0 1	5	0 1 0 1		
0 1 0 1	6	0 1 1 0		
1 1 0 1	7	0 1 1 1		
1 1 0 0	8	1 0 0 0		
0 1 0 0	9	1 0 0 1		

The nomenclature in Fig. 6.5*a* can be improved by substituting the dot for the coupling element symbol ⍀ . The result is the compact matrix of Fig. 6.5*b* that is more convenient to code. The dual ROMs of Fig. 6.5*a* and *b* are identical electrically.

The fundamentals supporting the design procedure used for Fig. 6.5 follow directly from a consideration of the Boolean expressions involved.[3] It is instructive to use Karnaugh maps and obtain the minterms for the Gray-to-BCD conversion. The two decimal lines selected by the *W*-bit appear in the Karnaugh map for the *W*-bit in Fig. 6.6. Note that the function for *W*, when related directly to the Gray code, reduces to $W = B\bar{C}\bar{D}$. The other minterm expressions are

$$\begin{aligned} X &= \bar{C}D \\ Y &= B\bar{C}D + \bar{B}CD \\ Z &= \bar{A}B\bar{C}\bar{D} + \bar{A}\bar{B}\bar{C}D + AB\bar{C}D + A\bar{B}CD \end{aligned} \tag{6-1}$$

If we do not wish to make available the simultaneous decimal output, these minterm expressions may be used to implement the Gray-to-BCD conversion. In Fig. 6.6 the desired conversion is implemented by using the double-NAND gate provided

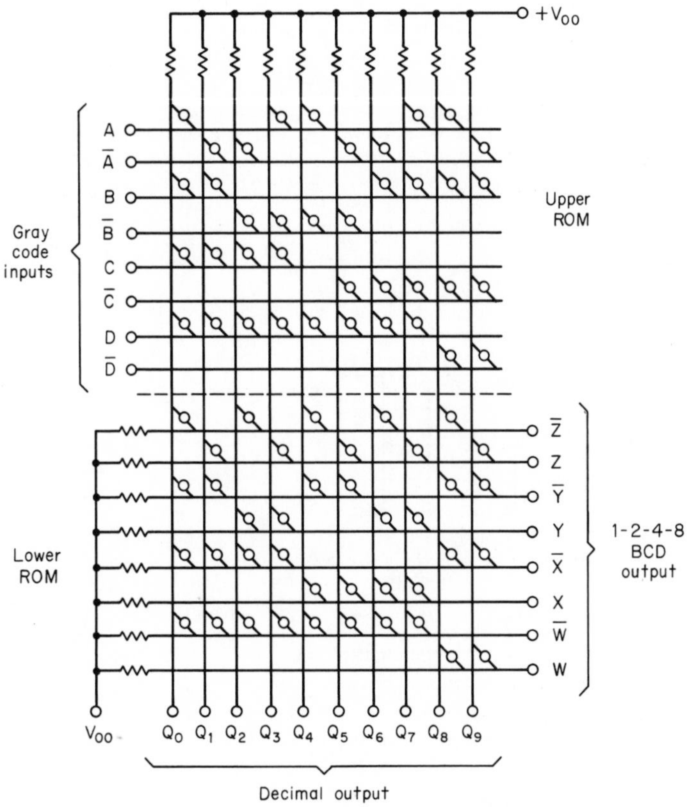

(a)

Fig. 6.5. (*a*) A double ROM matrix. Cross-coupling elements shown.

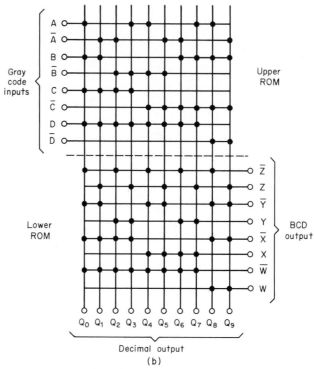

Fig. 6.5. (*b*) Same ROMs as in (*a*) but using a dot format schematic.

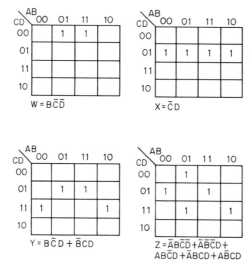

$W = B\bar{C}\bar{D}$

$X = \bar{C}D$

$Y = B\bar{C}D + \bar{B}CD$

$Z = \bar{A}B\bar{C}D + \bar{A}\bar{B}CD + AB\bar{C}D + \bar{A}BCD + A\bar{B}CD$

Fig. 6.6. Four Karnaugh maps.

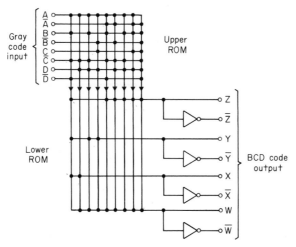

Fig. 6.7. Dual ROMs for converting the Gray code directly to the BCD code.

by two ROMs. The expressions for W, X, Y, and Z in NAND form for ROM design are

$$W = B\overline{CD}$$
$$X = \overline{C}D$$
$$Y = \overline{\overline{BC}D} \cdot \overline{B\overline{C}D}$$
$$Z = \overline{\overline{A\overline{BC}D}} \cdot \overline{\overline{A}\overline{B}\overline{C}D} \cdot \overline{\overline{A}BCD} \cdot \overline{A\overline{B}CD} \qquad (6\text{-}2)$$

For the circuit of Fig. 6.7 the upper matrix forms intermediate terms $\overline{B\overline{C}D}$, $\overline{\overline{C}D}$, $\overline{BCD}$, $\overline{\overline{B}CD}$, etc., which are used as input for the lower ROM. An inspection of Eq. (6-1) reveals that the upper ROM may be called the product generator. Notice that the lower ROM effectively sums the terms of Fig. 6.1 and thus may be called the sum generator. The ROMs in Fig. 6.7 require a total of 96 bits plus four inverters. This compares with the 160 bits required to provide the decimal and BCD outputs simultaneously in Fig. 6.5. In this example the ROM is used for up to 5-input NAND functions. It is generally impractical to use ROMs for so small a circuit as Fig. 6.5 or 6.7, but this example shows the technique.

Code conversions are readily implemented using ROM. Indeed, the most widespread application for ROM to date has probably been in the static logic implementation for the conversion of codes and generation of characters.

6.2.2 Implementing Random Static Logic

The implementation of Eq. (6-1) with the dual ROM connection demonstrates the ability of this circuit to provide random combinatorial (static) logic.[4,5] This is a powerful feature of the ROM and itself permits a host of applications. For instance, the high speed of the ROM can be used to provide control logic. The control logic of a digital machine consists of that complex of gates which decode various inputs, such as the contents of command registers, clocks, timers, status registers, and also provide further outputs to these and other circuits. The control function requires the high speed of ROM and is a fixed program function.

6.2.3 Random Sequential Logic

If we are to make the coupled ROM a truly universal design element, we must introduce a technique for performing sequential operations. This can be done by adding a feedback loop from the output of the lower ROM back into the upper ROM as shown in Fig. 6.8. An external feedback network consisting of flip-flop elements can be used to gate some of the output bits back into the product generator. This circuit is used with a single level of feedback to implement double-level random sequential logic. Circuits with this logic architecture are called *programmable logic arrays* or simply PLA.

When it's desired to extend the complexity of the PLA for more levels of random logic and add more clocking into the feedback circuits, the scheme shown in Fig. 6.9 can be used. In this scheme there are four levels of static ROM and three separate independent clocked feedback loops. Unfortunately, the logical design techniques which can take full advantage of the higher order of sequential complexity in Fig. 6.9 have not been perfected. Therefore, our discussion in this chapter will be restricted to the two-level PLA design configuration of Fig. 6.8.

6.2.4 Design of Modulo-10 Counter

The coupled ROM matrices may be used to perform counting functions. For this purpose we will design a modulo-10 counter using D-type flip-flops in the feedback loop. The Boolean functions required as inputs to the respective flip-flops for counting in modulo-10 are:

$$W^{n+1} = XYZ + W\bar{Z}$$
$$X^{n+1} = X\bar{Y} + X\bar{Z} + \bar{X}YZ$$
$$Y^{n+1} = \bar{W}\bar{Y}Z + Y\bar{Z}$$
$$Z^{n+1} = \bar{Z}$$

These Boolean functions are the minterms obtained from Karnaugh mapping or McClusky reduction of the counting sequence. The 4 binary bits W, X, Y, and Z all being true during the present time interval result in flip-flop outputs in the next time interval identified with the $n + 1$ notation. For example, the least significant

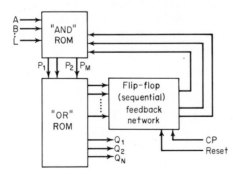

Fig. 6.8. Scheme used to implement double-level random sequential logic. This is called a programmable logic array (PLA).

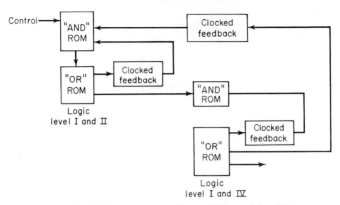

Fig. 6.9. Scheme to extend capability of the PLA.

bit Z is complemented during successive time intervals. The four Boolean functions given above are used as input functions for the flip-flops in the modulo-10 counter. The ROM coding is shown schematically in Fig. 6.10a with the flip-flops labeled $W, X, Y,$ and Z. The upper ROM matrix is the product generator and the lower matrix sums these products. The summing matrix is used to drive directly the 4 separate flip-flops, one for each of the 4 bits. Both true and complemented output values from the flip-flops are used. The input to the most significant W-bit flip-flop requires two separate product terms. One term is XYZ and the other term is $W\bar{Z}$. The X-bit flip-flop requires the three terms $X\bar{Y} + X\bar{Z} + \bar{X}YZ$. The three terms in X^{n+1} are obtained in separate product lines from the upper ROM. These three terms are summed by programming in the three coupling elements for the X-row in the lower ROM. The Y flip-flop has two terms which must be summed $\bar{W}\bar{Y}Z + Y\bar{Z}$. The input function for the Z flip-flop is especially simple since it consists of a single term, the complement of the Z level.

We have implemented in Fig. 6.10a a modulo-10 counter which will increment the next higher count with each successive clock pulse. Now we need some connection to the outside world to provide a useful utilization of this counting function. The output from the flip-flops could be used directly in a special design interconnection scheme. In an automated design, it may be more useful to bring the outputs from the summing matrix. This is done in Fig. 6.10b by selecting the lines $W, X, Y,$ and Z with the summing matrix for coupling to external circuitry. Now we have completed the design specification for the modulo-10 counter.

In an alternate design we may have desired to bring additional codes out of the modulo-10 counter. For instance, we might wish to bring lines from the summing ROM to provide a 12-bit Hollerith code, a Selectric code, a Johnson code, or others. The procedure for doing this is the same technique that was discussed above. Output in different codes can be provided by adding additional rows into the summing ROM. Additional output lines may also be necessary in case the complements of $W, X, Y,$ or Z become necessary. A modulo-10 counter using ROM can be especially effective when several output codes are required.

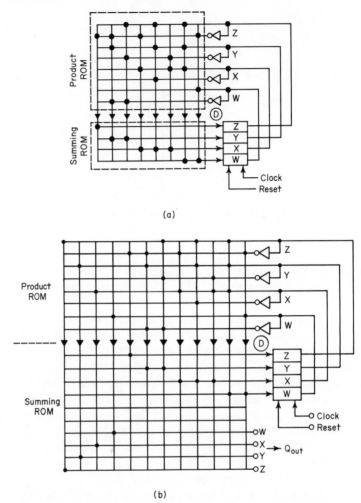

(a)

(b)

Fig. 6.10. (*a*) Single decade modulo-10 counter—counter only. (*b*) Single decade Modulo-10 counter—output lines included in summing matrix.

As an example of multiple output codes let's look at the requirement for modulo-10 counting with simultaneous output in BCD (weighted 8-4-2-1) and the Johnson BCD codes. These codes are shown in Table 6.3. The basic counter of Fig. 6.10*b* can be used to provide the simple BCD code and additional decoding added for the Johnson code. The 10 unique product lines are added to obtain the dual ROM design of Fig. 6.11. The added product lines correspond to decimal 0 through 9 counts. These decimal lines are summed to develop the specific Johnson code. If further, a third output code, decimal, is desired, it can be obtained by adding 10 rows to the lower matrix. Counting in multiple decades can be implemented by adding carry product lines to trigger counting into successively higher decades.[6]

Table 6.3. Coding for 8-4-2-1 BCD to Johnson BCD Conversion

Decimal	8-4-2-1 BCD				Johnson BCD				
Q	W	X	Y	Z	K	L	M	N	P
0	0	0	0	0	0	0	0	0	0
1	0	0	0	1	0	0	0	0	1
2	0	0	1	0	0	0	0	1	1
3	0	0	1	1	0	0	1	1	1
4	0	1	0	0	0	1	1	1	1
5	0	1	0	1	1	1	1	1	1
6	0	1	1	0	1	1	1	1	0
7	0	1	1	1	1	1	1	0	0
8	1	0	0	0	1	1	0	0	0
9	1	0	0	1	1	0	0	0	0

6.2.5 Trigonometric Function Generator

The ROM used as a look-up table can be used to generate a wide range of mathematical functions. Any single valued mathematical function that can be programmed as a look-up table can be generated through the ROM matrix. A specific example would be the generation of trigonometric functions. Figure 6.12 shows a 128-bit ROM used as a direct look-up table for the $\cos \theta$ function. This ROM is logically arranged as 16×8 and provides 8-bit $\cos \theta$ accuracy for 16

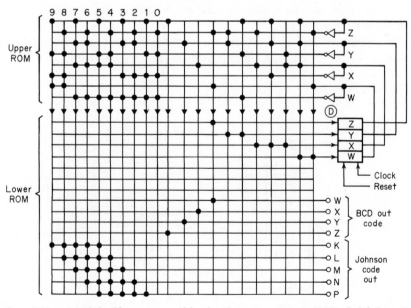

Fig. 6.11. Modulo-10 counter with simultaneous output BCD 8-4-2-1 and Johnson BCD codes.

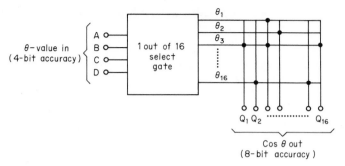

Fig. 6.12.   ROM used as a direct look-up table.

different θ values.   The direct look-up approach, as shown in Fig. 6.12, is sufficient for most applications, but the number of ROM bits required becomes uneconomical for situations requiring highest accuracy.   For instance, the direct ROM implementation of the θ-to-cos-θ conversion with 12-bit accuracy overall requires 2^{24}, or 16 million bits.   Accuracy can be made to increase rapidly with smaller memories coupled to full adders using interpolation.

An effective approach to high accuracy generation of mathematical functions uses one ROM to generate the approximate function and a second ROM to generate the interpolation value.   The outputs from both ROMs can be summed using a separate integrated adder to provide considerable increase in overall conversion accuracy than would have been obtained using a direct conversion using the same number of ROM bits in memory.   In Fig. 6.13 one ROM is used to implement the approximate θ-to-cos-θ conversion.   A second ROM in Fig. 6.13 provides the interpolation function which, when added to the approximate function, increases the overall conversion accuracy.

The interpolation approach divides the angle θ in two parts, θ_M and θ_L, corresponding to the most and least significant bits.   The trigonometric identity applies here.

$$\cos \theta = \cos (\theta_M - \theta_L) = \cos \theta_M \cos \theta_L - \sin \theta_M \sin \theta_L \qquad (6\text{-}3)$$

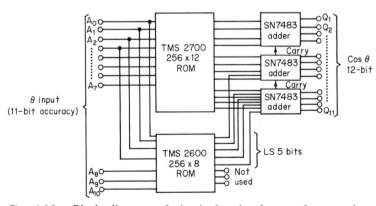

Fig. 6.13.   Block diagram of circuit for the θ-to-cos-θ conversion.

Assume the range is 0 to 90°. Let θ_M be the 8 most significant bits of θ, and θ_L be the least significant 3 bits (for a desired θ accuracy of 11 bits). The function $\cos \theta_L$ varies between 1 and 0.99998 for the small angles θ_L. So we may safely assume that $\cos \theta_L = 1$ and simplify the above expression

$$\cos \theta = \cos \theta_M - \sin \theta_M \sin \theta_L \tag{6-4}$$

Let's say our design problem calls for a θ accuracy of 11 bits and a $\cos \theta$ accuracy of 12 bits. Values of $\cos \theta_M$ are stored in a larger ROM of Fig. 6.13 which has a 12-bit output and an 8-bit input address. The second term in Eq. (6-4) ($-\sin \theta_M \sin \theta_L$) represents that small interpolation value $\sin \theta_L$ and is the output from the lower ROM of Fig. 6.13. The outputs from both ROMs are summed [as in Eq. (6-4)] using the full adders to provide the resulting $\cos \theta$ function with a full 12-bit accuracy. The total conversion time required for the implementation of Fig. 6.13 is that access time for the ROM plus the add time introduced by the adder circuits. Normally the adders would be much faster than the ROMs. If this conversion is implemented with ROMs of a speed approaching that of the adders, then one must be careful to avoid timing problems associated with the carry through the three adders.

The ROMs used in Fig. 6.13 contain 5,052 bits. Using the TMS2600 and TMS2700 ROMs in Fig. 6.13 results in a conversion time of approximately 700 ns using TTL full adders.

6.3 ON-THE-CHIP DESIGN TECHNOLOGY

6.3.1 General

The discussion of ROMs in this chapter has so far been limited to ROM application concepts. You the reader should now understand the general operational concepts of ROM. With that as background, the discussion of on-the-chip technology will be easier to follow. The MOS layout to be introduced consists of a double ROM structure. These concepts are extended to include an LSI chip with column select decode circuitry.

6.3.2 MOS Layout

The coupling of two ROMs is shown schematically in the series of views in Fig. 6.14. In Fig. 6.14a the NAND gate equivalent of each ROM is shown where $\bar{P}_1 = AB$ and $\bar{P}_2 = \overline{AB}$. The connection of ROM A into ROM B in Fig. 6.14b provides the logic function $Q_1 = AB + \overline{AB}$ and $Q_2 = AB$. The ROMs provide the AND and OR sections and constitute a PLA structure. The actual circuit schematic for the PLA using MOS p-channel enhancement devices is shown in Fig. 6.14c with input lines A and B and output lines Q_1 and Q_2. Each programmed 1 in the dual ROM consists of an active MOS transistor. In the AND or upper ROM, each input condition of A and B selected, both true and complemented, requires an active MOS transistor. In the OR or summing ROM, each node for the P_1 and P_2 lines requires an active MOS transistor. The total circuit of Fig. 6.14c requires 7 active transistors within the 6 × 2, or 12-bit, ROM structure. In addition each product term P and

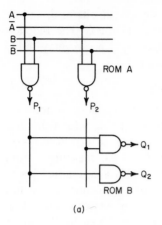

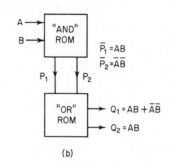

(a)

(b)

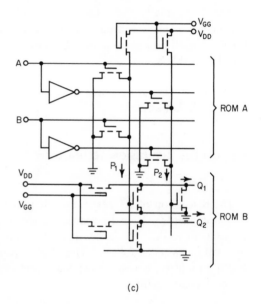

(c)

Fig. 6.14. (*a*) Two ROMs described as two positive NAND gates. (*b*) Coupled ROMs in a PLA configuration. (*c*) Two ROMs programmed with MOS technology.

each summing term Q_j require one external MOS load device as shown to complete the inverter action.

The NAND gates in Fig. 6.14*a* do correspond to the positive-logic case where the devices are p-channel enhancement MOS. If instead, n-channel enhancement devices were used, the NAND gates would correspond to the negative-logic equivalent.

Figure 6.15 shows the geometrical layout for the ROM A matrix of Fig. 6.14 expanded to include P_1, P_2, P_3, and P_4 product lines. The p-diffused lines running vertically are shown with cross-hatching. The metal lines run horizontally and provide the gate metalization for those transistors programmed with a thin gate oxide. Those cell areas where transistor action does not appear contain a thick gate oxide and a correspondingly high gate threshold voltage.

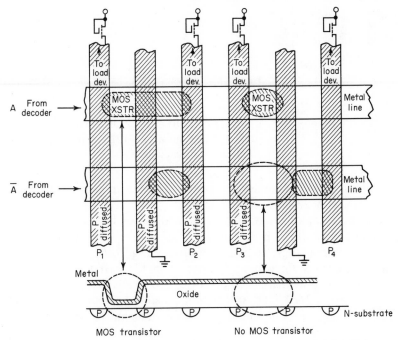

Fig. 6.15. Layout for individual ROM cell areas. Four product lines are shown here.

The metal line $\bar{A}$, coming across horizontally, does not have an MOS device programmed into its interception cell with the P_1 or P_3 product line. The oxide is programmed thick at this point and raises the gate threshold voltage level to that of the field oxide. The layout of Fig. 6.15 contains a very small number of bits, but is representative of the MOS/LSI memory matrix.

6.3.3 Programming the Standard MOS ROM

The standard MOS ROM of Figs. 6.14 and 6.15 is programmed using a gate mask which provides the unique arrangement of active MOS transistors within the storage matrix. In Table 6.4 the fabrication steps are summarized briefly for the manufacture of a ROM circuit. The process outlined here aligns the gate after the diffusion step. The gate mask step 3 programs the proper thickness of gate oxide for each

Table 6.4. Fabrication Steps Including Mask Programming for the ROM Memory

1. Source-drain deposition and diffusion
2. Field oxide formation
3. Gate masking and etching
4. Metal contact masking and etching
5. Metalization
6. Selective metal removal using mask

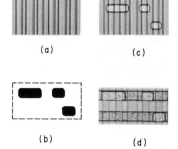

(a)   (c)

(b)   (d)

Fig. 6.16. Photomicrographs for the ROM section from Fig. 6.15 at various processing steps: (*a*) silicon with source and drain diffusions complete; (*b*) gate mask used to program the ROM; (*c*) silicon with thin gate regions programmed from mask (*b*); (*d*) completed ROM showing aluminum gate metalization.

individual MOS cell within the storage matrix. This is a unique gate mask generated with the particular fixed data storage desired.

The photomicrograph for the ROM region corresponding to Fig. 6.15 is shown, following fabrication step 1, in Fig. 6.16*a*. The gate mask (Fig. 6.16*b*) is applied through a photolithographic step and results in Fig. 6.16*c*. The portion of the completed ROM ready for packaging appears in Fig. 6.16*d*. These ROMs with different programmed data are each processed identically except for the processing step shown in Fig. 6.16*c*. The automation possible here provides excellent cost advantages for quantities of hundreds and above for identically programmed ROMs.

6.3.4 Row Select Circuitry

A typical ROM may contain dozens or hundreds of rows in the matrix. Since it is not feasible to bring each row out through separate package connections, an internal row select circuit is mandatory. An input of 2 control bits can select 1 of 4 rows, 4 control bits can select 1 of 16 rows, etc. For illustration, a 2-bit input function (A, B) is used to select 1 of 4 rows in Fig. 6.17. The row select circuitry uses multiple input gates with one gate for each row selected. This circuit selects a row (provides a negative voltage level in this case) for the corresponding input value positive-logic true. In this way an economy for package pin connections is provided by on the chip row decoding.

6.3.5 Column Select Circuitry

The motivating factor for column select circuitry is that it is more preferable from a yield point of view to process integrated circuits on chips which are approximately square. Since most ROMs require a large number of input combinations and relatively few output lines, some form of column select circuitry is needed. For instance, an ROM layed out with a 64 × 64 matrix geometry would provide a 64-bit output code. If we desired a logical equivalent of 4,096 × 1 for this chip, we would require a maximum amount of column select circuitry. An example of a column select circuit which selects 1 out of 4 columns and gates them to a single output node Q_0 is shown in Fig. 6.18. The column select circuit involves adding an additional MOS transistor in series with each column between the memory matrix and the load device. Here a 4-bit output is reduced to a single bit line Q_0. A more complete example is shown in Fig. 6.19 illustrating the use of column select circuitry. Here the basic ROM matrix uses a 4 × 4 cell geometry. The column

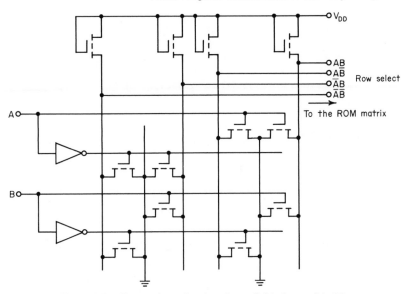

Fig. 6.17. Row select circuitry for a 2-bit input (A, B).

select circuitry provides two bits of logical output Q_1 and Q_2. The internal address to the ROM now requires 8 control lines or 3 bits. The ROM has a logical arrangement of 8×2 bits. Off-the-chip circuitry sees this ROM as an equivalent 8×2 bit structure and is unable to tell that the actual on-the-chip geometry is a 4×4 matrix.

The decoding in Fig. 6.19 can, of course, be extended for larger arrays. The circuit sections are identified for an MOS/LSI chip of physical size 111×118 mils in Fig. 6.20. This particular chip is a 4,096-bit read only memory (TMS4400). The basic memory matrix consists of MOS cells arranged in a 64×64 array shown in the

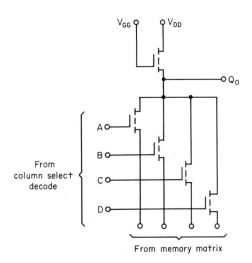

Fig. 6.18. 4×4 bit ROM matrix with decoding for 8×2 bit logical equivalent.

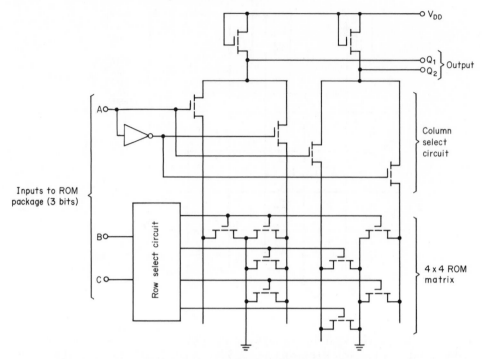

Fig. 6.19. Photomicrograph of MOS/LSI ROM chip (111 × 118 mils).

central portion of the chip. The word address section provides selection circuits for 64 gate metalization lines. The 64 column lines which provide the product term are processed in the column select circuit section on the chip. The column select devices appear, one for each bit or column line, together with the output drivers for interfacing to circuitry off the chip.

The basic memory array within the chip of Fig. 6.20 is arranged by the logic organization in a 1,024 × 4 or a 512 × 8 array. This is to say that there are either 1,024 or 512 (selected prior to packaging) different words or combinations that can be addressed by a 10- or 9-bit input address word. Similarly, output from the chip is decoded to a parallel 4- or 8-bit word.

The MOS ROMs discussed above provide a negative-going output signal with respect to the substrate. When the substrate is maintained at +5-V levels in a system, it is possible to interface directly with TTL circuits off the chip. Special drivers are required on the MOS chip to drive the active load presented by TTL circuits.

6.3.6 MOS Tree Matrix Circuitry

So far we have discussed the MOS ROM using only the rectangular matrix geometry. In the rectangular matrix those cells containing no active transistors represent stray parasitic capacitance which might be reduced in a more efficient layout. A different circuit where speed is a design goal may be implemented using a tree-type layout.

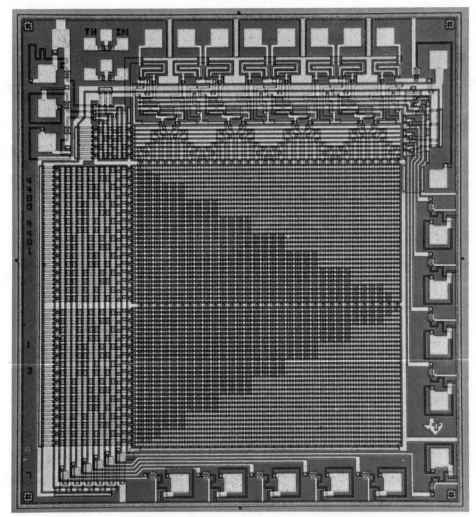

Fig. 6.20. Column select circuit for MOS.

The tree matrix is a direct implementation of specific product terms with no redundant unprogrammed cells. An example of the tree matrix is shown in Fig. 6.21. The switching speed is improved further by using a small value of resistance at R_L in place of high-impedance MOS load devices. The load resistor R_L in a tree matrix generally ranges 100 to 300 Ohms and permits switching times on the order of 50 ns for matrices containing several hundred bits.

The tree matrix is a direct implementation of specific product terms. These terms are summed at a single output node. In the design example, those product terms implemented with negative logic are $A_1B_1C_1 + A_1B_1C_2 + A_1B_2C_1 + A_1B_2C_2 + A_2B_1C_1 + A_2B_1C_2 + A_2B_2C_1 + A_2B_2C_2 +$ etc. from Fig. 6.20.

Figures of merit are summarized in Table 6.5. This circuit contains internal nodes of sufficient capacitance to cause voltage spiking at the output during switching

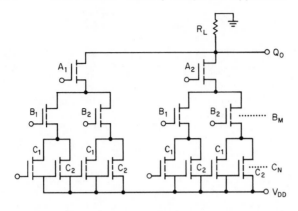

$Q_0 = A_1[B_1(C_1 + C_2) + B_2(C_1 + C_2)]$

$+ A_2[B_1(C_1 + C_2) + B_2(C_1 + C_2)]$

$+ \ldots\ldots$

Positive
logic

$Q = (A_1 + B_1 + C_1)(A_1 + B_1 + C_2)$

$\cdot (A_1 + B_2 + C_3)(A_1 + B_2 + C_2)$

$\cdot \ldots\ldots$

Fig. 6.21. Tree-matrix MOS circuit.

transients. Another disadvantage with this circuit is that an operational amplifier is required for interfacing to other MOS or bipolar circuits. The output voltage at node Q_0 is on the order of hundreds of millivolts. The advantage of this circuit is that it does provide a high access speed and can provide in some cases a more efficient layout than the rectangular ROM matrix.

6.3.7 Dynamic MOS ROM

Each of the ROM circuits discussed has been static. We have not discussed clocking of data on the chip. The high impedance level of MOS permits special clocking arrangements and storage of data at gate nodes. These special clocking arrangements reduce the power dissipation. The dynamic ROM can be clocked

Table 6.5. Comparison of Performance of Tree-type and Rectangular-type Matrix ROMs

MOS ROM CONFIGURATIONS	
Rectangular matrix	Tree matrix
Design may be readily automated	Voltage spiking appears at Q_0 during portion of readout
Logic swing sufficient for direct interface to MOS buffers	Reduced logic swing requires an external op amp fast access time

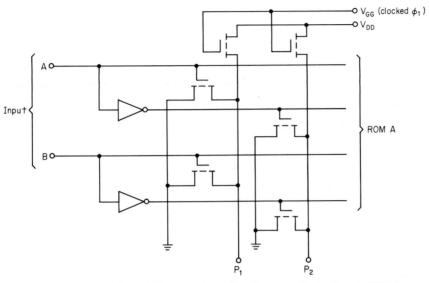

Fig. 6.22. Clocking of V_{GG} permits reduced power dissipation in ROM.

in various ways. The most direct way to clock is through the column select lines. The load devices in the circuit of Fig. 6.22 show external clocking ϕ_1. The output from the dynamic ROM must be carefully timed for sampling at external nodes to avoid loss of data.

6.4 BIPOLAR MEMORY DESIGN TECHNOLOGY

6.4.1 Memory Cells and Address Decode

The three basic portions of the bipolar ROM remain the same as for the MOS ROM. These are the (1) memory cell array, (2) X address decode or row select circuitry, and (3) Y address or column select circuitry. This is shown in Fig. 6.23.

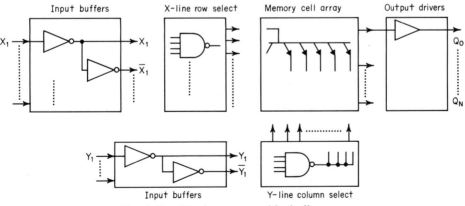

Fig. 6.23. Bipolar memory block diagram.

Output drivers are used to provide the degree of output drive desired for off-the-chip load circuits. Since bipolar devices have much lower impedance than MOS, more drive capability is required throughout the bipolar ROM circuitry. To start with, an input buffer inverter should be fast and capable of driving the multiple row select gates.

6.4.2 Address Decode Circuitry

An example of an input inverter with a totem output[7] is shown in Fig. 6.24. The use of an active load transistor T_3 provides a low impedance for the output 1, and T_2 provides a low impedance for the output 0. The resistors are selected to permit transistor T to turn on before T_2, eliminating the problem of output glitches and power dissipation during the switching transient. This circuit requires less area than the conventional bipolar TTL inverter.

The buffer-inverters drive multiple-emitter NPN devices which complete the X address or row select circuitry. Each row is selected through a multiple-emitter transistor as in Fig. 6.25. In Fig. 6.25a the input bits are used to uniquely select a given row in the memory. Three rows only are shown here. The row select transistors have $2L$ emitters where there are L X-input bits. One row select multi-emitter device is used for each row. In Fig. 6.25b a representative row or word line is shown together with the device T_3 within the memory matrix. The device in the matrix has one emitter for each of M columns or bit lines.

In Fig. 6.25b the bipolar X address decoding device is shown with 10 emitters as would be required for addressing 32 separate rows in the ROM array. Each of the 32 multiemitter row select transistors contains 10 emitters. True and comple-ment address levels are obtained from the input buffer-inverter via metal connecting lines to the emitters of the multiemitter transistor T_1. Programmable contacts provide emitter connections with either the true or complement input signals as necessary to generate the appropriate function at the decoder output node K. The

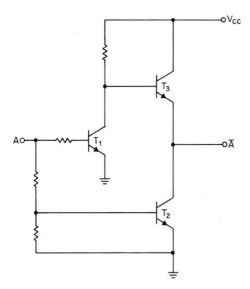

Fig. 6.24. Input buffer-inverter circuit.

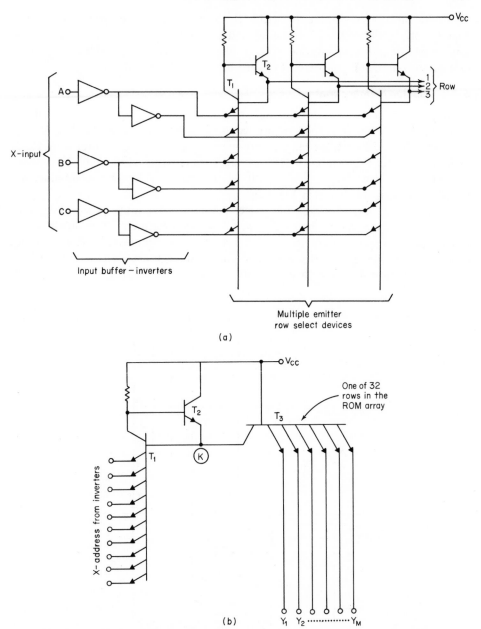

Fig. 6.25. Row select decoding circuitry: (*a*) 3-row drive; (*b*) single row including device in memory matrix.

emitter follower T_2 provides increased drive for the matrix device T_3. Pull-down drive is supplied by the input buffer T_2 through the emitter-base junction of device T_1. In this circuit, both T_1 and T_2 operate only in the active region and minimize delay and saturation storage effects. Propagation delay in the row select section of the circuit is a few nanoseconds.

For the selection of a single row within the 32×32 array, the row select decoding circuits hold 31 out of the 32 nodes labeled K at a high voltage. Node K for that single row selected causes device T_3 to conduct and therefore provides a logic high into those columns Y connected to transistor T_3 as programmed.

6.4.3   Bipolar Memory Matrix

Transistor T_3 of Fig. 6.25b is a single row of the memory matrix. Transistor T_3 is connected as an emitter follower and contains M separate emitters. For $M = 32$ we have a 32×32 or 1,024-bit memory matrix geometry. The outputs of the 32 emitter followers (T_3) are each fed through parallel connections into 32 separate column or bit select detectors. The bit select circuit acts like a NAND gate, and we can represent it as such in Fig. 6.26.

Notice that 31 out of the 32 row select devices do not cause power dissipation in device T_3, and therefore the total power dissipation for the memory array is held to a minimum. The entire array of 1,024 bits is encompassed within a single collector-isolation area, and the programmable emitter contact opening technique can be used to permit a very high bit density within the ROM array.

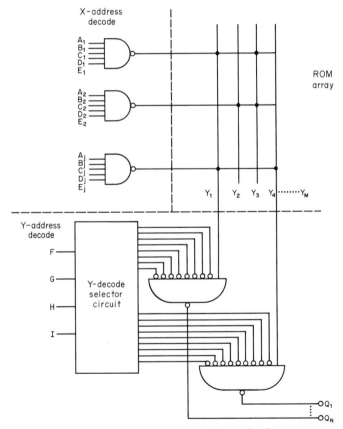

Fig. 6.26.   Typical bipolar ROM circuit.

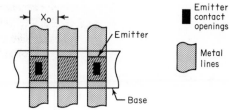

Fig. 6.27. Emitter contact mask programmed to form transistor emitters at specific points in bipolar circuit.

6.4.4 Mask Programming of the Memory Matrix

The separate multiemitter transistors within the ROM storage array consist of long base stripes into which emitters have been selectively programmed, using a photo-lithographic mask. Debiasing along this long base stripe has been minimized by the addition of an n^+ emitter diffusion which is diffused alongside this base and connected at intervals of 4 or 5 emitters using a metal shorting bar.

The emitters of these transistors T_3 can be programmed in two different ways. Figure 6.27 shows an emitter contact mask programmed to form transistor emitters at specific points along the base stripe. Another technique shown in Fig. 6.28 shows metal contacts to each emitter along the base stripe of transistor T_3 and programming of the metalization mask itself. The metalization mask can be opened in the area shown between the metal column stripes and the actual emitter contact to isolate any particular emitter connection on the transistor.

Memory cell area is minimized using the technique of Fig. 6.27 instead of Fig. 6.28. Emitter spacings may differ by a factor of almost 2 to 1 between the two techniques. The emitter contact mask programming does require a masking step prior to final metalization and therefore appears at an earlier time during the fabrication process. Metalization removal as suggested in Fig. 6.28 may occur after final processing and just prior to any lead coating depositions.

6.4.5 Column Select Circuitry

The column select circuitry consists of sensing the presence or absence of a high voltage in a selected vertical bus, and is accomplished using circuitry such as that shown in Fig. 6.29. Here the column select address decoders hold the bases of 28 out of 32 of the bit select transistors at a low voltage: the selected base is pulled high, turning on the bit select transistor. The column select circuitry here provides a 4-bit word output Q_1, Q_2, Q_3, and Q_4. For the selection of a single output bit,

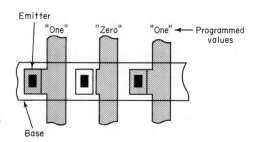

Fig. 6.28. Metalization with programmed emitter connections.

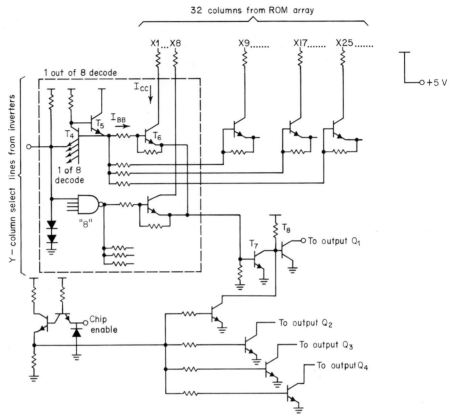

Fig. 6.29. Column select circuitry for 32-column matrix and 4-bit output word.

say Q_1, the column select decoders hold the bases of 7 out of the 8 devices Q_4 at a low voltage. The base of the selected transistor T_4 goes high, permitting T_5 to conduct and providing drive current to T_6. The column select transistor T_6 operates as an emitter follower. The emitter current from device T_6 consists of the summation of base and emitter current. The presence of a programmed 1 along any selected column is indicated by a conducting device T_6 and consists of current level $1_{BB} + 1_{CC}$. The sum of these two currents appears as drive for device T_7 and the inverter T_8. The output drivers, T_7 and T_8, are two cascaded inverters. Note that since 7 out of 8 bit select transistors are not conducting at any time, only 4 of the 32 columns of the memory cell array are selected, and power dissipation is thus minimized. The photomicrograph of a 32 × 32 bipolar ROM memory chip is shown in Fig. 6.30. The subject is the SN54187 bipolar ROM chip which measures 93 × 130 mils. This is a 1,024-bit memory containing an internal memory matrix arranged geometrically in a 32 × 32 fashion. The 32 separate transistors each with 32 emitters are placed within a memory cell matrix area measuring 30 × 80 mils. The total chip contains approximately 460 separate components and the average density over the entire chip is 12 sq mils per matrix bit. Individual bits within the memory cell array require approximately 2.4 sq mils per bit.

Fig. 6.30. Photomicrograph of a chip of the SN54187 bipolar ROM memory (93 × 130 mils).

6.4.6 Comparison of MOS with Bipolar ROM

Both MOS and bipolar ROM are being designed in capacities up to 8,200 bits. In Table 6.6 an advanced bipolar design is compared with the performance of the MOS TMS4400 circuit. Here the bipolar and MOS ROM circuits contain 4,096 bits of memory. The 50-ns access time for the bipolar circuit is a factor of 10 to 20 faster than that for the p-channel enhancement-type MOS. The power dissipation

Table 6.6. Comparison of Characteristics of Bipolar and MOS 4,096-bit ROMs

Characteristic	Bipolar	MOS TMS4400
Chip complexity, bits	4K	4K
Package pins	24	24
Access time, ns	50	<1,000
Power dissipation, mW		
Per bit	0.12	0.06
Total package	500	250
Cell area, sq mils	2.0	0.7
Chip area per bit, sq mils	5.6	3.3
Bar size, mils	150 × 150	111 × 118

of 0.12 mW per bit for bipolar memories is approximately twice that of the high-level MOS circuit. The cell area of 0.7 sq mil within the memory matrix of MOS is approximately one-third that required for the bipolar structure. Row and column decoding is more efficient using bipolar, and as a result the total average chip area per bit for bipolar is a closer match to MOS. The values in Table 6.6 are certainly subject to revision at any time. Future technologies can alter the balance for cost-effective design decisions in favor of either MOS or bipolar for specific applications. For instance, the speed advantage of bipolar ROM is practically eliminated with n-channel MOS technology.

6.5   PROGRAMMABLE ROM

6.5.1   Fusible Metalization

The ROMs discussed so far in this chapter have required a programmed mask to implement the write function. Masking steps are relatively expensive and often do not become cost effective unless a production quantity of chips with the unique memory pattern are desired. There are other techniques available which permit one to program the ROM after encapsulation and packaging. These techniques permit one to program very small quantities of ROM and therefore can be cost effective where production runs for a specific program are not desired.

If one uses a fusible metalization with bipolar circuits, the connections to the individual emitters for separate memory cells can be open-circuited in a controllable way and the memory may be programmed after packaging. A fuse metal such as nichrome is typically used and does provide an effective answer to requirements where a small volume of a particular bit pattern is required. These types of ROM are termed programmable ROM to distinguish them from mask programmed ROM, characteristically termed factory programmed. MOS ROMs are not programmable at the present time. Figure 6.31 shows the schematic for a programmable ROM array that uses bipolar transistors. In this configuration the Y column select circuit must be kept simple because a relatively large fusing current is required to program this ROM and a direct path between the V_{CC} line and the output node is required. Here the transistor is a multiemitter storage cell. The current path for fusing is shown with the arrow. The nichrome fuse is in series with each individual emitter in the ROM matrix.

One problem which presently exists for the fusible ROM relates to testing prior to programming. The packaged ROM prior to programming contains a memory matrix of all 1s. As a result, it is impossible in present design to determine whether each bit within the ROM is functioning properly. Malfunctioning devices can also provide the logic 1 at the output and are thus indistinguishable among the cells which are functioning properly. As new circuits are developed, it is possible that the programmable ROM can be more extensively tested prior to shipment from the manufacturer. At the present time the programmer must consider this problem in his system design and consider the yield loss in cost projections. At the present time it would be a mistake to design an integrated system into which programmable ROMs are mounted for programming on the printed circuit boards after system delivery in the field.

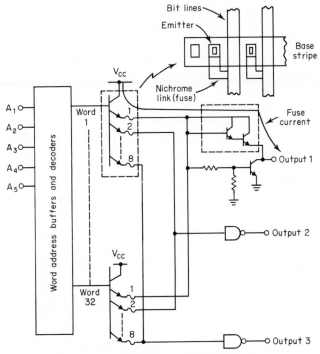

Fig. 6.31. A programmable ROM array.

6.5.2 Avalanche-induced Metal Migration

Another technique for electrically programming the ROM utilizes an avalanching approach. The cell structure is somewhat different from the fusing approach and involves avalanching the base-emitter junction of an individual transistor within the storage cell. The resulting metal migration sets a permanent base-emitter short and therefore programs the memory cell bit. The avalanching technique requires a higher voltage and higher current but the resulting metal migration is a fast mechanism.

6.5.3 Comparison of Programmable ROMs

Table 6.7 compares the programming features for the fusible link and avalanche programmable ROM technology. The fusing time for the nichrome ranges between 5 and 200 μs, while the closure time for the avalanching approach may be two orders

Table 6.7. Programmable ROM Fuse Technology

Technique	Link	Fuse current, mA	Fuse time, ms
Fuse apart	NiCr fuse	20–50	5–200
Fuse together	Base emitter avalanche short	200–300	0.02–0.05

of magnitude faster. The time and equipment required for electrically programming the ROM can become an important consideration in larger memory structures.

The vital statistics for programmable ROMs are summarized further in Table 6.8. For a chip complexity of 1,024 bits, access time on the order of 35 ns characteristic of bipolar ROM is obtained. Power dissipation per bit averages 0.5 mW. The speed and bit density is approximately the same for the nichrome or avalanche circuits. The cell size for a programmable ROM is of course considerably larger than that for the corresponding mask programmed ROM. For production quantities the unit cost for the programmable ROM is in considerable excess (presently a factor of 5 to 10) compared to mask programmed ROMs.

6.5.4   Other Techniques

Another technique for programming the semiconductor ROM involves a mechanical approach. Here the initial metalization provides logical 1s in each memory cell location. The 0s are programmed by scratching the metal emitters and hence open-circuiting the transistor or diode which is used as a coupling element for the ROM. The technique of scratching must be done using a micro-manipulator and is a slow and cumbersome task.

The MOS technology does not lend itself readily to fusing, avalanching, or mechanical scratching. There are some very interesting developments that permit programming the MOS ROM, however. These programming techniques utilize the fact that charge can be stored within the gate dielectric or within varied gate structures. This charge storage can be a semipermanent mechanism and provide for long-term programming of the MOS ROM. Figure 6.32 shows the cross section for a programmable MOS ROM structure. Figure 6.32*a* shows an individual device in cross section. This device contains a buried, electrically floating gate. The floating gate is generally a silicon structure which has been deposited epitaxially during the dielectric deposition process. This cell is used as the basic coupling element within the ROM matrix. The p-channel MOS transistor structure shown here contains the usual source and drain diffusions and the novel feature of the isolated gate. This gate can acquire a negative charge and permanently invert the surface of the silicon substrate. This provides a semipermanent channel between source and drain. Electrons are injected into the oxide layer from an avalanching drain junction as shown in Fig. 6.32*b*. These electrons are moved through the electric

Table 6.8.   Programmable ROM Vital Statistics

Chip complexity	1K
Package pins	16
Access time	35 ns
Power dissipation	
Per bit	0.5 mW
Total package	500 mW
Fuse technique	NiCr (or avalanche)
Cell size	4.5 sq mils
Bar size	140 × 140 mils

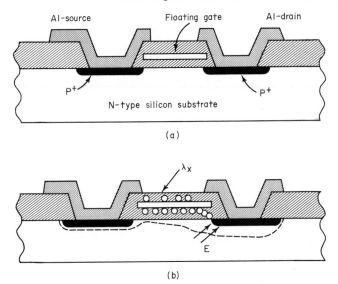

(a)

(b)

Fig. 6.32. A memory device using an MOS transistor with a buried, electrically floating gate: (*a*) cross-section geometry; (*b*) schematic illustration with charge storage on gate.

field toward the floating gate. A division by capacitance of the applied voltage makes the gate positive with respect to the drain. Thus, the operation of the memory requires the injection of hot electron into the silicon dioxide layer and subsequently an accumulation on the buried gate. It is possible to reprogram this particular cell by neutralizing the charge on the floating gate. Ultraviolet or x-ray sources can be used for this purpose. The use of x-radiation limits the number of times a given package can be erased and reprogrammed due to radiation damage.

The use of a second metal gate permits reprogramming a structure without the use of an ionizing erase radiation. The cross section of a structure which does include this second gate for erasing purposes is shown in Fig. 6.33. This cell is programmed by applying a negative voltage to both the source and the drain for inducing

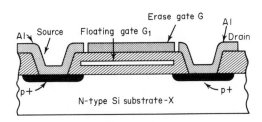

Fig. 6.33. Structure for use where electrical reprogramming is necessary.

	V_{G_2S}	V_{SX}	V_{DX}
Set-channel	Positive	$-BV_{SX}$	$-BV_{DX}$
Erase-channel	Negative	$-BV_{SX}$	$-BV_{DX}$

avalanche breakdown at both junctions. Simultaneously, a positive voltage applied to the second gate G_2 increases the rate at which electrons accumulate on the floating gate. As electrons accumulate on the floating gate, the transistor channel appears and the device turns on. The structure of Fig. 6.33 is erased by avalanching the source and drain junctions again but now reversing the electric field between the erase gate and the substrate. With a negative voltage on gate G_2, the electric field provides for an accumulation of holes on the floating gate and therefore a neutralization of existing charge on that same gate. The result accumulates the n-type silicon substrate surface and erases the conducting channel between source and drain.

Another programmable-ROM uses the gate dielectric itself for a charge storage. A class of dielectrics including alumina and silicon nitride may be used as gate dielectrics for the MOS transistor and can also provide a reprogramming feature. The cross section for a memory cell using alumina dielectric is shown in Fig. 6.34. This element is termed a MAOS memory element.

The MAOS element is programmed by the application of a positive or negative gate voltage pulse[8] above a critical polarization level. For p-channel devices, a positive gate voltage is used to write into the cell. A write voltage of 50-V amplitude requires 10 to 20 μs for programming prototype structures. The access times for readout are approximately the same as for standard MOS ROM arrays. Erasing requires an opposing polarity on the gate. This type of memory cell may be reprogrammed at a fast rate. We can call it read mostly memory (RMM) since it begins to take on the aspects of a random access memory structure in terms of reprogramming speed. We should emphasize that these devices are not available commercially at the time of this writing.

Table 6.9 lists the wide variety of technologies now available for ROM. These technologies provide various advantages and disadvantages. ROM technologies which do not lend themselves to monolithic fabrication processes can be expected sooner or later to yield to IC technology. Technologies such as the amorphous (noncrystalline) substrate devices[9] have so far provided a very low reliability function and have not found use in large-scale systems. The problem of accessing very small volumes within a 3D matrix appears to be reduced for future memories using holographic techniques.[10] Others have proposed ferroelectric and ferromagnetic ceramics[11,12] as providing an ultimate memory. In any event, at the present time the new ROM technologies which are not based upon silicon appear to be very much in the research stage.

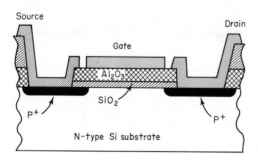

Fig. 6.34. Cross section of an alumina-dielectric device.

Table 6.9. Technologies Presently Available

Bipolar ROM	Bipolar PROM
Diode	Fuse
Transistor	Mechanical linkage
MOS ROM	Metal migration/avalanche
Transistor	MOS PROM
Other ROM	Avalanche
Optical (includes holographic)	MAOS interface-trapping
Capacitor	Mechanical programming
Inductor	Amorphous gate dielectric
Ferroelectrics	
Ferromagnetics	

REFERENCES

1. S. D. Harper, Computer Memories, *Honeywell Computer J.*, **5**(2): 51(1971).
2. R. Dussine, Evolution of ROM in Computers, *Honeywell Computer J.*, **5**(2): 79–88(1971).
3. G. E. Goode, "Design of Synchronous Sequential Logic Circuits," to be published by McGraw-Hill Book Company, New York.
4. F. Kvamme, Standard Read-Only Memories Simplify Complex Logic Design, *Electronics,* **43**: 88–95(January 5, 1970).
5. J. Linford, ROMs as Logic, *Electron. Eng.*, pp. 52–53, July 1971.
6. W. N. Carr and J. P. Mize, "MOS/LSI Design and Application," chap. 6, McGraw-Hill Book Company, New York, 1972.
7. J. C. Barrett, A. Bergh, T. Hornak, and J. E. Price, Design Considerations for a High-Speed Bipolar Read-Only Memory, *J. Solid-state Circuits,* **SC-5**(5): 196–202(October 1970).
8. D. Frohman-Bentchkowsky, The Metal-Nitride-Oxide-Silicon (MNOS) Transistor—Characteristics and Applications, *Proc. IEEE,* **58**(8): 1207–1219(August 1970).
9. J. Feinleib, J. de Neufille, S. C. Moss, and S. R. Orshinsky, Rapid Reversible Light-Induced Crystallization of Amorphous Semiconductors, *Appl. Phys. Lett.*, **18**(6): 254–256(1971).
10. J. W. Weil, An Introduction to Massive Stores, *Honeywell Computer J.*, **5**(2): 88–92(1971).
11. A. A. Snaper, The Ultimate Computer Memory, *Opt. Spectra,* pp. 28–28, March 1972.
12. J. A. Rajchman, Promise of Optical Memories, *J. Appl. Phys.*, **41**(3): 1376(1970).

7

Semiconductor Storage Element
Reliability

7.1 INTRODUCTION

This chapter concentrates on establishing a measure of confidence that semi-conductor memories built from semiconductor storage elements will maintain an acceptable level of reliability. Discussion concerns: first, the underlying factors of the reliability of dense products and their data base; second, the reliability required of storage elements used in memory systems; third, the in-house and field data base of bipolar and MOS, respectively; and fourth, some general comments concerning memory systems error correction techniques and on further screening of components to maintain higher reliability.

7.2 UNDERLYING FACTORS OF LSI
(LARGE-SCALE INTEGRATION)* RELIABILITY

As emphasized throughout the discussion of the technology arsenal and the design chapters, the motivating force for the SC integrated-circuit designer is to provide higher bit density (smaller area per bit and thus, more bits per chip) for the storage element. Such high density has called for greater utilization of silicon area via (1) closer component spacing, (2) simpler circuitry with wider design tolerances, (3) processing that reduces area for components, and (4) metalization techniques that accommodate interconnection of the closely spaced components.

The increased density of LSI requires a corresponding reduction in defect density per unit area if the yield is to be maintained at a level which will allow the manufacturer to economically produce the high density product.[1] Therefore, extensive effort is devoted to more uniform processing of the semiconductor material in order to maintain an acceptable yield.

The emphasis on density has a significant impact on reliability. The failure rate has the possibility of being much higher on the higher density products because the probability of a defect causing a chip failure is much higher due to the increased components and functions per unit area. However, if the failure rate per high

---

*Greater than 100 logic gates.

density chip can be maintained the same as for less dense chips, then the failure rate per function will decrease and the reliability of the system, based on a failure in the function, will be enhanced.

Certain guidelines are necessary to help maintain the same failure rate of the chip as the density of components increase per unit area. Some of these are:

1. Conservative circuit design with good design margins in voltage, current, temperature, and power dissipation
2. Adequate and uniformly enforced layout rules
3. Fully characterized device capabilities obtained from a given process
4. Rigid process controls
5. Adequate feedback to design and process engineering from failure analysis on early accelerated test failures
6. Adequate qualification tests

The process improvements that are incorporated as a result of factors 4, 5, and 6 will tend to help the higher density product follow a reliability learning curve of reduced failure rate with time similar to that experienced for the less dense component. The failure rate of the higher density product is determined in the manufacturer's facility by testing components on accelerated life tests, either operating or storage or both, at conditions that remain reasonably constant. This allows the comparison of failure rate over a long period of time.

The test of reliability, of course, that the designer and equipment user is interested in is the operating reliability of the end equipment.[2,3] This produces somewhat of a dilemma concerning the assurance of the component reliability. The in-house testing for assurance of a level of reliability may not directly correlate to the reliability of the part operating in the end equipment. Therefore, in many cases both in-house data and field data are required to establish the component reliability.

It takes a long time to establish a data base. The data base is diluted because:

1. The product is not uniformly manufactured due to variable processes in the early stages of development.
2. Multiplicities of technologies and circuit implementations have evolved which require somewhat independent verification rather than directly relatable data.

Presently, this is a significant problem with semiconductor storage elements, since insufficient time has passed to establish the data base on a uniformly produced product. Additional time will eliminate this because field data are now being established.

Before proceeding further, the reliability required of storage elements will be established by examining the requirements of memory systems.

7.3   MEMORY SYSTEM RELIABILITY REQUIREMENTS

7.3.1   MTBF for Memory Systems

There are several vital reliability requirements of memory systems. Digital systems that contain memory must operate error-free for extended periods of time in order for them to be used efficiently. Some equipment must operate for weeks without error, some months, and some, possibly, years. Obviously, if each would operate for years, that certainly would be desirable. However, as systems become more complex and contain hundreds of thousands of logic gates and millions of bits of memory, the probability of failure becomes greater and the system mean time between failures (MTBF)[3,4] becomes less.

Figure 7.1 lists the failure rates required of the components that make up various size memory systems. The minimum MTBF that was considered is one week. A convenient grouping of the components into segments of 1,000 bits will help relate these required failure rates to package reliability of MOS and bipolar storage elements.

The failure rate (FR) required for a particular MTBF in hours is calculated as follows:

$$\text{FR (\%/1K hr/1K bits)} = \frac{1 \times 10^2}{\text{MTBF} \times 10^{-3} \times N} \tag{7-1}$$

where N is the number of 1,000-bit units.

This, of course, represents the failure of any one of the components in the system as well as a failure of an assembly or connector interconnection. The assumptions are made that each component failure occurs randomly and independently and represents a system failure.

Detailed MTBF calculations can be made by knowing the failure rate at a selected confidence level for each component or an assembly operation used in the system. For example, Table 7.1 contains a calculation of the failure rate per 1,000 hours of a system on the basis of the failure rates of the individual components or of an assembly operation.

The MTBF is the reciprocal of the failure rate, therefore

$$\frac{1}{8.9 \times 10^{-5}} = 11,000 \text{ hours} \tag{7-2}$$

Memory size, bits	No. of units*	MTBF			Failure rate, %/1K hr/1K bits		
		Wk	Mo	Yr			
100K	100	X			5.9		
			X			1.4	
				X			0.12
1 million	1,000	X			0.59		
			X			0.14	
				X			0.012
10 million	10,000	X			0.059		
			X			0.014	
				X			0.0012
100 million	100,000	X			0.0059		
			X			0.0014	
				X			0.00012

*1,000 bits per unit.

Fig. 7.1. Memory system component failure rate.

Table 7.1.   MTBF Prediction

Component or operation	Number per system	FR, %/1K hours	System FR, %/1K hours
Tantalum capacitors	1,000	20×10^{-4}	2.0
Connector pins	10,000	0.43×10^{-4}	0.4
Solder connections	100,000	0.1×10^{-4}	1.0
Integrated circuits	500	1×10^{-3}	0.5
Storage elements	5,000	1×10^{-3}	5.0
			8.9

This calculation assumes that the IC and storage element are both at a 0.001 percent per 1,000 hour failure rate.   This is presently not the case, as will be shown later, but data show a trend toward this number.   Long-term field data are available on SSI and a mixture of MSI integrated circuits, but field data on the related LSI storage elements are just now starting and additional time is required before trend lines are really established.

Returning to Table 7.1 establishes this comparison.   Approximately 50 percent of the failure hazard is contributed by the storage elements, and the remaining 50 percent is due to the other components.   Again, the IC failure rate is 0.001 percent. The storage element failure rate is also assumed to be the same, 0.001 percent. These are the kinds of failure rates that seem to be reasonable to project for semiconductor components.

On this basis, an important assumption is made so that the failure rate goal required for storage elements in a memory system can be determined.   This assumption is: The storage elements contribute an equal amount of hazard to a system failure as the rest of the components in the system.   As memory systems become larger and larger in size, the contribution by the storage elements should probably be weighted heavier.   However, for this discussion the 50–50 ratio is maintained.

7.3.2   Storage Element Failure Rate

Recall that the failure rate calculated for Fig. 7.1 used 1,000 bits per package. Applying the 50–50 ratio to the failure rates in Fig. 7.1 provides the required failure rate goals for the storage elements in a given size memory.   These are shown in Fig. 7.2.   A 10 million bit memory system with an MTBF of one month requires a storage element with a failure rate of 0.007 percent per 1,000 hours for every 1,000-bit package.   Corresponding storage element failure rates for the other memory sizes are listed.

7.4   RELIABILITY PER FUNCTION

Chapter 1 delineated the lowest level function relatable across the technology as a gate for logic and a bit for storage.   In a memory system if each bit can make the system fail, then the failure rate per bit is an additional important measure to guide in judging reliability trends between components containing different numbers of bits.

Memory size, bits	No. of units*	MTBF			Failure rate, %/1K hr/1K bits
		Wk	Mo	Yr	
100K	100	X			3.0
			X		0.7
				X	0.06
1 million	1,000	X			0.3
			X		0.07
				X	0.006
10 million	10,000	X			0.03
			X		0.007
				X	0.0006
100 million	100,000	X			0.003
			X		0.0007
				X	0.00006

*1,000 bits per unit.

Fig. 7.2. Storage element failure rate goals.

The reason that MSI has made sense compared to SSI is because the failure rate per function, as well as the cost per gate, has decreased significantly. This is because the MSI chip containing the larger number of functions has the same magnitude of failure rate per 1,000 hours as its smaller predecessor. The same trend is apparently starting to be experienced with LSI and with the storage elements that have been discussed in the design and application chapters.

To illustrate the concept refer to Fig. 7.3. Six chip designs are shown. Each has twice the bit density of the one lower than it. If the reliability of the chip, measured in failure rate (percent per 1,000 hours), can be held constant, then the failure rate per bit halves as the bit density doubles.

Equation (7-3) expresses this in more general terms.

$$\frac{\text{FR/pkg}}{\text{Bits/pkg}} = \text{FR/bit} \qquad (7\text{-}3)$$

As density is increased the same failure rate for the chip may not be maintained, but if the failure rate per bit is lowered, then higher system reliability in terms of longer MTBF will result. This assumes, of course, that each bit failure randomly and independently causes a system failure.

	Chip Number					
	1	2	3	4	5	6
Failure rate, %/1K hours	0.01	0.01	0.01	0.01	0.01	0.01
Bits/chip	128	256	512	1,024	2,048	4,096
Failure rate $\approx$ per bit $\times$ 10^{-4}, %/1K hours	0.7	0.4	0.2	0.1	0.05	0.025

Fig. 7.3. Failure rate per bit.

7.5 BIPOLAR IN-HOUSE TEST DATA

In order to verify whether it is possible to increase density and reduce or maintain the failure rate per function, test data from accelerated operating life tests at 125°C for small-scale integration (SSI) and medium-scale integration (MSI) bipolar circuits are used as the base. These data, derated to 55°C by using an experimentally determined acceleration factor to simulate actual operating conditions of the system, are shown in Table 7.2. With the use of such an acceleration factor, a correlation is attempted between in-house accelerated testing and actual equipment use.

The acceleration factor in this case is 6.8.[3] The failure rate of SSI (SSI is classified as an integrated circuit with up to 12 gates) is 0.01 percent per 1,000 hours,[5] and the failure rate of MSI[6] (MSI is classified as an IC that has more than 12 gates but less than 100) is 0.015 percent per 1,000 hours. For Table 7.2, SSI has about 6 gates and MSI about 40 gates. Therefore, the failure rate per gate has reduced by a factor of 4.5 and the system using MSI would have an MTBF 4.5 times as long as when SSI is used, assuming, of course, that there is a direct replacement of gate-to-gate functions when switching from SSI to MSI. Similar improvement from MSI to large-scale integration of storage elements is predicted. Of course, when these denser packages are used, many external, less reliable interconnects are eliminated and an additional corresponding reliability improvement should be obtained.

7.6 COMPARISON TO RELIABILITY GOALS

The data in Fig. 7.2 are now reduced to failure rate per bit from failure rate per 1,000-bit package. This is shown in Fig. 7.4. Comparisons can now be made to presently available storage elements: first, per 1,000 bits by referring to Fig. 7.2 and second, per single bit by referring to Fig. 7.4. How well does the present storage element compare to these goals?

7.6.1 Bipolar In-house Test Data

Most of the data base that is available is bipolar SSI. It is from accelerated life test data at 125°C derated to 55°C. The calculations are for an upper confidence limit (UCL) of 60 percent. These data are plotted in Fig. 7.5.

As time has progressed, the failure rate has been reduced along a learning curve. This learning curve is projected to continue. Initially, the rate of decline was quite rapid while the process and design were being established. As the product matures, the slope of the learning curve flattens out.

Included in this also is a change in product mix from the large bar RTL ICs to much smaller chip DTL, modified DTL, and TTL. When this happened the average

Table 7.2. Bipolar SSI and MSI Reliability

Circuit	FR at 55°C, %/1K hours	Circuit complexity, avg. no. gates	FR/gate at 55°C, %/1K hours
SSI	0.010	~6	0.0017
MSI	0.015	~40	0.00038

Memory size	MTBF		FR/pkg., %/1K hr/1K bits	FR/bit, %/1K hr
	Mo	Wk		
1 million	X		0.07	0.7×10^{-4}
		X	0.3	0.3×10^{-3}
10 million	X		0.007	0.7×10^{-5}
		X	0.03	0.3×10^{-4}
100 million	X		0.0007	0.7×10^{-6}
		X	0.003	0.3×10^{-5}

Fig. 7.4. Failure rate goals.

complexity was much higher and the failure rate stabilized at a much lower learning curve rate. The data point for 1971 is plotted at 0.009 percent per 1,000 hours.[5] This is for TTL plastic SSI after 95.6 million device hours. These parts had no precap visual or burn-in. Additional testing through 1972 has increased the cumulative hours to 136.5 million device hours and the failure rate is plotted as 0.0088 percent per 1,000 hours.

7.6.2 Bipolar Field Data

Latest field data for TTL SSI for several equipment cases are plotted on Fig. 7.5 as:

1970—0.007 percent per 1,000 hours based on data at Texas Instruments on 397 million device hours for plastic TTL operated in a computer mainframe. Earlier data are averaged into a curve and this curve is extended through these points and passes through a projected point of 0.005 percent per 1,000 hours for 1972.

Now, that is bipolar SSI experience. Where do storage elements fall on the curve? Limited data from the field are just now being established, but one data point is established at approximately 0.01 percent per 1,000 hours for a 256-bit

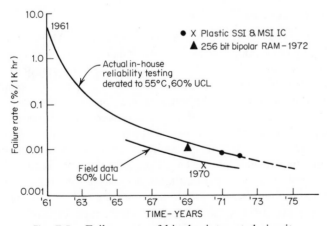

Fig. 7.5. Failure rate of bipolar integrated circuits.

bipolar used in a 128K-word by 33-bit memory operating in a system at Texas Instruments. This point is plotted on Fig. 7.5. These data are based on 85 million device hours. It is anticipated that the failure rate data from this part will travel down the learning curve of the field data, possibly at a faster rate than indicated for the SSI parts, because past experience is retrofitted into the memory chips and because of the regular and repetitive nature of the memory matrix in the chip layout. The time that it takes to travel down the learning curve is unknown. However, an estimate at this time indicates that the 0.005 percent level might be reached in a year or so.

7.6.3 Comparison—Data to Goals

The present 0.01 percent for the 256-bit chip yields a bit failure rate of 0.4×10^{-4} which is satisfactory, from Fig. 7.4, for a 1 million bit memory with an MTBF of almost two months but not satisfactory for a 10 million bit memory because the MTBF is less than one week.

The projected 0.005 percent yields a bit failure rate of 0.2×10^{-4}, which from Fig. 7.4 is satisfactory for a 10 million bit memory with an MTBF of greater than a week.

The 0.001 percent per 1,000 hours predicted for ICs would yield a 0.4×10^{-5} failure rate per bit which is quite satisfactory for a 10 million bit memory with an MTBF of almost two months and a 100 million bit memory with an MTBF of almost a week.

1,024-bit storage elements are already in equipment. When data are obtained, if they too indicated a 0.01 percent per 1,000 hours failure rate, then the failure rate per bit would be 1×10^{-5} percent per 1,000 hours. As shown in Fig. 7.4 this is not quite satisfactory for a 10 million bit memory with an MTBF of one month. Hopefully, enough system data for 1,024-bit units will be available to establish this point in 1973.

When data establish the field failure rate of 0.001 percent per 1,000 hours, this component is then satisfactory for a 100 million bit memory with an MTBF of almost one month (Fig. 7.4).

7.6.4 MOS In-house Tests

A reliability comparison based on the same volume of MOS devices produced as bipolar will help to pinpoint the relative position of MOS reliability data compared to bipolar. This is shown in Fig. 7.6. MOS reached the cumulative productive level in early 1970 that bipolar attained in 1962. Static shift registers of MOS standard p-channel high-threshold aluminum gate process were operated at 125°C for the device base data. 346,000 device hours were accumulated. The devices were cooled under bias to 25° and measured at periodic intervals. The device failure rate was then derated to 55°C in the same fashion and with the same factor as bipolar. Again the calculations are based on a 60 percent UCL.

Two points are plotted. A separate time scale is used for MOS. The failure rate in early 1970 was 0.6 percent per 1,000 hours and the failure rate was 0.08 percent per 1,000 hours in late 1971.[7] Additional testing through 1972 on a more complex

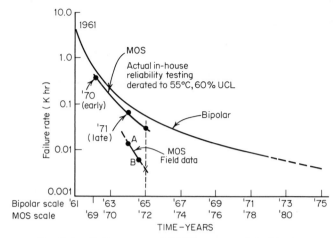

Fig. 7.6. Failure rate of MOS compared to bipolar.

device using the same standard p-channel aluminum gate process has increased the equivalent cumulative device hours to 16.9 million and when related back to the previous static shift register shows a failure rate of 0.05 percent per 1,000 hours. This point is plotted on Fig. 7.6. The failure rate improvement of MOS along the learning curve appears to be somewhat better than was experienced for bipolar ICs in the early production era. It is understood that the bipolar ICs were SSI parts and the MOS are classified as LSI because they contained greater than 100 gates. Therefore, these are positive data that show that more dense parts are being manufactured with the same reliability learning experience as for earlier simpler ICs.

The long-term in-house test data are limited on MOS devices. As previously mentioned, the proliferation of many technologies and many processes has delayed the long-term data on a given device with a given technology.

7.6.5 MOS Field Data

The field data for MOS products are limited for the same reasons as cited previously for the in-house data. However, some reasonably long-term data for storage elements are now beginning to be documented.

Two points are plotted on Fig. 7.6. Point A documents data through December of 1971. This is operating data for memory systems using a 1,024-bit dynamic MOS storage element.[8] These *add-on* memories showed 7 failures in 45.5 million device hours under standard commercial operating conditions. For the 1,024-bit package this is a failure rate of 0.015 percent per 1,000 hours.

Point B is data through mid-1972 on the same type units. 527 million device hours produced 40 failures from 144,000 devices operating in 118 systems.[9] This is a failure rate of 0.007 percent per 1,000 hours.

Additional very early data from a 128K × 33-bit memory system at Texas Instruments using a 1,024 dynamic MOS storage element through 1972 indicates a failure rate of 0.033 percent per 1,000 hours based on 16 million device hours.

7.6.6 Comparison of Data to Goals

The MTBF of a 10 million bit memory system using the 1,024-bit MOS storage element plotted as field data on Fig. 7.6 would be one month (Figs. 7.2 and 7.4).

It is difficult to predict how the field data curve is going to extend in time; however, it seems that a failure rate of 0.001 percent per 1,000 hours could be reached within five years. A 100 million bit memory system, as with bipolar, then would have an MTBF of almost a month (Fig. 7.2).

7.6.7 Error Correction

The MOS and bipolar data just reviewed indicate that 10 million bit memory systems should have an MTBF of about one month. However, if larger systems are required, data are lacking to substantiate an MTBF.

Operation of such a system can proceed, however, by using error correction peripheral circuitry.[10] Such circuitry detects that there is an error in a given number of bits—usually a word, or combination of words. After detecting, other circuitry is provided to correct the error in the bit location in which it was detected.

Error correction techniques allow the memory system to appear error-free to the CPU. This enhances the MTBF of the memory system because the memory system need not be shut down when an error does occur.

Error correction techniques can be on the basis of correcting single bit errors, or they can be extended to simultaneous errors in two bits. Correcting 2-bit errors would enhance the MTBF even further than for single bit errors. However, there is a compromise between the amount of additional circuitry that is required. Significantly expanded circuitry is required to correct 2-bit errors over that used to correct single bits. This does, however, provide a means to implement very large memory systems with satisfactory MTBFs with present storage elements. These systems are much too complicated to describe in this text but interested readers are referred to articles by Hamming[11] and Lignos.[12]

7.7 ADDITIONAL ITEMS TO ENHANCE RELIABILITY

There are several items that are worthy of mention that can be used to assure lower failure rates. These come under the category of tests or inspections that screen the product to select out units that are likely to produce failures or else sample the product to help maintain a level of reliability. Each of these is an extra, requested by the customer through special specifications and adding cost to the basic unit price.

The first of these is an inspection, under magnification, of the complete integrated-circuit chip or bar. This is called a bar inspect when the bar or chip is inspected before mounting, or a precap visual when the chip or bar is inspected after being mounted in a package.

Extensive criteria can be applied to the inspections that occur, and much has been learned from the high-reliability programs of the military on its component screens for the space and missile programs.

This inspection detects major physical defects such as overetching, cracked substrates or oxide, and scratched surfaces. If done as a precap visual it also includes an inspection of the bonding connections to the bar or chip and to the external pins. Inspection at 100X magnification seems to be quite adequate to screen out these major defects and reduce the component failure rate.

The second is an accelerated burn-in operating screen. Here units are put under bias and operated at a higher temperature than the end equipment will experience in order to simulate the early hours of equipment operation. If units are going to malfunction, many of them do it in the first early hours of operation. Therefore, effective burn-in screening can be applied to a product to lower the failure rate of the unit when it is installed in the end system. Again, the burn-in is at extra cost because of the sockets and burn-in racks that must be built to screen the product in this fashion.

The third of these is qualification tests. These are not a screen for reliability but a means of maintaining a reliability level through sampling. Products can be effectively sampled for reliability by subjecting them to a series of qualification tests. These tests are a combination of group A, group B, and group C tests. Through these specified tests, the product can be tested initially to indicate the failure rate level. After this qualification, the product is sampled on a regular basis (e.g., lot by lot) and these samples tested to the same kind of tests to assure that the initial reliability level is being maintained.

Through these methods, the failure rate for storage elements can be lowered from the in-house data previously recorded. Such lower failure rates then should be substantiated by lower failure rates in the field, and correspondingly longer MTBFs for the systems.

7.8 SUMMARY

The important reliability requirements of memory systems established the reliability of the storage elements.

In-house and field data experience indicates that the storage elements are presently quite satisfactory for 10 million bit memory systems and can be enhanced beyond this by the added methods discussed.

Present-day 100 million bit memory systems need error correction systems, but as the reliability trends are established, total dependence on this will diminish, and less peripheral circuitry will be required for this function for a given size memory.

REFERENCES

1. B. T. Murphy, Cost-Size Options of Monolithic Integrated Circuits, *Proc. IEEE,* **452**(12): 1537–1545(December 1964).
2. G. W. A. Dummer and N. B. Griffin, "Electronics Reliability—Calculation and Design," p. 40, Pergamon Press, London, 1966.
3. J. D. Adams et al., Reliability Assessment of Monolithic Microcircuits, "Reliability Handbook for Silicon Monolithic Microcircuits", **4**(May 1969), NASA Contract CR-1349.
4. D. K. Lloyd and M. Lipow, "Reliability: Management Methods and Mathematics," Prentice-Hall, Inc., Englewood Cliffs, N.J., 1962.
5. W. H. Gianelle, L. R. Amon, and J. D. Adams, "A World-wide Reliability Report on SSI Products," TI Brochure CR-107, April 1972.

6. Texas Instruments Internal Document, "Reliability and Engineering Report Summary Sheet," 1-31XX-72, 1972.

7. Texas Instruments Internal Document, "Reliability and Engineering Report Summary Sheet," M-102.

8. AMS (Advanced Memory System) Product Reliability Bulletin of March 1972.

9. AMS Product Reliability Bulletin of July 1972.

10. W. Keister, A. E. Ritchie, and S. H. Washburn, "The Design of Switching Circuits," D. Van Nostrand Company, Inc., New York, 1951.

11. R. W. Hamming, Error Detecting and Error Correcting Codes, *Bell Syst. Tech. J.,* **29**(1950).

12. D. Lignos, Error Detection and Correction in Mass Storage Equipment, *Comput. Des.,* **11**(10): 71–75(October 1972).

8

Fixed Program and Sequentially
Addressed Memory Applications

8.1 INTRODUCTION

MOS and bipolar fixed program (ROM) memory can implement functions such as random logic, code conversion, multiplication, division, exponentiation, and character generation. The first-mentioned application area, random logic, has been discussed in Chap. 6. The other functions will be implemented individually in this chapter. ROMs can be used to provide any function that can be stored in the form of a look-up table. Multiplication and division tables are examples. The generation of characters for display or printing, such as one finds in the matrix printer, CRT display, and scanning billboards, also requires a type of look-up table memory.

The sequentially addressed memory discussed in this chapter consists of shift registers. The semiconductor shift register elements presently available include the bipolar flip-flop, MOS multidevice elements, bucket brigade, and CCDs. These elements are listed in order of memory bit density (bits per sq mm) achievable with present technology. The CCD shift registers show promise of continuing to provide the maximum semiconductor serial memory bit density for some time into the future. The closest competitor for high density would be an MOS RAM memory of the single device per cell type which has been reconfigured for the data-shifting function. Sequentially addressed memory provides the economies of the shift register but is always slower than a RAM memory using comparable technology. The reason for the slowness is the built-in shift time required to permit data access.

8.2 THE ONE-CHIP CALCULATOR FUNCTION

The one semiconductor IC which has made the most significant use of the ROM has been the calculator-on-the-chip. The 1-chip calculator is especially significant because it is the first really widespread application of LSI outside the large computer mainframe. The most functionally complex LSI circuit in large-scale production to date has been the 1-chip calculator. This calculator, using MOS technology, makes extensive use of semiconductor memory circuits to provide data control, program storage, timing generation, random access memory, and input/output encoding on the chip. The calculator function provides addition, subtraction, multiplication, and division. A typical finished calculator product using the 1-chip calculator as the basic component is shown in Fig. 8.1a. The data display in this example is 10 segmented digits. The keyboard is a simple switch matrix. The displays used for these calculators generally require most of the total calculator power.

Display digits variously used are visible light emitting diodes (VLED), cold cathode gas discharge devices, fluorescent devices, liquid crystal devices, and incandescent segmented devices. The display digits are time multiplexed because (1) the number of connections to the MOS/LSI chip is limited and (2) display power dissipation

(a)

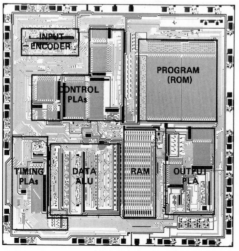

(b)

(c)

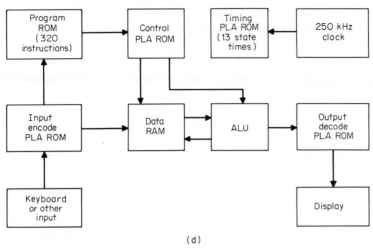

(d)

Fig. 8.1. One-chip calculator: (*a*) operational instrument; (*b*) photo-micrograph of silicon chip; (*c*) 28-pin package for TMS0100 NC series; (*d*) operational block diagram.

is to be minimized. Interface circuits are required between the calculator chip and the display digits to provide the required current/voltage level translation or buffering. The incandescent display is the most difficult to use with the calculator because the thermal inertia of the display does not permit fast multiplexing of multiple digits.

The specific circuit layout of the calculator chip appears in Fig. 8.1*b*. The chip, measuring approximately 230 by 230 mils in size, uses 30 bonding pads around the periphery. Additional peripheral bonding pads, together with other pads within the central chip area, are used as test pads or probe points during production testing. Twenty-eight leads are bonded to the chip for final encapsulation in the plastic dual-in-line package shown in Fig. 8.1*c*.

The circuit philosophy used for the 1-chip calculator provides a unique way of changing the circuit action for new applications. Customizing of the function is readily obtained through a single mask change which programs the several ROMs on the chip. ROMs are used to (1) store the program (up to 320 11-bit instructions), (2) decode the output for the display, (3) encode the input from the keyboard, and (4) determine the master control and timing function sequence on the chip. This mask programming approach permits changing the calculator function to meet a variety of applications while simultaneously retaining the economy of a single, basic chip design that can be mass produced and tested.

The versatility of the mask programming can be illustrated by noting how the output format can be changed. The output programmable logic array PLA ROM can be mask programmed to drive either 7-, 8-, or 9-segment display devices. Since 10 output lines are available, single-line selection is also available for driving a Nixie* cold cathode display. The PLA output decoder may also be programmed for codes such as BCD, excess-3, etc., as desired. The output lines are multiplexed externally to successive digits. Digit-strobe is obtained through 11 control lines which are

*Trademark of Burroughs Corp.

turned on individually for the multiplexing. Each calculator chip provides its output in only one code. By mask programming, the calculator chip can be readily changed in production for a variety of output formats.

The digit-strobe lines define 11 definite time intervals. The digit-strobe line is used to scan-encode the keyboard which is connected to an 11-column by 4-row array. The 11 keyboard columns are manually connected to a selected one of the 4 rows by simple switch action during depression of a key. The 4 row lines are multiplexed into an input-encoding PLA ROM on the chip to determine which key the operator depressed. The scan-encoding of the keyboard is accomplished on the chip. The input-encoding PLA memory can be used to receive a variety of keyboard or other input combinations such as BCD codes.

The control section of the 1-chip calculator consists of another PLA ROM circuit. The control section operates from the program ROM as shown in Fig. 8.1d. Up to 320 instructions are used in the program ROM to provide the microprograms for multiply, divide, add, and subtract. The control PLA ROM uses a simpler OP code that includes shift right, shift left, exchange operands, add, subtract, compare, and clear. A total of 26 1-bit flags are used in the control function. All flags can be set and reset.

The master clock operates at 250 kHz and is located off the chip. A state time is 12 μs. A digit time consists of 13 state times and is nominally 156 μs. The basic timing intervals for the control function are multiples of the digit time. Also a digit time is the amount of time during which each digit of the multiplexed display appears. The timing circuit furnishes a blanking pulse for the output to permit transitions from one digit to the next. The outputs from the timing PLA ROM in Fig. 8.1d connect throughout the chip.

The arithmetic logic unit (ALU) consists of BCD add/subtract circuits. Up to 13 digits can be processed from numbers stored in the 3-digit registers of the data RAM. In addition the status of the 26 flags is stored in the data RAM. Although 13 digits are processed, the output decoding selection permits a display maximum of 10.

The 1-chip calculator represents a very successful application of semiconductor memory integrated into a total circuit function. The high degree of programmability permits tailoring the 1-chip calculator to match specific requirements through a relatively simple ROM mask change. This design is the beginning of many similar digital MOS/LSI integrated memory circuit functions that will appear in the future.

In this chapter specific circuits such as the add/subtract units are presented for design illustration. These circuits are discussed to show general circuit features and are not necessarily the same circuits used in, for instance, the 1-chip calculator.

8.3 ARITHMETIC FUNCTIONS

8.3.1 Add/Subtract

The addition of two numbers A_i and B_i in a bit-by-bit time-serial fashion is implemented with a single full adder. When the subtract function is desired, two full adders are used, as shown in Fig. 8.2. The first adder provides the serial addition

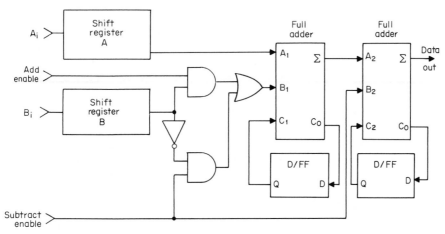

Fig. 8.2. Bit-serial circuit uses two separate full adders.

of A_i and $\bar{B}_i$. The second adder circuit provides the added 1 necessary to complete the 2's complement addition of the two numbers A_i and B_i. In Fig. 8.2 the D-type flip-flops (D/FF) are used to provide the delay carry for successive serial bits. In most circuits the full adder will contain a bit time of delay and therefore the feedback FF is not needed for synchronous operation. In such a case, output terminal C_0 is directly connected to C_1 and C_2, respectively, for the two separate full adders.

When one wishes to implement the add/subtract function for numbers not coded in binary format, the two full adders must be supplemented with special steering logic. The most common format is of course decimal. Figure 8.3 indicates schematically the circuitry necessary to add/subtract binary-coded decimal numbers appearing serially as A_s and B_s. This is a binary-coded decimal (BCD) add/subtract unit. In this circuit the same two full adders appear. But now the shift register with a parallel output is used to gate each BCD digit into the steering logic.

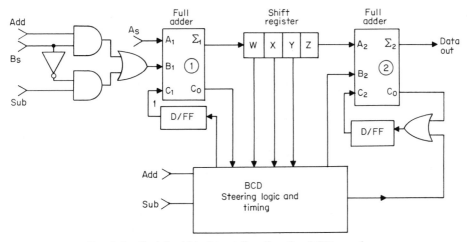

Fig. 8.3. Serial add/subtract function for BCD numbers.

The steering logic determines the carry levels C_1 and C_2 and the data bit B_2 on the second full adder. With three bit values C_1, C_2, and B_2 as output from the steering logic, several combinations are possible for proper circuit operation. Table 8.1 summarizes the special function desired from the steering logic. The special function is in addition to the normal gating of C_o to C_i for the carry levels. A circuit which will provide the desired function is given in Fig. 8.4a. The timing requires digit times of four intervals each. Figure 8.4b defines the four timing pulses T_1, T_2, T_3, and T_4 which define the digit time. ROM can be used together with flip-flops to provide the entire circuit action of Fig. 8.4a. A portion of this circuit has been singled out for implementation with ROM. The full adder section of Fig. 8.4a enclosed within the dotted line is a multiple-level logic function and has been implemented in Fig. 8.5.

Now let's go through the design sequence necessary to specify the ROM equivalent circuit within the dotted line. Input B_1 for the full adder is

$$B_1 = B_s \text{ (ADD)} + \bar{B}_s \text{ (SUB)} \tag{8-1}$$

The sum Σ output from the full adder is the combination of ABC inputs being true either one or three at a time,

$$\Sigma_1 = A_s \bar{B}_1 \bar{C}_1 + \bar{A}_s B_1 \bar{C}_1 + \bar{A}_s \bar{B}_1 C_1 + A_s B_1 C_1 \tag{8-2}$$

These functions are programmed into the ROM of Fig. 8.5. The left column in the matrix develops the product B_s (ADD). The second column in the matrix develops the product $\bar{B}_s$(SUB). These two product terms are summed to yield B_1 as desired. Since the sum Σ_1 value requires B_1, the B_1 line is fed back into the

Table 8.1. Steering Logic Required for BCD Add Function

BCD in shift register W X Y Z	Special steering logic requirement
0 0 0 0	Add 0 to next BCD
0 0 0 1	Add 0 to next BCD
0 0 1 0	Add 0 to next BCD
0 0 1 1	Add 0 to next BCD
0 1 0 0	Add 0 to next BCD
0 1 0 1	Add 0 to next BCD
0 1 1 0	Add 0 to next BCD
0 1 1 1	Add 0 to next BCD
1 0 0 0	Add 0 to next BCD
1 0 0 1	Add 0 to next BCD
1 0 1 0	Add 1 to next BCD
1 0 1 1	Add 2 to next BCD
1 1 0 0	Add 3 to next BCD
1 1 0 1	Add 4 to next BCD
1 1 1 0	Add 5 to next BCD
1 1 1 1	Add 6 to next BCD

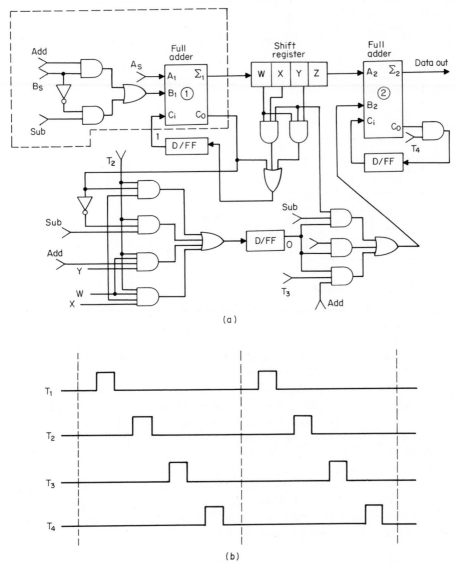

(a)

(b)

Fig. 8.4. (*a*) Detail circuitry for the steering logic and timing for bit-serial BCD add/subtract unit. (*b*) Diagram for timing pulses in (*a*).

product portion of the dual ROM. The third column of the product portion of the dual ROM generates the $A_s \bar{B}_1 \bar{C}_1$ term. This term together with the other three terms specifying Σ above are summed as output to the shift register in Fig. 8.5. Recall that a PLA is defined as two ROMs interconnected to perform the AND and OR function with feedback. This is exactly what the arrays are doing in this case and hence constitute a PLA connection. The circuit implements four-level logic when the B_1 feedback line is considered in Fig. 8.5.

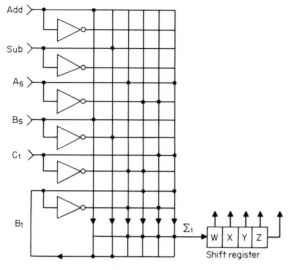

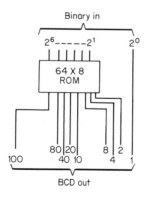

Fig. 8.5. Programmable logic array providing add/subtract control and the first full adder.

8.3.2   BCD Code Conversion

Figure 8.6 is an illustration of an ROM which directly converts a 7-bit binary number into BCD digits. There are 9 bit lines required for specifying the BCD range 0 through 127. The least significant binary digit does not require any decoding and is gated directly through. The ROM of Fig. 8.6 is addressed as 64 × 8 and therefore has 512 bits. The direct conversion of larger binary numbers into BCD becomes inefficient with ROM alone. For larger numbers the ROM becomes too large. For instance, the direct conversion of an 11-bit binary number into 4 BCD digits using a single ROM would require 28,672 ROM bits. If multiple ROMs are used, the direct conversion without using adder circuits requires 12,288 bits.

When the conversion is expanded into a multistep process, the number of ROM bits required is reduced for converting large numbers. One novel technique for converting binary to BCD coding uses a three-step process: (1) convert binary to the BCD excess-X code in individual ROMs, (2) add outputs from pairs of ROMs to obtain a BCD excess-6 code, and (3) utilize the relatively simple adder circuit to convert excess-6 code to the desired BCD.

Fig. 8.6. An ROM that converts a 7-bit binary number into BCD digits.

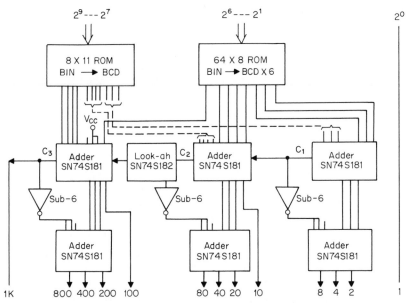

Fig. 8.7. Circuit for converting 10-bit binary to BCD.

This coding scheme is used in Fig. 8.7 for converting a 10-bit binary number to BCD. The BCD output consists of three complete decades plus one bit of the fourth decade. The least significant binary bit is gated directly through to the BCD output since no decoding or sampling is required of it. Two ROMs are used to convert 3 of the most significant bits and 6 of the least significant bits into straight BCD and BCD excess-6 codes, respectively. The 6 binary bits of lower significance are converted to 8 BCD bits. The most significant 3 binary bits can influence the full BCD output range and therefore are coded into 11 binary lines. At the second level the outputs from the two ROMs are added to obtain an excess-6 coded BCD number. A third level of processing is triggered by the carry bit from the excess-6 addition. Whenever a carry is observed, the quantity-6 is added to provide the desired straight BCD code.

In Table 8.2 the parts that could be used to implement the code converter of Fig. 8.7 are listed. This particular configuration converts with a typical conversion time of 75 ns.

**Table 8.2.   Parts Required for Implementing
10-bit Binary-to-BCD Circuit**

Part Number	Function	Quantity
SN7488A	(ROM)	3
SN74S181	(ADD)	6
SN74H00	(GATE)	1
SN74S182	(C-ADD)	1

The technique may be extended to larger numbers using the same design approach. For instance, a 16-bit binary number may be converted to a 4-digit BCD output using 2,300 ROM bits. Using parts similar to those listed in Table 8.2, the conversion time for 16 bits is typically 180 ns. These circuits permit simple layouts since the package count using MSI and LSI parts is low. No clocking is required within the converter.

8.3.3 Multiplication

Multiplication tables may be stored using ROM for fast look-up. The ROM offers the fastest circuits for multiplication available at the present time since the operation is fully parallel. The multiplication function has in the past been delegated to clocked arithmetic units which did not include ROM. With the availability of low-cost ROM we can expect to find an increasing usage of ROM multiplier designs.

The use of ROMs as multipliers is shown in Fig. 8.8. Here a 4-bit multiplier X_4 and a 4-bit multiplicand Y_4 are used to address two ROM look-up tables and provide the desired 8-bit product output function Z_8. In this case the two ROMs, each addressed with 8 bits, are each configured for 256×4 formats. The tabulation at the left of the circuit in Fig. 8.8 is a portion of the multiplication table stored in the ROMs. A total of 2,048 bits are used to provide the binary product for a 4-bit multiplier and multiplicand.

For larger numbers it is economical to divide the product coefficients into most and least significant terms. For instance, the product Z,

$$Z = XY \tag{8-3}$$

when expanded will have these component parts

$$Z = (X + X')(Y + Y') \tag{8-4}$$
$$Z = XY + X'Y + XY' + X'Y' \tag{8-5}$$

These terms can then be conveniently summed with adders. We will follow with design examples.

(a) Multiplication of 8-bit Numbers. A 16-bit product is obtained by working with the 4-bit components of the multiplier and multiplicand:

$$Z_{16} = (X_4 + X'_4)(Y_4 + Y'_4) \tag{8-6}$$
$$Z_{16} = X_4 Y_4 + X'_4 Y_4 + X_4 Y'_4 + X'_4 Y'_4 \tag{8-7}$$

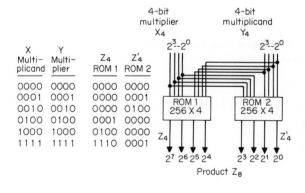

Fig. 8.8. Two ROMs used in 4×4 binary multiplier $(X_4)(Y_4) = Z_8$.

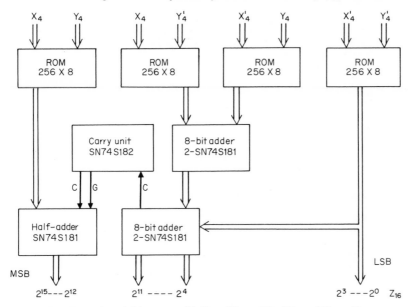

Fig. 8.9. 8×8 binary multiplier $(X_4 + X_4')(Y_4 + Y_4') = Z_8$.

In Fig. 8.9 the product Z_{16} is obtained by processing from four separate ROMs. The four ROMs provide separately X_4Y_4, X_4Y_4', $X_4'Y_4'$, and $X_4'Y_4'$. The least significant term $X'Y'$ is gated directly through to provide the least significant 4 product bits. The addition of contributions from the 4 terms is done in two stages. First the 2 middle terms $X_4'Y_4$ and X_4Y_4' are added. Last, this result is added to the contribution from the least significant term $X_4'Y_4'$ and from X_4Y_4. A carry bit provides the only contribution to the most significant 4 bits of the binary product.

In Fig. 8.9, each of 4 product terms is developed with a memory section organized as 256×8. The product of two 8-bit binary numbers can be obtained using SN74187 bipolar ROM packages. These bipolar ROMs have a typical access time of 50 ns. When used with carry look-ahead adders, the 16-bit product is obtained with a typical 100-ns time.

(b) Multiplication of 16-bit Numbers. The next step in complexity for multiplying two 16-bit binary numbers can be implemented by using the multiplier of Fig. 8.9 as a building block. The resulting circuit indicated in Fig. 8.10 provides a 32-bit product. At the input, the two 16-bit numbers to be multiplied are broken down into two separate 8-bit numbers. The adders, you will recognize, perform the same function as in the previous example. The difference here is that the adders are working with more bits, and the total conversion time will be increased. Table 8.3 is a performance summary of several multipliers using bipolar ROMs and MOS. The 16×16 multiplication using the SN74187 1,024-bit bipolar ROMs has a conversion time of 150 ns. If the TMS2600 MOS ROM is used, the time is approximately 1 μs for all conversions, corresponding to the delay time of the MOS chip. The four-term look-up approach of Eq. (8-3) involves processing the MSB and LSB portions of the multiplier and multiplicand separately. For instance, a four-term look-up for multiplying two 10-bit numbers ($m = 10$) uses 40,960 bits. In general,

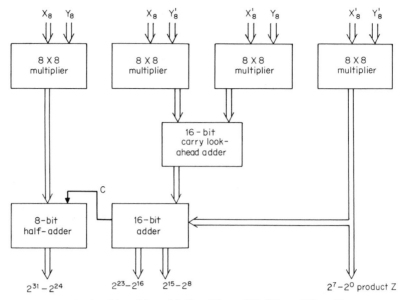

Fig. 8.10. 16×16 multiplier $(X_8 + X'_8)(Y_8 + Y'_8) = Z_{32}$.

the number of ROM bits N required to implement the four-term look-up product is

$$N = m2^{m+2} \tag{8-8}$$

where m is the number of multiplier bits. For a direct look-up the number of memory bits N_D needed increases to

$$N_D = M2^{2m+1} \tag{8-9}$$

These results are summarized in Table 8.4 for multiplication of 8- and 16-bit multipliers. The multiple-term look-up approach to fast multiplication of large binary numbers is clearly advantageous for many situations. The ROM multipliers can provide a speed advantage over other circuits.

8.3.4 Division

A look-up table approach can be applied to division also. For example, let's select an 8-bit number X and divide it by a 4-bit number Y to obtain a quotient Z accurate to 11 binary bits. Using a direct look-up table, the divisor and the dividend would

Table 8.3. Performance Summary of Three Multipliers Using Bipolar and MOS ROMs

Multiplier	MOS TMS2600JC, μs	Bipolar SN74187, ns
4×4	1.0	40
8×8	1.0	76
16×16	1.1	150

Table 8.4.   Comparison of ROM Multiplier
Bit-count

Multiplier	Memory size, bits
Direct look-up 8×8	1M (single ROM)
Four-term look-up 8×8	8K
Direct look-up 16×16	137M (single ROM)
Four-term look-up 16×16 . .	33K

require a total of 12 bits, and the memory would contain 4,096 words of 11 bits each, or about 45,000 bits. To get the bit total down to a more manageable size, a multiterm approach can be used. The divisor X_8 can be separated into most significant and least significant terms.

$$X_8 = X_4 + X'_4 \tag{8-10}$$

and the 11-bit quotient Z_{11} becomes

$$Z_{11} = \frac{X_4 + X'_4}{Y_4} \tag{8-11}$$

and

$$Z_{11} = \frac{X_4}{Y_4} + \frac{X'_4}{Y_4} \tag{8-12}$$

The term X_4/Y_4 contributes to the entire range of the 11-bit quotient. A circuit providing for summation of these ROM outputs is given in Fig. 8.11.

The least significant bits are supplied from the ROM to the right. These bits contribute to the least significant 7 quotient bits and provide components to be added. The X_4/Y_4 requires 2,816-bit storage. The X'_4/Y_4 term requires 1,792-bits. Three adders are used to sum these contributions. A high-speed look-ahead carry can be used to link the three adders and provide a higher-speed generation of the quotient Z_{11}. The look-ahead circuit is connected as shown in Fig. 8.11 when it is used. The binary "point" separates fractional from integer bits.

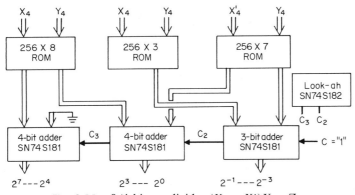

Fig. 8.11. 8/4 binary divider $(X_4 + X'_4)Y = Z_{11}$.

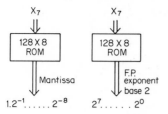

$$1.2^{-1}\ldots\ldots 2^{-8} \qquad 2^{7}\ldots\ldots 2^{0}$$

Fig. 8.12.   Generation of exponential function $Z = E^{x}$.

8.3.5   Exponential Functions

Raising values to an exponential power can be implemented with ROM.   Since the exponential function has such a large range of magnitude, floating-point notation should be used.   The circuit in Fig. 8.12 uses one ROM to generate the 128 different mantissas for a 7-bit number X_{7}.   Another ROM is used to generate the corresponding 128 binary floating-point numbers for the exponent.   Powers of 2 are convenient for the floating-point numbers for the exponent.   Powers of 2 are convenient for the floating-point base, but other bases, such as 10 with BCD, could be used depending upon the particular application.   The output in this case is binary coded to the form $C_{o}2^{k} = Z$.

8.4   SERIAL ACCUMULATOR

The semiconductor serially addressed memory is presently known as an accumulator or recirculating shift register.   In the future we can anticipate other types of semiconductor serially addressed memory.

In this section the serial accumulator using the shift register as an integral element will be expanded upon with a design example for multiplexing.   Figure 8.13 is an example of a serial accumulator.   The semiconductor shift register might contain bipolar, standard MOS, bucket brigade, or CCD type shift elements.

When sequential flow of data is required, the shift register accumulator is very useful.   The shift register section of serial accumulator shown in Fig. 8.13 uses gates at the input for data recirculation and bringing in new data, depending upon the logic level of the recirculation line.   This accumulator may be implemented using conventional MOS shift registers.   There is also a new semiconductor component, important to serially accessed memory of the future.   This is the CCD, or charge coupled device.

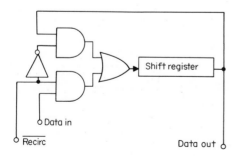

Fig. 8.13.   Serial accumulator.

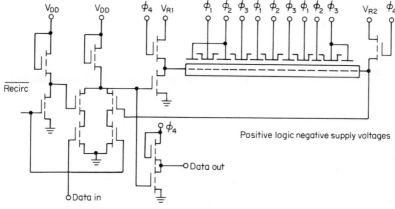

Fig. 8.14.   CCD serially addressed memory.

In Fig. 8.14, a CCD shift register with MOS gates on an n-type substrate is shown. The input selector gates are implemented here with static logic for simplicity in demonstration only. These are dynamic gates in actual practice. This particular CCD shift register is clocked with three phases along the delay path. A fourth phase permits matching levels in time for the desired recirculation and data input/output functions. Voltage reference V_{R1} sets the zero level for the register input. Reference V_{R2} sets the reference potential for the sense node.

The accumulator throughput data rate can be increased by multiplexing shift registers operated in a parallel time mode. This multiplexing operation is implemented in Fig. 8.15 using two shift registers. Multiplexing is required at both the input and output of the time-paralleled shift registers. The recirculate control for the accumulator function uses an OR gate with these techniques. Two shift registers each operating at 2.5 MHz repetition rate can be interleaved to provide output data at two times this frequency. Similarly, four shift registers can be multiplexed to provide a data transfer rate of four times that of the individual register.

Multiplexing of shift registers becomes much easier where multiphase clocking is used. In the next example, time division multiplexing is obtained by interchanging clock connections. The technique used in Fig. 8.16 makes use of the internal sample-and-hold nodes that are contained in each shift register circuit. This is a four-phase shift register circuit. If clocks 3 and 4 are interchanged with clocks 1

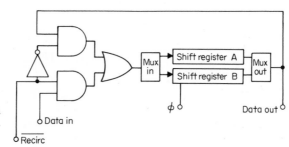

Fig. 8.15.   Multiplexing operation is implemented using two shift registers.

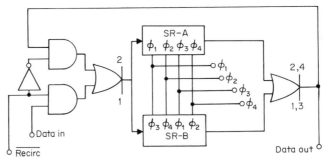

Fig. 8.16. Implementation of time division multiplexing by interchanging clock connections.

and 2 between the two registers, we gate information from shift register A during the first half of the clocking period and from shift register B during the second half of the clocking period. The direct connection for multiplexing in Fig. 8.16 does require special input and output circuitry on the chip for the two shift registers. The TMS3309 is a four-phase shift register which includes the special gating on the chip for this desired multiplexing. For other four-phase shift registers a more complex gating is required at input and output.

The upper portion of Fig. 8.17 shows a more precise connection of two four-phase shift registers connected for multiplexing. Shift register A and shift register B have phases 3 and 4 interchanged with phases 1 and 2 between the two shift registers. Data are clocked into the upper shift register during phase 2, and into

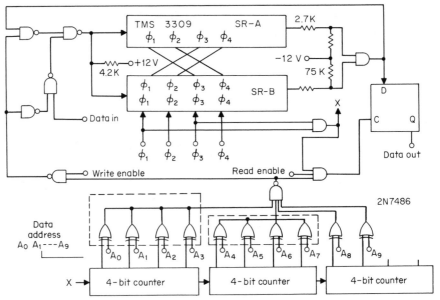

Fig. 8.17. Two 4-phase shift registers connected for multiplexing plus their data address section.

the lower shift register during phase 4. Output data are available at the output Q and are gated from the output back into the input for recirculation through the delay D.

The lowest portion of Fig. 8.17 includes the address section: The data address is derived from a binary counter with 10 bits resolution to specify separately each of the 1,024 states of the shift register combination. The write enable and read enable lines are NANDed with the modulo-1,024 counters. The TMS3309 shift register indicated in Fig. 8.17 operates with a 5 megabits per sec rate. Using the multiplexing techniques here, the data rate is increased to 10 megabits per sec.

8.5 CHARACTER GENERATION

Character generation is one of the best known, most important, and widespread applications for fixed program memory. Ease of programming with ROM for special situations allows the design engineer a choice of characters, coding, character formats, and output formats. Off-the-shelf ROMs are available with standard ASCII coding for row or column output. There are many character formats that may be coded into the ROM. The most popular format is the dot matrix.

8.5.1 Dot Matrix Format

Consider the 5 by 7 dot matrix shown in Fig. 8.18. It's coded for the letters N and S of the English alphabet. If each of the dot positions represents a light-emitting diode, then these same dot positions would have been coded as binary 1 values in the ROM. Similarly, the dark-field display points correspond to bits in the ROM coded with binary 0s. This type of display format applied to a CRT terminal uses the same two-state ROM control for blanking and unblanking the electron beam as it excites the phosphors on the face of the CRT. The output from an individual character generator may be used for either vertical or horizontal scanning of the CRT screen. The characters in Fig. 8.18 are, on the left, vertically scanned with blanking on the beam retrace, and on the right, programmed for faster plotting with display included during retrace. The display format on the left uses a dot matrix character and a raster with blanked retrace. The display matrix on the right uses full pedestal control without blanking on retrace. Both examples use a vertically scanned CRT beam.

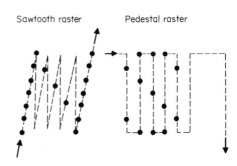

Sawtooth raster   Pedestal raster

Fig. 8.18. 5 × 7 dot matrices coded for the letters N and S.

The dot matrix format is useful for displays on billboards, printhead drivers, and electrostatic fluidic printers, in addition to the CRT display terminal. A 5 × 7 dot matrix provides the minimum resolution necessary for good legibility in presentation of the English alphabet and numbers. Other matrix sizes such as the 7 × 9, 8 × 10, or 12 × 16 may be used to provide special symbols and improved resolution. Each display point uses one bit of ROM storage. To store 64 different characters in a 5 × 7 dot format, 2,240 bits of ROM storage are required. If each character is to be designated with additional information such as the cursor (an intensified area of light under operator control), then the next standard ROM matrix size of 2,560 bits could be selected. If we were to implement this memory with diodes or bipolar logic, a memory of this size would be unreasonably expensive. The drive and sense circuitry required make core memory undesirable for these relatively small capacities. In contrast, MOS ROMs can be purchased off the shelf, or can be customized with a single gate mask. Production quantities can provide significant savings in cost, size, weight, and power consumption.

Figure 8.19 shows a block diagram of a CRT display terminal which includes the MOS ROM character generator. The direct addressing of the character generator is controlled by a serial shift register memory which circulates specified characters for refreshing an entire line to the ROM character select. The clock and position counters provide the timing for the various functions. Any CRT cursor requires special logic control. The circuitry in the circulating memory and the ROM section is shown in Fig. 8.20.

The 6-bit character address to the character generator is determined by the levels from 6 separate shift registers in Fig. 8.20a. This display uses the TMS2400 character generator with row output where the character bits are available for sequential

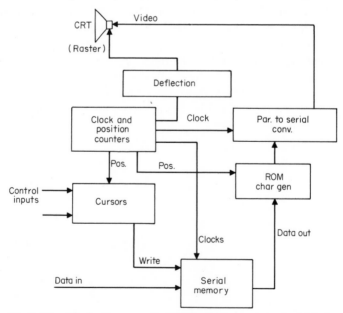

Fig. 8.19. Block diagram of a CRT display terminal which includes an MOS ROM character generator.

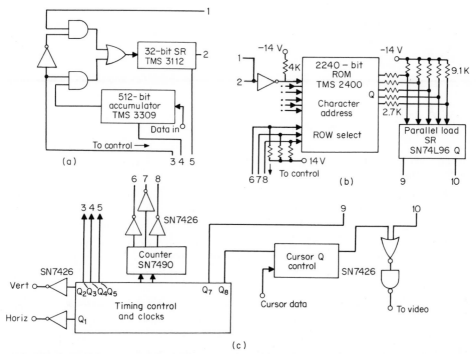

Fig. 8.20. Circuitry in the circulating memory and ROM section: (*a*) shift register and accumulator; (*b*) character address row select and load shift register; (*c*) sequential gating to CRT video amplifier.

display in a horizontal line. The short 32-bit shift registers contain 1 bit for each horizontal character position. The data to the line refresh memory are obtained from a separate circulating memory or accumulator. The larger 512-bit shift register memory contains the information necessary to display one entire CRT frame. To store a display frame with 16 lines of 32 characters each, we will need 6 separate 512-bit accumulators. The row output from the character generator requires that the character be selected and the specific row (one out of 7) be specified. In Fig. 8.20*b* the row select has decoding from 3 input bits to specify separately one out of 7 rows. The row output contains all 5 bits to specify a row of the 5 × 7 dot format character. The five levels are used to parallel-load a shift register which gates these same levels sequentially out to the CRT video amplifier, as shown in Fig. 8.20*c*.

Synchronization of all functions results in a fairly complex clocking requirement for the terminal. The timing control provides separate clocking for synchronizing the vertical and horizontal sawtooth generators, the circulating memories, the row select counters, the parallel-to-serial video signal conversion, and any cursor.

8.5.2 Vector Display Format

The vector display technique can greatly increase the resolution of the displayed character. As shown in Fig. 8.21, instead of generating the absolute coordinates X and Y at each stroke time, only the changes in coordinate locations need be

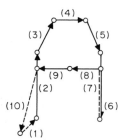

Fig. 8.21. Vector generation.

generated at each stroke time. The character begins at an initial position on the CRT. During the first stroke time, the CRT beam can move in any direction to new coordinates with the beam blanked or unblanked. During subsequent stroke times, the beam can again move to new coordinates with the beam on or off. The initial position of the beam for the second stroke time is the final position of the beam at the end of the first stroke time. Implementation of this vector stroke requires a means of holding a digital-to-analog output voltage at the end of each stroke. This voltage is summed with the change in voltage required during the next stroke period.

Figure 8.22 shows the seven outputs from the series 4100 of MOS ROMs being used to develop the character strokes. Three output lines are used to designate the X coordinate. The seventh bit controls the CRT beam intensity. The upper ROM generates half of the vectors for a character and the lower ROM generates the other half. By using more MOS ROMs, the number of strokes per character can be increased, resulting in a character display with higher resolution.

8.6 ROM ECONOMICS

Table 8.5 provides a design summary example which illustrates the gate reduction possible with ROM. We can replace control logic previously implemented with

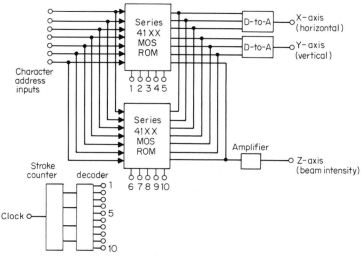

Fig. 8.22. Simplified schematic of a vector generator.

Table 8.5.   Design Summary Example

Replace control logic with ROM

1. Controller originally 2,500 bipolar gates
2. 1,280 of these gates replaced with ROM
3. Assume 12 ROM bits required for each gate function equivalent

Thus, 1,280 gates = 15 1,024-bit ROMs

bipolar integrated circuits by using ROM. The specific example here is a controller originally containing 2,500 bipolar gates. We find that we can replace 1,280 of these gates with ROM. Table 8.6 shows a component cost comparison. Bipolar ICs averaging 5 gates per package are compared in cost for two system production levels—a low-volume system and a high-volume system. Low volume corresponds to about 250 systems, high volume we'll define as being about 2,000 systems. The 1,024-bit bipolar ROM purchased in low volume is priced at $10 per package, corresponding to 1 cent per bit. In high volume this cost presently reduces to approximately 0.5 cent per bit. The average bipolar IC package cost by comparison is 17 cents. Inspection, printed circuit card cost, insertion cost, board checking, connectors, power supply, and other costs increase the assembled package total cost for the bipolar IC case to $1.17 for a total of $585. The manufactured controller cost using bipolar ROM is $463 for low volume and $388 for high volume using the values from Tables 8.5 and 8.6.

The cost per gate equivalent reduces to 23 cents for the bipolar integrated-circuits design, 14 cents for the low-volume bipolar ROM, and 8 cents for the high-volume bipolar ROM. The cost per equivalent gate for the controller of Table 8.6 is further reduced using MOS ROM at the expense of reduced switching speed. For the low-volume production case the cost per gate equivalent using MOS ROM is 8 cents. At the high-volume level the cost per gate with MOS ROM is 2 cents.

Table 8.6.   Component Cost Comparison between Bipolar IC and ROM

Item	Bipolar IC 5 gates/pkg.	ROM 1,024 bits (low volume)	ROM 1,024 bits (high volume)
Part	$0.17	$10.00	$5.00
Inspection	0.05	0.25	0.25
PC card	0.30	0.30	0.30
Insertion	0.10	0.10	0.10
Board check	0.10	0.20	0.20
Connector	0.05	0.05	0.05
Power supply	0.15	0.70	0.70
Other	0.25	0.25	0.25
Pkg. total	$1.17	$11.85	$6.85
Cost per gate equiv.	$0.23	$ 0.14	$0.08

REFERENCES

1. A. C. Davies, Design of Feedback Shift Registers and Other Synchronous Counters, *Rad. and Elec. Eng.*, pp. 213–223, April 1969.
2. R. R. Dussine and R. M. Zieve, Read-only-memories in Computers—Where Are They Headed? *Elec. Des. News*, pp. 24–30, August 1, 1972.
3. A. Hemel, Square Root Extraction with Read-only Memories, *Comput. Des.*, pp. 100–104, April 1972.
4. G. Hoffman, "MOS Character Generators," Texas Instruments Application Report, Bulletin CA-145, January 1970.
5. J. Springer and P. Alfke, Parallel Multiplier Gets Boost from IC Iterative Logic, *Electronics*, pp. 89–93, October 12, 1970.
6. D. M. Taub, A Short Review of Read-only Memories, *Proc. IEEE*, **110**: 157–161(January 1963).

9

Bipolar Random Access Memory
Applications

9.1 INTRODUCTION

Random access memory systems cover a wide range of applications as discussed in Chap. 1. In this chapter, the discussion will center on TTL bipolar random access memory systems ranging from small scratch-pad-size systems of up to 256 words to minicomputer mainframe-size systems with a minimum of 4,096 words. Commercial systems that have cycle times from 70 to 100 ns and operate over an ambient temperature range from 0° to 70°C will be the major concern. Military systems can be constructed from the same system diagrams, but the system packaging would probably have to be unique to the hardware requirement. Obviously, storage elements that operate over the extended temperature range required would need to be selected.

Throughout this chapter speed performance will be indicated in maximum limits that include worst case propagation delays. Typical performance will be significantly better and frequently these times will be indicated.

Memory systems for a variety of applications will have different specifications. For this reason, the general information and the system applications will be discussed in enough detail to provide a thorough understanding of the critical application areas. With this approach it should be easy to proceed with a specific design to a successful conclusion.

Three key subjects will be analyzed in general discussion. These are: loading, timing, and output fan-out. After these subjects have been discussed, specific systems will be designed.

9.2 LOADING

The first subject, loading, is analyzed to determine the load for external drive circuits required in a memory system in addition to the storage elements themselves.

A general diagram for a random access memory system is shown in Fig. 9.1. There is a matrix of storage elements, some form of decoding which may include

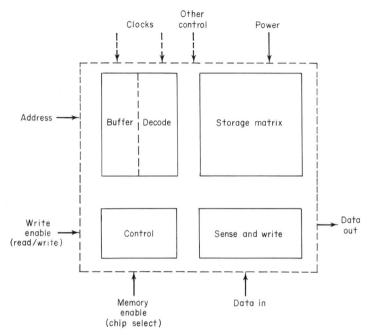

Fig. 9.1. Memory system block diagram.

buffering, circuitry to sense the contents of storage, circuitry to change or write new information into storage, and control circuitry to designate that the storage element is active (enabled) and that it is to be read or changed by writing. Power, of course, must be applied. Major input signals are address, read/write or write enable, memory enable or chip select, and data in. Other control signals and clocks may have to be provided. Data out is the major output. The TTL RAMS that will be discussed will not require clocks for the storage elements. They are static and need not be refreshed or clocked.

These storage elements will be used in combination to build larger memory systems. Proper support circuitry must be selected to provide the necessary drive for the lines. For this reason, one of the main concerns will be the loading on the lines. Of course, as the drive circuitry is provided, there is then a concern for the time relation of the signals. Has delay been added in the signal chain? Are the time relations of the signals at the storage element correct? Before these questions are answered, let's look at the loading.

An expanded memory system is shown in Fig. 9.2. It has N bits with M words. In this simple example there is one word per package; however, the normal case is to have many words in a package. To select the desired word in a package, the required address bits must be directed to each package. Therefore, the address loading will be a function of the number of words and the number of bits. For this reason, the first place that additional drive circuitry will be required is in the address and read/write path.[1] This is indicated by the additional buffer shown in this path in Fig. 9.2.

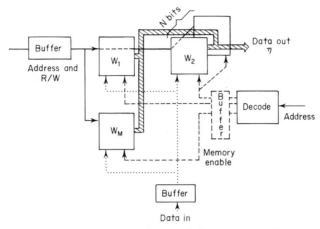

Fig. 9.2.   A simplified expanded memory system.

If the total words required is greater than the words in a package, then separate packages must be selectively activated for the expansion. This is accomplished by using a decoder in the address path, energized by the significant address bits that designate the packages to be selected by the decoder. The decoder selects a particular line out of a number of outputs. Each package connected to this line will be enabled through the memory enable or chip select input on the storage element. To obtain expansion, the decoder had to be inserted in the address path; therefore, the associated time delay must be accepted. The load on the decoder output line is a function of the number of bits in a word. Thus, for larger systems, buffering, as indicated in Fig. 9.2, may also be required on the output lines of the decoder. This adds additional propagation time delay.

The data-in lines will be isolated according to the specific bit in a word.[2] Common lines handle the same bit in all words. The loading is a function of the number of words. Buffering may be required.

The data-out lines will also be isolated by bits, and again, as with data in, common lines handle the same bits in all words.[3] The number of lines connected together is given by the Greek symbol η. The output lines are designed to be connected on common buss lines, and later discussion will point out that loading is most commonly constrained by the ac response rather than the dc limitations. If the data-out line loading is limited to less than the required loads, then common practice is to use multiple sense amplifiers, dividing the loads to a certain maximum per sense amplifier. The data are then combined at the sense-amplifier outputs.

9.2.1   Loading Factors That Occur in a Memory System

Designers will be concerned with the loading on lines that must be energized by drivers or logic gating or sensed with amplifiers. The loading factors for a memory system can be expressed as equations. (In fact, in later figures that describe memory system applications, circled numbers appear on the figures to signify the loading.)

For the address (A) and read/write (R/W) or write enable (WE), Eq. (9-1) specifies the loading.

$$L_A = \left(\frac{W_M}{W_I}\right)\left(\frac{B_N}{B_I}\right) \text{ILF} \tag{9-1}$$

where W_M = total words required
  W_I = words in an individual package
  B_N = total bits required
  B_I = bits in an individual package
  ILF = input load factor

The input load factor, ILF, needs clarification. It is a measure of the type of excitation that an input requires for activation. TTL inputs require a driver with a current sink; the input load factor is the amount of current per input. In like fashion the ILF for other circuits may be the amount of current that must be supplied, or the capacitance that will load the output to determine the ac response. The load on an input line is the number of loads times the input load factor.

Individual package address and read/write must go to each package in parallel. Therefore, from Eq. (9-1), the load L_A on the drivers for these lines is a function of the words and the bits required.

Examining the loading factors shows that the number of memory enable or chip select lines S_L that must be decoded are:

$$S_L = \frac{W_M}{W_I} \tag{9-2}$$

and the load on each decoded line L_D is

$$L_D = \left(\frac{B_N}{B_I}\right) \text{ILF} \tag{9-3}$$

where W_M, W_I, B_N, B_I, and ILF are as for Eq. (9-1). Equations (9-2) and (9-3) are applicable to only a single decode line. Matrix decoding of enable lines will have different loading equations.

Data input line loading is only a function of the number of words given by

$$L_{\text{IN}} = \left(\frac{W_M}{W_I}\right) \text{ILF} \tag{9-4}$$

Data output line loading is different than data in, even though common lines for specific bits from each word are used in the same manner. The load on data output lines is controlled by the number of lines that are connected to the same buss. In order to evaluate this loading, the number of lines η that will be connected together must be known. The number, which is a function of number of words required, is determined using Eq. (9-5).

$$\eta = \frac{W_M}{W_I} \tag{9-5}$$

Examining the loading factors shows that L_A is the largest factor. It is a function of words and bits; the other factors are just a function of either words or bits.

9.3   TIMING

The second subject, timing, concerns the propagation delays that will exist in a memory system.   There are three major times specified for memory systems: access time, write time, and cycle time.   Access time is defined as the time delay from the application of appropriate address signal levels to the presence of valid data signal levels at the output.[4,5]   Write time is defined as the time of application of a write enable signal level so that successful writing of new data is guaranteed in the storage element.   Obviously, the data-in and address signals must be present and in correct time sequence to write data into the selected cell.   Cycle time is the basic time period required by the memory system to accomplish its requested operation,[5] whether it be read then write, or read/read, or write/write, or write/read.

9.3.1   System Access Time

Access times, write times, and cycle times in a memory system are determined by a number of factors.   The various time delays associated with access time in a memory system are shown in Fig. 9.3.   System access time is made up of two portions: that internal to the storage element, and that external in the support circuitry.   The internal access times are characterized by three times.   The first is t_{pA}, which is the access time for valid data at the output after application of address. This is due to the decode and sensing delays in the storage element.   The second is t_{pAE}, which is the access time for valid data at the output after application of memory enable with address present.   The storage element takes time to respond after being enabled because of internal gating delays.   The third is a path determined by the application of the read/write mode signal, write enable.   This has been characterized as t_{pAWE}.   The write enable signal requires special timing which will be discussed shortly, but since this signal is buffered the same as address, it usually is not the determining delay path for access time.   The concern then will be with the first two.

To determine the system access time by including the external delays, two major delay paths can be expressed as

$$t_{pAT} = t_{pBA} + t_{pA} \tag{9-6}$$

or
$$t_{pAT} = t_{pME} + t_{pAE} \tag{9-7}$$

Both equations use the change of data at the address register as $t = 0$.

Equation (9-6) is the system access time t_{pAT} when the time delays are considered from application of address to valid data at the output.   It includes as terms t_{pBA},

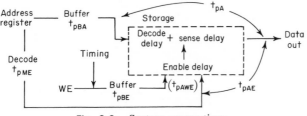

Fig. 9.3.   System access time.

the buffer delay in the address path, plus the internal access time for the storage element t_{pA}.

Equation (9-7) is the system access time t_{pAT} when the time delays in the enable path are considered. The terms t_{pME} and t_{pAE} are the time delay in the decoder for enabling selected storage elements and the internal enable delay, respectively. Of course, if additional sense amplifiers are placed externally, they will contribute additional propagation delay.

Memory system access time will usually be determined by these paths.[6] The longest time delay resulting from Eq. (9-6) or (9-7) will be the worst case access time. Since decoding delays are usually longer than buffer delays, if t_{pA} and t_{pAE} internal to the storage element are specified with nearly equal values, then Eq. (9-7) will usually determine the access time. In the latest storage element designs, it has been an objective to reduce the enable access time to a minimum such that a large delay can be added in the enable path before this path becomes the limiting path on access time.

Before proceeding with the delay paths that determine write time, a critical timing requirement and sense line recovery of the storage element must be analyzed.

9.3.2 Address, Write Enable, Data In, and Data Out Timing

Figure 9.4 shows the signals for address, write enable, data in, data out, and memory enable. To write information into the storage element reliably, the write enable signal must be active, in this case low, for a minimum time t_W while address is present and the storage element is enabled.[5] Also, address must be held for a given time t_{hold} after write enable returns to the high state. Special timing is required on the write enable signal to maintain this time relation at the storage element in the memory system. The data to be written must be set up for a minimum time from write enable and held after write enable; this timing is usually no problem.

There is a sense line recovery characteristic that manifests itself as noise on the output as shown. This is caused by a residual voltage left on the internal data lines.

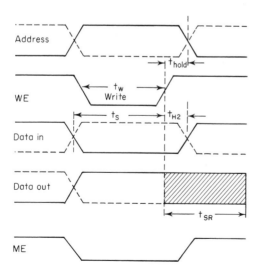

Fig. 9.4. Timing diagram showing signals for address, write enable, data in, and data out.

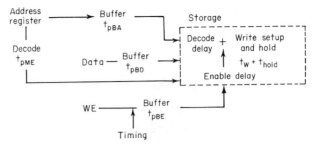

Fig. 9.5. System write time.

It occurs after write enable returns high. This sense line recovery happens in time as a new address is being established, so although there is noise on the output line, it occurs during the time that data are not valid and is a problem only in the most critical speed requirements. The most serious effect is when the memory is enabled, written into, and then without changing address, a check is made on the data by reading them. Here, t_{SR} can be the limiting time in the cycle.

9.3.3   Write Time

The write time, like the access time, is dependent on a number of time delay paths in the memory system.[4] Figure 9.5 identifies these. Again, the time delays are external and internal. In this case, the internal delays of the storage element are t_W and t_{hold}. These are the same times that have been discussed in the previous section. The external delays in several cases are the same as for access time.

One time delay path is that which enables the memory storage elements. The memory cannot be written into until enabled. This was shown in Fig. 9.4. The delay in the enable path t_{pE} is

$$t_{pE} = t_{pME} + t_W + t_{hold} \tag{9-8}$$

which is a sum of the internal delays and the external delay through the decoder in the enable path.

The write enable (or read/write) signal path is another delay path. The storage element will not write information until it receives the control signal to do so. The time delay t_{pWE} is

$$t_{pWE} = t_{pBE} + t_W + t_{hold} \tag{9-9}$$

Again, the internal delays, plus the buffer delay in the read/write signal path, are the major paths for determining write time. The address and data paths could also determine write time; but the address buffering is the same as write enable, while the data buffering is usually less. Obviously, the longest time delay of Eqs. (9-8) and (9-9) will determine the worst case write time.

9.3.4   Cycle Time

The cycle time period must be as long as the longest time of either access or write. Some design margin is usually added to provide a safety factor. However, in many cases, operating time in the cycle may be required for parity check, or other error detection and correction, or for other logical operations. This, then, extends the cycle time beyond the minimum determined from access or write time.

9.4 OUTPUT FAN-OUT

Proceeding with the general discussion, the third subject is output fan-out.

9.4.1 Comparison of Open-collector and Three-state Output Configurations

Normally, two types of outputs shown in Fig. 9.6 are available with TTL RAM storage elements: an open collector output and a three-state output. The memory outputs are shown dotted together on a common output line that feeds a TTL gate or gates. Only one output is low at any one time, and a transistor sinking current to ground is available for each output case. All other outputs are off to allow the output to go high as required for the two binary states. The number of outputs dotted together is η and the capacitance at the output mode is η times the capacitance of each output plus the input capacitance of the driven gate or gates. The values are approximately the same for both cases. Note that in Fig. 9.6a the open collector dot (connection of multiple gates in parallel on the same buss) requires a pull-up resistor, while the three-state output, because it has an active device pull-up, does not. This is the design feature of the three-state output. Even with the active pull-up it has a high impedance state where both totem pole transistors are off, allowing the connection to a common buss line. This is not possible with the standard TTL totem pole output.

The open collector pull-up resistor of Fig. 9.6a has a minimum value and a maximum value calculated from equations that consider the dc conditions when all outputs are high or if one output is pulled low. The maximum resistor value is given by[7]

$$\text{Max } R_L = \frac{V_{CC} - V_{OH}}{(\eta)I_{OH} + N(I_{IH})} \tag{9-10}$$

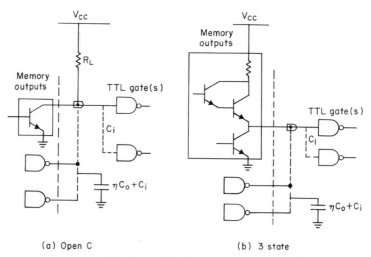

(a) Open C　　　　　　　　　　　　　(b) 3 state

Fig. 9.6. TTL RAM outputs.

and the minimum value by[7]

$$\text{Min } R_L = \frac{V_{CC} - V_{OL}}{I_{OL\ MAX} - (N)I_{IL}} \tag{9-11}$$

where η = number of dotted gates
N = number of driven TTL gates
V_{OH} = minimum high logic level (2.4 V for 54/74 TTL)
V_{OL} = maximum low logic level (0.4 V for 54/74 TTL)
I_{OH} = maximum output current at high logic level ($\leqslant 20\ \mu A$)
I_{OL} = maximum output sink current at maximum low logic level
  (54/74 TTL—16 mA)
I_{IH} = maximum input current at high logic level ($\leqslant 40\ \mu A$ for 54/74 TTL)
I_{IL} = maximum input current at low logic level (1.6 mA for 54/74 TTL)

Equation (9-10) can be used to solve for η, the number of dotted gates allowed. This is

$$\eta = \frac{V_{CC} - V_{OH} - NI_{IH}R_L}{I_{OH}R_L} \tag{9-12}$$

where R_L now is any value that is within the minimum and maximum values. The minimum value of R_L will give the largest allowed η. The minimum R_L is calculated using Eq. (9-11) and the selected TTL specifications.

With an output transistor sink capability of 12 mA and driving one TTL gate, the minimum resistor value is 475 Ohms, and the dc fan-out from Eq. (9-12) is limited to 246 dotted loads. Similar calculations for the three-state output limit the dc fan-out to 256 dotted loads.

Dc fan-out is not the problem: ac fan-out is. It is the transition from low to high level that limits the ac fan-out. The output signal transition from high to low is no problem because of the low impedance discharge path. To understand this, refer to Fig. 9.7.

The capacitance of the dotted loads is represented by ηC_o. For the open collector example of Fig. 9.6a, the capacitor is charged from a circuit with R_L to V_{CC}. At $t = 0$ the voltage across the capacitance is V_{OL} or a small value compared to V_{CC}.

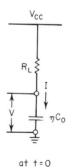

at $t=0$
$V = V_{OL}$

Fig. 9.7. Factors limiting ac fan-out for open-collector outputs.

If the capacitor is allowed to charge fully, it will charge to a voltage of V_{CC} and the charging current would be an exponential function. However, during the time of a voltage change from V_{OL} to a TTL high threshold level of, say, 1.5 V, it is a good approximation to consider the charging current to be constant.

Under these conditions, the time to charge the capacitance ηC_o with a constant current I to a final voltage V_F is

$$\Delta t = \frac{V_F - V_{OL}}{I} (\eta C_o) \qquad (9\text{-}13)$$

Now, to a first approximation

$$I = \frac{V_{CC} - V_{OL}}{R_L} \qquad (9\text{-}14)$$

and

$$\Delta t = R_L (\eta C_o) \frac{V_F - V_{OL}}{V_{CC} - V_{OL}} \qquad (9\text{-}15)$$

Therefore, the charge time is a function of the load-resistor load capacitance time constant. This is not true for the three-state output. Refer to Fig. 9.8. The current is limited only by the characteristics of the output pull-up transistor: that is, the amount of drive, the current gain, and the output impedance. Therefore, to a first approximation, the time for charging the capacitance ηC_o is given by Eq. (9-13) and is limited only by the constant current that can be supplied. For many three-state TTL RAMs, the output current is still 10 to 12 mA when the output voltage is 2.4 V and the average charging currents are 20 to 50 mA.

One can calculate the ac response load limit for the open collector by using Eq. (9-15) and solving for η. If R_L is the minimum value of 475 Ohms, and C_o equals 6 pF per output, the ac fan-out for the open collector output is limited to 20 if the output voltage is to change 1.5 V in 20 ns.

By using Eq. (9-13), the tri-state output would have a much larger limit of 40 if the average charging current is assumed to be 20 mA. Stated another way, if there are a given number of loads to be driven (representing a given capacitance), then the output response from low to high would be much faster with the tri-state output than with the open collector.

For the system applications in the remainder of this chapter and in Chaps. 10 and 11, the 20 ns will be assumed as adequate and no comment will be made on output loading unless the fan-out exceeds the above limits.

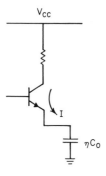

Fig. 9.8.   Factors limiting ac fan-out for three-state outputs.

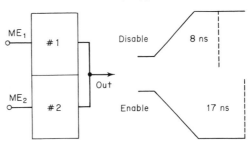

Fig. 9.9. Transient reliability of three-state outputs.

9.4.2 Reliability of Three-state Output

Dc Case. The question naturally arises: Is there a reliability problem with the three-state output? With the dc case, in the event that two memories are activated on a buss simultaneously with one active high and another active low, there is a current limit designed into the output stage, such that catastrophic failures will not occur. Of course, this condition does cause an error and must be located and eliminated, but the parts will not be destroyed. What about the transient case?

Transient Case. Figure 9.9 shows two storage elements dotted at the output. First of all, element number one is active and element number two is inactive. Now consider number one is disabled and number two is enabled. The number one element is disabled from the buss line in about 8 ns. The number two element is not enabled to the buss line until about 17 ns. Assuming the memory enables are activated simultaneously, there should be no short circuit generated between units as long as the skew between memory enables is maintained at less than 8 ns.

These general discussions have now established tools that can be used to guide the application of the storage elements in memory systems.

9.5 APPLICATION OF THE STORAGE ELEMENTS IN MEMORY SYSTEMS

9.5.1 Memory Systems up to 256 Words

The first memory system requirement is a small scratch-pad memory, 128 words by 16 bits. A cycle time less than 100 ns is desired. To implement this system, a storage element organized less than 256 words in a package must be used. A common element is a 64-bit TTL bipolar RAM (SN7489). In Chap. 4 a picture was shown of the integrated-circuit chip and some of the characteristics were discussed. These will be summarized again so that all parameters are understood before the application begins.

Organization	16×4 (16 words by 4 bits)
Decode	Fully decoded
Signal levels	TTL logic levels
Output	Open collector
Access time t_{pA}	< 60 ns
Access time t_{pAE}	< 50 ns
Power dissipation	375 mW total
	5.85 mW per bit
ILF	1.6 MA

Terminals
  4 address
  4 data in
  4 data out
  WE (read or write)
  ME (memory enable)
  V_{cc}
  GND

A block diagram is shown in Fig. 9.10. The storage element is in a 16-pin package. The inputs are buffered so the load is one standard TTL and are also clamped to suppress noise. The four data outputs have a standard TTL open collector output.

With the full decoding, each of the 16 words is selected with a straight 4-bit binary address. The maximum access time is less than 60 ns from address application, and 50 ns from enable application if address is present. Typical times are 35 and 30 ns, respectively. With these two access times nearly the same value, it becomes quite likely that the memory enable path delays will determine access time rather than the address path. The typical power dissipation is 5.85 mW per bit. Internal delays occur in the input buffers and 1-of-16 decode. The memory enable logic is implemented in the buffering circuitry and read/write control is on the output.

Table 9.1 lists the condition that exists at the storage element output for given signals on memory enable and write enable. In some cases outputs of storage elements that are not enabled can cause erroneous signals in a memory system.[4,5] Therefore, the conditions are checked as shown in the following examples.

To write into storage, write enable and memory enable must be low and, at that time, the complement of the data appears at the output. Of course, normally in storage applications, these data are not used at this time and are not necessary. But there may be cases where the memory could be used for a register at this time and this could be an advantage.

To read out the storage, and it is a nondestructive read, memory enable is low and write enable is high. The complement of the data stored is presented at the output. To disable the storage element, both memory enable and write enable should be high. In this mode the output condition is high allowing other memories that have been coupled on the output to control the condition of the bit lines.

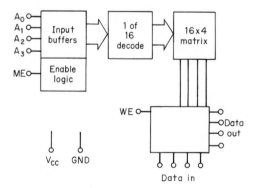

Fig. 9.10. Block diagram of a 64-bit TTL RAM (SN7489).

Table 9.1. Condition of Output for Specific Enable Control Signals (64-Bit RAM)

ME	WE	Operation	Output
L	L	Write	Data in
L	H	Read	Data stored
H	L	Inhibit store	Data in
H	H	Do nothing	H

With memory enable high and with write enable low, corresponding to inhibiting all storage elements except the ones that are enabled for writing, the output condition is the complement of data in. Therefore, the output for a given bit line is in concert with the bit line condition of the storage element that is enabled and receiving data for storage.

9.5.2 Checking the Loading

The system has 128 words and 16 bits; therefore, $W_M = 128$ and $B_N = 16$. The storage element has $W_I = 16$ and $B_I = 4$. The ILF equals 1.6 mA for one standard TTL load. With this information and the previous equations, the loading factors are calculated.

The address line and write enable (R/W) line loading is, from Eq. (9-1),

$$L_A = \frac{128}{16} \times \frac{16}{4} \times \text{ILF} = 32 \text{ ILF} \tag{9-16}$$

Or the driver must be able to drive 32 standard TTL loads. Correspondingly, from Eq. (9-2), the number of memory enable lines to be decoded is

$$S_L = \frac{128}{16} = 8 \tag{9-17}$$

because only one memory enable input is available.

In the diagrams this load will be identified with a triangle around the number, e.g., $\triangle 8$. Other loads will be circled.

The loading on the decoded lines is

$$L_D = \frac{16}{4} \times \text{ILF} = 4 \text{ ILF} \tag{9-18}$$

from Eq. (9-3), or four standard TTL loads.

The data-in line load is eight standard

$$L_{IN} = \frac{128}{16} \times \text{ILF} = 8 \text{ ILF} \tag{9-19}$$

TTL loads using Eq. (9-4) and the eight outputs are paralleled onto a buss line as defined in Eq. (9-5):

$$\eta = \frac{128}{16} = 8 \tag{9-20}$$

9.5.3   128 × 16 Memory System

Address Line Buffering.   Keeping in mind the load factors, the memory system can be expanded in two fashions: One is to buffer the address lines and the other is to parallel address registers.   The block diagram in Fig. 9.11 shows the address line buffering.

This system uses a 3-to-8-line decoder, one of 8 memory enable lines low.   Each decode line has a load of 4, per Eq. (9-18), to provide the 16 bits for each word. The 4 addresses going to all units in parallel are buffered by a driver which can drive up to 37 loads, well within the 32 required.   A buffer delay has been introduced in the address line and a decode delay in the memory enable line.

The write enable signal is also buffered by the same type driver as address, but at the same time it is used as a gate to control the write enable timing.   A board enable signal connects to the 3-to-8-line decoder (SN74155) and the write enable gate.   All ME enables are high when board enable is high and no storage elements are selected.

The address registers feed the address and read/write control signals to the drivers.   An extra register stage is available (SN74175) and its output can drive another board to implement a 128 × 32 system.   Or the complement of the address can be used to implement a 256 × 16 system by selecting the second board through the board enable.

A similar register to the address register can be used to drive the load of eight on the data-in lines without additional buffering.

The data outputs have 8 lines in parallel on each bit line buss.

Paralleling Address Registers.   The past discussions have considered supplying the address line load with a buffer.   This load can be supplied another way—by paralleling address registers.   This provides the address fan-out without a buffer delay, but does require additional loading on the source driving the register.   In addition,

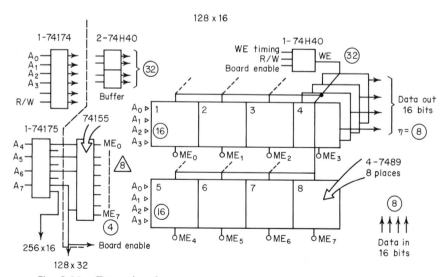

Fig. 9.11.   Expansion for a memory system using address line buffering.

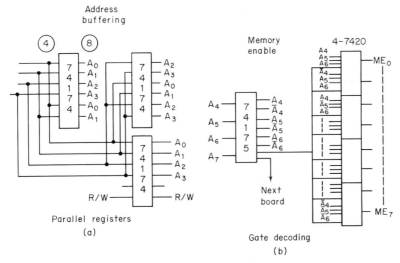

Fig. 9.12. Parallel address buffering and gate decoding.

if maximum speed performance is the objective and the decoder delay limits the performance, the memory enable decoding can be obtained with only one gate delay.

Both of these concepts are shown in Fig. 9.12. Instead of the buffer driver of Fig. 9.11, two more address registers are added for the addresses $A0$ to $A3$ as in Fig. 9.12a. Each register drives 8 loads times the address source fan-out of 4 results in satisfying the address loading of 32 for L_A in Eq. (9-16).

Since the address register used for $A4$ to $A7$ has both true and complement outputs, these could have been supplied to dual 4-input gates to provide the 1-of-8 memory enable decoding with only one gate delay. This is shown in Fig. 9.12b.

Performance Comparison. How do the two systems compare? First, worst case access times are shown in Fig. 9.13.

Refer to the access times using standard TTL [Fig. 9.13(I)]. The fastest times (70 ns) are obtained using case A, the parallel registers, and the gate decode. Note

Memory system	Access time	Address path, ns			Enable path, ns		
		t_{pBA}	t_{pA}	t_{pAT}	t_{pME}	t_{pAE}	t_{pAT}
I. Standard TTL							
A. Parallel registers		0	60	60	20	50	(70)
B. 74H40 Buffer 74155 Decode		12	60	72	34	50	(84)
II. Schottky TTL							
A. Parallel registers (74S20)		0	60	(60)	5	50	55
B. 74S40 74S138		7	60	(67)	15	50	65

Fig. 9.13. Access times of 128 × 16 memory system.

Times Memory system	Write, ns	Access, ns	Cycle, ns
I. Standard TTL			
A	65	70	75
B	79	84	90
II. Schottky TTL			
A	52	60	65
B	60	67	75

Fig. 9.14. Write, access, and cycle times for 128×16 memory system.

the worst case path is the enable path. Similarly, in case B, using the decoder and address buffer, the worst case access time is determined by the enable path. In this case, the external delay by the decoder is 34 ns of the 84-ns total. There is greater than a 15 percent improvement in access time by using parallel buffering in the system.

Additional improvement in access time can be obtained using faster peripheral circuits. As an example, in Fig. 9.13(II), the access times calculated from data sheet specifications are listed, using faster TTL circuits of similar types. The improvement in access time is 15 to 20 percent. Again, there are worst case times, and typical times are 60 percent of worst case times. Also, packaging delays are not included. The improvement between case A and case B is now only 10 percent, but note that the access time is now determined by the address path rather than the enable path because the decode delays have been reduced significantly.

A similar check is made on write time using the internal delay of t_W plus t_{hold} equal to 45 ns. These, along with the previous access times and resulting cycle times, are shown in Fig. 9.14.

The improvement in write time is again 15 to 20 percent between the parallel registers and the address buffer and 15 to 20 percent as a result of faster peripheral circuits. Note also that cycle times, with design margins added, are determined by access time and not write time. Even with packaging delays added, the system should meet the 100-ns cycle requirement.

Figure 9.15 summarizes the power used and the number of packages used (registers are included) as a further means of comparing the standard TTL systems. Recall that the A system is the fastest parallel register system and the B system is the buffer and decoder. More packages and power had to be used to get the increased speed. Also included are the packages and power used for a 128×32 or 256×16 system.

System	128×16		256×16 128×32	
	No.	P_D	No.	P_D
A	$43\frac{1}{2}$	13.7	88	27
B	41	13.4	81	26.2

Fig. 9.15. Package count and power dissipation of the system.

Later a comparison will be made with the packages and power used for another 256×16 system.

9.5.4 Memory Systems Larger than 256 Words

The requirement is now for a memory system which has 256 or more words. Many of the basic details stated in the general discussion have been applied and explained for the 128×16 system. Therefore, in the remaining applications, the memory system performance in many cases will be stated without repeating the detailed explanation. Large mainframe memories are covered in Chap. 11, thus the size in this chapter will be restricted to minicomputer mainframe size.[8,9,10]

Storage Element Characteristics. These systems can be implemented with a storage element that has 256 words or more. A common element is a 256-bit TTL bipolar RAM (SN74200), which was also shown in Chap. 4. Again the characteristics are summarized:

Organization. . . . . 256×1 (256 words $\times$ 1 bit)
Decode. . . . . Fully decoded
Signal levels . . . . TTL logic levels
Output . . . . Three-state output
Access time t_{pA} . . . . < 60 ns
Access time t_{pAE}. . . . . < 30 ns
Power dissipation. . . . . . . 500 mW total
                             1.95 mW per bit
ILF . . . . 1 mA

Terminals
  8 address
  1 data in
  1 data out
  WE (read or write)
  3 ME (memory enable)
  V_{CC}
  GND

A faster Schottky version of this same storage element (SN74S200) starting into production has the following improved speed/power characteristics:

t_{pA} . . . . < 50 ns
t_{pAE} . . . . < 35 ns
P_D . . . . 435 mW per total
                            1.7 mW per bit

Units built with oxide isolation have a similar performance.[11] These parts may be substituted in the following application for even faster times, but for the present the standard TTL unit will be used.

Several important differences are apparent with this storage element. The first is the access time. Even though the bit density is now 256 bits, the address access time is still not greater than 60 ns; what is more important, the enable access time is now only half this value. With the enable access time one-half that of address access, there will be fewer occasions where the enable path will determine the access times. There are three active low memory enable decode inputs rather than one for the previous storage element. These will aid in expanding into larger memory systems. Another difference is the low-level input current of 1 mA instead of 1.6 mA for a standard TTL gate. This means 40 percent more memory can be driven by the standard TTL support circuitry. There is one data output which has a three-state output instead of an open collector—again, an improvement. Another improvement is that the power per bit has been reduced by a factor of 3 compared to the previous storage element. All these are pointed out as the design directions that are significant improvements for the implementation of a system.[2]

Storage Element Block Diagram. As shown in the block diagram (Fig. 9.16), 5 of the 8 input address binary bits go to a 1-of-32 decode which selected 32 rows of 8 bits. The 8 bits are decoded by column with a 1-of-8 decoder operating from the remaining 3 input binary address bits. The enable logic is now in the output along with the sense and write circuitry. As before, all logic levels are TTL compatible.

This storage element uses diode coupling to the digit lines from the flip-flop cell as discussed in Chap. 4,[12] rather than a multiple-emitter cell,[13] which is used in the 64-bit RAM.

A check of the output conditions for various states of write enable and memory enable logic signals is made by referring to Table 9.2.

All memory enable inputs must be low, and write enable must be low to be in the write mode. The output is then in the three-state *off* or high impedance stage. In the read mode, all memory enable inputs are low and write enable is high. The output condition is then the complement of the data stored. With at least one memory enable high, the storage is inhibited and the output is in the three-state *off* condition—no matter what the state of write enable.

Storage Element Timing. In the system, the timing that was discussed for the storage element must be observed. t_W for the SN74200 is 35 ns and t_{hold} is 15 ns. These time relations control the special timing that must be put on write enable

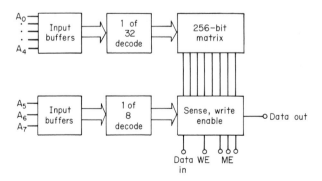

Fig. 9.16. Block diagram of a 256-bit TTL RAM (SN74200).

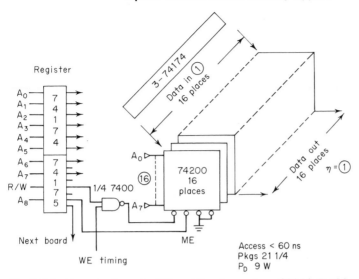

Fig. 9.17. Organization of a 256 × 16 system using a 256-bit RAM.

in relationship to address. For the 128 × 16 system, this timing input was shown as write enable timing. In the systems that follow this identification is continued. One very simple way of generating this timing is to use a monostable multivibrator (SN74121) triggered from the clock that times the registers. Another way, of course, is to generate phases from a master clock and use logic to provide the timing.

9.5.5 256 × 16 Memory System

Figure 9.17 shows the organization of a 256 words by 16-bit system using 16 storage elements and one 2-input gate for the memory proper. Four packages with six D-type flip-flops are used as address and data-in registers. A quad D flip-flop with complementary outputs (SN74175) completes the register. There is no buffering or decoder delays. This 256 × 16 system represents quite a saving in packages and power compared to the 256 × 16 system using the 64-bit RAM packages, about one-fourth of the packages and one-third of the power with improved performance. Of course, the use of the 64-bit RAM was because of a 128-word requirement which cannot be met with the 256-bit RAM without wasting capacity.

Table 9.2. Output Conditions for Specific Enable Control Signals (256-bit RAM)

ME*	WE	Operation	Output condition
L	L	Write	High Z state
L	H	Read	Data stored
H	X	Inhibit	High Z state

*L—All ME inputs low.
H—At least one of ME inputs high.
X—Don't care.

This system has the memory enable signal available for another board so that a 512-word by 16-bit memory with 60-ns access time can be implemented by just paralleling address registers. So much for the small memory; now a larger memory system is required.

9.5.6 XYZ **Decode**

As larger memory systems are designed using the individually packaged storage elements with more than one enable input, a choice must be made as to how many memory enable inputs are going to be used for decoding. For the 256-bit RAM only one may be used, or only two, or all three. Our choice is to design a system which uses all three. Such a decode system is usually called an XYZ decode and is illustrated in Fig. 9.18. One enable input is associated with each axis and each axis has various planes of units each with a memory enable input associated with it. The plane contains a matrix of storage elements. The X selection memory enable input not only selects a row of storage elements but it selects a full plane of storage elements determined by this row selection. Similarly for Y, the column selection by Y memory enable input determines a full plane of storage elements. The Z memory enable selection picks the full plane of Z storage elements to be activated. This Z plane contains the previously selected X row and Y column selected devices. Thus, the individual storage element, at the intersection of the X, Y, and Z plane, is activated.

The total number of storage elements to be decoded is a function of the number of planes decoded for each axis. Each plane parallel to the plane of the axis requires a decode line. If there are L planes parallel to each axis, then the total elements decoded are

$$\text{Total decoded elements} = X_L Y_L Z_L \tag{9-21}$$

Now this is quite a powerful technique, but care must be exercised because the load on the memory enable inputs increases rapidly. The load on each memory enable driver is the number of devices in the plane for that enable input. For example, if L_1, L_2, and L_3 lines are decoded respectively for the X, Y, and Z planes, then the load on the respective driver is

$$X \text{ load} = Y_{L2} Z_{L3} \text{ILF} \tag{9-22}$$

$$Y \text{ load} = X_{L1} Z_{L3} \text{ILF} \tag{9-23}$$

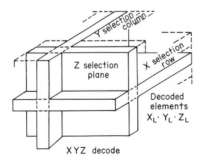

Fig. 9.18. XYZ decode.

Table 9.3. Application of XYZ
Decode to a Square Matrix

L	Load	Elements*	Words
2	4	8	2K
4	(16)	64	16K
8	64	512	128K
16	256	4,096	1,024K

*256×1.

and
$$Z \text{ load} = X_{L1}Y_{L2}\text{ILF} \tag{9-24}$$

ILF is again the input load factor and will be 1 mA for the 256-bit RAM.

Now what about a square matrix where the decoded lines are equal for each axis? Table 9.3 shows the loading.

The driver load is shown in the column titled "load." With only 16 decode lines per axis, one million words can be selected using a 256×1 storage element. The load per plane is 256 and has to be buffered accordingly. The system selected for this discussion is one where the load on each enable is a fan-out of 16 or 16 mA using the 256-bit RAM. This allows the use of standard TTL decoders without additional buffering. It provides up to 16 thousand words.

9.5.7   16K Word System

The matrix arrangement of storage elements to be assembled on a board to allow selection of up to 16K (16,384) words is shown (Fig. 9.19). In addition, for memory

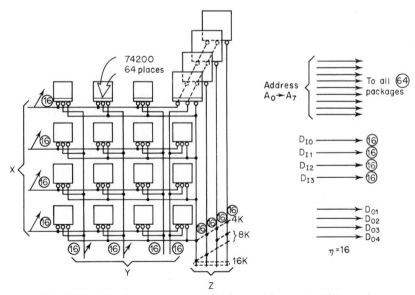

Fig. 9.19. Matrix arrangement which provides up to 16K words.

expansion, each board would contain identical segments of storage elements, driver circuits, logic gates, and decoders.

There are 64 storage elements arranged $4 \times 4 \times 4$. Each Z plane represents 4K words times 1 bit. This means that one data-in line and one data-out line serve each Z plane. With this arrangement, the organization of storage elements on the board can then be changed very easily. The circled numbers are the loads of devices on each line. Since the 256-bit RAM ILF is 1 mA, these numbers represent milliamperes of load. All Z memory enable lines connected together make the board a 4K-word by 4-bit with a Z load of 64. Pairs of Z memory enable lines connected together make the board an $8K \times 2$-bit with a Z load of 32. Activating each memory enable line separately makes the board a $16K \times 1$-bit with a Z load of 16.

The address and write enable must feed to all packages in parallel and, therefore, have a load of 64. The four data-in lines have a load of 16. The collector dot on each output bit line is 16.

9.5.8 4K × 4 Board

This matrix with the peripheral circuits is shown in the block diagram of Fig. 9.20. Two gates of a quad 2-input gate are paralleled to supply the drive for the address and write enable lines that feed all 64 packages. Write enable timing is ANDed with the write enable signal. The buffer delay is 20 ns.

Two address bits are decoded to four lines for both the X and Y axis, as previously discussed for Fig. 9.19. A board position for a similar decoder, which can drive 16 mA and has a 34 ns decoder delay, is provided if the board organization were to be changed. The organization chosen for the board is $4K \times 4$, and this decoder

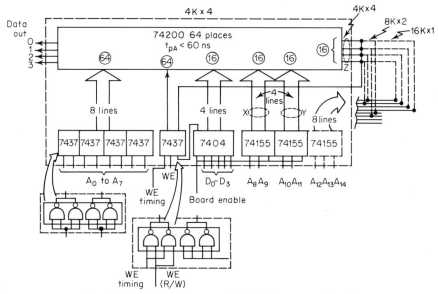

Fig. 9.20. Block diagram of 4K × 4 memory board.

Package	Type	Count
74200	Storage element	64
7437	Quad 2-input buffer	5
7404	Hex inverter	1
74155	Decoder	2
		72

Fig. 9.21. 4K × 4 package count.

is not required because all Z lines are driven in parallel. However, examples are shown for the 8K × 2 and 16K × 1 organizations if the additional decoder is used. For 16K × 1, the decoder (SN74155) shown is used as a 2-to-4-line decoder with the four output lines driving the Z lines. For the 8K × 2 organization, it is used as two 1-to-2-line decoders operating in parallel to handle the load. The 4K × 4 enable, identified as board enable, is inverted before it passes through the parallel SN7437 gates. At the same time the X and Y decoders are selected. All storage element enables are high if board enable signal input is at the high level. Therefore, this board is enabled when the input signal is at a low level.

The board is in a read mode when write enable is at a low level and, obviously, in the write mode when the level is high.

The four data-in signals are buffered through inverters. Also four data-output lines are provided due to the 4K × 4 organization. If the board is changed in organization, pairs of lines are dotted together for the 8K × 2 organization. All four lines are dotted together for the 16K × 1 organization. Care must be taken to consider the ac response desired on the 16K × 1 board organization because there are 64 dotted outputs. If these are dotted again, the load capacitance is greater than 640 pF and the ac response can limit the system performance.

The access time for valid information at the output after application of address to the board is 80 ns worst case. The write time is within this time so that system cycle time can be set on the basis of access time.

All the address and write enable buffer (SN7437) inputs are either two or four standard TTL loads. Broad enable has a load of three standard TTL loads. Other inputs are one standard TTL load. The board consists of 72 packages (Fig. 9.21) and dissipates 32.8 W of power.

9.5.9 4K × 16 Memory System

Further expansion is now possible with the use of the 4K × 4 board. A 4K × 16-bit memory is required for a minicomputer mainframe.

The 4K × 16-bit memory has four boards as shown in Fig. 9.22. Identical units are used for the four positions. Each position has its own 4 bits of data in and 4 bits of data out. The inputs common to all boards are the address lines, board enable, write enable, and write enable timing, which are provided with additional buffering. The addition of this buffering, of course, is a disadvantage because it increases the access time of the 4K × 16-bit memory to 100 ns from an 80-ns access for the boards by themselves. 292 packages are used for the memory system with 131.6 W power dissipation. This is 2.02 mW per bit compared to the storage ele-

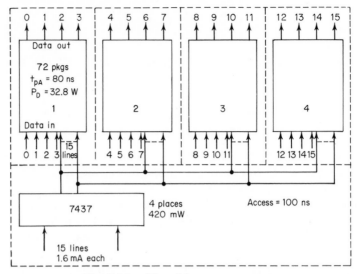

Fig. 9.22. 4K $\times$ 16 memory system.

ment per bit power dissipation of 1.95 mW. This illustrates the small power contribution by the peripheral circuitry. The major power dissipation is from the storage element itself and indicates again the emphasis placed on reducing the power dissipation per bit when designing the storage elements. Obviously, larger memory sizes to 32K words could be built with these boards with the extra decoder in place.

9.5.10 Higher Performance 4K $\times$ 16 Memory System

There is a simple modification that can be made to improve the performance: Replace the standard TTL with faster (Schottky) modules. This is shown in Fig. 9.23. For example, the SN7437 can be replaced with the SN74S40. The SN74S04

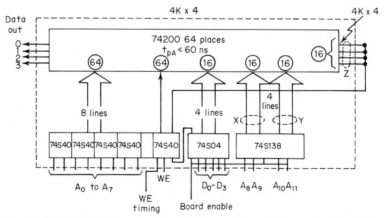

Fig. 9.23. Modification of 4K $\times$ 4 memory board (shown in Fig. 9.22) to improve performance.

Package	Type	Count
74200	Storage element	64
74S40	Dual 4-input buffer	5
74S04	Hex inverter	1
74S138	Decoder	1
		71

Fig. 9.24.   4K × 4 Schottky package count.

replaces the SN7404, and one SN74S138 replaces two SN74155 because the SN74S138 is a true dual 2-to-4-line decoder with separate address lines.   Each SN74S40 has a maximum output current specified at 60 mA.   It is being extended a bit to drive the 64 mA required, but this is no problem.   A dual 4-input gate (SN74S40) is replacing a quad 2-input gate (SN7437).

With these package changes, the board package count is now 71 packages (Fig. 9.24), the board access time is reduced by about 20 percent to 67 ns, but the power dissipation has increased by 0.4 W to 33.2 W.

The 4K × 16 memory is built the same as before (Fig. 9.22).   The dual 4-input Schottky buffer gate (SN74S40) is also substituted for the additional address and enable line buffering for the 4K × 16 memory system.   However, eight packages are used instead of four, but, because a package was saved per board, the number of total system packages is the same.

Refer to Fig. 9.25 for this comparison.   The system speed performance was improved by over 25 percent, using the faster TTL modules (73 ns).   For this only a little over a watt more power was dissipated (133.3 W) and, as stated, equal number of packages were used.   A straight reduction in access time of 10 more nanoseconds and further power reductions are possible using the faster TTL storage element (SN74S200).

9.6   SUMMARY

In this chapter, several very important general topics that apply to all memory systems have been developed and these have been applied to systems from 128 words to 16K words.   These concepts will continue to be used in the discussions that follow in the remaining chapters.

Type memory	Support circuitry	Max access, ns	Power	Pkgs.
74200	Std TTL	100	132	292
74200	Schottky	73	133	292

Fig. 9.25.   Speed, power, and number of packages of the 4K × 16 memory systems.

REFERENCES

1. J. K. Ayling, R. O. Moore, and G. K. Tu, A High-performance Monolithic Store, *ISSCC69 Dig. Tech. Pap.*, pp. 36–37.
2. M. G. Snyder, Bipolar Memories, *EEE*, **17**(11): 62–67(November 1969).
3. J. Gray, Design Considerations for a Bipolar 256 Bit RAM, *IEEE Comput.*, **4**(2): 18–22(March/April 1971).
4. J. Springer, Making Sense out of Delay Specifications in Semiconductor Memories, *Electronics*, pp. 82–88, October 15, 1971.
5. C. D. Talbert, Simplify Random-access Memory Selection, *Electron. Des.*, **18**(17): 70–74(August 16, 1972).
6. R. W. Bryant, G. K. Tu, T. C. Kwei, and R. H. Robinson, A High Performance LSI Memory System, *Comput. Des.*, pp. 71–77, July 1970.
7. R. L. Morris and J. R. Miller, "Designing with TTL Integrated Circuits," pp. 48–49, McGraw-Hill Book Company, New York, 1971.
8. R. K. Jurgen, Minicomputer Applications in the Seventies, *IEEE Spectrum,* **7**(8): 37–52(August 1970).
9. T. W. Hart, Jr. and D. D. Winstead, Semiconductor Memory Systems—What Will They Cost? *Electron. Eng.*, pp. 50–54, September 1970.
10. B. A. Kute, Design Considerations for Semiconductor Random Access Memory Systems, *IEEE Comput.*, **4**(2): 11–17(March/April 1971).
11. W. D. Baker, W. H. Herndon, T. A. Longo, and D. L. Pelzer, Oxide Isolation Brings High Density to Production Bipolar Memories, *Electronics*, pp. 65–70, March 29, 1973.
12. D. A. Hodges et al., Low-power Bipolar Transistor Memory Cells, *IEEE J. Solid-state Circuitry*, **SC-4**(5)(October 1969).
13. L. L. Vadasz, H. T. Chua, and A. S. Grove, Semiconductor Random-access Memories, *IEEE Spectrum,* **8**(8): 40–48(May 1971).

10

MOS Random Access Memory Applications

10.1 INTRODUCTION

This chapter concerning random access memory applications concentrates on MOS random access storage elements providing basic tools and techniques for the application of MOS storage elements to specific systems. Because of the scope of this subject, not every detail is covered. However, enough material is included to assist the designer to a successful conclusion of his memory design, even if a variety of storage elements are used.

The special requirements of MOS random access memory are discussed first. Then, the means to implement these needs are detailed. Next, two systems of 64K (words) × 16(bits) are developed to illustrate the application of different types of MOS random access storage elements. The chapter concludes with a discussion of continuing developments in both p-channel and n-channel, including some important systems applications.

To assure that everyone has a familiarity with MOS, the discussion of the special requirements of MOS random access memory begins with a review of several facts regarding MOS in general.

10.2 FACTS TO KEEP IN MIND ABOUT MOS

The first fact is that there are three basic MOS type devices:[1] p-channel,[2,3,4] n-channel, and complementary[2] (which includes both p and n channels). Application discussions focus on p-channel because these devices are in production and readily available, but the same techniques are easily applied to other types of storage elements. With the advent of n-channel[4] devices some of the interface circuitry illustrated for p-channel will be eliminated because of the direct interface to the storage element from available TTL peripheral circuitry. Again, this should not detract from the techniques and approaches presented, but specific examples are shown at the end of the chapter.

The second fact is that the MOS device is basically a high-impedance device with a transconductance of hundreds of micromhos. With an input that exhibits very high resistance, the MOS device is essentially a capacitive load. Therefore, input load factors (ILF) to MOS storage elements are characterized as capacitive loads that require charging to specified voltage levels. Thus, transient charging currents are generated at inputs and outputs. Output currents from MOS devices: (1) are direct functions of device physical size, (2) are generated from a relatively high impedance source, and (3) deliver only hundreds of microamperes per volt of input voltage change for the fractional device sizes used in high-density storage elements.

The third fact is that MOS usually requires some high drive voltage. For example, the p-channel storage elements used in the applications to be described later require at least 15 V drive. This means translation will be required from low-level logic voltages to the MOS drive levels. As mentioned, for n-channel devices, some of these interface circuits will be eliminated. However, many of the more economical p-channel devices will still require high voltage drive, especially on the clock voltages, even though other signal inputs are compatible with low level logic.

A fourth fact is that MOS storage elements are designed to provide either static or dynamic storage. Bipolar storage elements provide static storage. With the advent of n-channel MOS, static designs that are directly compatible with low-level logic levels may offer much more density advantage than the present p-channel designs, which offer little density advantage over bipolar. Therefore, bipolar has served this market.

Dynamic MOS storage elements have small cell areas and provide high-density packing.[3] These features allow economical fabrication and enable them to compete with and exceed core for mainframe memory applications. Because of these benefits, the applications in this chapter concentrate on MOS dynamic random access storage. Static MOS designs would follow very closely the bipolar designs of Chap. 9. A simplified example is included later in the chapter.

Dynamic MOS storage, because the information can deteriorate, has the extra requirement that it must be refreshed to maintain information.[5,6] Therefore, a portion of the support circuitry required provides the control and timing for refreshing the storage element.

Dynamic MOS storage also has an additional support circuitry requirement—timed driving voltages that are called clocks. These are not required for the static bipolar storage elements.

To summarize, then, MOS is characterized by: (1) high resistance inputs, (2) capacitive loading, (3) small output currents, and (4) need for refresh and clock circuitry.

It will be beneficial to look at several of these, because they apply on a general basis to the applications.

10.3 HIGH DRIVE VOLTAGE

10.3.1 Typical Input Conditions

Figure 10.1 shows some of the types of inputs that load a driver. Note that input loads are capacitive as a result of gate input lines or as a result of input lines that go to diffused junctions that form the drain or source of an MOS transistor.[7] These diffused junctions are normally diodes to substrate. Gate inputs are normally metal

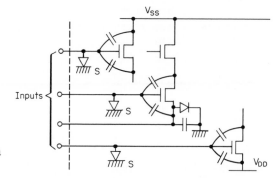

Fig. 10.1. Types of inputs that load a driver.

connections and have the overvoltage input protection for static electricity. However, many of the input lines that go to gates must first have their paths completed with diffused tunnels that pass under other metalization. Therefore, a diode may also be on each of these lines. If the line is made more positive than substrate, which can occur due to noise, then the diode conducts, charges are injected into the substrate, and satisfactory operation of the chip is impaired.

This is illustrated in Fig. 10.2, which shows the voltage waveform at the input to a p-channel MOS gate. The amplitude of the drive voltage is from 10 to 20 V.

The high logic levels (for positive logic) are identified as V_{IHA} and V_{IHB} for the maximum and minimum, respectively. These levels are usually no higher than V_{SS}. The low logic levels are identified as V_{ILA} and V_{ILB} for the maximum and minimum, respectively. These are usually more positive than V_{DD}.

It is important that input voltage be bounded by certain limits. As already mentioned, V_{IHA} must not be exceeded; if it is, the diode described will be forward-biased. The input voltage, however, must be above the V_{IHB} level to ensure that the p-channel devices are turned off. If a lower V_T (threshold) MOS structure is used, then the V_{IHB} limit must be specified closer to V_{SS}.

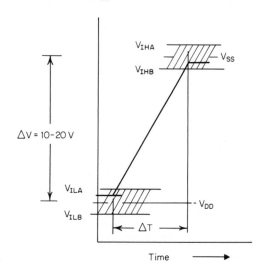

Fig. 10.2. Input voltage drive.

The low level must be bounded at V_{ILB} to prevent exceeding breakdown voltage limits or field threshold turn-on and at V_{ILA} to maintain the desired circuit performance from the MOS device, since current in the MOS transistor is a function of the gate-to-source drive voltage.

In Chap. 9, Eq. (9-12) gives the time that it takes to charge a given capacitance (ηC_o) to a given voltage change $(V_F\text{-}V_{OL})$ with a constant current I. This equation is used in simpler form and rearranged as

$$I_D = C_L \frac{\Delta V}{\Delta t} \tag{10-1}$$

where I_D is the current that is supplied by the driver that drives an MOS input; C_L is the capacitance load on the line; ΔV is the voltage change identified in Fig. 10.2; and Δt is the time required, also shown in Fig. 10.2.

If the capacitance is 200 pF and the voltage change is 20 V in 20 ns, then the average charging current is 200 mA. The peak currents are higher, so the driver power supply must be designed to provide these. Also, adequate power supply bypassing at the unit is very important.

10.3.2 Power Considerations

With such large currents, significant power must be dissipated. Consideration must be given this dissipation.

As the capacitor is charged, a negligible amount of power is dissipated in the capacitor, but significant power is dissipated in the driver. When the capacitor is discharged, the driver again dissipates significant power—the energy stored in the capacitor.

Now, if the capacitor is charged and discharged at a frequency f, then the average charging current is

$$I_{AVG} = C\Delta Vf \tag{10-2}$$

where f now describes the time period. Since

$$P = VI \tag{10-3}$$

then, with a voltage change equal to the supply voltage $(\Delta V = V)$, the power dissipated to charge and discharge the capacitance is

$$P_D = CV^2 f \tag{10-4}$$

This added power dissipation must be considered for the driver and the memory system.

10.3.3 Interface Driver for MOS

Low-level logic is usually used for control circuitry, address registers, input data registers, and other support circuitry; therefore, a voltage translation is required from the control low-level logic to the output of the driver. In many cases, discrete components have been used to solve this interface drive translation,[7,8] or a combination of integrated logic circuits and discrete components.[7,8] Advances are being made in this area, as mentioned in Chap. 1, and complete monolithic drivers are now designed to satisfy this interface. The system applications that follow in this chapter use such a driver (Fig. 10.3). There is a dual driver in an 8-pin package and a quad driver in a 16-pin package. Each circuit has an independent input, but there is a common strobe for two circuits. It provides the voltage translation from TTL to MOS, it is designed to provide the high charging currents, and it delivers drive voltages from 5 to 20 V.

To help reduce power dissipation, the input circuit is operated at standard TTL V_{CC} levels of 5 V, and the output circuit V_{CC} can be varied from 4.75 to 20 V depending on the magnitude of the drive voltage required. The output is a totem-pole circuit with an active pull-up. A current-limiting resistor is provided. As previously discussed, the V_{IHB} logic level is very important to the turn-off of the p-channel devices; in this monolithic driver the V_{OH} level pulls up to at least 1 V of V_{CC2} even with 50 μA flowing. As explained, the driver dissipates power when charging the line capacitance. An example of the charging power dissipation in the driver follows using Eq. (10-4) where $C = 500$ pF, $V = 16$ V, and $f = 1$ MHz.

$$P_D = 5 \times 10^{-10} \times 16^2 \times 10^6$$
$$= 128 \text{ mW} \tag{10-5}$$

Additional internal driver circuit power dissipation brings the total to 225 mW at 70°C. There is an important design feature that can be incorporated into such drivers; i.e., low power dissipation when the output is high. This represents a common condition in the system whether the driver is used as an address, or enable, or clock driver. For the device of Fig. 10.3, the power dissipation with the output high is only 10 mW.

The propagation time delay through such drivers is very important because, as discussed in Chap. 9, such delays contribute to the system access time, write time, and cycle time. Figure 10.4 demonstrates the method of measuring the propagation time delay for a monolithic IC driver (Fig. 10.3). The propagation delays are listed at various temperatures with the capacitance as a variable. Times are measured from the 50 percent point on the input to either the 10 or 90 percent point on the output to assure that the times are to the correct levels required for MOS. The drivers, when used for address, data input, and timing and control inputs, will have typical propagation delays from 40 to 50 ns.

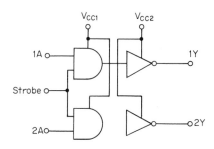

Dual

SN 75361A

8−pin P−dip

Quad

SN 75365

16−pin P−dip

Fig. 10.3. Details of a monolithic IC driver for MOS.

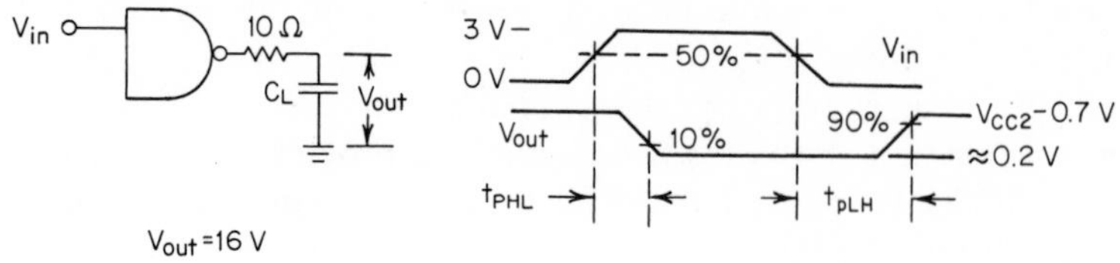

V_{in} — [NAND gate] — $10\,\Omega$ — C_L — V_{out}

$V_{out} = 16\ V$

3 V —
0 V —
— 50% —
V_{in}

V_{out}
10%
90%
$V_{CC2} - 0.7\ V$
$\approx 0.2\ V$

t_{PHL}
t_{PLH}

C_L	t_{PHL}(TYP)			C_L	t_{PLH}(TYP)		
	25°C	40°C	70°C		25°C	40°C	70°C
pF	ns	ns	ns	pF	ns	ns	ns
100	18	17	16	100	25	27	32
500	35	34	32	500	40	42	46
1,000	52	50	48	1,000	52	54	58

Fig. 10.4. Propagation delays at various temperatures with capacitance as a variable.

10.4 REFRESH

10.4.1 What Is Refresh?

Several times in previous chapters it has been stated that dynamic MOS memory needed to be refreshed. A brief review will clarify what is meant by the term "refresh."[1,6,9] Figure 10.5 shows a dynamic MOS 3-transistor cell from the TMS1103 1,024-bit random access storage element, which will be applied in a system. The heart of the storage element has information stored as charge or no charge on capacitor C_s. Charge deteriorates due to a leakage current, and new

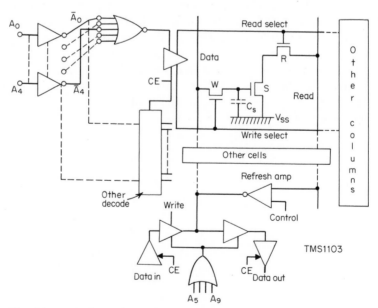

Fig. 10.5. A dynamic MOS 3-transistor cell from a random access storage element.

current must be applied to restore the charge.   Application of such current is known as "refresh" or "refreshing."

It must be noted that the charge deteriorates to a design tolerance margin after which the cell will no longer be successfully refreshed.   Two factors determine the rate at which refreshing must occur: a specific value of charge and the amount of leakage current, which is a function of temperature.   A common refresh rate at $70°C$ is every 2 ms.

The read select line (Fig. 10.5) is pulled low and a complete row of storage cells is interrogated; each cell is refreshed through its respective column refresh amplifier. Therefore, to refresh a total 1,024 storage element (32×32), all 32 read select lines must be pulled low for the complete matrix at least every 2 ms at $70°C$.

Only when a system is operated such that the address lines are activated in a binary sequence at the required rate can the designer be sure that each cell is being refreshed in time to retain the information.   For the most common case, a special refresh procedure is necessary.[5]

10.4.2   How Refresh Is Accomplished

To select the 32 lines required, the 5 address lines A_0 to A_4 (Fig. 10.5) must be sequenced through all their 32 binary states.   This is accomplished with a binary counter as shown in the refresh address counter of Fig. 10.6.   Four binary bits are generated by the synchronous binary counter and the additional bit by a D-type flip-flop and additional gating.

A refresh access high level enables the counter for counting.   The counter counts when the clock input transition is positive.   Each clock cycle advances the counter 1 state of its 32 states.   The transition that causes the count occurs at the end of the refresh cycle.   Therefore, addresses A_0 to A_4 are presented to the storage element as the refresh address at the start of the refresh cycle; at the end of the cycle the counter is advanced one step.   Note the burst control input; it also enables the counter to count.

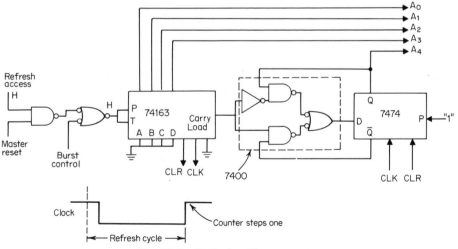

Fig. 10.6.   Refresh address counter.

There are two operating modes for refreshing. One is to perform a refresh cycle every 62.5 μs such that each line of 32 is refreshed every 2 ms, or all 32 lines can be sequenced in a burst—32 refresh cycles in a row. If the memory cycle is 750 ns, then the last mode would require 24 μs every 2 ms. Normally, in operation, it is not satisfactory for the CPU to wait for 24 μs while the memory is refreshed. It is better to delay the CPU for one cycle every 62.5 μs. However, it is useful to refresh in the burst mode when the memory is idling. This is the reason a burst control is provided.

10.4.3   Analysis of Refresh Address and Timing Control

The refresh counter has generated the address, but now it must be routed to the storage element.[10] The refresh address, because it is different than the CPU address or some other source requesting memory, requires an address selector. Such a selector is shown in Fig. 10.7. For this purpose 4-input-to-1-output data selectors are used, with one input not being used; instead, it is tied to ground. The state of the control inputs A and B determines which source address is fed to the output. Table 10.1 details which address source is being used. With both A and B high, the refresh address for address bits A_0 through A_4 from the refresh address counter is presented to the storage element through drivers and buffers as required. When A and B are other than both high, source I or source II addresses for address bits A_0 to A_4 are presented to the storage element. Other selectors are present to change bits A_5 through A_9 from source I to source II, but only bits A_0 to A_4 are changed for refresh.

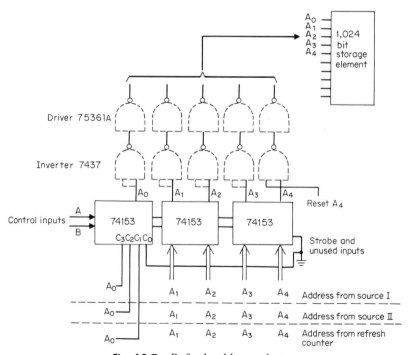

Fig. 10.7.   Refresh address selector.

Table 10.1. Control Functions for Address Selector

Control C (Fig. 10.8)	A	B	Address source
L	L	H	I (CPU)
H	H	L	II (DMA)
X*	H	H	Refresh

*Don't care.

Note the reset control put on A_4 address. A_4 is reset to a high at the end of a refresh cycle to save power dissipation in the TMS1103 storage element.[10] To select the refresh address every 62.5 μs and meet the requirement that 32 rows (for a 1,024 storage element) are to be refreshed every 2 ms, the control input status of A and B, indicated by Table 10.1, must be generated. Figure 10.8 contains the circuitry for such control.

Recall from Table 10.1 that A and B are both at the high level to select refresh address and that the refresh access is high (Fig. 10.6) to enable the refresh counter. These conditions are met when both D-type flip-flops have low outputs into the NAND gates that drive A and B. A low input from the 7400 NAND gate (identified as R and circled on Fig. 10.8) feeding the flip-flop inputs through an AND gate establishes the flip-flop output low level required. The low-level R from the 7400 gate has priority over the control signal identified as "control access for (source) I and II." This is identified with a C on Fig. 10.8 and on Table 10.1. Any time the refresh timing circuit produces a low level at R, it overrides the control at C. In other words, if the memory is tied to the CPU or DMA and it needs to be refreshed, the control signal R generated by the refresh timer takes over and refreshes the memory after the memory finishes its present cycle. Every 62.5 μs the refresh oscillator generates a low-to-high transition that sets the first stage of the timing shift register on the next clock cycle to generate the low control signal R and provide

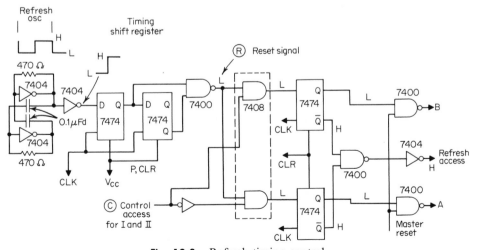

Fig. 10.8. Refresh timing control.

the address counter and refresh address selector with the correct control signals. The shift register ensures that timing is synchronized to clock; it also recognizes a refresh cycle request that occurs while memory is busy with a cycle for source I or II. The clock driving the refresh timing shift register and the access flip-flops is gated off during memory cycles so that memory cycles in progress cannot be disrupted by a change of the access signal or a refresh cycle request.

10.5 TIMING

The last general subject is timing. As previously mentioned, timed signals must be provided to dynamic MOS storage elements. Some of these signals have critical time relationships, which means these signals must be generated and distributed with these relationships maintained.

There are a number of ways that these timing signals can be generated—delay lines, shift registers, and monostable multivibrators are common ways.[10] However, a somewhat more versatile system is to generate phased signals from a master clock and logically combine these signals to produce the timed intervals.

10.5.1 Timing Generator

An example will help illustrate phased signal generation. Figure 10.9 is a portion of a memory controller that contains, in addition to the access and selector circuitry that has already been discussed, a timing generator outlined with dotted lines. It also includes memory request and read/write control circuitry. Source I or source II may request a memory cycle to either fetch or store data as required. Selector

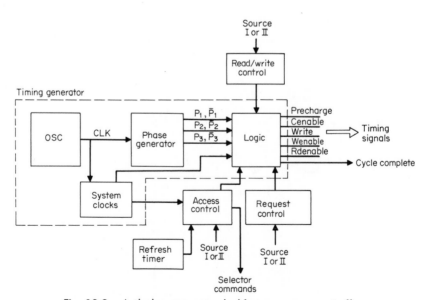

Fig. 10.9. A timing generator inside a memory controller.

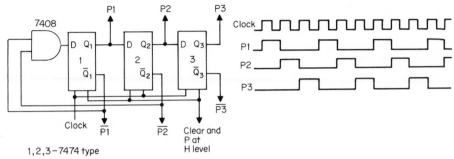

Fig. 10.10. Three-phase generator.

commands are given to apply the correct address to the memory. When a memory cycle is requested, the timing generator provides the timing signals in correct sequence. In addition, a "cycle-complete" signal is changed in state to indicate that a cycle is in progress. When it changes back, the cycle is complete. The overriding feature of a request for a refresh cycle has already been explained. All the logic of the timing generator need not be discussed because looking at several basic parts will provide the understanding that is necessary to implement the technique.

For timing, a master oscillator generates a clock for a three-phase generator and for any other system clocks required in the controller (Fig. 10.9).

10.5.2 Three-phase Generator

From these three phases and other signals generated from them, the basic timing is generated with logic. Figure 10.10 shows the three-phase generator. Three D-type flip-flops with complementary $\overline{Q}$ and Q outputs and a positive AND gate provide P_1, P_2, and P_3 as shown. Each flip-flop is clocked on the positive transitions. The complementary signals are used for state control as well as for signals for other logic.

Table 10.2 contains the states of the three-phase generator. These correspond to the timing chart of Fig. 10.10.

Table 10.2. States of Three-phase Generator

Time	P_1 $\downarrow$ $D_1 \; Q_1 \; \overline{Q_1}$	P_2 $\downarrow$ $D_2 \; Q_2 \; \overline{Q_2}$	P_3 $\downarrow$ $D_3 \; Q_3 \; \overline{Q_3}$	$\overline{Q_1} \cdot \overline{Q_2} = D_1$
0	1 0 1	0 0 1	0 0 1	1 1 = 1
1	0 1 0	1 0 1	0 0 1	0 1 = 0
2	0 0 1	0 1 0	1 0 1	1 0 = 0
3	1 0 1	0 0 1	0 1 0	1 1 = 1
4	0 1 0	1 0 1	0 0 1	0 1 = 0
5	0 0 1	0 1 0	1 0 1	1 0 = 0
6	1 0 1	0 0 1	0 1 0	1 1 = 1
7	0 1 0	1 0 1	0 0 1	0 1 = 0

The clock phases P_1, P_2, or P_3, or their complements, are combined logically with other signals to produce the timed signals required.

10.5.3   Timing Logic

For example, Fig. 10.11 is a portion of such logic that will be used in a timing generator for the memory systems that follow. Basically flip-flops Q_0 and Q_1 with the associated input gating form a simple four-state controller. The various states of the controller are used to produce the timing signals required by the MOS memory networks. A brief explanation will suffice to understand the technique.

The J and K inputs to the Q_0 and Q_1 flip-flops are functions of the logic controlling them. For example, for Q_0

$$J_0 = Q_0\, Q_1\, P_2 \tag{10-6}$$

and
$$K_0 = Q_0\, Q_1\, P_3 \tag{10-7}$$

when there is a high-level output from the D NAND gate that feeds the B gate.
    Correspondingly, through F gates,

$$J_1 = Q_0\, Q_1\, P_1 \tag{10-8}$$

and
$$K_1 = \bar{Q}_0\, Q_1\, P_3 \tag{10-9}$$

The K_0 input to the Q_0 flip-flop will be a function of both the B and the D gates if the output of the D gate is not at the high level. A cycle request (memory request) produces a high logic level at the indicated input (Fig. 10.11) to gate E which produces the high logic level into gate B so that K_0 is the logic function of Eq. (10-7).
    Table 10.3 is a state diagram of the logic shown in Fig. 10.11. The outputs Q_0 and Q_1 are the outputs of interest. Table 10.3 begins with all inputs to the flip-flops at a 0 level and each output Q_0 and Q_1 at a 0 level. It proceeds through clock time until the logic states repeat themselves.

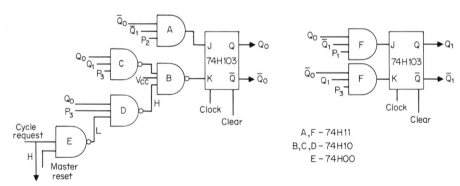

Fig. 10.11. Logic diagram showing how signals are combined to produce particular timing signals.

Table 10.3. States for Q_0 and Q_1 Control Logic

Clock time	Phases $P_1\,P_2\,P_3$			$\overline{Q_0}\,\overline{Q_1}\,P_2 = J_0$				$Q_0\,Q_1\,P_3 = K_0$				$Q_0\,\overline{Q_0}$		$Q_0\,\overline{Q_1}\,P_1 = J_1$				$\overline{Q_0}\,Q_1\,P_3 = K_1$				$Q_1\,\overline{Q_1}$	
0	0	0	0	0	1	1	0	0	0	0	0	1	0	0	0	0	0	1	0	0	0	0	1
1	1	0	0	0	1	0	0	0	0	0	0	1	0	0	1	0	0	1	0	0	0	0	1
2	0	0	1	1	1	0	0	0	0	0	0	1	0	0	0	1	0	1	0	0	0	0	1
3	0	0	0	0	0	1	0	1	1	0	1	0	1	1	0	1	0	0	1	1	0	0	1
4	1	0	0	0	0	0	0	1	0	0	1	0	1	0	1	1	1	0	0	0	0	0	1
5	0	0	0	0	0	1	1	1	1	0	1	0	1	1	0	1	0	0	0	1	0	1	0
6	0	0	1	0	1	1	1	1	1	0	1	0	0	1	0	0	0	0	0	1	0	1	0
7	1	0	0	0	0	0	0	1	0	1	1	0	0	1	1	0	0	0	1	1	0	1	0
8	0	0	1	0	0	0	0	1	1	0	1	0	0	1	0	0	1	0	1	1	0	1	0
9	0	1	0	0	1	0	0	1	0	0	1	0	1	1	0	1	0	0	0	1	1	1	0
10	1	0	0	0	0	0	0	0	0	0	0	1	0	0	1	0	0	1	0	0	0	0	1

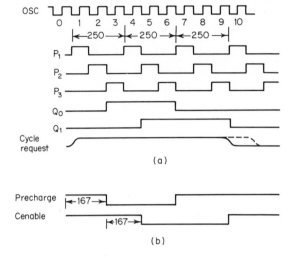

Fig. 10.12. Timing diagram for Q_0 and Q_1.

10.5.4   Timing Diagram

Figure 10.12a is a timing diagram relating the master oscillator, the three phases of the timing generator, and the outputs Q_0 and Q_1. The system application of the timing generator uses a 12-MHz master oscillator assuring that the high level of each phase is 83 ns and the low level is 167 ns. Other systems use other frequencies and/or more phases.

A timing signal identified as PRECHARGE in Fig. 10.12b is required for the system. This can be generated quite simply by feeding the signal CYCLE RE-QUEST and Q_0 into a NAND gate. Q_0 is gated with cycle request to prevent an erroneous PRECHARGE signal should the CYCLE REQUEST signal be slow in returning to the zero level as shown by the dotted line in Fig. 10.12. Signal CEN-ABLE is generated by Q_1.

Timing generation for a wide variety of applications can be implemented by these techniques. In many cases they are not as simple as using a monostable multivibrator, but they are much more versatile, and timing is highly accurate in that it is determined by the system clock crystal oscillator.

10.6   ANALYSIS OF A ONE MILLION BIT MAINFRAME MEMORY

The remaining portion of this chapter is devoted to the application of MOS dynamic storage elements to specific systems. The use of two 1,024-bit storage elements in a mainframe memory of up to one million bits (64K words by 16 bits) will be detailed and a comparison made between the two systems. The applications are in commercial systems with a temperature range of 0 to 70°C ambient.

10.6.1   Storage Element Characteristics

The characteristics of the first 1,024-bit storage element (TMS1103) which uses a 3-transistor cell—the so-called 3-2-2 cell of Chap. 2—are summarized again as follows:[7]

Organization. . . . . 1,024 × 1 (words × bits)
Decode. . . . . Fully decoded
Signal levels . . . . V_{IH}: +16 V
                                 V_{IL}: 0 V
Output . . . . Single ended with sense current > 0.5 mA
Access time t_{pA} . . . . < 300 ns
Read cycle . . . . ≥ 480 ns
Write cycle . . . . ≥ 580 ns
Refresh time . . . . 2 ms (70°C)
Power dissipation . . . . 400 mW total operating
                                 0.4 mW per bit
                                 50 mW standby

Terminals
   10 address
   Data in
   Data out
   Timed signals
      1. R/W (read/write)
      2. CENABLE (chip enable)
      3. PRECHARGE
   Power
      1. V_{SS}: +16 V
      2. V_{BB}: +19 V
      3. V_{DD}: 0 V

All inputs are protected against static charge and, in addition to address and data-in input signals that are present during the largest part of the cycle, there are three timed signals or clocks: R/W, chip enable, and precharge. Precharge does just what it says; it precharges capacitance on nodes inside the storage element. The precharge and chip enable were generated previously in Fig. 10.12*b* and are discussed in detail later. One single-ended data output, which can be OR-tied, provides at least 500 μA of current for identifying the data, data which are a complement of the data stored.

P-channel MOS devices operate between a power-supply voltage of V_{SS} and V_{DD}. V_{SS} can be ground and V_{DD} a negative voltage, or V_{DD} can be ground and V_{SS} a positive voltage.

In the application that follows, the source voltage is plus 16 V, and V_{DD} is at ground, allowing easier interface with TTL. A substrate bias voltage of 19 V is required. Peak currents to 60 mA during precharge and chip enable average to a supply current of 25 mA and a power dissipation of 400 mW (V_{SS} = 16 V).

The refresh time at 70°C is 2 ms, but if the environment of units of this type is controlled to a much lower temperature, the refresh time will be significantly longer.

Portions of the block diagram and a schematic of the TMS1103 were presented in Chap. 5. Figure 10.13 is the complete block diagram of this circuit. Note that the timing signals go through additional distribution circuitry on the chip. The unit is fully decoded, and only 10 binary address bits need be applied to all storage

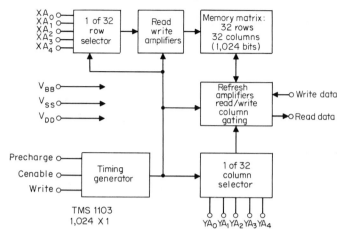

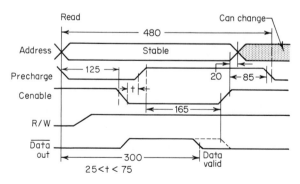

Fig. 10.13. Block diagram of a 1,024-bit dynamic MOS storage element.

elements in order to select 1 word from the 1,024 available. Eighteen pins are required to provide all signals and power to the storage element.

10.6.2 Timing Diagram—Read Cycle

There is critical timing that must be maintained. To understand this critical timing, refer to the read cycle timing diagram of Fig. 10.14. In a memory cycle, whether read or write, a low level on precharge must be maintained for a minimum time of 125 ns before the chip enable signal is brought low. This results in the selection of a row of cells in the 1,024 matrix, determined by the binary address input. The address signals must be stable during this time. If the cycle is a read cycle, then the read/write signal (R/W) must be at the high level (near V_{SS}). These clocks, R/W, precharge, cenable (chip enable) are routed through additional on-chip circuitry to provide inversion and on-chip timing. The chip enable signal is similar to that for the bipolar storage elements in Chap. 9, but it has the time relationship with precharge and read/write as shown in Fig. 10.14.

Note that an enable access time t_{pAE} has not been called out. The reason is that chip enable, now a timed signal, must be in a given time relationship with the other

Fig. 10.14. Timing of a read cycle.

clocks and therefore already contributes to t_{pA}, the access time from address application.

There is an overlap between precharge and cenable. This is the critical timing indicated (t in Fig. 10.14).[3,7] The voltage level on the data line in the cell is a function of the overlap time. Insufficient overlap, or conversely, too much overlap, will cause improper operation of the cell and data will be lost. At least 25 ns, but not more than 75 ns, of overlap must be present for proper operation. The chip enable signal must be low for at least 165 ns after precharge ends; another cycle cannot start before 85 ns from the end of chip enable. With a rise time of 20 ns and the minimum overlap of 25 ns, the read or refresh cycle time must be at least 480 ns for the storage element itself. The access time is 300 ns minimum. Address must be stable when the storage element is enabled and must be held for at least 20 ns after enable goes high.

One important point concerning the output current must be emphasized: If the storage element is enabled and the element is in the read or refresh mode, current will flow from the data output to the sense amplifier. If a 1 is read from the cell, a high current is available; if a 0 is read from the cell, a high current appears as the cell is addressed and then decays to a low level. During refresh a combination high current appears from all columns and care must be taken that this does not cause lost time due to sense amplifier saturation.

10.6.3 Timing Diagram—Write Cycle

Similar timing is required when writing in the storage element (Fig. 10.15). A write cycle has the write pulse included and the signal must be low for a minimum of 80 ns. In addition, this must occur after chip enable has been low 165 ns; therefore, chip enable must be extended accordingly. A storage element write cycle must be a minimum of 580 ns under the same conditions as the read cycle with valid input data overlapping the write pulse.

The time relationship of the clock signals is generated by the timing generator, which was previously discussed.

These are the characteristics of the standard 1103. There are other specially selected units for faster access times. These can be specified separately.

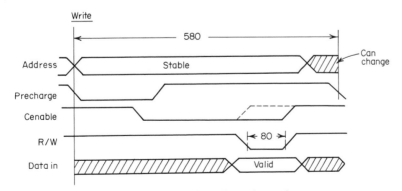

Fig. 10.15. Timing of a write cycle.

10.6.4 Memory System

8K × 16 Board. The one million bit memory system will be made up of multiple boards of the same type, as was done in Chap. 9 with the bipolar storage elements. The board size, in this example, will be 8,192 words by 16 bits (8K × 16). It is shown in Fig. 10.16.

In addition to the support circuitry shown (Fig. 10.16), the storage matrix has 128 1,024-bit storage elements on the board. It will be beneficial to look at the loading on the drivers for this board, as bipolar system loading was examined in Chap. 9.

Loading Factors. W_M = 8K words, W_I = 1K, B_N = 16 bits, and B_I = 1. It has been pointed out that the input to MOS storage elements is capacitive. Table 10.4 lists representative values.

In Chap. 9 the loading equations for a memory system were developed and now will be used for the MOS memory. The address line loading is, from Eq. (9-1),

$$L_A = \frac{8K}{1K} \times \frac{16}{1} \times 7 \text{ pF} = 896 \text{ pF} \qquad (10\text{-}10)$$

Propagation delays would exceed 40 ns in the drivers if each one were to drive this full load. Therefore, two drivers in parallel will be used to limit the load to 450 pF on each driver.

Equation (9-2) determines the number of lines to be decoded when only one chip enable is used. Therefore,

$$S_L = \frac{8K}{1K} = 8 \qquad (10\text{-}11)$$

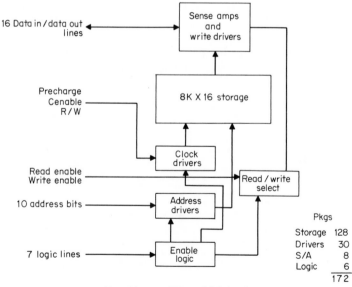

Fig. 10.16. 8K × 16 board.

Table 10.4. Input Loading Factors (Capacitive) for TMS1103 (picofarads)

Address	7
Cenable	18
Precharge	18
R/W	15
Data in	5
Data out	3

and the load on the lines will be

$$L_D = \left(\frac{B_N}{B_I}\right) \mathrm{ILF} \tag{9-3}$$

From Table 10.4, the ILF for chip enable and precharge is 18 pF and for R/W it is 15 pF; therefore

$$L_{\mathrm{CEN}}, L_{\mathrm{PREC}} = \frac{16}{1} \times 18 \text{ pF} = 288 \text{ pF} \tag{10-12}$$

and
$$L_{\mathrm{R/W}} = \frac{16}{1} \times 15 \text{ pF} = 240 \text{ pF} \tag{10-13}$$

Each time the timing signals force the driver through a voltage transition the driver dissipates power. Therefore, to conserve power, as well as provide the storage element decoding for memory system expansion, chip enable, precharge, and write pulse are decoded. One driver (SN75361) for each of 8 lines handles the capacitive loads of 288 and 240 pF, respectively, on these lines.

From Eq. (9-4) the data-in loading is

$$L_{\mathrm{IN}} = \frac{8K}{1K} \times 5 \text{ pF} = 40 \text{ pF} \tag{10-14}$$

This presents no problem because there is a separate driver for each bit line.

Data-output load capacitance resulting from outputs being connected together on a common buss is determined from Eq. (9-5) and the capacitance of the output line given in Table 10.4. Therefore,

$$\eta = \frac{8K}{1K} \times 3 \text{ pF} = 24 \text{ pF} \tag{10-15}$$

The 8K × 16 memory board of Fig. 10.16 contains the 128 1K packages, but in order that ringing in the lines be held at a minimum and coupling noise from high-voltage transitions be restricted, all MOS-level voltage drivers are contained on the same board. Also, following good practice, sense amplifiers are contained close to the storage element matrix.[11,12]

The board also contains some enable logic and read/write select logic which discussion of the system decode will clarify. All interface to the board is at low-level logic signals (TTL).

Total System Decode Structure. The overall diagram for decoding 64K words is shown in Fig. 10.17. Six additional addresses are used in addition to the 10 addresses required for the 1K decode in each package. Three 2-to-4-line decoders convert the 6 address lines to 12 selection lines. The blocks represent a board with 8K words and the number of bits required—in this case 16—plus a parity bit if desired, to increase the total bits to 17. The 8K board is divided into 4K segments. One decoder (bits 0 and 1) selects two 8K boards. Another decoder (bits 2 and 3) selects a 4K segment from the 16K selected. The remaining decoder (bits 4 and 5) selects a 1K row from the 4K segment. The 10 addresses to each package then select the desired word.

Logic is placed between the decoders and the board inputs such that all boards, segments, and rows are activated to select all modules during a refresh cycle.

Board Select, Segment Select, and Row Select. Additional details of the board select, segment select, and row select logic are shown in the next three figures. Figure 10.18 shows the board select, the segment select, and the row select. The board select and segment select signals are at a high level when active, as is the RS select line.

A high level on BS (which may be BS_0, BS_1, BS_2, or BS_3 of Fig. 10.17) will allow a high level to be present on SA or SB as dictated by S_0 and S_1, the segment select signals. S_0 and S_1 could also be S_2 or S_3, depending on the board position on Fig. 10.17. One of either RS_0 through RS_3 or RS_4 through RS_7 will be selected based on a low level on one line of R_0 through R_3 and the state of SA or SB.

Read/Write Enable. Figure 10.19 shows the logic for address driver enable and read and write enable on the board. Write enable energizes write select, which in turn energizes the write drivers when information is stored. Similar action occurs in the read mode: read enable energizes read select, and read select strobes the sense amplifiers. Write select and read select are high when active, are complementary,

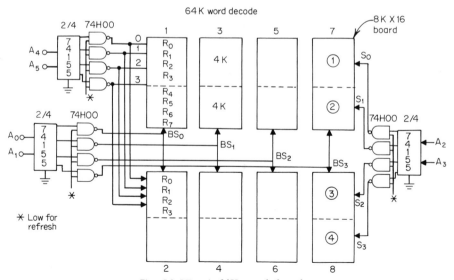

Fig. 10.17. A 64K-word decode.

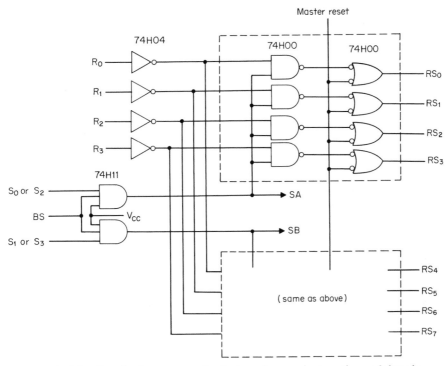

Fig. 10.18. Board select, segment select, and row select portions of decode.

and cannot be generated on the board unless the board is selected; i.e., either *SA* or *SB* must be high, which is only allowed if *BS* (Fig. 10.18) is high. A high on *SAA* or *SAB* corresponding to the high on *SA* or *SB* enables the address drivers of the selected 4K segments of memory.

Selection of 1K $\times$ 16 Bits. Figure 10.20 shows the selection of the row of 1K $\times$ 16 bits of memory by selecting the timed signals of precharge and chip enable required.

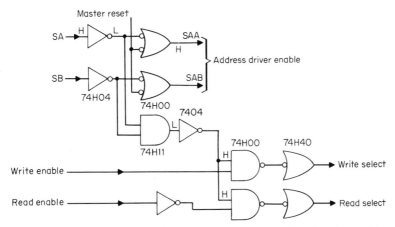

Fig. 10.19. Logic for address driver enable and read and write enable of decode.

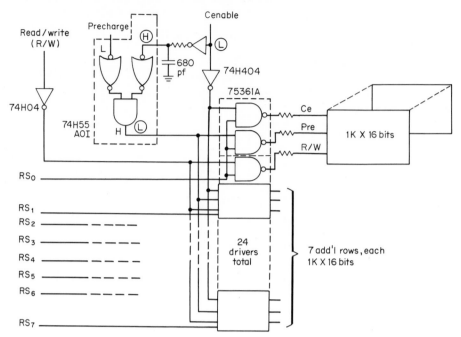

Fig. 10.20. Selection of the row of 1K × 16 bits of memory.

Drivers for chip enable, precharge, and write are selected by a high level on the row lines—one of which is activated as discussed (Fig. 10.17). The precharge signal—at the low level at the input to the AND-OR-INV gate (marked AOI) during its active time period—is fed through the driver (75361) as a low level to activate 16 storage elements. Chip enable—again low during the active period—also feeds through the driver as a low level to the storage element.

Recall that there is a critical time period between the overlap of chip enable low and precharge low at the storage element. To assure that this timing is between the 25- and 75-ns window specified, an RC time constant circuit and inverter couples the chip enable signal to the precharge gate. A chip enable low causes the precharge signal to return to a high level at the storage element after a set delay even though the precharge timed signal is still low. To help maintain this timing, the drivers for precharge and chip enable should be circuits from the same package. Similarly, two write drivers should be in the same package.

You'll note there is a 10- to 50-Ohm resistor shown in the line from the driver to the storage element. This is for damping the ringing on these lines on the board. Because this resistor does effect transition times, its value should be selected for the particular assembly conditions.

The read/write signal, generated as a high level for read and as a low level for write during a write cycle, also is gated through a driver. During refresh, all the *RS* lines are high and all modules have chip enable and precharge signals applied. However, the write signal is not generated during refresh. Therefore, although the write driver is selected, its output level is in the required high state for the read-refresh mode. This control is easily generated by logic from the control signals already shown.

Address Drive Selection. The selection of the row of packages for 16 bits is complete, but further decoding is required because the individual word from the 1K in a package is what is desired. This decoding is accomplished in the package from the address bits applied in parallel to each package. The 10 addresses come from the source (CPU, DMA, or REFRESH) selected through the address selectors (Fig. 10.7). The loading factors require that address drivers be limited to driving half the modules on the board, or 64 modules (4K × 16), as shown in Fig. 10.21. Recall that for Fig. 10.19 it was stated that SAA and SAB enable address drivers. This is accomplished with the driver (75361) which has a dual input and also allows the use of the segment signals SAA and SAB to energize only the drivers that are selected. This saves power because unnecessary drivers are not charging and discharging capacitance.

All functions of the memory board of Fig. 10.16 have now been discussed except the sense amplifiers and the write drivers.

Sense Amplifiers and Write Drivers. As shown in Fig. 10.22, a common line for each bit connects all 8 data outputs of the 8K words on a board. Similar connections are made for the data input.

On the multilayer board used for interconnection, the sense line is separated from the input signal lines by a ground plane. In addition, a dummy sense line is run in parallel with the real sense line and connected to the reference input of the sense amplifier, causing common-mode noise induced on the sense lines to be rejected by the sense amplifier.

The output current of the storage element is at least 500 μA, and typically will be above 1 mA. The voltage developed is proportional to the load resistor at the sense amplifier input. However, large values of resistors cause long time constants to exist on the sense line, and these add directly to access time.

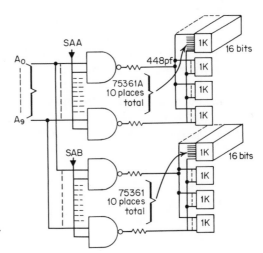

Fig. 10.21. System for selecting the address for the individual word desired.

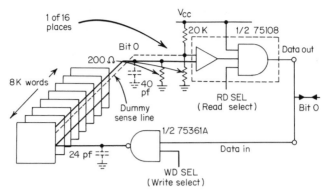

Fig. 10.22. Common data line.

The one half of a SN75108 dual line receiver shown is an excellent sense amplifier. A 25-mV differential signal is required for guaranteed operation with the most-positive input drawing 75 μA of input current.

The reference voltage, established by the 20K and 200-Ohm resistor divider, must be at least 25 mV for proper detection of a 0; i.e., no current from the storage elements. The storage element current must develop 50 mV across the input sense resistor in addition to supplying the 75 μA. Capacitance on the output line—40 pF in this case—must be charged by the storage element current to assure reliable detection. This is no problem until a large number of units are coupled together; η, which determines the number of units, is a function of W_M/W_I.

A low at the input to the storage element stores information such that a high current is available at the data output when that cell is interrogated. The data-in line determines this level via the data-in driver (SN75361).

The driver is gated by the write select input which, if you recall, is a function of the board select logic and the write enable signal. The strobe gate on the output of the sense amplifier is gated by the read select signal, which is a function of board select logic and the read enable signal. This arrangement requires only one line for data transmission to the read register or from the data source for storing information. Therefore, for the 16 bits of data only 16 lines, instead of 32 lines, need be coupled between the board and the data registers.

Summary of 8K $\times$ 16 Board. In summary, all the functions of the board block diagram (Fig. 10.16) for the 8K $\times$ 16 board have been discussed including the enable logic, the address and clock drivers, and the read and write support circuitry. The board contains 172 packages defined as shown.

In order to select a word of 16 bits and read out its contents these circuits must be active and selected:

    16 storage elements
    10 address drivers
     3 clock drivers
    16 sense amplifiers
     6 logic packages

112 storage elements remain unselected.

Under these conditions the power dissipation for a board is 21 W, or 167 μW per bit.

Controller. The system block diagram is not complete until a memory controller is added to control the boards. This controller is shown in Fig. 10.23. Multiple storage element boards are added to the controller to expand the memory system to 64K words. There are 43 possible low-level signal lines coupling between boards and controller. However, only 7 of the 12 between decode and enable logic go to each board. Therefore, there are 38 lines.

Thus far in our discussion the following units have been discussed in the controller:

Timing generator
Refresh timing
Refresh address
Address selectors
Buffers
Decode

The write data selectors have not been discussed, but they operate the same as the units for address selection with one exception: The data input is selected from source I or source II; there is no data selection on refresh. The address and read data registers consist of D-type flip-flop modules either of standard TTL (SN7474 type) or of faster Schottky TTL.

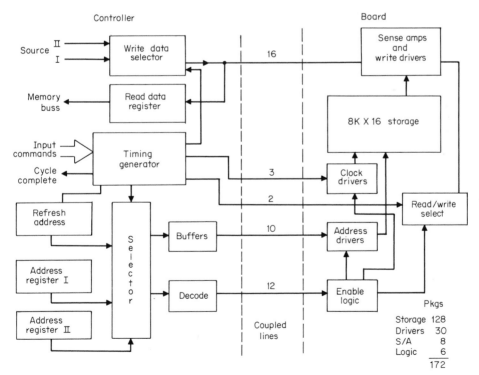

Fig. 10.23. Memory controller coupled to a board.

Summary of System Using TMS1103. A summary of the performance of the system can be obtained by examining the system timing diagram which is shown in Fig. 10.24.

The basic time signals that were previously generated are shown in Fig. 10.24a. Recall that the master oscillator frequency is 12 MHz and each phase of the three-phase generator is 83 ns with the basic cycle time of the memory system being 750 ns. The cycle request signal initiates a cycle. If it is a read or refresh cycle, for example, 167 ns are allowed for the propagation of signals through the decode logic external to the storage element, for the selectors to be energized, and for the address signals to the storage elements to stabilize. Precharge is activated. Then, 167 ns later, chip enable is activated and terminates precharge at the storage element within the overlap specifications. This is indicated by the dotted portion on the PRE-CHARGE timing diagram. Chip enable and read enable (Fig. 10.24) continue to be activated to provide data at the output. As shown, data are valid 430 ns after precharge to the storage elements is activated. From the start of the cycle request, data are valid approximately 600 ns later. In refresh, the addresses from the refresh counter for A_0 to A_4 are routed to the storage element with all modules enabled.

Fig 10.24c shows the time position of the write enable and write signals. Of course, data in must be valid during the write time.

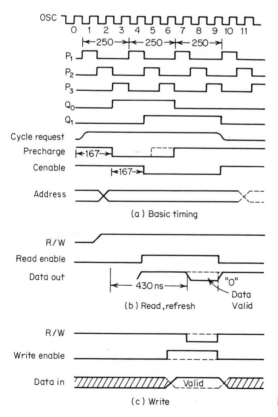

(a) Basic timing

(b) Read, refresh

(c) Write

Fig. 10.24. System timing diagram.

Fig. 10.25. Picture of 8K × 17 memory board.

Figure 10.25 is a picture of a memory board using the 1,024-bit dynamic MOS memory. This board has 8K X 17 bits. It was mentioned that a parity bit could easily be added. Of course, parity check modules must be added to the controller.

Other features could have been included in the design. One of the main optional features is to "power down" when the memory idles, as it would if it were not being used, or if main power had failed and battery backup were used.[13] In such a mode, only refresh circuitry, operating in the burst mode, is activated periodically, in addition to the storage elements, to keep the information stored. Even logic power can be turned down between refresh cycle to keep the idling power at a minimum. The desired system described requires as simple a system as possible. These additional features add extra circuitry but can be easily implemented into the basis system when required.

10.6.5   System Using TMS4062 1,024-Bit MOS RAM

Recall in Chap. 5 that a 1,024-bit dynamic storage element using a 4-transistor cell was described. This is the storage element used in the TMS4062 system—a system very similar to the TMS1103 system. In this section the TMS4062 system will be described and then compared to the TMS1103 system.

Storage Element Characteristics. It was pointed out in Chap. 5 that the TMS1103 is processed with a p-channel self-aligning silicon gate process; the TMS4062, on the other hand, is fabricated using a standard p-channel aluminum gate process. Even with this simpler processing, this TMS4062 1,024-bit storage element has an access time that is twice as fast as the TMS1103. The characteristics of the TMS4062 are:

```
Organization . . . . . . . . . .  1,024 × 1
Decode . . . . . . . . . . . . . .  Fully decoded
Signal levels . . . . . . . . . . .  V_IH: 20 V
                                     V_IL: 0 V
Output . . . . . . . . . . . . . .  Differential with sense current
                                     >100 µA
Access time t_pA . . . . . . . .  ⩽150 ns
Read cycle . . . . . . . . . . .  ⩾290 ns
Write cycle . . . . . . . . . . .  ⩾290 ns
Refresh . . . . . . . . . . . . .  2 ms (70°C)
Power dissipation . . . . . . .  180 mW total
                                  0.18 mW per bit
                                  2 mW standby
```

Terminals
   10 address
   2 I/O lines

Timed signals
   1. Reset
   2. Clock
   3. Chip select
Power
   1. V_{SX} (V_{BB}): 22.5 V
   2. V_{SS}: 20 V
   3. V_{REF}: 7 V
   4. V_{DD}: 0 V

The characteristics of the two 1,024-bit storage elements, although they use different cells, are similar in input protection, number of timed signals required, number of address lines, full decoding, organization, and refresh time. Despite these similarities, significant differences do exist.

When analyzing the TMS4062, the first difference noted is speed performance. Access time t_{pA} of the TMS4062 is 150 ns with correspondingly faster and equal read and write cycle times. The second difference is power dissipation. Operating power is 180 mW and standby power is only 2 mW for the 1,024 bits. The third significant difference of the TMS4062 is the type of output data. A differential sense current of at least 100 μA is obtained on the two digit lines that are provided directly on the package pins through a chip select transistor at the output (*cf.* Fig. 5.13). Another difference, if you recall from Chap. 5, is that refreshing is simpler and that chip select (chip enable) does not have to be activated in order to refresh. The fifth difference is the voltage drive required, with this 1,024-bit storage element requiring 20-V signals. Finally, note that a reference voltage V_{REF} is required.

Block Diagram. The block diagram shown in Fig. 10.26 identifies the X and Y decode structure used for the full decode of 1,024 bits, but note the digit lines only have multiplexing, no refresh amplifiers, and no write amplifiers. The reset, clock, and chip select signals are timed signals (clocks). Reset precharges node capacitance within the storage element, and therefore, it is the same as precharge. Writing is accomplished by forcing one I/O line to V_{SS} when a bit is selected and holding the other at V_{REF}. This extra reference supply means that 19 terminal connections must be made and, therefore, a 22-pin package must be used. Again, in the system application of this unit, it will be more convenient for interfacing to low-level logic to operate the storage element from $V_{DD} = 0$ V to $V_{SS} = 20$ V.

When applying this 1,024-bit storage element (TMS4062), there are several negative factors. These are:

1. No on-chip circuitry for separating read/write modes or writing into cell.
2. No on-chip circuitry for amplifying the current output from the cell.
3. An extra reference supply is required.
4. A 22-pin package is required.

However, it must be noted these may not be "disadvantages"; the system application must be evaluated first.

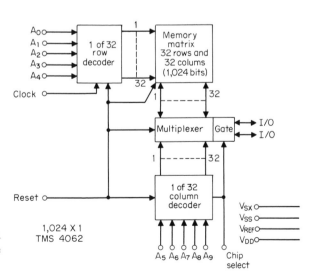

Fig. 10.26. Block diagram of a 1,024-bit dynamic MOS storage element with a 4 XTR cell.

In the system, the same basic controller support circuitry will be used, as well as the same technique for decoding and generating the clocks. However, differences will occur in the write and sense circuitry, and the timing will be much easier.

Timing Diagram. The timing chart of Fig. 10.27 identifies the time relationship of the three clock signals—reset, clock, and chip select—with address. The reset pulse must be low, a minimum of 130 ns. This is especially critical after writing because one digit line has been disturbed to V_{SS} and must be returned to V_{REF}. If a longer cycle time than the minimum can be tolerated, then variations in access time can be held to a minimum with a longer reset time.

The clock and chip select pulse should occur at the same time, but not before 60 ns after the reset pulse returns high. As mentioned previously, the reset pulse period is a precharge. The on-chip decode circuitry must be set before the clock and chip select signals are activated. This is the reason for the 60 ns.

Data in must overlap the clock and chip select pulses when in a write cycle.

When reading, the output current is a slowly rising ramp because of the charge of internal nodes by the cell. The 150-ns access is when the differential current is at least 100 μA. Access time can be reduced by accepting a lower differential current for the sense amplifier trigger level. However, if higher sense impedances are used to accomplish this, the input time constant nullifies the gain.

But in this analysis there is no critical overlap timing as with the previous 1,024-bit storage element. This is a significant advantage. Because address can change all during reset, optimum positioning of the reset pulse in the cycle is possible. Even though this timing chart shows the reset pulse starting the cycle, reset could just as easily be at the end of the cycle. Later discussion will show that clock and chip select can be tied to the same pin and be the same signal. In fact, new versions of this 1,024-bit storage element are being manufactured in an 18-pin package (TMS4063).

The drive voltages for clocks and for the address inputs swing from ground to $+20$ V. The same drivers as used for the previous system can be used. The write voltages will be different. The two digit lines must swing from V_{REF} to V_{SS}.

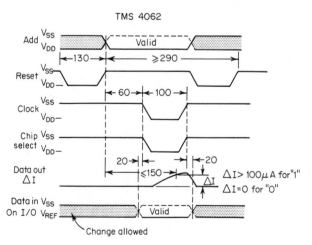

Fig. 10.27. Timing chart of a 1,024-bit storage element.

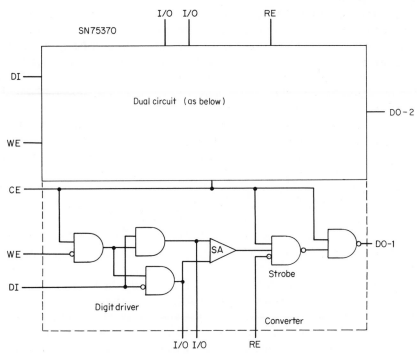

Fig. 10.28. A monolithic sense amp and write driver.

Controller. Referring to the controller for the previous system (Fig. 10.23), it can be seen that the timing generator can use the same techniques as before to generate the reset, clock, and chip select pulses. Logic would change to adjust the timing and to eliminate chip select on refresh. The refresh timing, refresh address counter, refresh address selectors, selectors for source I and source II addresses and for write data, are all the same as previously. Even the buffers, decode, and registers remain unchanged. Therefore, the same basic controller used previously is used for this system.

8K × 16 Board. On the 8K × 16 board signficant changes are made in the sense and write circuitry. To simplify the interface required for the sense amplifiers and write driver, monolithic integrated circuits have been designed to perform the required functions shown in Fig. 10.28. This provides a great advantage because one package contains dual circuits that provide the functions required instead of the functions being implemented with discrete components or a combination of discrete and monolithic circuits.

Reading the differential current from the storage element (TM4062) requires the write enable (WE) signal to be high and the read enable (RE) to be low. Under these conditions, the I/O lines and the input to the sense amplifier are at reference voltage potential. The differential current of 100 μA is detected, passes through the enabled strobe gate, and is converted to a TTL output DO-1. This output can be an open collector or have a pull-up resistor allowing 20 outputs to be bussed or dotted together.

Writing into the storage element requires the WE signal to be low and the RE signal high. Under these conditions, the I/O lines will have complementary states— one will be near V_{SS} and one will be at the reference voltage. Their state depends on the level of the data input. The sense amplifier inputs are protected from the high input voltage and the output is disabled by the strobe gate. All loads have an ILF of one standard TTL load. A chip enable is available if required for additional gating. In our system application, it is tied to a high level.

Specifications of the monolithic sense amplifier and write driver (SN75370) that are a concern for the system application are:

Write propagation delay—50 ns with 60 pF load
Sense amplifier—Converter delay—60 ns
Power dissipation (per circuit)—(Read)—225 mW
                              (Write)—350 mW
                              (Standby)—175 mW

The load of 60 pF represents driving 16 storage elements. The system requirement is for 8.

Examining the block diagram of the board (Fig. 10.29), the changes are indicated by a shaded block. The monolithic sense amplifier and write driver has replaced the individual sense amplifier and individual data-in drivers. This saves 8 data-in driver packages. A change also occurs in the read/write select logic. The two SN74H40 gates of Fig. 10.19 feeding write select and read select are eliminated because the inversion is no longer required with the sense amp/write driver package (SN75370). However, the SN74H00 gate in this same logic (Fig. 10.19) must be changed to a SN7437 in order to handle the load of 16 standard TTL loads.

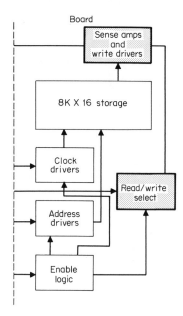

Fig. 10.29. 8K × 16 board block diagram.

Table 10.5.   Input Capacitive Load (picofarads)

Address	3.5
Reset	40
Clock	18
Chip select	18
I/O	3.5

It was mentioned previously that chip select need not be enabled to refresh; thus, driver power could be saved. By driving chip select and clock together, four drivers can be saved, eliminating the possibility of reducing the power on refresh. These drivers are eliminated in the system that follows.

The loading on the drivers needs to be checked to determine if any overloading occurs because of a new storage element. Table 10.5 lists the storage element input and output capacitive loading (ILF).

Loading factors using these input capacitive loads can be calculated as before. These are listed in Table 10.6.

The address capacitive load is reduced in half from the TMS1103. This means that the number of drivers can be reduced in half. However, to minimize power dissipation, a choice is made to continue to enable only those address devices for the 4K segment of memory that is selected. Therefore, 20 address drivers are still required. The clock and chip select drivers are similar to the load for the TMS1103, but if combined, will present a load of 576 pF—still quite acceptable for the driver (SN75361). The big load difference is in the reset load—640 pF—however, the driver can still handle this with an increase of only 5 to 10 ns in delay. Parallel units can be used if this is critical.

With this large load on reset, it would seem that the dynamic power dissipation would be higher than the previous system under normal operation. It is, but the difference is small because the address capacitive load has been reduced in half and compensates. On refresh, approximately the same total capacitance is being driven, so power dissipation is the same—unless chip select is disabled.

Total System. In Fig. 10.30 the controller and the 8K × 16 board are combined. As mentioned previously, the controller is considered the same; the only significant changes are in the boards.

What are the results? First, a comparison of the 8K × 16 board package count. This is shown in Fig. 10.31. Recall that the first system has 172 packages. This system has a total of 158 packages, 14 less packages. This reduced number results from 8 less packages of data-in drivers, 4 less packages of clock drivers, and 2 less

Table 10.6.   8K × 16 Loading Factors (picofarads)

Address	448
R	640
C, CS	288
I/O	28

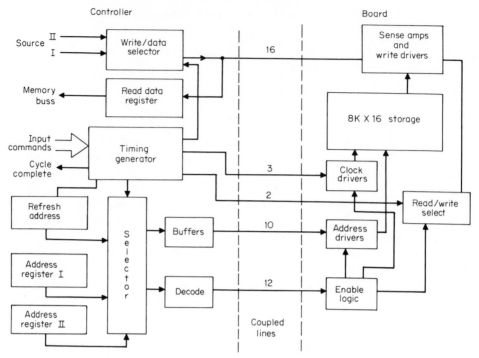

Fig. 10.30. System diagram—controller and board.

logic packages. Since the special timing circuit for turning off precharge in the first system is no longer required, another logic gate package is also saved in addition to the previous one.

Second, performance can be defined by examining the timing chart (Fig. 10.32). The time provided for the external decode logic, the address selectors to energize, and the stabilization of the address is 111 ns from the start of a cycle due to cycle

	TMS1103	TMS4062
Storage	128	128
S/A (plus write)	8	(8)
Drivers		
R/W	4	
Pre (reset)	4	(4)
Cen (Clk, CS)	4	(4)
Address	10	10
Data in	8	
	30	18
Logic	6	4
Total	172	158

Fig. 10.31. Package count on the board (8K $\times$ 16 packages).

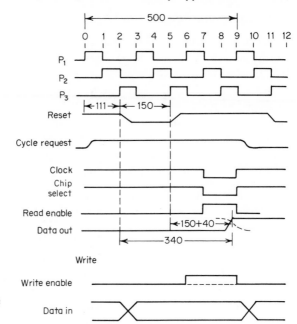

Fig. 10.32. A timing chart for the system.

request. The system access time is 340 ns from the start of reset—precharge—rather than 430 ns previously. The cycle time is now 500 ns instead of 750 ns.

The count of selected packages for a word of 16 bits is:

16 storage elements
10 address drivers
 2 clock drivers
16 S/A, write driver
 4 logic packages

One hundred and twelve storage elements are unselected.

Power dissipation is 10.3 W (83 μW per bit), approximately half the power dissipation of the previous system under these conditions.

Summary of the Two Systems. The 8K $\times$ 16 board for the second system uses 14 less packages, dissipates about one-half the power, and has an access time which is at least 30 percent faster. So the storage element with the four negative factors really provides some significant performance advantages when designed into a system. The extra power supply required does not seem a deterrent, but the large package may influence some system designers. However, as mentioned, an 18-pin package is available. The much simplified timing and the reduction to only two clocks certainly are advantages that are very significant.

Semiconductor mainframe memory using MOS random access storage elements is here today. The techniques and approaches that have been discussed provide million bit memory systems which are easy to use and which provide speed performance and low cost that exceed cost-effective core systems by a factor of 2 to 1.[11,14]

10.7 CONTINUING DEVELOPMENTS

Developments are continuing at a rapid pace in four areas: faster speeds, higher density, more low-level logic input compatibility, and n-channel processing. P-channel is not to be discarded, for, as previously mentioned, it has been the early leader in lower cost devices and progress is continuing. For example, the 1103 storage element has faster speed versions with access time under 200 ns ($t_a = 150$ ns).[3] Additional developments by the industry also have pin compatible 1,024 p-channel units that do not have the timing constraints that exist for the 1103.[3,21]

P-channel advances in density have produced a 2,048-bit storage element (TMS6003) with these major characteristics:

Organization . . . . 2,048 × 1
Decode . . . . Fully decoded
Signal levels
    Clock . . . . V_{IHB}: +4 V
                              V_{ILA}: − 14 V
    Inputs except clock . . . . V_{IHB}: +3.5 V
                              V_{ILA}: +0.5 V
Output . . . . Single ended with
                              output current at   One level 0.6 mA min
                                                     Zero level 0.1 mA max
Access time t_{pA} . . . . 360 ns
Read cycle . . . . 595 ns
Write cycle . . . . 595 ns
Refresh time . . . . 2 ms (70°C)
Power dissipation . . . . 160 mW operating
Terminals
  11 address
  Data in
  Data out
  Write enable (R/W)
  Chip select
  Timed signals
    1. Clock 1
    2. Clock 2
    3. Clock 3
  Power
    1. V_{SS}: +5.0 V
    2. V_{SX}: +8.0 V
    3. V_{DD}: − 15 V
Package . . . . 22 pin dual-in-line

Besides its increased density, another important feature of such a storage element is the compatible drive with low-level logic on all inputs except the three clocks, thus removing the requirement for many special high-voltage translators on the address, write enable, and chip select input lines. The clock voltages must still be typically 20-V signals, and they do require translation. In addition, level shifting must be provided from the driver input low-level logic. A rather inexpensive approach is shown in Fig. 10.33*a*, using a driver similar to the one for the 1103 system (Fig. 10.3) coupled with a discrete PNP transistor. The pull-down time constant is dependent upon the value of R_L and therefore can be a limiting item for maximum speed performance.

If the high level of the drive voltage to the discrete PNP needs to be a value closer to +5 V, V_{CC2} on the driver can be raised to a voltage greater than +5 V or a pull-up resistor can be added in the input line as shown. Obviously more power dissipation results.

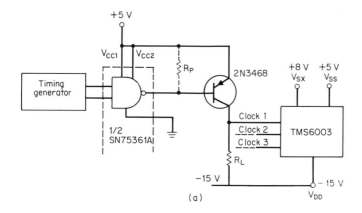

(a)

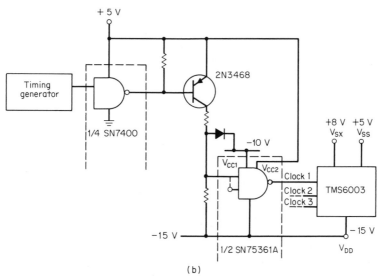

(b)

Fig. 10.33. Driver, translator, and level shifter: (*a*) simple resistive load; (*b*) active pull-up and pull-down.

A translator configuration that has much better drive capability is shown in Fig. 10.33*b*. An additional power supply line is required, but the gate interface to the PNP is now a simple low-level logic gate.

Other features are incorporated in the 2,048-bit storage element to eliminate support circuitry. The data-out and address lines already have latches built onto the chip; therefore they are not required externally. The output drive can be fed directly into a TTL gate, a sense amplifier with a TTL output, or a discrete device.[15] The 3-transistor cell is of the complementing type discussed in Chap. 5 and contains a data control register to keep track of the data as they are refreshed.

Certainly the increased density per package, the low power dissipation, and the peripheral circuit savings are distinct advantages to the designer. Added to these is the implied increased reliability because of less system external interconnection.

However, the desire for more density continues, and a 4,096 p-channel storage element has been reported by Lambrechtse, Salters, and Boonstra.[16] Such a storage element is expected to have an access time of 300 ns and a cycle time of less than 450 ns with the dissipation to be 150 mW. Again, address and input/output lines would be low-level logic compatible. Only one clock is required at a 10-V level, but other clocks are generated within the storage element. The 1-transistor cell size falls within the sizes discussed in Chap. 5: 1.35 sq mils.

Obviously such density, low power, and easy-to-use features are quite important, as we have emphasized many times, and the standard p-channel technology is important from an economic standpoint. However, the remaining area of intense development activity—n-channel processing—adds another dimension of increased speed performance to these advantages.

10.8 N-CHANNEL RAMS

In Chaps. 2 and 5 the advantages of n-channel MOS devices for RAM cells and storage elements were discussed. Let us review these.

First, the higher mobility provides an increased transconductance, g_m, and thus faster speed performance (by a factor of 2; see Chap. 2). Second, lower voltage operation is possible, resulting in higher density packing. Third, the lower voltage operation provides the interface compatibility with low-level logic that makes n-channel storage elements easier to use because of the simplified peripheral circuitry. Two significant additional advantages result from the n-channel developments: simplified refreshing and simplified timing.

Developments have occurred in both the static and the dynamic area. Following the lead of Altman,[3] these can be summarized into three application segments as shown in Table 10.7. The fastest performance with moderate density and moderate power dissipation is for segment I, the simplest to use for segment II, and the lowest cost and highest density for segment III.

10.9 INTERFACE WITH N-CHANNEL

Before proceeding with the application of specific n-channel storage elements, it is necessary to look at the difference between the interface of typical NPN bipolar integrated circuit drivers and the n-channel MOS RAMs.

Table 10.7   Product Segments for n-Channel

Segment	Cost	Speed performance, ns	Density, bits	Power dissipation, mW	Power supplies	Interface
I	High	Fast (50–80)	Moderate (1–2K)	Moderate (150–500)	More than one	Moderate to easy
II	Medium	Slow (300–1,000)	Moderate (1–2K)	Moderate (150–300)	One	Simple
III	Low	Moderate (150–500)	High (4–?)	Moderate (400–800)	More than one	Easy

Figure 10.34 compares a typical p-channel and n-channel gate being driven by a bipolar driver with active pull-up on the output. Note that the output of the NPN bipolar driver IC is high (near $+ V_{CC2}$) when the p-channel device is held off but must be low (near ground) when the n-channel device is off. The normal NPN bipolar driver IC dissipates a large amount of power when the output voltage level is low but much less power when the output voltage is high. As explained for the driver of Fig. 10.3, for example, typical power dissipation is approximately 173 mW when the output level is low and 13 mW when the output level is high.

Under the same operating conditions and voltage swing, the operating power for a given duty cycle for driving the input capacitive load for either the n-channel or p-channel would be the same. It is made up of the typical operating power dissipa-

MOS Input logic level	V_0 value	State of p–channel gate
V_{OH} V_{OL}	Near V_{SS} ($+ V_{CC2}$) Near V_{DD} (GND)	Off On

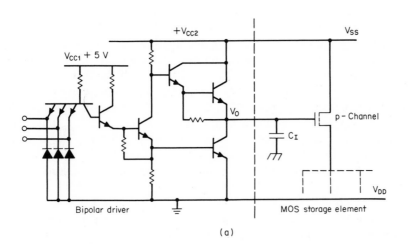

(a)

MOS Input logic level	V_0 value	State of n-channel gate
V_{OH}	Near V_{DD} $(+ V_{CC2})$	On
V_{OL}	Near V_{SS} (GND)	Off

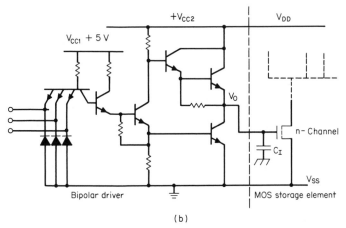

Fig. 10.34. Bipolar to MOS interface: (*a*) p-channel; (*b*) n-channel.

tion of the driver itself (for Fig. 10.3 approximately 95mW for a 50 percent duty cycle) and that given by Eq. (10-4) due to the dynamic power dissipation.

Under standby conditions or conditions of unselected storage elements, the situation is different. Under these conditions, as demonstrated in Figs. 10.18 to 10.21, the system design is implemented in a majority of cases to keep the driver power dissipation to a minimum. Because the standby level or level for holding the internal n-channel devices OFF is the high dissipation state, additional design features must be added to keep the dissipation to a minimum. Other gating or new PNP integrated circuit drivers must be developed and applied to accomplish this.

Several examples of other gating are shown in Fig. 10.35. In Fig. 10.35*a* the driver output stage voltage supply line, V_{CC2}, is gated to all the drivers on the board only when the board is enabled. This saves 66 percent of the power dissipated when the driver output is in the low level. In Fig. 10.35*b* both the driver output stage and low-level logic voltage supply lines are gated. This saves considerably more power, another 29 percent, because the input stages to the drivers dissipate significant power. This configuration gates a separate voltage supply line, V_{BB}, that supplies the base of the output stage driver transistor (SN75365). Thus the V_{BB} voltage can be greater than V_{SS} and the output voltage pulled closer to V_{SS} for more design noise margin. Again the control input could be board enable. Resistors R_2 must be added to the output line of the driver to discharge the MOS control line to ground when the driver supplies are disengaged. R_1, of course, is just to prevent ringing on the lines. In Fig. 10.35*c* the voltage supplies of the driver are not gated, but a PNP inverter is placed in the logic path so that a high level output from the NPN

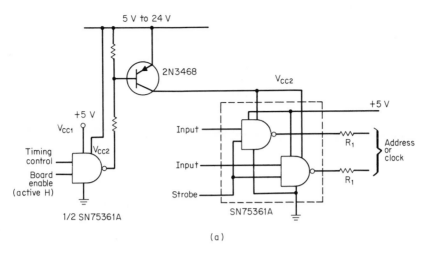

(a)

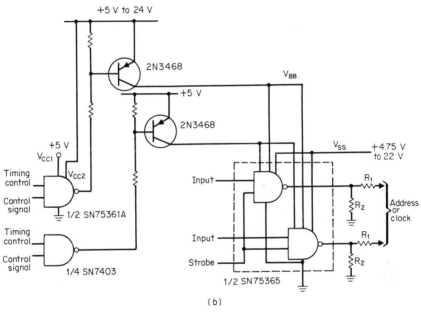

(b)

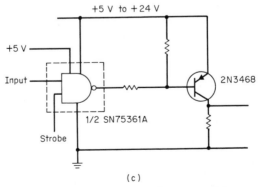

(c)

Fig. 10.35. N-channel drivers with low standby power: (*a*) output stage voltage only; (*b*) output stage and input logic; (*c*) low standby.

integrated circuit driver is now a low level to the n-channel MOS. Both these stages are then in a low-power dissipation state. The drive time constant is limited by the load resistor and line capacitance [see Fig. 9.7 and Eq. (9-15)].

10.10   APPLICATIONS

10.10.1   Simplest to Use

Now let us expand on the application of the product segments which were illustrated in Table 10.7. First, segment II. The developments of n-channel RAMs that operate from a single $+5$ V power supply make them completely compatible with bipolar low-level logic. The advantages cited for n-channel due to low voltage operation have resulted in the design of static MOS RAMs with 1,024 bits with little more chip area than used for a p-channel with 256 bits.[3] Since these are static they need no refreshing and no excess interface circuitry. They are, however, much slower than the fast dynamic RAMs of segment I. With features similar to bipolar, such n-channel units are in direct competition with their bipolar counterparts in equipment where speed performance is of no concern. For example, Table 10.8 contains data of a simple system such as shown in Fig. 9.17. It has been converted to a $1K \times 16$-bit memory system with four times the capacity with the addition of the necessary address signals (substitute 74174 register for 74175). The number of packages is the same. Note the access time is something greater than 500 ns, rather than less than 60 ns. In exchange for the loss in speed performance, there is almost seven times less system power dissipated per bit of storage. Similar conversions can be made for the other bipolar systems of Chaps. 9 and 11 with corresponding reductions in power dissipation and much slower access times.

10.10.2   Fastest Speed Performance

Segment I of Table 10.7 is the product segment that has the fastest speed performance. As indicated in the table, the access times are 50 to 80 ns. In Chap. 5 the internal refresh dynamic RAM cell was discussed: first, the system is simplified because extensive refresh circuitry is eliminated; second, there is more availability of the memory because there is no down time for refreshing.

All 1,024 bits of a storage element made from these cells are simultaneously refreshed by the application of a write pulse, and one such pulse can refresh an entire system because storage elements that are not enabled are also refreshed.[17] Therefore, on write cycles the total memory is refreshed and, by including a write

Table 10.8.   Bipolar versus Static n-Channel

System	Packages	Access time, ns	P_D, W	P_D/bit, mW
Bipolar 256 $\times$ 16	$21\frac{1}{4}$	<60	≤ 9	≤ 2.2
N-channel MOS RAM 1,024 $\times$ 16	$21\frac{1}{4}$	>500	≤ 5.8	≤ 0.3

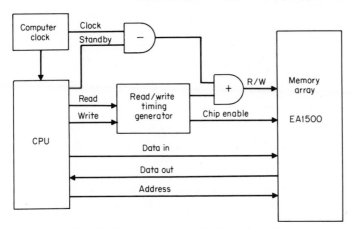

Fig. 10.36. Automatic refresh each cycle.

pulse at the end of a read cycle, or in other words every system cycle, no memory system interruptions result. This of course extends the cycle time typically from 200 ns to 500 ns. For fastest speed, a single pulse can be used every 2 ms. No address selection is required and the memory is busy due to refresh only 0.01 percent of the time. Systems of this type, described by Walther,[17] are shown in Figs. 10.36 and 10.37. A timing diagram (Fig. 10.38) identifies the time sequence of pulses applied to the storage elements from the control circuitry shown in Fig. 10.37. The timing for refresh is now simply providing a memory busy pulse which enables a write pulse and disables the chip enable control signal, with this occurring if there has been no write cycle for 2 ms. The same generation technique referred to previously for timing can apply. Because of the simplicity, one-shot multivibrator integrated circuits are well suited for this application.

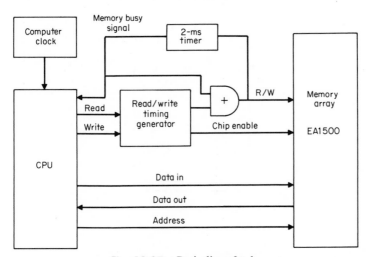

Fig. 10.37. Periodic refresh.

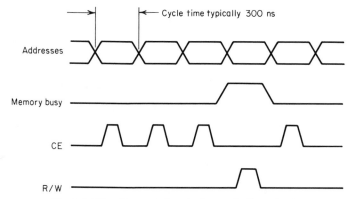

Fig. 10.38. Control signals for periodic refresh.

However, the interface is somewhat complicated. In this particular design (EA1500) plus and minus power supplies of 12 to 15 V must be used, and the address signals and control signals must have translators and level shifters from low-level logic to +12 to 15 V and −12 to 15 V. Therefore, the interface requirements are comparable to the p-channel high-voltage system discussed and are not as simple as indicated in Figs. 10.36 and 10.37.

In Chap. 5 the charge pump RAM cell was discussed (see Fig. 5.17). This concept has been applied to the 4-transistor cell illustrated in Figs. 5.5 and 5.6. Figure 10.39

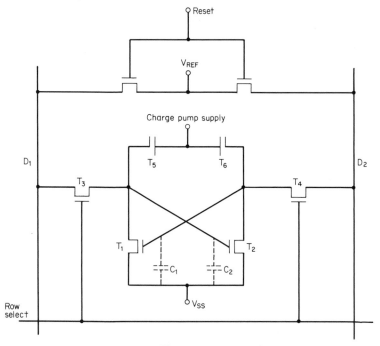

Fig. 10.39. Charge pump refreshing.

shows such a cell. The addition of devices T_5 and T_6 to each cell performs the charge pump function and keeps the data continuously refreshed onto C_1 and C_2 as appropriate. Such an MOS RAM cell, when used in a storage element, now has the characteristics of a static RAM storage element but the density and power dissipation of a dynamic storage element. For example, a 1,024-bit storage element has demonstrated access times of 55 ns and a cycle time of 180 ns for both read and write.[18]

Considerable power—450 to 500 mW—is dissipated in the storage element when it is operating to obtain this speed. Normal standby power would be high also, but with the charge pump refreshing, the power down standby mode power is only 2 mW. This represents a power dissipation of the same order of magnitude as the previous p-channel 1,024 chip with row selection refresh (*cf*. TMS4062).

The interface to all input signal lines except clock is compatible to low-level logic; however, pull-up resistors must be provided on normal TTL driver outputs to make sure the MOS input voltage high-logic level is greater than 3.5 V. Such a storage element, because of the speed performance, is more likely to be used with ECL logic. The input interface to ECL 10K is shown in Fig. 10.40.

The clock level must be a 15 V signal and can be interfaced as shown in Fig. 10.40. The reference voltage and substrate bias voltage must also be provided.

The output is a differential output that must be referenced to $+8$ V. Its interface is shown in Fig. 10.40, again to ECL. A voltage-controlled oscillator whose output is a square wave is used as the charge pump source. Its frequency can be adjusted by varying the V_{RANGE} voltage; 100 kHz seems to be a recommended frequency.

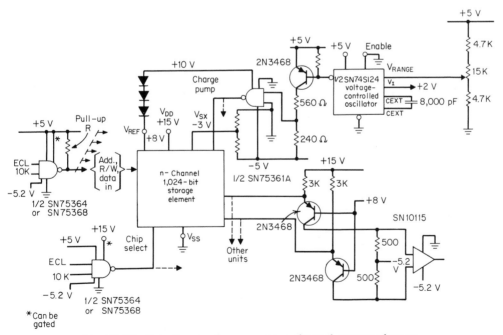

Fig. 10.40.   Interface to charge pump n-channel storage element.

Of course, gated power lines can be used to reduce driver power, as previously discussed and as indicated on Fig. 10.40.

Many interfaces may be required with IBM's 370 systems. Converters are available (AC1736, AC1737) from these ECL logic levels to TTL, and vice versa. The TTL input drivers previously discussed can then be used.

Besides the high-speed performance, input signal compatibility and simplified refresh circuitry are added benefits of the use of such a unit.

10.10.3 Lowest Cost, Highest Density

The third product segment (segment III) is one designed for lowest cost per bit of storage. Highest density per package is the tool and, of course, at the fastest speed and the lowest power. The design approaches were outlined in Chap. 5 and there are many approaches being followed,[19] so let's look at a specific unit. Our choice is a unit using a 1-transistor cell, the TMS4030. It has the following characteristics:

Organization . . . . 4,096 × 1

Decode . . . . Fully decoded

Signal levels

    All inputs other than

      clock . . . . V_{IH}: 2.4 V

                      V_{IL}: 0.6 V

    Clock . . . . V_{IH}: +12 V

                      V_{IL}: 0 V

    Output . . . .   Three-state:

                      High level—2 mA @ 2.5 V

                      Low level—3.2 mA @ 0.4 V

                      High impedance—clock low or C/S high

Access time t_{pA} . . . . <300 ns

Read cycle . . . . ≥470 ns

Write cycle . . . . ≥470 ns

Refresh time . . . . 2 ms (70°C)

Power dissipation . . . . . . 660 mW total operating

                      400 mW typical operating

                      0.1 mW per bit

                      2 mW standby

Terminals

  12 addresses

  Data in

  Data out

  R/W (read/write)

  Clock

  $\overline{\text{C/S}}$ (chip select)

  Power

    1. V_{DD}: +12 V

    2. V_{CC}: +5 V

    3. V_{SX}: −3 V

    4. V_{SS}: GND

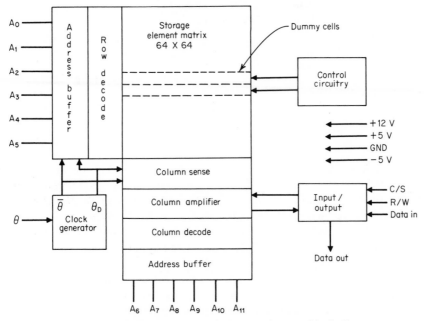

Fig. 10.41. A 4,096-bit n-channel storage element block diagram.

All signal lines are true TTL low-level logic compatible except clock. Note that even with the density of 4,096 bits the access time is 300 ns, and the cycle time of 470 ns and the power dissipation of 0.10 mW per bit are the same range of performance parameters as for the low-cost p-channel dynamic storage elements.

The block diagram (Fig. 10.41) shows a square matrix such that each one of 64 rows must now be accessed every 2 ms at 70°C in order to refresh the storage element. Note the rows of dummy cells and the control circuitry. These are used for internal control of the data. The output now is a three-state output with a high impedance state when the chip is not enabled or selected.

The line capacitances are shown in Table 10.9. This storage element can now be substituted for the 1,024-bit storage element used for the systems previously discussed. For example, the 8K $\times$ 16 board (see Figure 10.16) now becomes a 32K $\times$ 16 board. The package size has changed to a 22 pin dual-in-line package, increasing the board area required.

The loading on the lines can be checked by using the loading equations of

**Table 10.9.   4,096 n-Channel
Line Capacitance**

Line	Max. capacitance, pF
Clock	27
C/S	6
R/W	7.5
Address	7.0
Data in	6.0
Data out	7.0

**Table 10.10. Comparison of Driver
Loads for Two Systems**

Line	8K × 16, pF	32K × 16, pF
Address	896	896
Clock	(Pre) 288	432
C/S	(Cen) 288	96
R/W	(R/W) 240	120
Data in	40	48
Data out	24	56

Chap. 9. The results compared to the previous loading for the 8K × 16 board (TMS1103) are shown in Table 10.10. The address load is the same in both cases and the only significant load difference is in the load on the clock. This, however, is still well within the capabilities of the drivers used.

Referring to Fig. 10.16, it can be seen that the sense amplifiers and write drivers can now just be straightforward TTL gates since the output and input current and voltage levels are TTL compatible. A TTL gate with a three-state output on the data-out line can be an advantage (SN74S134). All the address drivers should still be SN75361 drivers because of the current output for fast charging and discharging of the line capacitance. However, the voltage supply is now +5 V rather than the high-voltage level. The same is true of the R/W and C/S driver. The only one that is high voltage (+12 V) is the clock driver. On all these drivers the gating of the power supply to provide a low dissipation state can be implemented. Of course, two more address signals are required because of the larger number of bits in the storage element. Since the address drivers must be doubled because of the capacitive load, four more drivers are required.

The other logic can remain the same as before if the power supply gating is not used.

Table 10.11 gives the package count comparison and the power dissipation of the board for the two systems. The power dissipation is with 16 memory modules selected and 112 unselected and the associated logic, drivers, sense amplifiers, and write drivers activated. Note the very small increase in packages (four) for a very large increase in memory capacity and a 5:1 reduction in power dissipation per bit. Approximately the same speed performance is obtained as with the p-channel TMS1103.

The timing generator must be changed because of the much simpler timing. The refresh address times must be made to run faster, for now 64 lines must be covered in 2 ms and, of course, another refresh address must be selected.

**Table 10.11. Comparison of Boards for p-Channel
and n-Channel Systems**

System	Packages	P_D total, W	P_D/bit, μW
8K × 16 board (TMS1103)	172	21	167
32K × 16 board (TMS4030)	174	16.2	31.6

10.11   FURTHER DEVELOPMENTS

Already projections are being made for 8K and 16K storage elements. Hoffman and Kalter[20] reported on an 8,192-bit p-channel silicon gate storage element using a 1-transistor cell. Initial access time is 1,730 ns but subsequent access time is 540 ns. Other units of the same density and beyond using n-channel are certainly likely in the next few years. Such progress in design of products that are easy to use, promote system simplicity, and have low cost potential will continue into the foreseeable future and provide exciting product developments to assure that the mainframe memory designer will continue the innovative and pervasive application of semiconductor storage elements.

REFERENCES

1. L. M. Terman, MOSFET Memory Circuits, *IEEE Proc.,* **5:** 1044–1057(July 1971).
2. W. N. Carr and J. P. Mize, "MOS/LSI Design and Application," chap. 2, McGraw-Hill Book Company, New York, 1972.
3. L. Altman, Special Report: Semiconductor RAMs Land Computer Mainframe Jobs, *Electronics,* pp. 63–77, August 28, 1972.
4. L. Altman, N-Channel MOS Bids for Mainframes, *Electronics,* pp. 90–91, July 31, 1972.
5. L. Boysel, W. Chan, and J. Faith, Random Access MOS Memory Packs More Bits to the Chip, *Electronics,* pp. 109–115, February 16, 1970.
6. W. M. Regitz and J. Karp, Three-transistor Cell 1,024-bit 500 nS MOS RAM, *IEEE J.,* **SC-5**(5): 181–182(1970).
7. M. E. Hoff, Jr., The 1103–1024 Memory Bits on a Chip, *Electron. Des.,* pp. 40–45, January 20, 1972.
8. D. Leonard, MOS Memories, *EEE,* **12**(11): 54–61(November 1969).
9. W. F., Jordan, Jr., Main Memory: Past, Present and Future, *Honeywell Computer J.,* **5**(2): 52–57(1971).
10. M. E. Hoff, Jr., Assembling Large Array IC Memories, *Electron. Des.,* **4:** 76–81(February 17, 1972).
11. W. M. Regitz and H. F. Bodio, A MOS Main Memory System, *Honeywell Computer J.,* **5**(2): 66–71(1971).
12. L. L. Vadasz, H. T. Chua, and A. S. Grove, Semiconductor Random-access Memories, *IEEE Spectrum,* **8**(5): 40–48(May 1971).
13. M. E. Hoff, Jr., 5W Per Million Bits of Memory, *Electron. Des.,* **5:** 50–53(March 2, 1972).
14. R. Graham and M. Hoff, Why Semiconductor Memories, *Electron. Prod.,* **11:** 28–34(January 1970).
15. M. Geilhufe, More Bits/Chip Lead to Economical Semiconductor Memory Systems, *EDN,* **18**(4): 76–81(February 20, 1973).
16. C. W. Lambrechtse, R. H. W. Salters, and L. Boonstra, A 4096 Bit One-transistor per Bit RAM with Internal Timing and Low Dissipation, *ISSCC73 Dig. Tech. Pap.,* pp. 26–27.
17. T. R. Walther, Dynamic N-MOS RAM with Simplified Refresh, *Comput. Des.,* **12**(2): 53–58(February 1973).
18. Product review, *Electronics,* **46**(5): 36–38(March 1, 1973).
19. H. Wolff, 4,096 Bit Rams Are on the Doorstep, *Electronics,* pp. 75–77, April 12, 1973.
20. W. K. Hoffman and H. L. Kalter, An 8K Bit Random-access Memory Chip Using a One-device FET Cell, *ISSCC73 Dig. Tech. Pap.,* pp. 64–65.
21. G. Sideris, The Intel 1103: The MOS Memory That Defied Cores, *Electronics,* pp. 108–113, April 26, 1973.

11

Large Mainframe Memories

11.1 INTRODUCTION

Although semiconductor storage had its initial applications in the smaller memory systems for minicomputers and small data processing systems, semiconductor storage is also entirely applicable to large mainframe memory systems.[1,2] In fact it is more than applicable; it is cost effective for large systems being designed today. In this chapter discussion concerns the application of semiconductor storage elements in large mainframe memory systems.

During several generations of computers, CPU speeds have increased by a factor of 1,000; such high speeds have provided the ability to handle larger problems and have resulted in demands for much larger memory capacities. No longer is memory capacity limited to thousands of words; memory capacity is now in millions of words. Moreover the memory system designer not only wants large capacity; he wants fast-speed operation also, speeds comparable to those of the CPU. But these desires for high-speed performance and large capacity are contradictory. Large-capacity memory has been large *physically,* and the propagation time of data, even at the speed of light, results in time delays from CPU to memory and back again that are two or three *times* the access time of the basic storage module itself. For example, the IBM 360/95 has a basic storage-module access time of 60 ns, yet the CPU's *true* access time to 128K, 64-bit words is 180 ns.[2]

The two-level memory concept made possible by the advent of high-speed semiconductor storage elements has changed this. The fact that semiconductor integrated-circuit technology made possible SC storage elements and systems with sufficient capacity to match the CPU speed was the key to successful application of a two-level main memory.[3]

11.2 TWO-LEVEL MAIN MEMORY

A multilevel memory system, properly organized, can resolve the clash between the desire for CPU memory speeds and the physical factors limiting the performance. The two-level main memory consists of two memories as illustrated in Fig. 11.1. One memory is a buffer store identified as M_C, with the C designating this

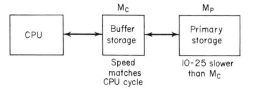

Fig. 11.1. A two-level main memory block diagram.

buffer as a *cache* memory. The buffer memory is small, *fast* to match the CPU cycle and close-in for quick accessibility. The other memory is the M_P, or primary storage, which is a large-capacity memory whose cycle time is 10 to 25 times slower than that of the M_C. To the program and the CPU, the cache memory looks like the main memory, and the cache, containing instructions and data immediately required for processing, exchanges these directly with the CPU.

Information is transferred from M_P to M_C in blocks with more information being transferred to M_C from M_P than is immediately requested by the CPU. Therefore, most of the time the information required by the CPU is in M_C and accessible at the CPU's cycle speed. The concept is feasible because *programs* usually consist of lists of instructions in successive locations, to be executed in sequence with blocks of *data* usually in adjacent locations. Stated another way, most of the information required by a program at a given time is found together in a relatively small segment of storage. If the information required by the CPU is *not* in M_C, then the request is sent to M_P and the block of information containing the desired data is transferred to M_C. This does call for slowing down the CPU to the M_P cycle speed until the data are transferred, but subsequent information will then most likely be in M_C, and the CPU once again requests and receives these data at the rate of the CPU cycle.

Three features of this two-level concept contribute to increased processor performance.[3] First, it increases the useful bandwidth of M_P. Second, valuable information is prefetched and present in M_C. And third, information contained in M_C is frequently reused. Of course, one of the requirements of the system is that the request for information from the CPU must be compared with the data in the cache memory to determine whether the information is present in the cache or must be fetched from M_P.

11.2.1 Analysis of Two-level Systems

The techniques of organizing the data flow are of interest to allow the characteristics of the buffer storage and the primary storage to be identified.

Four types of buffer designs have been analyzed: fully associative, sector, direct mapping, and set associative. Several articles by Conti,[3] Mead,[4] and Scarrott[5] survey these various two-level memory systems. In the discussion in this chapter the details of the direct mapping and the set-associative approach will be described as they relate to a small computer system and a large computer system, respectively. The fully associative buffer and sector buffer designs will then be compared, generally, to the other two designs.

Direct Mapping. Although the two-level memory has been applied most efficiently to *large* computer systems, as will be discussed for the set-associative design, it also has been utilized in small computers by using the direct mapping design. Bell and Casasent[6] described such a system.

Block Diagram. Figure 11.2 shows an M_P of 2^n words and a buffer storage M_C of 2^m words. M_P is divided into sectors of 2^m words or blocks, identified by tag bits for each sector from 0 to $2n/2m - 1$. In effect, each "buffer-full" is numbered.

When sector S is stored in M_C from M_P, all 2^m words or blocks of sector S are transferred and stored in M_C and identified with tag bits for sector S. Block X of any sector of M_P will be contained in the same X position in M_C. The address for block X for each sector remains the same—only the sector tag bits change. The location of the word in M_C locates the block in the sector, and thus the block in M_P that contains the word. Identifying the tag bits locates the sector of M_P from which the block was taken.

The CPU requests one of the 2^m blocks of information via an effective address which contains the block address and the sector tag bits. The address locates the block in M_C. We need only compare the tag bits of the accessed data from the M_C block, with the CPU effective address tag bits, to determine whether the data in M_C can be used by the CPU. If the data are in M_C, the CPU uses them. If not, the data must be brought from M_P. Note the write tag bit. When new data are written into a particular block, this write tag bit is made a 1. Now when new data from M_P are exchanged in M_C, the blocks with the write tag bits of 1 must be rewritten into M_P to update the data in M_P.

Other schemes of accomplishing the rewrite or update are possible. For example, every time new data are written in M_C, they are also written into M_P. Everytime the data in M_C are replaced, all data in M_C are rewritten into M_P. The particular technique depends on the choice of the designer for the specific application.

Controller. A controller block diagram[6] for direct mapping for the small computer is shown in Fig. 11.3. A comparator is shown between the registers of the CPU and M_C to compare the effective address (M_A) and the data out (D_O) of M_C. The memory address from the CPU goes to M_C; if the D_O from M_C contains tag bits that *match* M_A, then the CPU proceeds. If the data *do not* match, then M_A is sent to M_P, and that sector of data is brought into M_C. The distribution of data-in (D_I), effective memory address (M_A), and data-out (D_O) is indicated from the I/O lines to the primary memory M_P and to M_C.

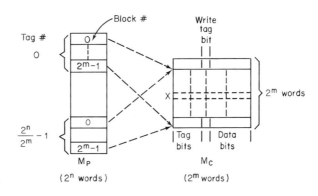

Fig. 11.2. Direct mapping.

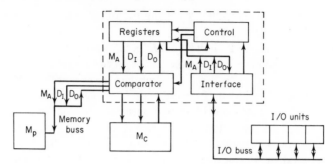

Fig. 11.3. Block diagram of a small computer controller.

Note that in such a direct mapping scheme there is no content addressable memory;[7] only a comparison circuit is present, thus avoiding the complexity inherent in CAM circuitry.

A timing diagram (Fig. 11.4) relates the various decision times to the M_C cycle time. At $t = 0$, a memory address is received. At t_1, the data out are valid and tag bits are compared to determine if the data are in M_C. If they are, the CPU proceeds with the next instruction and the next memory address, M_A, through times t_2 and t_3. If the CPU proceeds, M_A and D_I must be valid and the write or read mode line for the next cycle must be valid by t_2. If tag bits do not compare, the M_C cycle is stopped, sometime before t_2, and the M_A goes to M_P for retrieval of information, doing this at the slower time cycle of M_P.

Since the block of data in M_P can only exist in one, and only one, block in the buffer, resulting in easy comparison and fast access to the buffer, the major disadvantage is that information for the next program step might require the same block in the buffer store as the preceding information except from a different sector. This would require every step be a slow M_P cycle because the data would have to be rewritten into M_C.

Set-associative Design. A buffer design used for larger computers is called the set-associative buffer. The capacity of the M_C used for the larger machine is, of course, much larger than that used for the small computer. Figure 11.5 shows the set-associative design as described by Conti.[3] This design alleviates the contention for the same block in the buffer storage as described for the direct mapping. Specific blocks in M_P are still in specific locations in the buffer storage, but the difference is that there is more than one slot at the specific location in the buffer. For example, in Fig. 11.5 M_P is a memory of 2^n blocks or, in this example, 8,196. M_C is a buffer storage that can hold a given number of blocks, but it is organized differently than

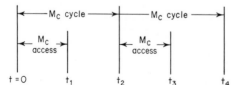

Fig. 11.4. Controller timing diagram.

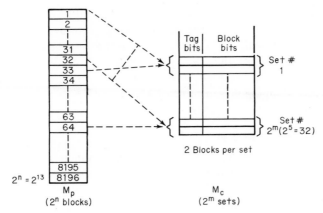

Fig. 11.5. Set-associative two-level memory system.

in Fig. 11.2 for direct mapping. Now the blocks are grouped in sets (in this example there are two blocks to a set). The capacity of the buffer is 2^m sets—with two blocks per set—and if there are 2^5 sets (32), then the buffer storage contains 64 blocks.

When the data are mapped into the buffer from M_P, if block 1 maps into set 1 then block 32 will map into set 32. Similarly, block 33 will map into set 1 and block 64 into set 32. However, there is no distinction which of the two blocks in the set holds the respective blocks of 1 and 33 or 32 and 64.

In operation, if data are required by the CPU, the effective address from the CPU contains the address for the set number plus the tag bits to identify the block number in addition to the other data bits. The buffer storage, corresponding to the set location, contains tag bits for the two block numbers as well as the word number in that block plus other data bits.

A comparison of the tag bits from the two blocks with the tag bits in the effective address from the CPU determines if the data required are in the buffer storage. If a match occurs, the selected data are gated through. If a match does not occur, then the data must be selected from M_P and written into M_C.

In set-associative design twice as many tag bits must be compared as for direct mapping but, again, the storage for the tag bits need only be random access[4] and not content addressable. This again eliminates the complexity necessary with content addressable storage.

Fully Associative Design. With the fully associative design, the M_P and M_C are again divided into blocks. Any block in M_P can be mapped into any block in M_C. A fully associative comparison of the tag bits for the block of data must be compared to every tag in the buffer storage calling for a content addressable storage of the tag bits.[4] This produces a very slow access to the data and a very complex circuit package.

Sector Buffer Design. In sector buffer design, M_P and M_C are divided into sectors much larger than the block size of the other designs. Any sector in M_P can map into any sector in M_C. The sector is further subdivided into blocks, but only sectors, one at a time, can be mapped into M_C from M_P.

Considering its advantages and complexity, sector buffer design can be placed between the fully associative and the other designs. Its advantage is that it uses relatively few tags, but it should be noted that it still needs the content-addressable or full simultaneous comparison.

Because the set-associative design combines advantages of both the fully associative and the direct mapping designs, the set-associative design seems to be the most popular design for the large systems.

11.2.2 Memory System Cost and Performance

Size and Performance Ratios. The size and performance of the buffer and the primary memory for the small and large computer are shown in Table 11.1. These are actual sizes cited in articles by Bell and Casasent[6] and by Gibson and Shevel.[2] M_P is the primary memory, M_C is the buffer or cache, and t_{cp} and t_{cc} are the primary memory and buffer memory cycle times, respectively.

For the minicomputer, a 512-word M_C and a 4,096-word M_P were used. The M_C cycle time was 100 ns, while the M_P cycle time was 1 μs, a ratio of 10 to 1. A system cycle time of 200 ns resulted from this combination.

For the large computer, the ratio of M_P speed to M_C was 12 to 1 (960 to 80 ns). In this example, the system speed was 100 ns, using an M_C of 16K bytes and an M_P of 4 million bytes.

Note that the buffer sizes range from 8 to 256 times *smaller* than primary storage, depending on the system with the buffer being from 10 to 12 times as *fast* as the primary storage. The size ratio may be as large as 1,000 and the speed ratio as large as 25 in some system designs.

Simulated programs for large machine designs have indicated that, with a buffer of 16K to 32K bytes, this capacity is sufficient to hold, on an average, 95 percent of all storage requests from the CPU. Theoretically, this type cache system attains between 64 and 96 percent of the system performance that could, theoretically, be achieved with a single memory having the speed of the M_C and the capacity of the M_P.[2]

Cost-Performance Ratios. Following the lead of Bell and Casasent,[6] relative cost, relative performance, and a cost-performance ratio of two types of two-level memory systems are shown in Table 11.2. Again, the two systems are the small and large computer systems that have been discussed. The single-level core main memory system is used for reference for all the relative comparisons, with comparisons made for present conditions and projected to 1975.

Table 11.1. Two-level Memory System Size and Performance

Computer	Size			Performance			
	M_P	M_C	Size ratio M_p/M_c	t_{cp}	t_{cc}	System	Cycle time ratio M_P/M_C
Small	4,096 words	512 words	8	1 μs	100 ns	200 ns	10
Large	4M bytes	16K bytes	256	960 ns	80 ns	100 ns	12

Table 11.2. Two-level Memory System Relative Cost and Performance

Computer	P Speed performance		C Cost per bit		P/C ratio all core = 1	
	1972	1975	1972	1975	1972	1975
Small						
All core	1	1	×	×	1.0	1.0
S C MOS	2	3	×	0.5×	2.0	6.0
Cache/core	5	5	1.5×	1.2×	3.3	4.1
Cache/MOS		5		0.7×		7.1
Large						
All core	1	1	×	×	1.0	1.0
S C MOS	2	2	1.5×	0.5×	1.3	4.0
Cache/core	10	10	1.1×	1.1×	9.0	9.0
Cache/MOS		10		0.6×		17.0

Comparisons are made between a single-level core main memory and:

1. Cache/core which is a two-level memory system with a semiconductor M_C and a core M_P
2. Cache/MOS which is an all-semiconductor two-level memory system in which both M_C and M_P are semiconductors (M_P uses dynamic MOS)
3. SC MOS which is an all-semiconductor single-level main memory using dynamic MOS

Performance. At present, for the small computer, the cache/core memory is five times faster than an all-core memory; the all-MOS memory is two times faster. Projected to 1975, and considering that the performance of core memory will increase slightly, the relative speed ratio between cache/core and an all-core memory will be the same, five times. However, because of n-channel MOS, the speed performance of the all-MOS main memory will be three times better than the single-level core system. The cache/MOS system, with a very economical dynamic MOS M_P, will have the same relative performance as the cache/core system since the performance depends heavily on the performance of the high-speed cache buffer.

At present, the large computer cache/core system is 10 times faster than the single-level core; the all-MOS system is two times faster. The same relationships should continue through 1975, since the cache/core and cache/MOS systems are basically the same, and since n-channel MOS performance will not have much impact before 1975 on the very large economical mainframe memory, a memory will likely continue to be designed and built with p-channel MOS. The n-channel systems designed next year will start to have their impact after this.

Cost. An all-MOS memory and a core memory for the small computer presently are considered at a size where the cost is the same as discussed in Chap. 1.[8] For the large computer, core is presently less expensive than all-MOS. The factor shown is 1.5 higher cost for MOS. For 1975, in both the small and large computer, the all-MOS memory will be half the cost of core, as was explained in Chap. 1.

A premium is paid for the high-speed cache memory. Presently, for the small computer the cost of the two-level cache/core is 50 percent more than core itself.[6]

Since semiconductor memory will continue to decrease in price as volume increases (Chap. 1), the cost differential for high-speed cache will decrease such that the relative cost for the cache/core is 1.2 in 1975. Note the cache/MOS relative cost for the small computer. Considering that the cache cost adds 0.2X per bit to the total, the relative cost for the cache/MOS in 1975 is 0.7X.

Costs of the large computer follow the same pattern as those for the small computer. The cache is a smaller percentage of the total cost of the system because of the system size. Therefore, the cache/core relative cost is 1.1X and the cache/MOS is 0.6X. Note that in both systems all-semiconductor memories have an excellent cost picture.

Performance-Cost Ratio. A ratio is formed between the relative performance and the relative cost per bit for each system type for each year. This ratio compares the cost effectiveness of the memory system to provide a given performance at a given price versus the performance-price factors of an all-core system—the higher the ratio, the better the efficiency of the system.

In both the small computer and the large computer system, the cache/core system has the highest present performance-cost ratio, 3.3 and 9. However, the comparison is quite different in 1975. The all-MOS main memory is more cost effective than core or cache/core for the small computer. But cost effectiveness of the *all-semiconductor two-level memory system* is even more attractive. With bipolar buffer for M_C and dynamic MOS for M_P, the relative performance-cost ratio is 7.1 for small computers and 17.0 for large computers—almost twice as effective as cache/core. As n-channel MOS high-speed units move into production, some of them will likely be used for the buffer.

11.2.3 Summary

Thus far the discussion has shown that using a fast buffer memory and a relatively slow primary memory simulates a virtual memory that has speed performance approximating that of the buffer memory. Also, it has been shown how a two-level memory, which is now a combination of semiconductor and magnetics, will probably be *all-semiconductor*. This will occur in the very near future when the MOS storage elements can be purchased at a lower cost per system bit than core.

11.3 ECL MEMORY

A key to a two-level memory is the buffer storage element. The TTL bipolar random access memory systems previously described in Chap. 9 can be used for these buffer storage systems and will provide access times between 60 and 100 ns. However, if even faster performance is desired, the systems designer can turn to ECL (emitter-coupled logic) integrated circuits. By design, emitter-coupled logic circuits operate the active transistors out of saturation, which avoids the common saturation time delay and restricts logic propagation delays to only a few nanoseconds. In addition, the circuit outputs are designed to drive transmission line impedances of from 50 to 100 Ohms. Thus, the system designer who wants increased speed must accept increased power consumption per function.

SC storage elements, fabricated using standard as well as isoplanar processing (Chaps. 2 and 4), and having input drive requirements and data output levels compatible with ECL logic levels, are available in sizes of 64, 128, 256, and 1,024 bits. Several units also have TTL or ECL levels at the input.[9]

To demonstrate the use of ECL storage elements in the design of a high-speed buffer, common available elements will be used. They are of the 64- and 128-bit capacity because the buffer requirements are for shortest access time.

11.3.1 ECL Memory Storage Elements

The memory cell and the characteristics of ECL memories were discussed in general in Chap. 4. Following is a summary of the characteristics of a specific storage element (SN81002) presented here to allow it to be used in a system design. As previously stated, it has a capacity of 64 bits.

64-bit ECL Storage Element

Organization	64×1 (64 words by 1 bit)
Decode	Fully decoded
Signal levels	ECL levels developed from a single negative supply
Output	Open emitter for OR tie Drives 50 Ohms
Access time t_{pA}	< 10 ns
Access time t_{pAE}	< 7 ns
Power dissipation	420 mW total @ -5.2 V 6.5 mW per bit
ILF	$I_{IH} < 50\ \mu A$ $C_{IN} < 3$ pF

Terminals
  6 address
  1 data in
  1 data out
  2 cenable
  1 R/W
  V_{EE}: -3.5 to -6.5 V
  GND

Organized 64×1, the storage element requires only 6 binary bits for addressing since it is fully decoded. It has a maximum access time from application of address of 10 ns, and an enable maximum access time of 7 ns. The buffered inputs of address, data in, two active low chip enables, and a read/write have a dc input load factor of less than 50 μA for the worst case high logic level. In parallel with this load factor is a 3-pF capacitor. Because 13 terminals are required, a 14-pin dual-in-line package is common.

With ECL, as with MOS, the input capacitance load is the primary factor determining speed performance, and consequently, overall system performance. More-over, input capacitance, 3.0 pF input in this example, rather than the dc loading, determines fan-out. The output is an open emitter of an emitter follower, which allows OR tieing and driving 50-Ohm loads.

Designed to operate over an ambient temperature range of 0° to 70°C, this 64-bit element requires a single power supply from -3.5 to -6.5 V for V_{EE}, and dissipates 6.5 mW of power per bit when operated at -5.2 V. Significant power savings result when the memory elements are operated at lower voltages. Speed performance degrades by less than a nanosecond over the full range of voltage while the current remains constant.

128-bit ECL Storage Element. A 128-bit storage element (SN81003), similar to the 64-bit element, has these characteristics:

Organization . . . . 128 × 1
Decode . . . . Fully decoded
Signal levels . . . . ECL levels developed from a
single negative supply
Output . . . . Open emitter for OR tie
Drives 50 Ohms
Access time t_{pA} . . . . < 15 ns
Access time t_{pAE} . . . . < 10 ns
Power dissipation . . . . 410 mW total @ −5.2 V
3.2 mW per bit
ILF . . . . $I_{IH} <$ 50 μA
$C_{IN} <$ 3 pF

Terminals
7 address
1 data in
1 data out
2 cenable
1 R/W
V_{EE}: −4.5 to −5.5 V
GND

This device contains twice the bits per package as the 64-bit element, but in other respects the two storage elements are quite similar. The 128-bit element has the advantage of one-half the power dissipation per bit, but this advantage is somewhat offset by a small degradation in speed performance. In addition, the 128-bit element operates over a lower power-supply range because it has a more efficient temperature compensation circuit. Incidentally, the two active low chip enable inputs of this device are useful for changing organization of a given memory board.

11.3.2 Application of ECL Storage Elements

ECL storage elements present several application differences compared to other bipolar units discussed previously. The output of an ECL storage element is an open emitter of an emitter follower, as shown in Fig. 11.6, and thus can supply current to the node to charge capacitance C_L, but a pull-down resistor must be provided to discharge C_L. To preserve waveforms and prevent ringing and reflections caused by fast wavefronts, terminated transmission lines are used for coupling between stages if the transmission path is greater than 3 or 4 in. A pull-down resistor is used for this termination. Maximum capacitive loading on the line, either from clustered short stub loads or from distributed single loads as shown in Fig. 11.6, must be restricted to a value of about 20 pF per 4.5 in. Otherwise reflections, which

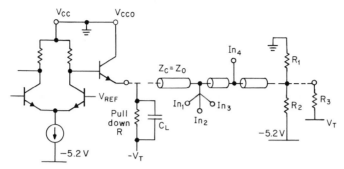

Fig. 11.6. Application requirements of ECL storage elements.

represent noise, will be too large. Most commercially available ECL circuitry operates between a minus voltage (typically -5.2 V) and ground. Termination can be accomplished in a number of ways with the most common ways shown in Fig. 11.6. A Thevenin equivalent output impedance of Z_o to a voltage V_T is formed by the resistor network of R_1 and R_2 between ground and -5.2 V. Z_o is

$$Z_o = \frac{R_1 R_2}{R_1 + R_2} \tag{11-1}$$

and V_T is

$$V_T = \left(\frac{-R_1}{R_1 + R_2}\right) 5.2 \text{ V} \tag{11-2}$$

Or, as shown in Fig. 11.6, a resistor R_3 equal to Z_o is terminated to a regulated voltage of V_T.

In the following systems the R_3 termination to V_T is used.

11.3.3   A 1,024 × 9 ECL Memory System

The application of ECL storage elements will be demonstrated in a system, organized 1,024 × 9, with a cycle time of less than 30 ns. The design procedure begins by checking the loading factors.

Loading Factors.   The equations of Chap. 9 will be used again. From Eq. (9-1),

$$L_A = \frac{1,024}{128} \times \frac{9}{1} \text{ILF} = 72 \text{ ILF} \tag{11-3}$$

This is also the load on read/write (R/W), 72 times the input load factor.

Dc loading is not a problem, but to maintain ac performance, the fan-out is restricted to less than 10; this represents a capacitive load of 30 pF due to the ILF of 3 pF plus stray wiring which boosts the capacitive load to 50 pF. For this reason, 8 drivers will be required.

The number of decode lines S_L from Eq. (9-2) is

$$S_L = \frac{1,024}{128} = 8 \tag{11-4}$$

and the load on each line is

$$L_D = \frac{9}{1}\,\text{ILF} = 9\,\text{ILF} \qquad (11\text{-}5)$$

from Eq. (9-3), or 27 pF plus stray wiring, within the fan-out requirement of 10. Data-in lines have a load of

$$L_{\text{IN}} = \frac{1{,}024}{128}\,\text{ILF} = 8\,\text{ILF} \qquad (11\text{-}6)$$

from Eq. (9-4). This is at least 24 pF.

Data out is dotted into η lines determined by Eq. (9.5). Therefore,

$$\eta = \frac{1{,}024}{128} = 8 \qquad (11\text{-}7)$$

This means that 8 outputs are dotted together, terminated by the characteristic impedance of the transmission lines used—in this case, 50 Ohms.

The System. The first part of the system is a storage matrix (Fig. 11.7) consisting of eight packages in each row and nine packages in each column. Terminating resistors are at the ends of the transmission lines, and each of the packages must have address bits distributed to it.

As shown in Fig. 11.8, address lines are driven in parallel by seven buffer amplifiers. The in-phase output of these buffer amplifiers drives seven drivers for each of two columns of nine modules, as shown in Fig. 11.8. An advantage of ECL circuitry is that both in-phase outputs (identified with no circles on the gate symbol) and out-of-phase outputs (identified with a circle on the gate symbol) are available with these outputs cross-coupled to provide mirror-image addressing to the two

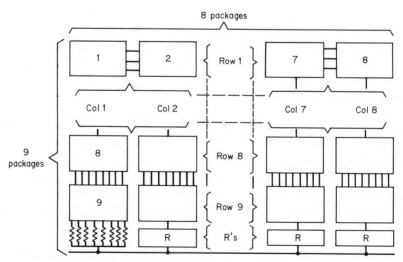

Fig. 11.7. Storage matrix for 1,024 × 9 ECL memory system.

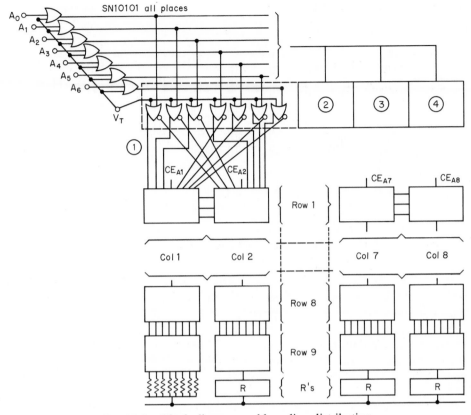

Fig. 11.8. Block diagram—address line distribution.

columns. These stages are repeated for the other three pairs of columns. Terminating resistors are at the end of the transmission lines.

As shown in Fig. 11.9, a 1-of-8 decoder is implemented. It provides a low chip enable signal on one of eight lines (CE_{A1} through CE_{A8} shown on Fig. 11.8) which selects one column of 128 words and 9 bits. Again, the added versatility of in-phase and out-of-phase outputs from the same gate is shown. The decode is implemented with OR-NOR gates. $CS1$ and $CS2$ are board-enable signals that must both be low to select the board. If either input is high, all enable lines will be high, and all storage elements will be disabled. Note the terminating resistors to V_T, and the connection of all unused inputs to V_T.

The system diagram is now simplified in Fig. 11.10. The address buffer and driver circuitry of Fig. 11.8 are contained in the address buffer block shown. The decoder of Fig. 11.9 is contained in the block identified as array column select. Note the address inputs and board enable signals (chip enable $CS1$ and $CS2$). These two blocks use 14 packages.

In the data-in and R/W section, a separate driver is provided for each row of storage elements and quad 2-input gates are used. R/W is buffered by an in-phase

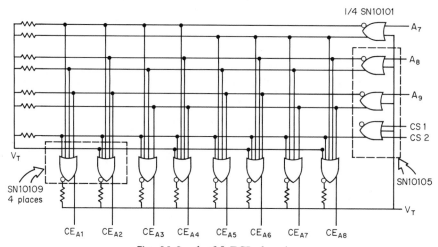

Fig. 11.9. 1-of-8 ECL decoder.

gate to an in-phase driver for each row of storage elements. Data output from each row of eight storage elements is dotted together and terminated with a resistor at the input to an output gate, to provide both in-phase and out-of-phase output signals. Read strobe must be low to gate the data through the output gate. The unused read strobe input is terminated to V_T. The performance characteristics for the total system using 128-bit storage elements are outlined in Fig. 11.11.

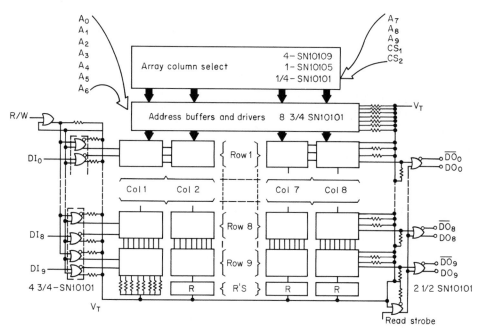

Fig. 11.10. Complete $1,024 \times 9$ ECL memory system.

Speed and P_D	*Packages*	
t_A = 20 ns typ	SN81003—	72
t_C = 30 ns typ	SN10101—	$16\frac{1}{4}$
Total: 40 W	SN10105—	1
Per bit: 4.3 mW	SN10109—	4
		$93\frac{1}{4}$

Fig. 11.11. Performance characteristics for total system using an ECL 128-bit storage element (1K $\times$ 9).

Access time is 20 ns typical, and cycle time is 30 ns typical. Wiring delays might contribute another 5 ns, but, of course, could be longer depending on the layouts and type of PC boards. Note that the power dissipation is 4.3 mW per bit compared to 3.2 mW per bit for the storage element itself.

Obviously, sufficient air-cooling (at least 300 linear ft per min) must be provided. Timing must be carefully controlled. Address, R/W, and data signals are assumed to have transition times of 2 ns, and the write and hold times for these storage elements are 8 and 3 ns, respectively.

11.4 A LARGE-CAPACITY, HIGH-PERFORMANCE MAINFRAME SEMICONDUCTOR MEMORY

The very fast buffers using ECL and the medium-speed buffers using TTL are available. These, coupled with MOS primary storage, can satisfy a wide variety of two-level storage requirements. However, there is still the nagging question, "Does the two-level memory really provide as much efficiency as the simulated programs indicate?" Some designers of large-scale high-speed processors do not think so, and feel there is still a strong need for a large-capacity mainframe semiconductor memory with as much performance as possible. This seems to be especially true for multi-programmed machines.

The physical factors of size and propagation distances have been mentioned. These still exist and are limiting items, but, again, the SC memory with its 4-to-1 advantage in physical size compared to core memory tends to alleviate these factors somewhat. In addition, the possibility of more easily distributing smaller segments of high-speed memory throughout the machine without paying a premium in cost encourages the application of bipolar semiconductor memory in this area.[10]

Let us consider a requirement for a large-capacity mainframe memory of 8 million bits organized 128K $\times$ 64 bits. The cycle time should be less than or equal to 200 ns. The discussions of previous chapters on design and process certainly emphasize the desirable characteristics for the storage element for this application; i.e., high density of storage bits, lower power dissipation, and high-speed performance.

A storage element that meets the requirement is a 1,024-bit TTL RAM (SN74S204). Previously, in Chap. 4, this storage element was discussed, but, as done in previous sections, the characteristics are summarized before a description of the system application begins.

11.4.1 1,024-bit Storage Element

Organization . . . . 1,024 × 1 (1,024 words × 1 bit)
Decode . . . . Fully decoded
Signal levels . . . . TTL logic levels
Output . . . . Three-state output
Access time t_{pA} . . . . ⩽70 ns
Access time t_{pAE} . . . . ⩽40 ns
Power dissipation . . . . 425 mW total
    0.42 mW per bit
ILF . . . . 0.5 mA
    3.0 pF

Terminals
  10 address
  1 data in
  1 data out
  1 cenable
  1 R/W
  V_{CC}: +5 V
  GND

The high density is met with the 1,024 bits organized 1,024 × 1 and the package pins are kept to 16 by having full decoding. Only 10 binary bits are required to select one word from the 1,024.

Although the density is now 1,024 bits, the access time is still only 70 ns maximum from address and 40 ns from enable. Typical access times are 45 ns from address application and 15 ns from chip enable with address present. The 10 address, one data in, one active low chip enable and one R/W input, are buffered and clamped. The input load factor is 0.5 mA maximum, a significant advantage for reducing the number of drive circuits required.

The output is a three-state output, discussed in Chap. 9, which can be OR-tied for easy memory expansion.

The memory requires one power supply of +5 V, and enjoys a factor of 5 reduction in power dissipation per bit, compared to the 256-bit TTL RAMs. At 0.42 mW per bit, the total package dissipation is 425 mW typical, showing a significant improvement in speed/power product (Chap. 4) for this application.

Block Diagram. Figure 11.12 shows the block diagram of the 1,024-bit TTL RAM. Two 1-of-32 decoders provide X and Y decode of the 32 × 32 storage matrix. In the write mode, write enable activates the data buffers which bring data into the cells. In the read mode, these buffers are disabled and the sense amplifiers determine the output state.

Table 11.3 details the output conditions. The control conditions are generally the same as for the 256-bit RAM. Memory enable (chip enable) and write enable (R/W) must be low for writing, and with write enable high the storage element is in the read mode. A high on memory enable inhibits the storage element and the output condition is high impedance due to the three-state output. The only sig-

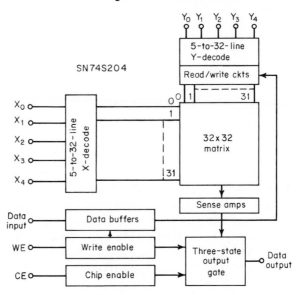

Fig. 11.12. Block diagram of the 1,024-bit TTL RAM.

nificant difference between 1,024-bit RAM and 256-bit RAM conditions (Table 9.3) is that the output of the 1,024-bit RAM is the data stored on reading instead of the complement of data stored, as for the 256-bit RAM.

Timing. Like the 256-bit RAM, the disable of the three-state output of the 1,024-bit RAM is faster than the enable, to prevent output OR-tie problems. The write time is 30 ns and the hold time is 15 ns. These are discussed under critical timing in Chap. 9. In the system application, because t_{pA} is almost twice t_{pAE}, the system access time is determined by the address access path.

This storage element uses a Schottky-diode coupled cell and Schottky on-chip peripheral circuits.

11.4.2 An 8 Million Bit Memory System Board

Organization of the Board. Like the previous applications, the memory system consists of a board containing a segment of memory which is used many times in the system to build up the total memory system. Such a board is shown in Fig. 11.13. It contains 8K × 16 arrayed in the matrix 8 packages by 16 packages. No buffering is required at the output; the data-out terminals are available directly as board terminals. Of course, the 8 packages are dotted together on the common

Table 11.3. Output Conditions for Specific Enable Control Signals (1,024-bit RAM)

ME	WE	Operation	Output condition
L	L	Write	High Z state
L	H	Read	Data stored
H	X*	Inhibit	High Z state

*X—Don't care.

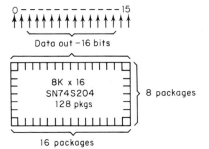

Fig. 11.13. Organization of 8K $\times$ 16 board.

bit line and the circuits have a three-state output. The system is for the commercial temperature range of 0 to 70°C ambient, and since the objective is for maximum speed performance, Schottky interface circuits are used.

Care must be exercised when using the Schottky interface circuits. Drivers, such as the SN74S140, can drive 50-Ohm lines, and therefore, drive and maintain proper waveform integrity over long transmission lines of twisted pair. However, other Schottky circuits must be restricted to driving short lines on the same board. If they drive long lines, then it is difficult to maintain waveform integrity.

The designer must be aware of these factors concerning Schottky circuits when packaging a memory system; he may have to include additional drivers and inverters to maintain performance for the specific packaged system. For this reason, the performance comparison of the following system assumes particular wiring delays with the computations based on the results. No particular packaging (except good engineering practice) is assumed except for multilayer boards; standard packaging techniques are assumed for printed circuit boards and connectors.

The Address Distribution. Figure 11.14 shows how the address is provided. Since each module is 1K words, 10 address lines must go to each module to select the desired word from the 1,024 words. The 10 address lines for this decoding and the R/W lines are driven by dual 4-input NAND gates. As mentioned, this Schottky gate (SN74S140) can drive a 50-Ohm line. Because of the ILF of 0.5 mA, the 128 packages represent a dc load of only 64 mA. The SN74S140 is specified at 60 mA

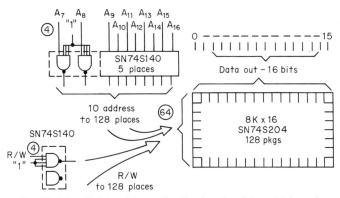

Fig. 11.14. 10-bit address distribution for 8K $\times$ 16 board.

of sink current; however, it can supply the 64 mA without a problem. More important, it can supply the same magnitude of peak current to charge to the high level the hundreds of picofarads of line capacitance. The circled numbers represent the milliamperes of load.

In addition to the dc current of 0.5 mA, the ILF also has 3-pF capacitance. If wiring capacitance is included, the capacitive load on the driver is from 600 to 700 pF. Therefore, the data sheet propagation delay is only a small portion of the total delay due to the additional time needed to charge the capacitance.

This illustrates how 1 word out of the 1,024 words is addressed; the next section describes how the 1K segment of 16 bits is selected from the 8K.

Memory Enable Decoding. The selection of a 1K segment from the 8K on the board is accomplished with the memory enable (cenable) line and a 1-of-8 decoder. The decoder (SN74S138) decodes 1 line of 8 low from 3-input address signals. The low line enables the sixteen 1K packages in a row, so that all 16 bits are active, which is accomplished with the chip enable input on the storage element packages. Figure 11.15 shows the decoder added to the block diagram. Note the board enable input. All eight decoder outputs are high until this line is low, and no storage elements on the board are selected until the board enable input line is low.

Data In. The peripheral circuitry on the board is completed by adding the necessary buffering for data input. The 16 bits are buffered by two input gates. All unused inputs on the board are terminated to a high level (Fig. 11.16).

Complete 8K × 16 Board. The completed 8K × 16 board is shown in Fig. 11.16. The normal ILF for the Schottky inputs is 2 mA with the driver for address (SN74S140) having an ILF of 4 mA. Figure 11.17 lists the characteristics of the completed board.

The access time is 70 ns typical and 100 ns maximum. There are 139 packages used, dissipating 0.425 mW per bit, for a total dissipation of 55.7 W. A 17 × 13 in. board will hold the components nicely with, as mentioned previously, adequate air flow required for the amount of dissipation.

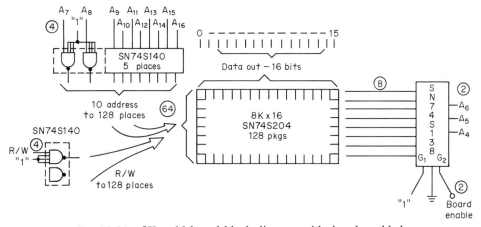

Fig. 11.15. 8K × 16 board block diagram with decoder added.

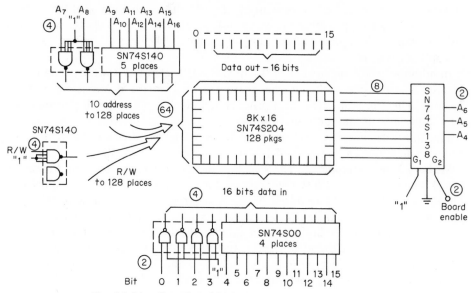

Fig. 11.16. Complete block diagram of 8K × 16 board.

11.4.3   Expanding to an 8 Million Bit System

As with our other applications, the 8K × 16 board is now duplicated over and over again to build up a larger memory system (Fig. 11.18). To provide the 64 bits, basic modules of 4 boards are used to provide 8K × 64 bits.

Four basic modules are grouped together for 32K × 64 bits, and two of these groups are combined to form a row of eight modules or 64K × 64 bits. There are four boards behind each block. Each select line, S through Z, will be used to select one 8K × 64-bit module: S_1 through Z_1 for the top modules and S_2 through Z_2 for the bottom.

10-bit Address Distribution (Plus R/W). The address bits that go to each 1K unit to decode the desired word are distributed through drivers as shown in Fig. 11.18. R/W must also be distributed in the same manner. Again, dual 4-input NAND gates are used as drivers to buffer the address lines and R/W except that the input address to the system goes to four gates in parallel rather than to just one gate. Each gate drives 32K × 64 bits, which is 16 boards. With each board input at

t_A		P_D	Packages
			SN74S204—128
Typ	Max	Total: 55.7 W	SN74S140— 6
70 ns	100 ns	Per bit: 0.425 mW	SN74S00 — 4
			SN74S138— 1
			139

Fig. 11.17. 8K × 16 (128K bits) board characteristics.

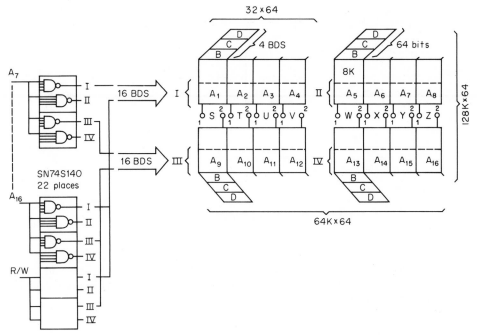

Fig. 11.18. 128K $\times$ 64 memory system with 10-bit and R/W address distribution added.

4 mA, the load on the driver is 64 mA, which taxes the driver a bit, but poses no problem. The outputs of the address drivers are codes identified with I, II, III, and IV. Corresponding inputs to the 16 board groups are identified with the same Roman numeral as the output. Each Roman numeral group is composed of 10 address lines from the 10 address bits A_7 to A_{16}. R/W also has its separate lines. Each board input is considered as a 5-pF capacitive load; therefore, excluding the additional connection capacitance, the address driver must drive at least 80 pF.

Example of Load and Delay Calculation. To determine the propagation delay in the system, the various external delays must be added to the internal delay of the storage element itself, [11] as explained in Chap. 9. The several paths of Chap. 9 need to be calculated separately.

To illustrate such a calculation, the address path of the 10-bit address that goes to each individual storage element will be used.

Figure 11.19 diagrams the delays that exist in this data access path. The total propagation delay from input address to data output consists of the storage element delays plus the buffer delays on the input and the output. Since the output is usually controlled by a strobe which may be timed to occur after the data are valid at the storage element output, the total address access time t_{pAT} for this discussion is taken only to the output of the storage element. There are delays indicated for cabling between peripheral circuits and the boards, t_{pw_1} and t_{pw_2}. t_{pw_2} on the boards is accounted for as an additional capacitance of 2 pF into the storage element inputs. t_{pw_1} is accounted for by adding an addition capacitance of 100 pF for each board.

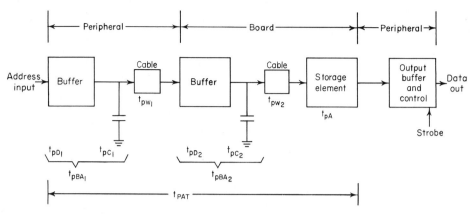

Fig. 11.19. 10-bit address data access path.

However, each of these will depend on the specific assembly used and should be varied accordingly. Thus, the system numbers are based upon engineering calculations, not actual measured data.

The total access time t_{pAT} is

$$t_{pAT} = t_{pBA_1} + t_{pBA_2} + t_{pA} \qquad (11\text{-}8)$$

The buffer delay consists of an internal propagation delay (t_{pD}) at data sheet conditions plus the added delay due to the capacitive load (t_{pC}). Therefore,

$$t_{pBA_1} = t_{pD_1} + t_{pC_1} \qquad (11\text{-}9)$$

and

$$t_{pBA_2} = t_{pD_2} + t_{pC_2} \qquad (11\text{-}10)$$

For the drivers used for buffers t_{pD_1} and t_{pD_2} are 6.5 ns maximum. t_{pC_1} and t_{pC_2} must be calculated using Eq. (9-13) and an average charging current of 50 mA to a threshold level of 1.5 V. For example, C_1 results from 16 board inputs as the load on the driver. Each input has an ILF of 4 mA plus a capacitance of 5 pF (3 pF for input + 2 pF wiring). When the driver sinks current, the discharge is a low impedance. The 4-mA load must be sinked to ground. For the high level the driver must supply current to charge the capacitance; therefore, the ac load is the important propagation delay load. As a result, with C_1 as

$$C_1 = 16 \times 5 = 80 \text{ pF} \qquad (11\text{-}11)$$

the time delay t_{pC_1} is

$$t_{pC_1} = \frac{80 \times 10^{-12}}{50 \times 10^{-3}} \times 1.5 \approx 2.5 \text{ ns} \qquad (11\text{-}12)$$

The total delay is, from Eq. (11-9),

$$t_{pBA_1} = 6.5 + 2.5 \approx 9 \text{ ns} \qquad (11\text{-}13)$$

A corresponding capacitive load is calculated for the ac load on the buffer driver on the board, C_2. This is

$$C_2 = 128 \times 5 = 640 \text{ pF}$$
$$+ \quad \frac{100 \text{ pF wiring}}{740 \text{ pF}} \tag{11-14}$$

since this driver has 128 loads and an additional 100 pF is added for wiring.

This C_2 [Eq. (11-14)] is then substituted into Eq. (9-13) as for C_1 and the propagation delay t_{pC_2} is

$$t_{pC_2} = \frac{740 \times 10^{-12}}{50 \times 10^{-3}} \times 1.5 \approx 23 \quad \text{ns} \tag{11-15}$$

and the total buffer delay t_{pBA_2}, from Eq. (11-10), is

$$t_{pBA_2} = 6.5 + 23 \approx 29.5 \quad \text{ns} \tag{11-16}$$

t_{pBA_2} will be considered as 30 ns and t_{pBA_1} as 10 ns. The results of the substitutions into Eq. (11-8) for the total access time t_{pAT} are

$$t_{pAT} = 10 + 30 + 70 = 110 \quad \text{ns} \tag{11-17}$$

This, of course, has the maximum t_{pA} of the storage element as 70 ns. Note that the board access time is 100 ns. This is the same as Fig. 11.17; therefore, this path has determined access time of the board, rather than an enable path.

Selecting 1K × 64 Bits. Recall from Fig. 11.16 that a decoder on the board selected 1K × 16 bits. Distributing these address bits to all boards (Fig. 11.20) will then select the 1K × 16 bits on each board. With four boards in the 8K module selected at one time, 64 bits are activated. The 10 bits of address select the desired word in the 1K packages; therefore, the selected word with its 64 bits is activated.

The same driver used previously buffers the three address lines to 32 boards with each address line distributed according to the 1, 2, 3, 4 notation shown. The first group of three gates feed to 1 and 2 in parallel and the second group of three gates to 3 and 4 in parallel.

Selecting the 8K × 64 Module. The row of 1K words has been selected on the boards from 8K available, and the desired word has been selected from the 1K words in the storage element. Remaining action requires selection of the 8K module desired from the 16 modules available. Recall that when a module is selected, four boards, each containing 16 bits, are selected providing the 64 bits in the word.

The decode circuitry is shown in Fig. 11.21. To select one 8K module, a 1-of-16 decoder is required consisting of two 1-of-8 decoders and an inverter. The 1-of-8 decoder accepts three address lines and decodes 1 of 8 lines low. The low line enables the module of 8K × 64 by enabling four boards. The control for the decoders are the bits A_1 through A_3. A_0 is the address bit that activates the particular decoder. All outputs of the decoder are high, and no modules are enabled when its enable input is at the high level. Propagation delays through these decoders are typically 9 ns and a maximum of 14 ns. This could be a trouble spot in the

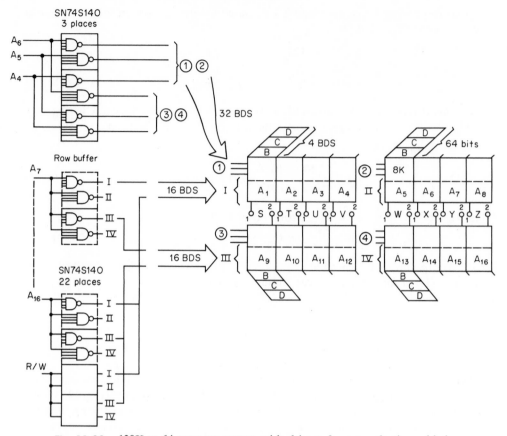

Fig. 11.20. $128K \times 64$ memory system with drivers for row selection added.

system distribution if the length of transmission line is extensive. The decoder output drives four boards which represents 8 mA of dc load and 20 pF of ac load, but if the transmission path is long, the waveform could deteriorate, as previously discussed.

The decode is now complete. A 1-of-16 decoder selects the 8K module, a 1-of-8 decoder selects the 1K words, and the 10-bit address selects the individual word.

Data In. With the decode complete, the data-in distribution is now added to the system as shown in Fig. 11.22. Sixty-four bits of data must be provided. The module has four boards identified as A, B, C, D, with each board containing 16 bits, and the same 4-input driver described previously is used to handle the load of 16 boards. Each gate drives a bit, and the first 16 bits are located on the A boards of each module, the second 16 bits on the B boards and so on for C and D boards. The total delay through the data-in path to the storage element is two gate delays plus capacitive load. Data out must be added to complete the system.

Data Out. The output from the storage element was OR-tied to seven other packages on the board for each bit. Therefore, each bit line from each $8K \times 64$

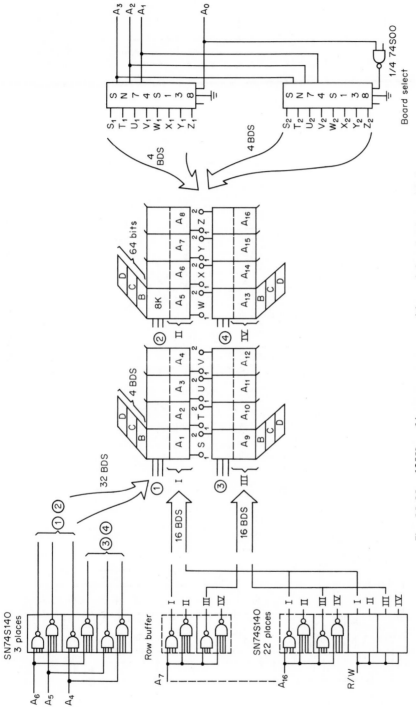

Fig. 11.21. 128K × 64 memory system with module selection added.

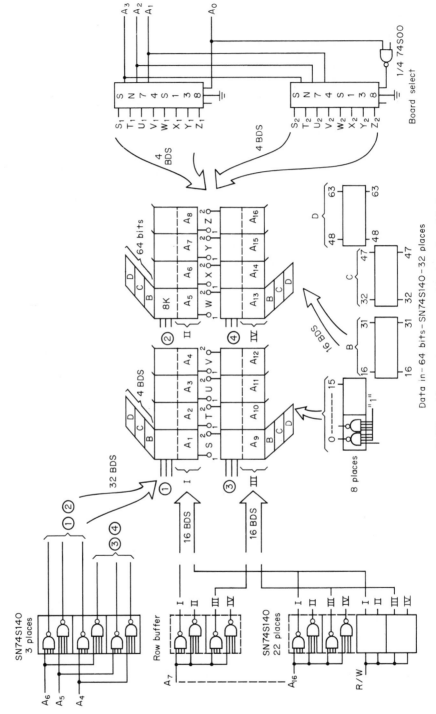

Fig. 11.22. 128K × 64 memory system with data in added.

module has a dotted load (η) of 8. If the bit lines of the 16 modules are dotted together, the η would be 128 lines. Each line might have from 5 to 10 pF of capacitance; thus the load could easily be 1,000 pF. The storage element output has a good drive capability but its average output current is only about 20 mA for charging capacitance rather than the 50 mA for the high power driver used previously (SN74S140).

Therefore, the output delay to be added to the t_{pAT} of Fig. 11.19 could easily be 70 to 80 ns. This might be acceptable, but in the system described maximum speed is sought and it is desirable to have only a 5- to 7-ns delay. For this reason, a 12-input NAND gate with a three-state output is used to accept all the data outputs for a given bit. This is shown in Fig. 11.23.

Only the outputs from the A boards are shown. Two board outputs are connected to an input. For the 16 boards, 8 inputs are used, and the other 4 inputs are tied high. A resistor to $+5$ V is tied to each input to eliminate any possible noise problems. The η on each line is 16. The output from this gate is a three-state output; therefore, it can be dotted again and have the high-impedance feature. The three-state control can then be used as a read strobe as shown.

Figure 11.24 further clarifies how the remaining boards feed the data out from 64 bits.

In summary, the use of this gate provides minimal delay in the output path, a three-state output for further memory expansion, and a read strobe control.

Complete 128K $\times$ 64 Memory System. Adding the data output distribution in a simplified fashion completes the 128K $\times$ 64 bit system (Fig. 11.25). All unused gates should be terminated. Obviously, all such detail cannot be shown on the simplified block diagram.

Characteristics of this memory system are shown in Fig. 11.26. Remember that these numbers are engineering design numbers; the actual wiring and interconnec-

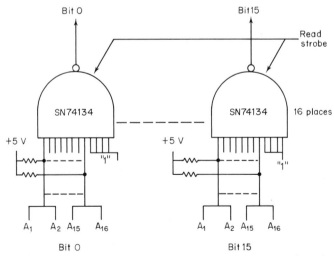

Fig. 11.23. Data output distribution for 16 bits from A boards.

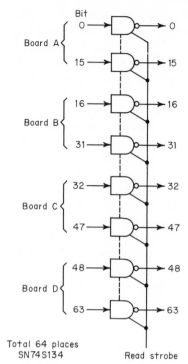

Total 64 places
SN74S134

Read strobe   **Fig. 11.24.** Complete 64-bit data output.

tion delays depend on the physical assembly chosen for packaging. First, the speed performance: The access time of the 8 million bit memory is approximately 120 ns, and allowing 20 ns more for wiring delay, the total is 140 ns. If 10 ns is enough design margin, then the cycle time is indicated as 150 ns.

There are 8,192 1,024-bit TTL RAM packages used for storage. Adding 828 drivers, buffers, and logic gives a total of 9,020 packages. There are 3,600 W dissipated by the total system. And the 5-V power supply must supply 720 Amps. This calculates to 0.44 mW per bit, of which 0.42 mW per bit is just for the storage. Thus, the support circuitry is incidental in the amount of power dissipation it contributes—0.02 mW per bit, less than 4 percent of the total.

Obviously, care must be exercised to provide enough pins on boards to handle the 11 to 12 Amps of current per board—1 Amp per pin is a satisfactory rule of thumb. Care must be taken to satisfy the heat exchange problems, but 50 to 60 W per board is not unusual for air cooling. Of course, it is even better for the memory system environment if some form of cold plate cooling can be used. As pointed out in Chap. 10, n-channel MOS storage elements can significantly reduce the power, especially in standby. Speed performance requirements, of course, must be carefully evaluated.

11.5 SUMMARY

The chapter discussion has pointed out two systems for use as large mainframe memories for computers. The characteristics of the two-level memory system and

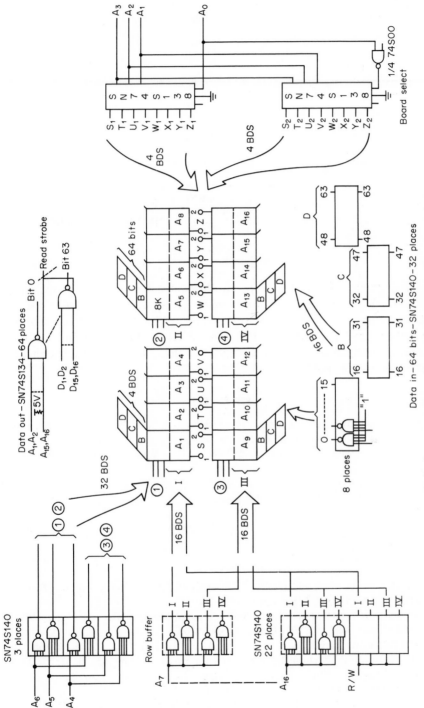

Fig. 11.25. Complete block diagram of 128K × 64 memory system.

Speed, ns

Time	Typ	Max	Wiring delay	Total
t_A	80	120	20	140
t_C				150

Packages

Storage elements (74S204) 8,192
Other 828
9,020

Power

5 V	Total: 3,600 W
720 Amps	Per bit: 0.44 mW

Fig. 11.26. System characteristics [8M bits (128K × 64)].

the analysis point toward the use of an all-semiconductor two-level memory for the systems where this approach can be used. It appears quite cost effective.

The all-semiconductor single-level mainframe will most likely have its emphasis on excellent speed performance, therefore dictating the use of bipolar RAMs. However, it will be interesting and exciting to watch the impact of n-channel MOS on this bipolar stronghold.

REFERENCES

1. J. R. Hillegass, Memory Upgrades Provide 360s with More Processing Punch, *Comput. Decis.,* **3**(12): 28–32(December 1971).
2. D. H. Gibson and W. L. Shevel, "Cache" Turns up a Treasure, *Electronics,* **42:** 105–107(October 13, 1969).
3. C. J. Conti, Concepts for Buffer Storage, *Comput. Group News,* pp. 9–13, March 1969.
4. R. H. Meade, Design Approaches for Cache Memory Control, *Comput. Des.,* pp. 87–93, January 1971.
5. G. G. Scarrott, The Efficient Use of Multilevel Storage, *Proc. IFIP Congr.,* **1:** 137–141(1965).
6. C. G. Bell and D. Casasent, Implementation of a Buffer Memory in Minicomputer, *Comput. Des.,* pp. 83–89, November 1971.
7. A. G. Hanlon, Content-addressable and Associative Memory—A Survey, *IEEE Trans. Comput.,* **EC-15**(4): 509–521(August 1966).
8. T. W. Hart, Jr. and D. D. Winstead, Semiconductor Memory Systems—What Will They Cost? *Electron. Eng.,* pp. 50–54, September 1970.
9. W. D. Baker, W. H. Herndon, T. A. Longo, and D. L. Pelzer, Oxide Isolation Brings High Density to Production Bipolar Memories, *Electronics,* pp. 65–70, March 29, 1973.
10. D. C. Gunderson, Advances in Memory Systems Technology on Computer Organization, *IEEE Comput.,* **3**(6): 7–11(November/December 1970).
11. R. W. Bryant, G. K. Tu, T. C. Kwei, and R. H. Robinson, A High Performance LSI Memory System, *Comput. Des.,* pp. 71–77, July 1970.

Index